D1443044

What Democracy Is For

By the Same Author

The Possibility of Politics: A Study in the Political Economy of the Welfare State (3rd ed. 2006)

Citizens, Families, and Reform (2nd ed. 2005)

What Democracy Is For

ON FREEDOM AND MORAL GOVERNMENT

Stein Ringen

PRINCETON UNIVERSITY PRESS
PRINCETON AND OXFORD

Library of Congress Cataloging-in-Publication Data

Ringen, Stein
What democracy is for : on freedom and moral government / Stein Ringen.
    p.   cm.
Includes bibliographical references and index.
ISBN-13: 978-0-691-12984-6 (cloth : alk. paper)
ISBN-10: 0-691-12984-3 (cloth : alk. paper)
1. Democracy. 2. Political ethics. 3. Social justice. 4. Corporate power. 5. Business
and politics. 6. Globalization. I. Title.
JC423.R516 2007
321.8—dc22   2006030854

British Library Cataloging-in-Publication Data is available

This book has been composed in Sabon

Printed on acid-free paper. ∞

press.princeton.edu

Printed in the United States of America

10 9 8 7 6 5 4 3 2 1

For Mary

Contents

Acknowledgments

THE TWISTED road towards this book started during a year of sabbatical leave in 1996–97, which I spent in Paris with La Maison des Sciences de l'Homme (MSH) and L'École Normale Supérieure de Cachan as my generous hosts. During that year some colleagues and I convened a little group that we called "the Paris Group on social policy and political theory." We were able to do that thanks to financial support from La Mission de recherche du Ministère des affairs socials and the MSH. I am glad here to express my thanks to Maurice Aymard, Marianne Berthod, and Catherine Paradeise for making this possible.

The Paris Group met first in May 1997 and again in the two following years. We had no strict agenda but shared work in which we were engaged that sought to bridge the gulf between the worlds of philosophical reflection and empirical observation, and to some degree between theory and action. For me, these were important and inspiring exchanges. The members of the group were Bruce Ackerman, Robert Boyer, Maurizio Ferrera, Bob Goodin, Anne-Marie Guillemard, Amy Gutmann, Des King, Jean Leca, Jane Lewis, Bernard Manin, Bernd Marin, Francois-Xavier Merrien, Ulrich Mueckenburger, Julia O'Connor, Claus Offe, Einar Øverbye, Bruno Palier, Victor Pérez-Diaz, Gilles Pollet, Bo Rothstein, Alan Ryan, Dominique Schnapper, Bernd Schulte, Bram de Swaan, and Dennis Thompson. I am thankful to them all for ideas, lively debates, and inspiration.

In 1998 I was asked by the government of Norway to serve on a Royal Commission on Human Values. We worked three years in studies, dialogues, consultations, hearings, debates, and other ways to try to take stock of how that little and tightly knit—and prosperous—population sees itself and its future. Some of what I have written here reflects what I learned through that kind of direct observation—for example, about freedom and reason, about democratic values and local democracy, about being skeptical when people in position complain about the ugliness of an assertive press, and not least about the great challenge of multiculturalism and the need for dialogue. My brief visit to the Sami minority, in the conclusion, comes from this work. To my colleagues on the commission and in our secretariat I am ever grateful, perhaps in particular to Inge Eidsvåg for our very rich discussions and friendly disagreement that continue to this day.

In chapter 3, I mention Research Committee 19 of the International Sociological Association. This committee has been and is a powerhouse for comparative research on welfare states, social policy, and poverty. I've attended most of our annual workshop conferences over the last twenty years, always with much benefit. From 1994 to 2002 I had the honor of serving as its president, a post now held by Ann Orloff and before me by Walter Korpi. To my colleagues on RC19: warm gratitude for their cooperation and friendship.

I have been fortunate to be able to discuss the ideas I pursue here as they have evolved in lectures and seminars in many places. Most of those opportunities are mentioned in the chapters. I want to add a particular note of thanks to some institutions that have welcomed me for periods of work as a visiting professor or fellow: the Sir Arthur Lewis Institute for Social and Economic Studies of the University of the West Indies in Barbados, with thanks in particular to Andrew Downes and Elsie Le Franc; the School of Social Studies of Masaryk University in Brno, with thanks in particular to Ivo Možný, Ladislav Rabušic, and Tomáš Sirovátka; the Institute of Sociology of the Academy of Sciences of the Czech Republic, with thanks in particular to Marie Čermáková, Jiří Večerník, Marek Skovajsa, and Petr Matějů; the Faculty of Social Sciences of Charles University in Prague, with special thanks to Martin Potůček; NOVA Norwegina Social Research, with special thanks to Magnus Rindal, Axel West Pedersen, and Aksel Hatland; and the Wissenschaftszentrum Berlin für Sozialforschung, with special thanks to Jens Alber. The long project on good government, to which this book contributes, started while I was at the Swedish Institute for Social Research at the University of Stockholm from 1983 to 1986. I remain heavily in debt to the stimulation that comes from working in so exceptional an academic community.

My own university is still a fine community of scholars and a great place to work. There is not a day in Green College without stimulating if often quirky conversation between colleagues and with a string of always interesting visitors. I say "still." We too, of course, are becoming ever more managerial and streamlined. What that means it is too early to tell, but there does not seem to be much value added to the account "a place where it's fun to be." My students have been a source of ideas and corrections, in particular in my course on the history of the welfare state.

I am grateful for permissions to reprint previously published material to *Democratization* (chapter 2), the *Czech Sociological Review* (appendix A), the *Times Literary Supplement* (appendix B), and the *British Journalism Review* (appendix C). Some close links in the form of further developments of previous work are acknowledged in the respective chapters.

Jens Alber and Neil Gilbert both read a draft manuscript for the book and made invaluable suggestions for its improvement. Irving Louis Horowitz has read this and other works of mine in a spirit of true friendship and generous guidance. Ian Malcolm, my editor, and his always excellent colleagues in Princeton and Oxford have worked with me so that I could not possibly have hoped for more.

My wife Mary Chamberlain, who is an oh-so-productive historian, has been unfailingly helpful and supportive, more recently with encouragements such as "Aren't you finished with that damned book yet?" It is dedicated to her, with love.

Oxford, December 2006

What Democracy Is For

DEMOCRACY IS VICTORIOUS. The competition has collapsed. Most countries have made themselves democracies of sorts and the remaining outright nondemocratic ones count only a handful. But citizens are turning away. They care less for democracy, believe less in it, participate less in it, and have less trust in its governance.

In this book I look inside the democracies that are usually thought to be the most robust and find them wanting—and possibly on the decline. Even those that are best by a comparative measure, such as the Scandinavian ones, do pretty poorly by an absolute standard. If we think democracy is now assured, we are mistaken. Democracy is strong in quantitative terms, in the number of democracies in the world, but weak in qualitative terms, in how well those democracies perform.

If democracy should decline, the loss would be immeasurable. It would be in the freedom and security of ordinary women and men and children and families to live their lives by their own ambitions and aspirations. It would be in our well-being.

We may not think that what we have won can be lost. But it can, in particular if those of us who have had the good fortune to live under democratic rule for some time slip into forgetfulness about what it means for us. Democracy can be taken away, of course; that is always a danger. Or it might just wither; that is perhaps a more imminent danger. It could disintegrate into despotic reality within democratic formality, the *despotisme doux* that Alexis de Tocqueville warned against in the 1830s, with a perceptiveness later unmatched by any student of politics, when he observed democracy in action in its then most advanced form, in America. Perhaps we are already deep into this *despotisme*; it was after all Tocqueville's genius to see that citizens could fall into a trap of unfreedom while still believing themselves to be free. His time was not unlike ours: a postrevolutionary one with democracy spreading and the direction of its inner development in the balance. The danger he saw was subtle, not so much that democracy might give way to violent or cruel government as that centralized government would become overwhelming and that citizens, out of convenience, selfishness, comfort or misunderstanding, would allow themselves to be degraded even if not tormented. In chapter 6, I suggest we may well be there.

Danger comes from two quarters: from defects in the machinery of democratic politics and from citizens themselves in how they practice and understand democratic citizenship. The first danger I address in chapters 1 to 3 and the second one in chapters 4 to 6. Throughout, my message is that we need to set up against the dangers both to and in democracy not only a defense of it, although that too, but a determined effort to *improve* it. The way to protect democracy is not to cheer it, which we do too much, but to reform it, which we do too little.

I start with questions about what democracy is and what makes one better than another. We have but the vaguest notions of democratic quality, and I hope to add to our understanding of that core concept. Then I turn to the economy. In a brilliant little book, *Equality and Efficiency* (1975), the economist Arthur Okun warned against the transgression (as he called it) of economic power into the domain of politics and argued that this in the United States had caused a political acceptance of poverty, which did not reflect American values. To counter such transgressions, I seek to breathe new (and, I hope, realistic) life into the notion of economic democracy. Finally I consider governance and the question of how democratic governments can and should provide necessary rule without becoming overpowering. My prism is the welfare state, that great civilizing project in modern capitalism which nevertheless also contains the danger of excess. I lay out ideas for a "welfare state for investment."

In the last three chapters, I consider democratic citizens. While they depend on democracy for freedom and well-being, democracy depends equally on them—on their capacity to be citizens and on their beliefs about citizenship. Poverty is destructive of freedom. The United Nations has majestically agreed on "millennium goals" to rid the world of the scourge of poverty. Let's take that mission seriously. In chapter 4, I seek to explain what freedom from poverty means. I then turn to the arena where most people live most of their lives, to families. Those little organizations are exceptionally productive, materially but also morally, in the nurturing of values and norms. Finally, I turn to the core concept of value in democracy, to freedom. Isaiah Berlin famously warned against ideas of freedom that could pervert to ideologies of unfreedom. In that spirit I recommend a concept of real freedom, which I think is helpful, indeed necessary, for us who struggle with the blessings and burdens of being free citizens.

WHAT PURPOSE DEMOCRACY?

What is democracy for? The question is not as easy to answer as one might think. Democracy is for many things, no doubt, and there are clearly many valid answers to the naive question. But I have come to see that the many potential purposes of democracy can be arranged in a sort of hierarchy and that it is possible to identify among the various democratic values one that is ultimate and defines its moral purpose.

Democracy, it is often said, is for government by popular consent, but that is not much of an answer. Government by consent is perhaps what democracy *is*, but then what is consent for? To enable the ruled to control the rulers? If that is the case, well and good, but just why should you and I be concerned to hold an intangible fraction of collective control over those who govern? Perhaps because this is the only way to assure rule by *popular* consent. Unless the power to control the rulers is spread out broadly through the citizenry, control will at best be in the hands of a small group of citizens and we will have a minority of controllers controlling a minority of rulers. But again, why is control important and why popular consent?

A classic answer is that power corrupts, in which case the purpose of consent is to prevent arbitrary or oppressive rule. But what is it that makes rule arbitrary? And if we are afraid of oppressive rule, what is it we fear? Rule is supposedly arbitrary if it goes against the will of the ruled, but what is it the ruled want from their rulers? Rule is perhaps oppressive if it denies or takes away from the ruled what they value. But what is it we value and that governments can give or deny?

One thing we obviously expect of a government is protection. But protection of what and against whom? Of life and limb clearly, but that does not tell us much about democratic governments specifically; a democratic government deserves no special praise for doing what any government should. Against domination, as Ian Shapiro argues in *The State of Democratic Theory*? Probably, but why? What is it we are made to sacrifice if others are able to dominate us?

We can start to pin down an answer by going back to basics and being reminded that no man is an island, entire of itself. We depend on dealing with others and on each other; we perforce live in community. Therefore we have to cooperate in various ways. Cooperation is difficult, however, and with the need to cooperate comes risk. It is difficult because we all know that often it is to our benefit that others cooperate but that we do not. It is dangerous because in cooperation we commit ourselves to paying attention to others. That creates bonds of dependency, which the strong and fortunate can use to harass the weak and unfortunate. Society therefore, at least civilized society, depends on some form of governance to help people to cooperate and to regulate for fair and orderly cooperation. But once we allow others the power to govern, we are at risk that they will use the power we grant them to make themselves the ones that harass us in their own interest. For the sake of our well-being and security, we should therefore want necessary government to be under our control to ensure that it governs precisely for our well-being and security and not against our interests.

That is a start towards an answer, but no more than a start. Concepts such as well-being, security, and interests are still elusive. Just what is it we want a good government to do and deliver, and just what is it a good government does not threaten?

We want many things from our government, and never more so than in the advanced democracies where we enjoy unlimited freedom to make demands on those who rule. We are not terribly worried that we demand more than governments can possibly deliver and we do not hesitate to demand different things that cannot come in the same package. We want economic growth and environmental protection and we expect our governments to deliver both, although we know it is impossible to maximize both at the same time. We want more and better services and lower taxes, and we expect the government to square the circle. All that is in the nature of the democratic tug of war and not something anyone should get themselves worked up about. But beneath our many and often contradictory claims on governments and expectations of goods we want them to deliver, there must be some yardstick of value. Good governments deliver goods, but we must hope there is something more to it. Presumably we want democracy because we need governance and because we believe democracy encourages good government. But what, finally, is it that makes governments good?

The answer I have arrived at is this. It starts from well-being, from the living of good lives. Everyone wants to live a good life. That is true because it is self-evident. The good life, however, is not found in any specific way of life. There is no recipe that tells everyone everything about what is good for them and for everyone else. Well-being can only be found person by person in the realization of a life that is good for him or her in the phase of life where he or she happens to be. Some ways of life are incompatible with any notion of a good life—for example, a life utterly devoted to doing evil or dominated by greed and egoism or one that is thoroughly frivolous and unreflective—but for the rest the life that is good for Mr. Jones is the life that is good for him. That is likely to be different, at least to some degree, from the life that is good for Mrs. Smith. This is true because we know it from experience. Some live to work, others work to live. And some of those who for a while live to work later find that working comes to stand in the way of living.

Well-being, then, the business of realizing good lives, depends on the Smiths and Joneses of this world being able to find the lives that are good for them, being able to change their minds about how they want to live, and then being able to modify their ways of life accordingly. That, again, obviously depends on many conditions—resources, competence, markets, friends, family, and much more—and we will visit all of those as things unfold below, but is in the end something individuals must sort out for themselves. What they must do for themselves, they must have the opportunity to do. Our well-being is ultimately of our own making, but we cannot make our lives good unless we have the tools to do it. Since well-being is in the realization of the life that is good for each person, we must all be free to shape our lives in ways that are good for us. It comes down, I take it, to the freedom of the individual. That's what governments can and should foster and protect, what oppressive governments refuse, and what arbitrary rule perverts. That's what we are denied when we suffer under domination.

Democracy has a purpose. It is (or rather, should be) for the good of the persons who live under its governance. It is to help them to live in autonomy and security and to get on reasonably with their lives as they wish. And it is to enable them to trust that they and their children can live as their own masters also in the future. It is, in short, for the freedom of the common man. It's *freedom* that democracy is finally for. That's the idea this book is built around: to analyze democracy according to its purpose, to find that purpose in the lives of persons and to think of it as ultimately a matter of freedom.

What Freedom?

One way to think about freedom is to imagine that it is the natural state of affairs in human life, but that trouble has come into paradise and deprived us of the freedom that is really there for us. In that case, the task is to clear away trouble so that we can reclaim our natural freedom. Or we might think, with Hobbes, that human life inclines to being nasty, brutish, and short and that freedom must be created, recreated, and delivered. I am of the second persuasion.

That leads me to a discussion that circulates around the difference between liberty and freedom, between *having* liberty and *being* free. Liberty is a mysterious quality. Not to have it is to be damned, but when you do have it you find that it does not do much for you. To run around and make choices all over the place is time wasted, silliness, and the stuff of neurosis—and a far cry from a life in freedom.

A free life could possibly be an easy life since when we are free we can do as we wish. But that is not how I see it. I believe a free life is potentially a good life, but I also think that freedom is difficult. The benefit is that you can live according to your own ideas about what it means to live well, but the cost is that you yourself have to sort out those ideas and resolve which ones are sound and worth living by.

In the liberal tradition that harks back to John Stuart Mill, freedom is the liberty to do as one wants without interference or coercion. The difficulty of freedom then comes into consideration after the fact in the *use* of liberty. I think that's too late. It leaves the *definition* naked, as no more than "do as you like." From that concept, it is (to use Isaiah Berlin's words) "no very great distance" to an idea that freedom comes from more of everything, from ever more rights and ever more abundance. But that makes freedom insatiable and renders it destructive to the individual who pursues it. It is also a dangerous idea in society. Before we know it, we are, in the name of freedom, parading an ideology of greed and selfishness to a world of mass poverty, environmental depletion, and cultural antagonisms.

My alternative is to bring the difficulty of liberty into the definition. Freedom—and here I follow Joseph Raz in *The Morality of Freedom*—is being your own master. That depends on the liberty of the liberals but does not stop there. To be master of yourself means to be able to do as you want, provided what you want is worth wanting. The challenge and difficulty lies not primarily in the choice of actions according to your wants but in being in control of what to want. If you live for the satisfaction of wants you just happen to *have*, you are not living a life of your own making. Freedom is power, but it is power over meaning, purpose, and ends as well as over means and choice. This understanding of freedom contains, inside the definition, wisdom, restraint, and self-control—what I call *reason*.

These ideas I consider in the final chapter. There I search for the foundations of freedom in the inner life of individuals. In earlier chapters I consider social foundations: How well do democracies perform in the promotion and protection of freedom? Is there an escape from economic domination? Can the welfare state empower citizens? Is poverty avoidable? Are families the source of values and norms that are in turn at the core of reason? It is democratic culture as much as democratic politics I am in search of.

GOOD GOVERNMENT

This book is my third from a project on "good government," following *The Possibility of Politics* (1987 and 2006) and *Citizens, Families, and Reform* (1997 and 2005). I now complete a journey that started with the economics of the welfare state and continued through a political analysis of social issues with a moral analysis of democracy.

The problem from which I started was the power of piecemeal reform, Karl Popper's bastion against tyranny in *The Open Society and Its Enemies* (1945). The prevailing view at the time was that reform was either socially futile or economically destructive. Those opinions were mainly grounded in theoretical logic, including a good serving of Marxist theory. I approached the matter from an empirical platform and tried to form a verdict on reformist redistribution by balancing effectiveness in relation to goals against costs in the form of (unanticipated) side effects. My experience has made me a determined defender of the heroic idea of reform.

It was immediately clear that the problem of reform was only a convenient entry into a broader problem and that what I was really on to was the meaning and capacity of democratic governance, given the constraints that democracy imposes on the exercise of political rule.

As I moved on, however, it gradually came to me that even the problem of democratic governance, big and unruly as it is, was in turn wrapped into a yet broader *problematique*. There is a grand idea about recent social history that we may refer to as *the liberal vision*—a fundamentally affirmative confidence in the genuineness of progress. The liberal vision starts from economic advancement and sees, or hopes for, rationality in the use of prosperity through a unity of democracy and benevolent government whereby economic potential translates into improved life chances for more people. Not surprisingly, an outlook on history as bright and optimistic as this has been of shifting credibility but has always had a following of hopefuls, myself with my confidence in reform being one of them. It has recently been brought to front stage again in Benjamin Friedman's courageous book, *The Moral Consequences of Economic Growth*. The reform skeptics I took on at the start of this project were obviously on the other side of this vision. In their camp, the economy was something that either could not be tamed without being destroyed or had to be tamed with more powerful tools than pitiful reform.

I came to see my project as an inquiry into the validity of the liberal vision. That caused my attention to shift step by step from public policy to democratic values and performance. For democratic rule to be effective, that effectiveness would, if we follow Max Weber, have to come from authority more than from power. Authority in turn originates in democracy itself rather than in governance. That begs the question not only of effectiveness in rule but of the solidity of the democratic architecture that underpins rule. In *Citizens, Families, and Reform* I started to drift in that direction, and in this book I take the plunge and try to consolidate.

In the first part of the project, during twenty years of careful, step-by-step research, I explored welfare-state reform against the dismal predictions of its detractors.

First proposition: The distribution of income in industrial societies tends towards stability and is insensitive to (weak) policy interventions, at least in the long run. My reply: Advances in comparative research on income since about 1970 have shown that income distributions fluctuate strongly within nations and differ strongly between nations, and that such fluctuations and differences are associated with changes and differences in government policies.

Second proposition: Although the distribution of income is not stable, the incidence of poverty is, the implication being that reformist policies are not sufficiently powerful to rectify injustices at the bottom of the distribution. My reply: This proposition has been shown to rest on weak definitions of poverty that make empirical results noninterpretable, to be not robust for alternative methods of measurement, and to be unable to stand up to stricter and more appropriate criteria of definition and measurement.

Third proposition: Although the distribution of income and the incidence of poverty are not insensitive to reformist policies, class inequalities of opportunity are, the implication being again that deep, hard-core inequalities persist unabated. My reply: Support for this last stand of the antireformists has been sought in elaborately estimated statistics that propose to show long-term stabilities in class inequality. These statistics have, however, proved no less fragile than those on stable income distributions and poverty rates. Stability results rest on excessively relativized methods of measurement that are biased in favor of the preferred hypothesis; the results are nonrobust for tests against alternative methods and are disconfirmed by methods of unbiased measurement.

Of these propositions, the most difficult one to resolve was the one on class inequality. That took about ten years of work, in fruitful collaboration with my colleague Ottar Hellevik, but has now been brought to a successful conclusion. The process of disentangling the substantive consequences of intricate methodological choices in the technology of reading the descriptive information contained in mobility tables is chronicled in appendix A, where also the final conclusion is given: that we can now consider the stability thesis of class inequality overturned.

This conformity of findings on income, poverty, and class vindicates, I think, my instinctive optimism about reform and, by extension, the power of democratic governance—of government with its hands tied. That resolves to my satisfaction the validity of the liberal vision as far as the potential for effective governance goes. However, the liberal vision rests on the double act of democracy and benevolent government. I had been able to deliver one of the partners but the second one was still missing. If potent rule is *possible*, what does it take in the democratic foundations to make it more assured? It is to that question I have turned in the works summarized in this third book from my long project.

A NOTE ABOUT THE STUDY OF POLITICS

These works are inspired by some ideas about fruitful ways of studying politics or more broadly, society, for that matter.

One is an idea of individualism. By this, I mean that we should observe persons in order to reflect informatively on goodness or badness or progress or decline in politics and society, and that observing persons means ultimately to observe individuals. Thus, for example, I think we should pronounce on the quality of democracies by their impact on people more than by, say, some principle of "democraticness" in the political regime. In the study of poverty, I think it is essential for our ability to tell truthful stories that we observe the lives of individuals. Valid accounts of poverty cannot be created from above—for example, from the distribution of income—but can come only from below, from putting together what is known about how persons have it.

A second idea is one of reason. I defend the basic idea that people are themselves the best judges of their well-being, and I put that in the language of reason rather than of rationality. The concept of rationality has been badly damaged by *rational-choice theory*, a strange concoction that has people making life choices on the basis of a mental calculus of utility, by which is meant the ability of a choice to add positively to the satisfaction of one's preferences, whatever they may be. A model of that kind may be useful as a methodological assumption, but the trouble is that some advocates of rational choice have come to see it as a guide for moral pronouncements. "I don't vote," a prominent colleague from the rational-choice school said in a recent conversation, and regrettably not in jest, "I'm rational."

A third idea is to look beyond procedures, processes, and structures to results, outcomes, and consequences. The democratic way to study politics, I think, is to study it from the angle of how people live and how it affects the way they live. The three institutions or superinstitutions under scrutiny here are democratic regimes, democratic governments, and families. In each case, I ask what they *do* and try to assess them by how well they do what we should think they should do for us.

A NOTE ABOUT METHODOLOGY

Social scientists are prone to having strong opinions about methods. My opinion on the matter is not in favor of this or that methodology but one that can be formulated as a double principle: the right methodology is always the one that is right for the job at hand, and the right methodology for the job at hand is always the simplest one that will do the job.

It is my experience that empirical social science is often at its best when it is simple and descriptive and easily goes astray when it makes itself too fancy for its own good. Of course, we must be prepared to use the most advanced techniques of analysis, including mathematical analysis. I am an admirer and practitioner of advanced statistical analysis of complex data sets. In previous work, I've gone to great lengths in that direction, and I think with good results. I build on some of that work here, in particular in the family analyses in chapter 5.

But I'm at the same time deeply skeptical of fancy sophistication. Where I here use statistical analysis, on poverty and democratic quality, I go to the opposite extreme and use the simplest methodology anyone could imagine. I seek to analyze complicated phenomena with elementary indicators and no more mystery in computation than percentages. I know from previous work that methodological simplicity is often analytically powerful. I present an example of that experience in appendix G. I argue, and I think show, that in some cases methodological simplicity can produce findings that elude more complex procedures.

The simplicity of indicators is to some degree deceptive. The indicators approach rests on its own theoretical logic, and I try to explain that logic in particular in chapter 4. Indicators take us beyond strict measurement towards drawing a statistical portrait of a thing the complexity of which may be lost when squeezed into the straitjacket of measurement. On poverty in particular, I question what has hitherto been seen as completely obvious—that the scientific job is to measure it. I argue that measurement just cannot tell us what society needs to know about it.

I hope that methodological eclecticism and simplicity has paid off in these works. Through conceptual analysis, I have been able to establish that freedom is not the same as liberty and that it rests also on the self, on skills and control and the ability to use liberty well. By subjecting families to economic and organizational analysis rather than sociological discourse, I show that they remain immensely productive institutions but that their productivity is slowly slipping. And I find out why: it has to do with subjective and almost imperceptible changes in the family project around the sense of purpose and trust. Economic democracy, I find, is not a dead end. If we reshape the question from one of centralized power to one of decentralized redistribution, a good serving of it is available and there for the taking.

With the use of indicators, I am able to offer statistical findings that are original and robust. Poverty is not an ambiguously relative something that there is a bit of here, there, and everywhere with little difference and that perpetually recreates itself irrespective of development and economic affluence. It is a real thing; there is terrifyingly much of it in some countries and wonderfully little in some others. It *can* be eradicated—and therefore it should be. Democracies are not only different in the way they do democracy, they are also different in how well they do what we ought to expect of them. Countries that appear to be equally democratic are enormously different in democratic quality. When ranked by quality, the big model ones are not the best ones. Since democracies are differently good, democracy could be better.

These findings are significant and respond to good substantive questions. They are, of course, not final and eternal and are certainly not offered without qualifications. But they *are* interesting and pretty strong. I consider them to be well established and satisfying.

As always, there is more research to do. I hope to do some of it, including further methodological work on the indicators approach: better indicators and better data that can be treated with additional sensitivity. The term, "social indicators" has had some bad press. It is an uphill struggle to defend simplicity in an environment where sophistication is the methodological order of the day, if often for its own sake. I take delight in rehabilitating an idea it is now time to take seriously, and I recommend the indicators approach as a vehicle for further statistical research.

My two cases of indicator analysis are easy to criticize in the way indicator analysis can always be criticized: Why those indicators and why not some other ones? Why not crunch the data into more refined parameters? That should be done and ought to yield additional knowledge, or at least the reconfirmation of findings some might still consider hypotheses. But I also know with some confidence that there might not be much payoff in some forms of elaboration. The index of democratic quality, for example, could be more finely grained or be estimated from more indicators, but that would not matter much for the range of difference on display or for the ranking. A choice of indicators must, of course, be theoretically sound but is also, if we are honest about it, inevitably a bit intuitive and arbitrary. Usually, as in my cases, we have to do the best we can with the data that happen to be available. Imperfect as all this is, much has been learned in these experiments in simplicity and much of what is to be learned is already there in the first-order analyses.

A NOTE ABOUT COMPOSITION, READING, AND CONTEXT

I offer here some reflections on democracy today and in the future, reflections grounded in the idea that the final purpose of it all lies in the freedom that citizens need to live well. Democracies come in many shapes and forms, are always imperfect, and are constantly in need of being reinvented and improved. Citizens depend for their freedom on something that is dangerous to their freedom: on governance. Governance—or rule, if you will—should therefore be both effective and constrained.

The six chapters constitute six essays, all related but adding up to less than a unified treatise. Each deals with its own big question, which in turn deserves a book of its own. I have sought brevity in form as well as in methodology. There is a great deal of invisible work behind these essays in other publications and lectures (see the chapter footnotes and entries in references). I have thought of that work as experiments, and I think of this book as a summary of what has survived experimentation.

One way of keeping things reasonably short has been to push some material into appendixes. They are a mixture of background, additional evidence, and methodological follow-ups. I hope they contain interesting analyses and perspectives, but the appendixes are not strictly necessary reading.

The last chapter contains the philosophical platform I have worked from. The guts of it are explained here in the introduction, and that is probably enough for many purposes. The full chapter is perhaps heavy reading—at least it was heavy going to write it—and those who are not specifically interested in the political philosophy of freedom may be excused for making do with my summary above. On the other hand, the nonreader of that chapter will have missed what I have to say about, for example, faith and freedom and about evidence-based faith.

My context is advanced contemporary democracy, although we should perhaps be cautious about advertising democracy as "advanced." I have in mind democracy as it is where it is established and where it has come to at the beginning of the twenty-first century.

CHAPTER 1

How Good Are the Good Democracies?

> Democracies have always been, and still are, failure prone.
> They were short lived and ill suited for survival
> —Giovanni Sartori, *The Theory of Democracy Revisited*

DEMOCRACY IS BETTER than nondemocracy. The reason I can say that with confidence is that we now know what to look for in order to compare systems of rule by quality. Democracy is a better form of rule than any known alternative because it is better for the people whose life chances depend on the rule they live under. If that system is democratic, they are more likely than otherwise to be able to live in freedom and enjoy some comfort of well-being.[1]

It has not always been accepted that democracy is better than autocracy, nor is it universally accepted today. For example, democratic rule is sometimes thought to be less efficient than some forms of autocratic rule and therefore less suitable in countries that are up against serious problems, such as underdevelopment or overpopulation. That, as it happens, is probably not true; the evidence is that democracy outperforms the competition also in efficiency.[2] But this disagreement depends not only on facts and figures, it also goes back to different ways of assessing quality. I say that democracy is better than nondemocracy because it is better for people. The case for autocracy is usually made on the argument that it is potentially a more powerful form of rule.

A first version of this essay was delivered as a lecture at the University of the West Indies, Cave Hill, Barbados, on 19 May 2004 while I was a visiting professor at the Sir Arthur Lewis Institute of Social and Economic Studies. Revised versions were given as lectures at the University of Iceland in Reykjavik on 8 October 2004, on the occasion of the centenary of home rule in Iceland, and to the Graduate School of Governance at Sungkyunkwan University in Seoul on 13 April 2005. I am grateful to those universities for the invitations to present these ideas for discussion, and to Andrew Downes, Jonathan Lashly, Don Marshall, Lynette Eastmond, Torfi Tulinius, Gunnar Helga Kristinsson, Páll Skúlason, Sandrine Rui, Huck-ju Kwon, Chulwoo Lee, Sung Hyun Moon, and others for helpful comments on those occasions. I have benefited greatly from conversations with and suggestions from Øyvind Østerud, Frederik Engelstad, Ruud Luijkx, Miles Corak, Tim Smeeding, Bruce Bradbury, Guillermo O'Donnell, Laurence Whitehead, Gianfranco Pasquino, John Keane, and Larry Diamond on matters dealt with here.

[1] As argued persuasively by Dahl 1998.
[2] For a summary of evidence, see UNDP 2002.

These are different ways of answering the same question, different in methodology. In the first case, we insist that the quality of a system, in this case a system of rule, should be assessed by what it does for people. In the second case, systems are assessed by how they work without any direct observation of what they produce. That kind of analysis is clearly relevant but in my opinion incomplete, at least for the present purpose. Of course we need to know something about how political systems work in order to make any kind of judgment about them, but if we want to judge them by quality we need to follow through and observe not only how they operate and run the machinery of politics but also what they actually do, deliver, and produce. Democracies are supposed to be for the people they serve. It is because I go by and trust that kind of analysis that I feel able to say with confidence that democracy is the better form of rule.

That's democracy versus nondemocracy. Presently I want to compare democracies among themselves. Again, my concern is with the normative issue of quality. I want to measure democracies by quality and compare them so as to see which ones are better than others. My argument will be that we must use the same kind of analysis when comparing democracies that has enabled us to establish the superiority of democracy to nondemocracy. We need to follow through and see what they do for people.

The analysis in this chapter is comparative; I say something about which democracies are better than others but less about just how good any of them finally are. In appendix B, I reproduce a summary of what is perhaps the most careful assessment ever of a single democracy. That is the case of Norway, which not surprisingly happens to do comparatively well on my scale of quality. The Norwegian review is critical and finds much that is inept in a democracy that is of very good standing in the world. Comparatively good, then, is not necessarily very good (while, by extension, comparatively bad really is bad). This juxtaposition of comparative evidence against the backdrop of a strategic and more absolute case study proves helpful when I come to questions of democratic reform in the concluding chapter, and I make full use of it there. In appendix C, I compare press quality in two neighboring European countries, Britain and France. This is to underscore a message of difference. Both Britain and France obviously have a free press but are, surprisingly perhaps, far from being on an equal pegging in press freedom. That shows up again in my comparative data where the fragility of press freedom in France is one of the factors that contributes to its relatively low rating on democratic quality overall.

GETTING THE METHODOLOGY RIGHT

Political scientists have in recent traditions been reluctant to take on the question of "the good democracy." While the world was divided in a competition between democracy and autocracy, that comparison attracted the most attention. In addition, many of them probably did not think it a very good question in the first place. Rather they may have thought the right democracy to be the one that is right for each country, depending on its historical experience and cultural heritage, and that it is simplistic to want to order them along a single dimension of quality. Or that democracies have different qualities, that democracy A may be better than democracy B by one criterion and B better than A by another criterion, and that no more can usefully be said.

One way in which this skepticism has been expressed is in a widely shared view that there is a built-in trade-off in democracy between representativeness and efficiency: perfection in representativeness costs something in the efficiency of governance, and vice versa. If that is right, a country cannot have a democracy that is excellent in both these qualities; it has to choose what it considers to be the most important quality.

This theory of contrasting qualities has now been put to careful testing and in an important breakthrough work shown to be false. Lijphart Arend has compared two types of democracy that differ in the way they work; he calls them *majoritarian democracies* and *consensus democracies*. By the conventional theory, consensus democracies should be better in representativeness and majoritarian democracies better in the efficiency of rule. Using a rich set of indicators—including indicators of what democracies produce for people—he found that consensus democracies tend to outcompete majoritarian democracies in both ways, not only in representativeness and in being "kinder and gentler," but also in efficiency of governance, such as in macroeconomic management and the containment of violence.[3] This finding undermines the trade-off theory and establishes that it is possible to get further than has usually been assumed towards positioning democracies along a scale from better to worse.

Lijphart introduces the *quality of democracy* concept, but not as an overarching one. He considers quality to be one of several dimensions for comparing democracies but not a matter of final assessment. More recently, however, the concept of quality has started to be used in this general way.[4] That, I think, reflects a renaissance of interest in "the good democracy." With the resolution of the competition between democracy and autocracy in favor of democracy, we can now devote more attention to the democracies themselves. That stronger focus internally on democracy has drawn attention to weaknesses even in the established democracies.[5] With the recent rapid expansion of democracy in the world, we

---

[3] Lijphart 1999.

[4] See, e.g., Altman and Perez-Liñán 2002; Iazzetta et al. 2004.

[5] See, e.g., Parr et al. 2000 and Lagos 2003 on confidence, Klingemann and Fuchs 1995 and Siaroff and Merer 2000 on participation, Dahl 2001 on the U.S. case, Østerud et al.

need to get a better grip on what democracy is capable of.[6] The scholarly literature on democracy is now steeped in the language of quality—democracy is consolidating, evolving, developing, retracting, improving, weakening, strengthening, broadening, deepening and so on—and a new branch of research is emerging under the name of *democratic audit*.[7]

The question of goodness having been asked, the task is of course to answer it. A recent review of the state of the art, however, shows that we are like blind men searching in the dark. It is not just that we are unable to answer the question; we have so far not answered the question of how to answer the question.

The October 2004 issue of the *Journal of Democracy* published the proceedings of a symposium on the quality of democracy held at Stanford University the year before, with the aim of exploring what constitutes quality in democracy and how to measure it.[8] This collection of papers by leading authorities in the field contains a mass of information about contemporary democracy and a range of original analyses and insights. But as to the question before the symposium—how to evaluate democratic quality—it makes for discouraging reading. A reflective afterword by the journal's editor reverts to the skeptical view that the question is probably not a very good one.

For my part, however, I read these papers in a different way. They show that the question is on the table and in search of an answer. If we are, like this symposium, unable to get very far towards answering it, that is not for want of knowledge about democracy and democratic governance, either theoretically or empirically, but because we are not in control of how to use that knowledge to answer *this* question. The symposium plunged right into the effort of compiling information about democracy with next to no consideration of what methodology to use to answer the research question. Democracy was sliced up into eight "dimensions" that were treated one after the other by separate authors, with the inevitable result that each dimension was subdivided further into as many subdimensions.[9] The effort became one of amassing information without a methodological

---

2003 on the Norwegian case, and Offe 2003 on the German case. See also appendices B and C below.

[6] The number of countries that hold multiparty elections had by 1999 reached 140 (of 189 countries in all); cf. UNDP 2002. See also Huntington 1991.

[7] For an overview, see OECD, "The Future of Democracy," www.oecd.org/futures. See also, e.g., Proyecto Estato de la Nacíon 2001; Beetham et al. 2002; Boix 2003; Iversen 2005.

[8] The contributors are Larry Diamond, Leonardo Morlino, Guillermo O'Donnell, Philippe C. Schmitter, David Beetham, Dietrich Rueschmeyer, G. Bingham Powell Jr., and Marc F. Plattner. See also Diamond and Morlino 2005.

[9] The dimensions identified on which democracies are thought to vary in quality are freedom, the rule of law, vertical accountability, responsiveness, equality, participation, competition, and horizontal accountability. Each dimension is in principle explored in three re-

apparatus to bring it together towards some kind of consolidated conclusion. The question was no doubt seen to be complex, and it was therefore tempting to think that its answer must depend on bringing together as much as possible of data. But measurement is never about piling up data. It is about considering carefully what the relevant data are and then arranging those data with plan and economy.

It is without question correct that the right democracy is the one that is right for this or that country. Democracies are, must be, and should be vastly different. Methodologically, this means there is an awful lot of information about democracy that is irrelevant to the assessment and comparison of their quality. The job at hand is to sort out what information *not* to use and then to organize what remains relevantly. We need first a methodology that can tell us where to look and what to look for.

Until recently, the theory of social measurement took it to be more or less obvious that the site of social change was, in one way or other, "the system." Development, for example, was seen to be something that happened in "the economy." The consequence of that view was that measurement approaches used "the system" as the unit of observation. Development was observed for countries, usually with the gross domestic product (GDP) per capita indicator.

In the last couple of decades, however, there has occurred what amounts to a change of paradigm in this branch of measurement theory. That has come about through a better understanding of just what the site of quality is and from there a better understanding of what is the appropriate unit of observation. We are now inclined to argue that social quality resides ultimately with the persons who belong to or live in a system and not exclusively in the system itself (at least, so we will argue if we work within a framework of democratic values). Systems have *potential* but the *value* contained in that potential is manifested or not in the lives of persons. If development is for people, it needs to be measured in how it manifests itself in the lives of persons.[10] If that is the case, we need to use the person as a relevant unit of observation. The change of paradigm is in this meaning towards methodological individualism.[11]

This has not made the system irrelevant as a unit of observation, but we would now see measurement approaches that observe only the system as insufficient. The measurement of development, to stay with that example, would observe first the system and its potential, using the GDP per capita indicator, for example, and then in addition the value that flows

---

spects: the empirical definition, the conditions for the dimension to develop and thrive, and the means by which it is commonly subverted.

[10] As in development as freedom; cf. Sen 1999b.

[11] Elster 1989.

from that potential into the lives people live, using poverty as an indicator, for example.

There is a specific logic behind the change of paradigm according to which the robust measurement of social quality depends on a kind of double bookkeeping in which information both about the system and the lives of those who live in it is recorded. Neither one nor the other is on its own enough. In the case of development, again, it is not enough to observe the living conditions of persons. These could theoretically be better than what is assured in the potential of the economy, for example, if poverty is held back by development aid rather than by the economic potential of the country itself. Such well-being would be precarious, and this country should therefore not be considered an economically developed one. Nor is it enough to observe the country's economic potential. Two countries that have the same economic potential but differ in their performance on poverty should not be considered equally developed. We observe two things—potential in the system and quality of life for persons—and measure development by a combined use of both observations. The obvious example is the Human Development Index (by the United Nations Development Programme). Development is here measured in an index based on the economic potential of each country and the standard of health and education in its people. That change in approach makes a very considerable difference in measurement results.[12]

Another area of research that has moved forward in authority and versatility thanks to having matured into post-paradigm-change methodology is the measurement of income inequality and poverty. Here, the double bookkeeping regards the household as the unit for the measurement of income and the individual as the unit for the measurement of the economic well-being that is contained in the economic potential of the household.[13] This, together with improvements in the database, has enabled us to attain much safer knowledge about comparative income inequality and poverty.[14]

Pre-paradigm-change methodology used single bookkeeping: information about the system only. Post-paradigm-change methodology does not offer a different kind of single bookkeeping but has advanced to double bookkeeping.

My argument here, obviously, is that we should take on board this change in methodological paradigm for the measurement of democratic

[12] Some countries have a higher ranking in human development than in economic development in recent reports (e.g., Sweden, Australia, Greece, Cuba, and Costa Rica), while others have a lower ranking (e.g., the United States, Switzerland, Ireland, and Denmark). See the annual *Human Development Reports*.

[13] See Ringen 1996, 2005a.

[14] See, e.g., "The Luxembourg Income Study," www.lisproject.org.

quality. Approaches of the *Journal of Democracy* kind are stuck in single bookkeeping mode; they observe only the system, that is, the regime. If we get the methodology up to post-paradigm-change scratch, we are halfway there. In fact, once we get the methodology right, we can, as we will see, get pretty far towards robust comparisons with the help of simple and rudimentary indicators. The Human Development Index is proof of that. It, deservedly, carries heavy authority in spite of being estimated from a few rough-and-ready indicators. On the other hand, unless we get the methodology right, not even the most refined and complete data will do the job.

THE MEASUREMENT OF DEMOCRACY

There is an extensive literature on the empirical comparison of democracies.[15] The most authoritative source is the Polity project (presently Polity IV).[16] This project measures the "degree of democracy" on a year-by-year basis, covering a period of roughly two hundred years, for all independent states (with populations of more than 500,000). The indicators are:

- Existence of a functioning polity (a functioning central political authority having been established and not interrupted)

- Openness (democracy) or closeness (autocracy) of political institutions

- Durability of the polity (number of years since the last regime transformation)

- Institutionalized procedures for the transfer of executive power

- Competition in executive recruitment

- Independence of/constraints on the chief executive

- Institutional structures of political expression

- Competitiveness of participation

The regime classification, based mainly on expert assessment, is on a scale from +10 (most democratic) to −10 (least democratic).

---

[15] The early standard reference is Inkeles 1991. For a later overview, see symposium articles in *Comparative Political Studies* 35 (February 2002), in particular Munch and Verkuilen 2002. See also Bollen and Jackman 1989; Bollen and Paxton 2000; Casper and Tufis 2002; and, for a summary of evidence, UNDP 2002.

[16] www.cidem.umd.edu/inscr/polity.

The aim of this project is to maintain long time-series of data on what makes countries more or less democratic within a simple and powerful framework. Its method is to compare countries using information on the shape of their political regimes.

The Polity comparisons show, not surprisingly, vast differences between the countries of the world in how democratic they are but little or no difference in the degree of democracy among the established democracies, for example those of Western Europe and North America. That would suggest that once countries are established democracies, they are pretty similar in how good they are as democracies.

My hypothesis is that democracies, even the established ones, are vastly different in quality. That does not seem to be the case from what we can read from the Polity data, but that reading is not persuasive for my purpose. Methodologically, projects of the Polity type are pre-paradigm-change. They look to the political regime—the system, in other words—and use that as the unit of observation. Such projects do not directly take in information on the situation of persons. Some comparisons do use information of that kind.[17] But the Polity project is representative of the mainstream measurement effort in taking the regime to be the appropriate unit of measurement.[18] It observes how political regimes are constituted and work but does not follow through to observing what they deliver for people.

My question is not how democratic the democracies are, but how good they are. That question, in my opinion, cannot be answered with the use of the Polity-type methodology. We need to start from Polity-type observations, which in my terminology go to the potential of regimes, but then to move on from there and follow through to observations of what the regimes produce of value, using the person as the unit of observation.

Guillermo O'Donnell has criticized mainstream political science for a "narrow focus on the regime."[19] That, I think, is a valid criticism of comparative democracy. In Polity-type comparisons, it is simply taken to be obvious that the regime is where the action is and where we should look for the "democraticness" of a country. The same obviousness informed the *Journal of Democracy* symposium (to which O'Donnell was himself a contributor). The dimensions into which democracies were sliced were regime dimensions.

But this regime focus is not at all obvious. There is a need to reflect more carefully on where to look for what kind of information. We do need to look to the regime, but we need to know just what we are looking

---

[17] See, e.g., Huber et al. 1997; and, as seen above, Lijphart 1999.

[18] For a review, see Reich 2002.

[19] In Iazzetta et al. 2004.

for there. And it is not enough to look to the regime. We need also to look to the people who live under the regime and again to know just what to look for there. Until we sort out what to look for and where, no knowledge about how democracies work, no dimensions of democraticness, and no piling up of data can lead us to a persuasive answer to the question of how good the democracies are.

FOUR QUESTIONS

The task is to compare systems. The first question, then, is what systems do we compare; what is it that is or is not democratic?

After that, the second question is to decide which systems qualify to be included in a comparison of democratic systems; what is it that makes a system democratic?

Once those matters are resolved, we can start to uncover the goodness of democratic systems. In post-paradigm-change methodology, that goes via two separate questions. First, what potential does the system have? That is a regime question, and the regime is the right unit of observation. Second, what flows to persons from that potential in the system? To answer this question, we need to step out of the regime and into observations with the person as the unit.

WHAT IS IT THAT IS OR IS NOT DEMOCRATIC?

Democracy applies potentially to any kind of community in which there is collective decision making and governance. That could be large communities, such as countries (or even the world, in the case of world government), or small ones, such as neighborhoods; it could be all-embracing communities (countries again), or ones that deal with only a limited part of their members' lives, such as voluntary associations or workplaces. It is convenient to use the term *polity* as the generic name for all communities with collective decision making and governance, of whatever size and kind. Generally, we should think of comparative democracy as a study of polities of whatever shape and size.

Polities consist of members. They are obviously made up of more than members—for example, of institutions, rules, conventions, and so on—but what finally constitutes a polity is the persons who are its members. Members of democratic polities are usually referred to as *citizens*.

While the polity is the thing that is or is not democratic, its citizens are those it is democratic for. Pre-paradigm-change approaches to comparative democracy measure the democraticness of political regimes in democratic countries. But a polity is not democratic for the purpose of being democratic. The purpose of democracy is to serve citizens. In order to establish descriptively whether or not a polity is democratic, it is enough to observe its political regime. But if we want to praise or blame democratic polities normatively, that is not enough. It is not for their elegant running of the machinery of politics we should thank democracies but for what they do for their citizens.

When we come to the empirical part of this exercise, I will follow suit in the comparative literature and compare countries. That is what I am interested in here, but other kinds of polities are in principle equally relevant objects of comparison.[20]

What Makes Polities Democratic?

This seemingly simple question is in fact very difficult to answer. It's the problem of defining democracy.

The standard approach to democracy in national polities is to use minimalist definitions built around the arrangement of competitive elections. Schumpeter famously defined the democratic method as "that institutional arrangement for arriving at political decisions in which individuals acquire the power to decide by means of a competitive struggle for the people's vote." Dahl gave his minimalist definition the name *polyarchy*: high officials are elected in free and fair elections based on inclusive suffrage, the rights to compete for office and of free expression are assured, and citizens have associational autonomy and access to alternative sources of information.[21] A country is considered democratic if its political regime operates on the basis of free and fair elections.[22]

As I have decided to compare countries, this definition of democracy is adequate for the purpose of the present study and it is the definition I will go by in the empirical comparisons below. The countries I compare will be considered to be democratic because they are electoral democracies. By this definition, a country is democratic if its political regime is run democratically, and that is the case if it works on the basis of free and fair elections.

There are very good reasons to use the election definition of democracy. The institution of free elections simply *is* the litmus test of democracy in today's world. Furthermore, the election method is a brilliant invention

---

[20] For example, subpolities within national polities, say municipalities or states in federal systems; cf., e.g., Hill 1994; Heller 2000.

[21] Schumpeter 1952; Dahl 1971, 1989.

[22] Of course, just what makes elections free and fair is not easily said; cf., e.g., Elklit and Svensson 1997.

for democracy and has attained its superior status in democratic thinking for good reasons. It is ingenious in the way it sorts out decisions, dangers, and protections. Those who acquire the power to decide by winning the people's vote have a real incentive to get on and produce decisions. They owe it to those who have given them power by voting for them. They know that they will have to face elections again quite soon. They have their mandate from their voters and that clarifies to some considerable degree what they are entitled to do and what is off-bounds. Their mandate is a more or less reasonable compromise between the divergent interests in the population as that has materialized in the process of a fair competition. Blatantly dictatorial decisions are obviously excluded from the mandate of any elected or majority government. Citizens can reasonably trust their representatives not to stray too far from legitimate rule because they have the power to deselect them in the next round. The election method is thus likely to bring about governance by consent and thereby legitimate rule, which is to say decision making that citizens have good reasons to accept and obey even when the decisions made are not those they themselves would have preferred.

But there are also problems. The election method, for all its cleverness, is still only a method. It hardly has the status it has because it *is* democracy, but because it delivers democratic value. Other methods—including possibly methods not yet invented—can and could produce the same magic. We consider the election method to be democratic because it has been proved to deliver democratic value; the inclusion or not of other methods would depend on the experience of delivery.

The problem is again a methodological one: where should we look to decide whether or not a polity is democratic? The election definition says that we should look to how the machinery of politics is run: by elections or not? As I've said, I am satisfied with the election definition for the present purpose. But in theory I do not think the election definition does the job of defining democracy in polities more generally.

For one thing, small polities would not depend on elections for being democratic. Families, for example, can clearly be more or less democratic or autocratic, but not depending on whether or not they hold elections. The same would probably apply to some workplaces and other small groups that could manage their affairs democratically without elections. The election definition is clearly not universally valid.

In national polities, democracy is done in infinitely different ways, and no two democracies are the same in the way they do it. Even elections are not *necessary* for a country to be democratic. The very idea of elected representative assemblies of legislation is an invention of modern democracy, known neither in the ancient world nor in the early Nordic quasi-democracies in Europe. In Switzerland, although an electoral democracy, the supreme method of decision making is by referendum. With direct democracy, decisions are made democratically without elections. Direct democracy in some form is where democracy started and is, although not widespread, still in use, for example, in local affairs in some towns in New England in the United States.[23] One can obviously ask how well such methods work, but that is the same question we put to the method of elections. Direct democracy, just like electoral democracy, is, with or without flaws, democracy.

Another nonelection method of decision making is by elaborate arrangements of consultation, veto, and consensus, as appears to have been the case in some city-states in Mesopotamia centuries before ancient Athens "invented" democracy, in a subsequent tradition in parts of Asia of public participation in decision making by discussion and consensus, and possibly also in precolonial "tribal democracy" in Africa, a tradition Nelson Mandela would invoke as an inspiration for his own style of conciliatory leadership.[24] Such methods may not be current today, but that is not to say they could not reemerge as democratic methods, for example, in some new democracies that come out of different historical or cultural traditions than today's established ones. Some commentators see the route to better democracy to go not so much through better elections and institutions of representation as through procedures and institutions of participatory, nonadversary, and deliberative democracy.[25]

Is direct democracy, consultative democracy, or deliberative democracy really democratic? If so, by what standards? If not, why not? If Switzerland gave up elections but retained referendums, would it still be a democracy?

And there are intermediate methods between electoral and direct democracy. Historically, the original democratic way of selecting officials was by lot in a system of rotating offices, which was the method in ancient Athens and one used widely in the Italian republics up to the fall of Venice in 1797.[26] When we think of elections today we usually think of arrangements in which *parties* compete, but party elections are a rather new invention historically and not the universal system today. Even modern electoral democracy is older than political parties as we now know them (for example, in core democracies such as Britain, the United States, and the Scandinavian countries), and there are democracies today that seem to function well enough without political parties.[27] Indirect election is a well-established democratic method, for example, in republics where

---

[23] See, e.g., Bryan 1995.

[24] Evans 1958; Jacobsen 1970; Finer 1997; Mieroop 1999; Nash 1999; Fleming 2004; Sen 2005.

[25] Mansbridge 1980; Barber 1984; Gutmann and Thompson 1996, 2004; Elster 1998; Ackerman and Fishkin 2004; Rui 2004.

[26] On the importance of lot in the democratic tradition, see Manin 1997.

[27] As documented by Anckar and Anckar 2000.

the president is elected by, and sometimes among, the elected members of the legislature.

Nor do elections necessarily assure the order and legitimacy that we usually think of as characteristics or even the purpose or meaning of democratic rule, even when the elections themselves are reasonably free and fair, resulting sometimes in hybrid regimes that have elections but are not really democratic.[28] By the election definition, present-day Iran might conceivably be classified as a democracy, which of course it is not. The experience in many parts of the former Soviet Union is that it at best takes time for the introduction of electoral democracy to produce even a semblance of real democratic order. In Latin America, some democracies are so intrinsically volatile and turbulent that they seem to represent a regime type of their own, for which the label "dysfunctional democracies" has been suggested.[29]

These examples suggest that there are shortcomings in the election definition (at least theoretically if not practically for the present purpose) because it finally does not look to the right place to identify polities unambiguously as democratic or not. It says that a country is democratic if it uses the election method. But since other methods are available that could make countries democratic, and since elections do not necessarily assure democracy, there must be something else behind any given method that really decides whether or not a country is democratic. It would seem that we should look deeper into the regime, or possibly behind it, for the definition.

My suggestion would be to define democracy as a structure of power rather than in a procedure or method: *a polity is democratic if its citizens hold the ultimate control over collective decisions in a securely institutionalized manner.* That is democracy because that is what is required for citizens to have good reasons to trust that collective decisions are made and will continue to be made on the basis of respect for their interests. Power sits with citizens (collectively, of course). Either citizens exercise their power themselves in some form of direct democracy or they delegate it to elites who then hold it in trust and use it under the knowledge that citizens retain the ultimate power to retract delegated power or to shift it to other elites of their choice. This definition obviously includes electoral democracy but does not limit democracy to that form.

This is a minimalist definition in its own right. It specifies the minimum requirement for a polity to be considered democratic but does not include in the definition itself any further particulars about the way or shape of the political regime. It is more open than the Schumpeter-Dahl definitions

---

[28] Diamond 2002.
[29] By Whitehead 2004.

but equally robust in requiring of polities that there is institutionalized popular control over collective decision making in order to qualify for membership in the democratic family. It is a safe definition that allows no autocratic rule to parade as "democratic in a different way." It is in that respect possibly safer than the election definition. For example, if by the election definition there should be some doubt about whether to classify Iran as a democracy, the matter would be resolved by this definition because, although there are elections and even if they were reasonably free and fair, ultimate power over collective decisions is wielded by an elite of unelected clerics from above and not by citizens from below. Or imagine a country with free and fair elections for political power but in which economic power overwhelmingly trumps political power; this would be a democracy by the election definition but not by the power definition.[30]

By my definition, the thing that finally makes a polity democratic is located deep inside or behind the regime.[31] The method by which the democracy works, say the election method, now becomes an intermediate variable between the democraticness of the regime by structure and the consequences of that democraticness for citizens. If O'Donnell is right to criticize mainstream political science on democracy for a narrow focus on the regime, that criticism should probably go both ways. On the one hand there is a failure to observe what regimes do for people, and on the other hand there is also a failure to look behind the methods of the regime to the real structure of power.

What Makes Democratic Polities Good?

Regime approaches to comparative democracy ask how democratic countries are and seek to identify that by the way they do democracy. However, it is elementary that countries differ and must differ in the way they do

---

[30] In *How Democratic Is the American Constitution?* Dahl puts a question mark against the democratic credentials of the U.S. regime on the argument that its system of representation is so unfair as to make it (nearly) undemocratic. I am not persuaded by that argument (as I would, for example, not be persuaded by an argument that Britain is undemocratic because it has an unelected upper house in the legislature). I think we should always recognize that democratic forms are historically and culturally determined and that the peculiarities of the U.S. constitution are simply "American" (as, for example, the House of Lords is a very "British" institution). I think a more persuasive question mark against American democracy (and probably British and other democracies as well) can be raised on the argument that economic power is allowed to trump political power. I return to that issue, although not specifically the U.S. case, in chapter 2.

[31] The right formulation would depend on the definition of "regime." If the regime is the apparatus of politics and governance, the structure of power would presumably sit behind it.

democracy, and it is therefore difficult to establish how democratic they are, never mind how good they are, by observing the way they do it.

For example, is the way the chief executive or cabinet members are recruited a criterion of democraticness, as is widely assumed (including in the criteria used in the Polity project)? It is sometimes considered democratic if they are elected, or at least chosen from among the elected members of the legislature. In the British case, for example, only members of Parliament are eligible for cabinet office (although that does include the nonelected members of the House of Lords). The democratic logic would be that citizens should be ruled by representatives they have themselves chosen. But in other parliamentary systems, such as the Scandinavian ones, the prime minister could in principle be chosen from outside of the legislature, and cabinet members frequently are. In the United States, the head of government (who is also the head of state, the president) is elected (in an intricate arrangement of indirect election), but cabinet members are usually not recruited from among the elected members of Congress (and if they are, they resign their post in the legislature, which in Britain they do not). These methods are all democratic in that they are used in established and respected democracies. Do these differences make some counties more democratic, or in other ways better democracies, than others?

Or take the principle of division of power. A claim to excellence in the U.S. Constitution is the formal division of power between the legislative, executive, and judicial branches of government. But the separation of legislative and executive power does not apply to parliamentary systems. Are they therefore second-rate democracies? Hardly, but just why is that so? The autonomy of the judiciary is generally taken to be essential in a democracy, but what then about the British case in which the judiciary is not formally separate from the legislature? The highest court in Britain has its site in Parliament and is made up of the Law Lords, who are members of the House of Lords and hence also legislators (and who, when meeting as a court, sit in the legislative chamber). The head of the judiciary, the lord chancellor, was until recently also both the speaker of the upper house and a member of cabinet. These arrangements are currently under reform, but was Britain undemocratic before those reforms or less democratic than, for example, the United States? The British judiciary has long been autonomous in fact, although that autonomy was not formally institutionalized. In terms of method, then, British democracy would seem to be wanting but, at least on this account, to be sound enough in practice.

In current writings about democracy, a high level of popular participation in elections and otherwise is generally taken to be an important criterion of democratic vitality.[32] That has not always been an agreed-upon

---

[32] This is, for example, a core criterion in the democracy issue of *Human Development Report* (UNDP 2002).

view. For example, the relatively low participation rates in elections in the United States has been seen as a sign of relaxed confidence in the system, and "an increase in the level of participation may reflect a decline of social cohesion and [even] the breakdown of the democratic process."[33] Personally, I'm of the opinion that a high level of popular participation is usually a good thing in a democracy, but I think it *can* be argued that it is not a *necessary* criterion of a good democracy and that democratic rule can function well enough without much popular involvement. Again we see how difficult it is to pronounce on the democraticness or quality of a democracy by the way it does democracy.

What we want to identify in the regime, once we have sorted out that it is democratic, is what I have called its *potential*. Post-paradigm-change approaches ask us to start by first identifying the quality potential that sits in the system and then to follow through to see what quality is in fact delivered to persons.

Mainstream approaches (to follow O'Donnell again) are insufficient, I have said, because they look to the regime only without following through to observing what is delivered. I am now inclined to think there is a problem also in *how* they look to the regime and what they look for there. They look to how democracy is done and try to assess how democratic a country is in the way it does democracy. But democracy is done in so many ways that there probably is no such thing as the most democratic way. Therefore, if we put the question of the good democracy as one of democraticness, I go along with the skeptical view that it is not a very good question.

Theoretically, I now lean to thinking that comparative democracy, when it aims to be normative, should *totally* disregard the way democracies do democracy. We should not look to any specific method for the definition of democracy, but look behind methods and to the structure of power. If we know that a polity has a democratic structure of power, we know that it is democratic and there is no need to be concerned with how it then chooses to operate the machinery of politics, not even whether or not it uses the election method. Nor should we look to any specifics about the way democracy is done to identify how good a democracy it is. What additional information we need for that assessment, once we have established its democratic credentials by the structure of power, is to be found in what it delivers to citizens. Everything that lies between these two observations—elections, the way elections are organized, the way the legislature operates, the division of authority between the branches of government, citizenship involvement, and much more—we can consign to the category of irrelevant information for this purpose. For other purposes,

[33] Lipset 1960, p. 32.

of course, this is important information but not for this one. In all these things, democracies differ, but those differences are not the ones that make them good or bad democracies. They are good if they are capable of delivering democratic value and if they actually do that. If we look at a country, establish that it has a democratic structure of power, and see in its political regime the potential to deliver democratic value and in its citizenry such value delivered, why should we be further concerned with the practicalities of just how this country has come to arrange the details of the doing of democracy and governance?[34]

That position is a radical departure from the mainstream. It says that most of what tends to be observed in comparative democracy is not of much relevance for the normative comparison of democracies by quality and that most of what needs to be observed for that kind of comparison has tended to be ignored. It is a theoretical recommendation that I myself will not be able to fully obey in the empirical comparisons below—I do follow it in everything except that I practically start from the election definition—but it is the position and approach I think comparative democracy should strive towards.

WHAT IS DEMOCRATIC VALUE?

In polities, collective decisions are made that are necessary for and binding on citizens. Decisions are needed in order for those who belong to the community to be able to cooperate and get on with life and business.

This necessity of binding decisions means that citizens are always in danger. They are in danger of necessary decisions not being made, or if made of not being implemented, or if implemented of not being obeyed. Such deficit of decisions is a danger to citizens because joint matters that they depend on being resolved in order to be able to work, travel, sell, buy, get married, raise children, and so on are not resolved. Liberties are left unprotected. Rules and procedures are not put in place that give citi-

---

[34] One of the problems with trying to assess the democraticness of democracies by how they do democracy is that one easily falls into the trap of postulating *the* best way of doing democracy, or even that everyone should do it the way *we* do it. In the introduction to the *Journal of Democracy* symposium on the quality of democracy, Diamond and Morlino ask how "efforts to think about democratic quality can avoid becoming paternalistic exercises in which the older democracies take themselves for granted as models . . . ?" (2005, p. 19). My answer is that as long as we think about democratic quality as a matter of how democracy is done, such paternalism is inescapable and that it can only be avoided by moving beyond that way of approaching the assessment and into post-paradigm methodology.

zens security against the threat they represent to each other, from traffic rules via the regulation of property rights to criminal justice.

But they are also in danger if decisions *are* made. They are in danger of having arbitrary or unduly restricting or dictatorial decisions imposed on them and of being subjected to decisions that put their health, liberty, or life in danger. Such excess of decisions is a danger to citizens because those who hold power are unavoidably tempted to use that power to give themselves advantage or to coerce others.

The danger that citizens are exposed to is, in the final analysis, the danger of not being free to live their lives as they themselves wish and choose. That includes, since life in community cannot be absolutely free, the danger that liberties are limited in arbitrary or unjust ways.

Here, I suggest, we are at the core of what democracy is for: freedom, the necessity of binding decisions, the dangers to citizens that are endemic in any kind of governance, the protection they need against the insecurities they are exposed to by living in community with others.[35] Democracy is about getting decisions made, getting the right ones made, averting the wrong ones—all from the point of view of citizens' quest for freedom and the need to regulate the exercise of freedom rationally and fairly. It is ultimately about the *security* of freedom—the experience of freedom today and the ability to trust that there will be freedom tomorrow and into the future.

Security of freedom means two things. It means that citizens have freedom and that that freedom is protected. The freedoms citizens have or do not have need to be observed in the lives they live. The degree to which freedoms are or are not protected needs to be observed in the political regime. To assess democratic quality we need both these observations, not one or the other but both. We need to move from single to double bookkeeping.

The relevant potential in the regime is its potential for ensuring and continuing to ensure citizens freedom. That's what we should look for in the regime. The relevant delivery is observed in the degree to which citizens are able to live in freedom here and now and to be able to feel confident that their freedoms are ensured into the future. That's what we should look for in the lives of persons. It is necessary but not enough to observe whether or not citizens live in freedom; we need also to see how well that freedom is protected and ensured. It is also necessary but also not enough to ascertain that there is potential for freedom in the political regime; we need also to see how well freedom is delivered. In the same way that an economy should be considered a good economy only if it has economic potential *and* that potential is translated into well-being for

---

[35] For a related argument, see Sen 1999a.

persons, a democratic polity should be considered a good democracy only if it has the potential to promote and protect freedom *and* that potential is translated into free lives for persons. Freedom without adequate protection in the institutions of the regime is transitory and unsafe. Potential for freedom that is not distributed in the form of free lives for persons is not the stuff of democratic quality.

Since I argue that democracy is for citizens and that what it is finally for is their freedom, we might think it sufficient simply to ask citizens if they consider themselves to be free and if they are content with the way their freedoms are enshrined in democratic institutions. I do think it follows from the logic I am arguing that a democracy is in some ways as good as citizens hold it to be, and I will include that kind of subjective assessment in my empirical comparison. But I don't think it is enough to ask citizens. It would be hard to give a democracy a high rating on quality unless its citizens consider it to be a good democracy that does for them what they think it should do, but citizens *could* be wrong, shortsighted, or manipulated. We should ask citizens but also make sure that their subjective judgments have an objective basis.

TOWARDS MEASUREMENT

We now have some clues to go by for taking the next step into empirical measurement.

First, the criterion of democratic quality is freedom. A democratic country is a good democracy if its political regime contains the potential to deliver security of freedom and if citizens actually have freedom and are able to feel confident that that will endure.

Second, the principle of double bookkeeping. We need to observe both the potential for freedom in the regime and the realization of freedom in the lives of citizens. In more methodological language: We are looking for an approach that combines macro and micro measurement. Quality is identified not in one or the other level but in the interplay of potential and realization. A country whose political regime contains the potential for freedom but does not deliver is not a good democracy. Nor is a country in which citizens may enjoy a fair degree of freedom but where their freedoms are not ensured in the institutions of the regime.

Third, methodological individualism. The relevant potential of quality in a democratic regime is its potential for delivery to persons, and the delivery that is realized is what shows up in the lives of persons. The assessment of democratic quality should be as seen through the eyes of citizens. It is not enough to look upon the polity from above or outside; we need to try to see what it looks like through the life experiences of those who live in it and whom it is for. The question is whether citizens, when they look to their lives see freedom in it and when they look to the political regime see laws, institutions, and conventions that give them good reasons to feel confident that their democracy is capable of delivering and protecting freedom today and into the future.

Fourth, a political regime has the potential we would ask of a good democratic one if basic liberties are protected in its institutions and if it has the capacity of decision making for efficient democratic governance. Democratic quality *is* a matter of "kind and gentle" governance, but even kindness in governance depends on effectiveness in governance. A democratic regime cannot do kindness unless it has capacity to do.

The concept of freedom I work from is explained in some length in chapter 6. Here, it is sufficient to define the minimal conditions of freedom as consisting of the liberties that are contained in basic civil and political rights and the resources that are needed to make practical use of such rights.

AN EXPERIMENT IN COMPARISON

My ambition now is a limited one. The hypothesis is that democracies are vastly different in quality. That hypothesis I will be able to test, but I do not, to repeat, pretend to be able to offer the final word on how good the contemporary democracies are.

This is an experiment in measurement that will take us a step forward in the comparison of democracies by quality, but much research remains to achieve more definitive results. I have argued that we need a very different approach for the measurement and comparison of democratic quality from the mainstream one, but I am not in a position to offer the final word on that alternative. The claim I would make for the present exercise is that it answers the question of how to answer the question, but not that it gives the final answer.

This is a first stab at a comparison that I consider to be by the right methodology, a first stab because it has to be done with inadequate data. I have not sought or been able to collect data specifically for this purpose and have had to make do with what I have been able to find in existing sources. I would, of course, have preferred more and more tailor-made data for the purpose and more detailed analyses, but these will have to wait. In fact, the problem of data is such that for one essential indicator I have next to no hard data to go by at all and have had to make do with a relatively impressionistic classification.

I compare only democracies and among them only democracies whose regimes are rated as highly democratic by a mainstream assessment of democraticness. All the democracies I include are at or near the top of the Polity scale. From that I take it to be given that these are all democracies in which citizens enjoy basic civil and political rights and in which these rights are ensured in the institutions of the regime. I therefore do not include information about basic rights in the comparison.

The language of delivery, which I have used in the discussion above, is a causal language. Regimes deliver and citizens are delivered to. That causality I will not be testing. I will observe potential in the regime and freedoms in the citizenry, but only descriptively. I do not doubt the causal link, but I do not observe or test it directly.

The approach I will use is an elementary indicators approach. I discuss the methodology of indicators in more detail in chapter 4 and appendix F.

I start by looking to the regime. Does it have the potential to deliver security of freedom? I then look to the life situation of citizens. Do they live in freedom, and are they able to feel safe about their freedoms? The decisive test under obvious principles of democracy is the degree to which freedom and the security of freedom extends to *everyone* in the citizenry.

I have two units of observation, the regime and the person. For each kind of observation, I have identified two dimensions. For each dimension, I will use two indicators. That will give me eight indicators in all: four to display the quality of potential in the regime and four to display the quality of delivery to citizens. For each indicator I will define a single cut-off point between good and not-good quality. To countries on the good side of the dichotomy I allocate a score of 1, to the others a score of 0. From this I will estimate a final index of democratic quality as a simple additive index from the eight indicator scores. The final index will then have a range from 8 (high quality) to 0 (low quality).

The choice of operational indicators is dictated by what I have been able to extract from existing sources. Not all that much is available to choose from, but I have been able to find enough to put together a relevant and reasonably robust battery of indicators. I treat the data with the respect I argue for in appendix F of not imposing on them more analysis than they can tolerate. The use of dichotomies, for example, is obviously pretty rough, but that does not make much difference here. With more flexible data, I might have been able to suggest a more fine-grained distribution of democratic quality but probably not more than the observed spread in quality.

The ambition of any indicators approach is to capture the thing the indicators are indicative of, in this case the quality of democracy. What is displayed then is not primarily a set of indicators but a portrait, drawn in the simplest possible way, of the thing of underlying concern. A set of indicators does not add up to a measure of the underlying thing in a strict meaning of measurement but does, when relevantly sensitive, capture true variations and movements in that thing. In this case, I think the choice of indicators is good and logical according to the theoretical and methodological principles I have sought to develop above. As for the simplicity in the treatment of the indicators—each is dichotomized and given equal weight—this recommends itself by the methodological principle that simplicity is the best procedure unless there is a solid basis for more complex methodological choices. It is probably a simplification of what really constitutes democratic quality to consider all the eight indicators below to be equally important and hence to give them equal weighting in the final index. But if we have no safe way of deciding which ones are how much more or less important that the other ones, which I at this stage of research do not have, the methodologically correct way is to treat them as equal. For example, I think a case might well be made for giving the subjective indicators of confidence and trust more than equal weighting compared to the objective indicators, but I would not know with the available information how that could be done persuasively.[36] Under the circumstances, "keeping it simple" would seem to be safe and advisable.

The first dimension of the regime I refer to as the *strength* of its democratic institutions, and the second dimension its *capacity* of decision making. The first dimension in the life situation of citizens I refer to as their *security* of resources for freedom, and the second dimension their *trust* in democracy and freedom.

INDICATORS OF STRENGTH

(1) Democratic regimes have the potential to deliver security of freedom when they are consolidated, which is to say that citizenship rights and democratic procedures are safely institutionalized in laws, conventions, and mind-sets so that democracy is "the only game in town."[37] Ideally, I would have wanted to start with a measure of consolidation, but the literature on consolidation deals mainly with issues in the transition to democracy. The democracies I am interested in comparing are those that in this literature are considered consolidated. The most authoritative effort to measure consolidation is the Bertelsman Transformation Index, which ranks 116 countries in the world by their progress towards market-based democracy, but the democracies that are already consolidated are not in-

---

[36] Although implicitly I am giving the subjective indicators extra weight in force of the strictness used in their operational definition. In reality, four statistical indicators are used to construct the two ones that appear in the comparison and the score of 1 is in each case allocated only to countries that satisfy both a trend and level criterion on both underlying indicators.

[37] On consolidation, see Linz and Stepan 1996.

cluded (roughly the OECD countries).[38] That brings us back to the Polity comparisons: it is assumed that once democracies are consolidated, there is not much to distinguish between them.

I do not think we should consider democracies equally consolidated if we see the core of it to be a matter of delivering security of freedom and that again for everyone. To illustrate, take the case of Australia, by all accounts a long consolidated democracy. One basis for that claim is that the country was among the earliest to introduce female suffrage, in 1902. However, universal suffrage was not attained in Australia until very late, in 1962 when the de jure inclusion of the aboriginal population was completed. This, then, is in many ways an admirable democracy, but one in which the exclusion from democratic citizenship of one section of the population is within living memory. Similarly, in the United States, universal suffrage in some Southern states was not finally attained until 1965. Again, this is a democracy in which the basic security of freedom that is contained in the democratic vote was denied to a section of the population until very recently.

If we look at their regimes, the Australian and American democracies appear to be solidly consolidated. But if we look at the situation of persons, these are only recently consolidated democracies in their ability to deliver security of freedom to *everyone*, and democracies that delayed that process conspicuously. In these countries a section of the population will, when they look to the regime they live under and their experience of it, have reason to see a somewhat shaky potential of security.

I have no direct measure of consolidation in this meaning to apply and must therefore resort to a proxy. I use as my first indicator the timing of finality in the establishment of universal suffrage. That is usually the timing of universal female suffrage but in some cases, as those mentioned above, it is the final extension of the vote to minorities. All the democracies I compare now have universal suffrage as we usually understand it. I will consider them firmly consolidated if universal suffrage is long established.

That is clearly not an ideal indicator. It pronounces on democracy today by looking at something that in most cases happened long ago. It is not a durable indicator, not one that can continue to be used, and may be one that is already excessively historical. But as a proxy it is still pretty good. It is relevant, it distinguished well, and durability is a well established indicator, for example in the *Polity* project.[39]

---

[38] www.bertelsman-transformation-index.de.

[39] An alternative criterion, suggested by Samuel Huntington, is to consider a democracy established or consolidated when it has had two consecutive peaceful changes of government.

Universal suffrage can come late for two reasons. The polity may be democratic but delay the final step to universal suffrage. By around 1920, the intellectual case for universal suffrage had been won. Democracies that then or shortly thereafter introduced universal suffrage have a proven history of being democratically responsive. Those that delayed have a historical record of being democratically resistant, as illustrated by the cases of the United States and Australia. In France the introduction of female suffrage was delayed until 1944. These are democracies in which at least some citizens have reason to see recent evidence of disregard for their rights and interests.

The other way is that democracy itself comes late, for example in India because of the timing of independence. In that case the problem may not be one of a delay in finalizing democracy—it is not a fault in a democracy that it is young—but that democracy has had a short time to become consolidated and citizens therefore have less reason than otherwise to be confident about the durability of their democracy. The case of India would seem to bear out that logic. Although universal suffrage could hardly have been introduced earlier than it was (although it was introduced in other British colonies before independence), India is nevertheless a new, "unsafe" democracy. That subsequently proved to be the case when Prime Minister Indira Gandhi was able to institute emergency rule in 1975 (and her son Sanjay felt bold enough to recommend a prolonged suspension of democratic procedures for the purpose of, inter alia, implementing a population-control policy of forced, or at least forcefully encouraged, sterilization). In the event, Indian democracy proved itself resilient by shaking off that challenge after nineteen months when it inflicted electoral defeat on the Congress Party, but Indian citizens had clearly had a warning, and it is a fact of Indian history and contemporary awareness that its democracy was recently suspendable.

However, in countries that could not introduce universal suffrage earlier than they did—for example, because they were or had been colonies—what is lateness on a mechanical scale of chronology may historically speaking be early. That may be the case in Barbados, for example, which introduced universal suffrage in 1950 for the 1951 elections, fifteen years *before* independence. That was clearly an achievement and might reasonably be seen as a historical record that gives Barbadians reason for confidence in their democracy.[40] In the empirical comparisons below, I will for this reason classify Barbados among the consolidated democracies in spite of its lateness in becoming a democracy. (This goes to show that even in a statistical comparative framework, one may not fully avoid concessions

---

[40] On democracy in Barbados, see Beckles 2004b.

to historical specificities. Some other concessions of that kind are made in the data, as explained in the technical notes.)

(2) A robustly free press exists. In electoral democracies, democratic rule is exercised by elites but, in principle, under the oversight and control of citizens. The most important instrument citizens have for so doing, in addition to the vote, is a free press. A free press informs elites about the wishes of citizens and citizens about the doings of governing elites, and holds elites to answer for how they exercise power. A democracy is hardly thinkable without a free press. A good democracy is one in which the press is not just free but robustly free (cf. appendix C below).

Indicators of Capacity

(1) Citizens depend for protection on the ability of their legislatures and governments to make and implement the decisions that are needed for the appropriate regulation of economic and social life. That is also a necessary condition of economic order and of progress in other ways. This invites us to take government effectiveness as an indicator of capacity: the ability of the government to get decisions made and implemented.

(2) In addition, citizens depend on their governments to make the right decisions, which is to say decisions that appropriately reflect citizens' interests and demand for security. That depends not only on the technical effectiveness of decision making but also on democratic efficiency, which is to say decision making without distorting influences in the processes. The most important source of distortion is what Arthur Okun called the transgression of economic power into the processes of democratic politics.[41] The second indicator here is the degree to which the processes of governance are protected against the political use of economic power.

Indicators of Security

Security of freedom depends, once rights are given, on access to adequate resources for citizens to be able to shape their own lives according to their own goals and aspirations (as discussed in more detail in chapter 6). Resources in this dimension are in the form of physical and human capital, which means purchasing power and health (as discussed in more detail in chapter 4). We should therefore expect a system of democratic governance to perform well in translating available economic resources in the economy into protection for citizens against poverty and in favor of care and treatment in the case of injury or ill health. Two indicators follow: (1) the level of income poverty and (2) the security of health care.

[41] Okun 1975.

Indicators of Trust

Democratic delivery is ultimately as experienced by citizens, and the way citizens experience delivery is in confidence, safety, and trust: confidence in government, trust in the security of rights and liberties, trust in an order that enables people to trust each other. Two indicators follow: (1) the degree of confidence the population has in political institutions, and (2) the degree of trust in the future of freedom. Confidence and trust are not straightforward indicators to apply. In a vibrant democracy, we should expect citizens to be critical of those who rule and therefore to award them no more than optimal confidence.[42] In today's democratic world, however, confidence and trust is very thin, and the problem is not too much of it but too little.[43] Therefore, the view taken here is that, relative to the overall state of confidence and trust, more is better than less. Even in those populations in which levels of confidence and trust are relatively high, none are uncritical. These indicators are defined so as to allocate quality scores to democracies in which the level of confidence and trust has been stable or increasing in recent years (against a general trend of decline) *and* is on a higher level than the average for all the democracies included in the comparison.

The more detailed definitions and sources are given in the technical notes to Table 1.1 at the end of the chapter. All indicators are operationalized demandingly. Democracy is consolidated when it has had a *long* period of consolidation. Press freedom is *robust* press freedom. Capacity is *above*-average capacity among reasonably well organized democracies. Security is *below*-average poverty and *above*-average public spending on health care. Trust is *both* in institutions and in citizens vis-à-vis each other and *both* on a high and sustained level.

Comparative Findings

Table 1.1 gives relative quality scores on these indicators for twenty-five democracies at the entry into the twenty-first century. The countries included are all solid democracies. (Most score 10 on the Polity scale, except Botswana, Chile, France, India, Poland, and South Africa, which score 9; and Korea and Mexico, which score 8. Barbados has no Polity score.) They are selected so as to represent a broad variety of types of democracy: old, new, large, small, federal, nonfederal, presidential, monarchic, rich, poor, from all continents and in Europe a broad spread.

---

[42] As argued by Rose 1994.
[43] See, e.g., Norris 1999; Boudon 2002; O'Neill 2002.

To read these results, consider, for example, the case of Iceland, which obtains a high quality score on seven of eight indicators. The story told for that country through this set of indicators is that when the Icelanders consider their political system and what it does for them, they see a democracy that they have reason to believe is here to stay and will endure and one in which they have the protection of a robustly free press. They see a regime with decision-making institutions that are comparatively effective in producing decisions and with political processes that are comparatively well protected from distorting influences of economic power. They are themselves comparatively well protected against poverty and for health care. However, in their final assessment of confidence and trust, there is nevertheless something in their polity that causes them to withhold an element of trust. What that is, we cannot know, except that the Icelanders report a high and increasing level of confidence in both Parliament and the civil service, and also in their feeling of personal freedom, but they report a declining level of "trust in people."

These findings come with the many qualifications and reservations mentioned above and are presented here as experimental. Nevertheless, a range of striking results are contained in this comparison. First, all these countries are solid democracies, and there is little to distinguish among them in an assessment of how democratic they are. Yet they are very different in democratic quality, distributed over the whole scale of the index, four at the bottom score of 0 (India, Italy, Mexico, and South Africa) and two obtaining the top score of 8 (Norway and Sweden). The two democracies in the group that have the Polity score of 8, Korea and Mexico, have quality scores of 3 and 0 respectively. Of those that rank 10 on the Polity score, the lowest quality scores are 0 (Italy), 2 (Costa Rica, Spain, and the United States) and 3 (the Czech Republic and Britain). Chile obtains a Polity score of 9 but no more than a score of 2 on the quality index, the latter probably being more believable given the remaining authoritarian enclaves from the Pinochet regime.[44]

As in other areas of social measurement, the move from a pre- to a post-paradigm-change approach makes a very considerable difference for measurement results. The how-good-they-are methodology is more sensitive to pertinent differences between democracies than the how-democratic-they-are methodology. My hypothesis that even established democracies differ vastly in quality is confirmed.

Second, the results are in part unexpected—notably the low quality scores obtained by the model democracies of the United Kingdom and the

---

[44] Iazzetta 2004. Chile obtains a score of 0 on both subjective indicators. That is partly a result of a drastic decline of confidence in Parliament from 1990 (the year of reintroduction of democracy) to 2000, the response score falling from 53 to 35 percent.

United States (3 and 2 respectively)—and clearly also by Italy (0) and France (3), for example. The relatively high score obtained by the postco-lonial democracy in Barbados is possibly also unexpected. On the side of more expected results, the Nordic democracies of Iceland, Norway, and Sweden obtain high quality scores.

Third, scores of 0 are numerous across the table, which goes to show that low democratic quality is the rule rather than the exception in the family of countries that are generally seen to be solid democracies. Below-par performance is widespread.

This picture of relatively low democratic quality is strongly influenced by low scores on the two subjective indicators. That again is influenced by a trend in most of the democracies of a decline in confidence and trust.

Fourth, generally (with only two or three exceptions) the smaller de-mocracies tend to be in the upper range of the quality index and the larger ones towards the lower range.

Finally, only two of these twenty-five democracies obtain the highest possible score, as compared with four at the very bottom of the range. We cannot know from this how good those at the top of the scale are—again, consult appendix A—but those at the bottom of the scale are clearly pretty poor. That is evidence to suggest that the way things work in the real world of democracy falls short of what might be expected of good democracies. On the other hand, the fact that some democracies perform to a relatively high standard of quality shows that where that is not the case, improvements are realistically possible.

Skeptics might think it preposterous to want to measure something as complex as democratic quality with a small battery of indicators and very little analysis of the indicator data. That is understandable—but I argue here, as I will do again in chapter 4 on poverty, that while it is obvious to anyone, including myself, that this is methodologically almost embar-rassingly simple, what is surprising is how sensitive this simple form of measurement turns out to be. Not only does it capture a degree of differ-ence between the democracies that has eluded previous work, it also re-sponds to detailed differences within that overall pattern. For example, it is well recognized that there are subtle differences in the quality of press freedom between Britain and France; that is picked up here. Most observ-ers would probably agree that German unification has come with an ele-ment of stress in German democracy; that is picked up here. In the last few years, Britain has made some progress in reducing child poverty and improving health-care services. The effects would have been picked up by this instrument in a comparison over time. I am the first to recognize that the methodology I am using here, and in particular its specific operational indicators, is far from perfect. But compared with known alternatives it is, even at this level of simplicity, in fact pretty good.

CONCLUSION

Real democracies are obviously not perfect, but are they good enough? The verdict of citizens seems to be that they are not. To some degree, that goes against both elite and academic assessments of contemporary democracy. Political elites often (in my observations of political life) tend to see the democracies they serve as better than citizens see them. This is a part of the contemporary clash between the people and the politicians and of the decline of trust and confidence. Elites are also often, or sometimes, inclined to blame citizens for not sufficiently appreciating the benefits of democracy. Citizens are said to be indifferent, unwilling to participate, unrealistic in demands and expectations, or victims of new values, such as postmodern individualism. The academic assessment of democracy has mainly been by the how-democratic-they-are standard, and that standard has, by and large, given at least the established democracies a clean bill of health and thus aligned itself with elite assessments.

While both elite and academic assessments have been based predominantly on the way democracy is done, citizens in the main experience democracy in delivery. The clash of people and politicians, then, is probably not so much over the interpretation of the same facts—for example, that citizens see also what elites see but through the distorted lens of new values—as resulting from the observation of different facts: the way democracy is done versus what it does. If citizens are increasingly critical or distrustful of democracy, which they probably are, we know that does not come from a decline in adherence to democratic values. It comes from their experience of shortcomings in the democracies they value.[45] From the results of the present exercise, I would warn against comparing and judging democracies normatively by how they do democracy—by how democratic they are—and recommend that we base our comparisons and judgments more on what they do, on how good they are by criteria of quality.

There is an apparent paradox in modern democratic culture. At the moment in history when the standing of democracy in the world is stronger than ever, its standing in the eyes of citizens is weak and probably weakening. That is not easily understandable in a tradition of reflection that judges democracies by how democratic they are. But if we instead judge them by quality of performance, it would appear that they largely are of pretty fickle fabric and the paradox evaporates in what would seem to be fair and realistic assessments by citizens. It is not that democracy is sophisticated and citizens are not, but rather that citizens are sophisti-

---

[45] For supporting evidence from as far apart as Costa Rica and Norway, see Proyecto Estado de la Nación 2001 and Verdikommisjonen 2001. For an analysis of the question in comparative value data, see Boudon 2002.

cated and their democracies are wanting. It is in democracy that improvements are needed, more than in citizens and their expectations.

TABLE 1.1
Relative Democratic Quality in Selected Democracies (at the entry into the twenty-first century)

	Strength		Capacity		Security		Trust		INDEX
	CON	PRS	EFC	ECP	POV	HCR	GOV	FRE	
Australia	0	1	1	1*	0	0	0	1*	4
Barbados	1	1	1*	1*	0	0	1*	0*	5
Belgium	0	1	1	1*	1	1	0	0	5
Botswana	0	0	0	1*	0	0	0*	0*	1
Canada	0	1	1	1*	0	1	1	0	5
Chile	0	0	1	1*	0	0	0	0	2
Costa Rica	0	1	0	1*	0	0	0*	0*	2
Czech Republic	1	0	0	0*	1	1	0	0	3
France	0	0	1	0*	1	1	0	0	3
Germany	1	1	1	0*	0	1	0	0	4
Iceland	1	1	1	1*	1*	1	1	0	7
India	0	0	0	0*	0	0*	0	0	0
Italy	0	0	0	0*	0	0	0	0	0
Korea	0	1	1*	1*	0*	0	0	0	3
Mexico	0	0	0	0*	0	0	0	0	0
Netherlands	1	1	1	1*	1	0	0	1	6
New Zealand	1	1	1	1*	0	1	0	1*	6
Norway	1	1	1	1*	1	1	1	1	8
Poland	0*	1	0	0*	0	0	0	0	1
South Africa	0	0	0	0*	0	0	0	0	0
Spain	0*	1	1	0*	0	0	0	0	2
Sweden	1	1	1	1*	1	1	1	1	8
Switzerland	0	1	1	1*	0	1	1*	0	5
United Kingdom	1	1	1	0*	0	0	0	0	3
United States	0	1	1	0*	0	0	0	0	2

* Scores allocated by best adjustment and/or with some missing data.

TECHNICAL NOTES TO TABLE 1.1

There are four dimensions of quality, with two indicators for each dimension. For each indicator, each country is allocated a score of 1 (better quality) or 0 (worse quality). The final score for each country is an unweighted additive index of the eight indicator scores.

The table shows the comparative picture of democratic quality circa year 2000. It has been compiled from a variety of sources. Primary among these is the UNDP *Human Development Report 2002*, in which democracy was the special theme and available research and statistics on the state and performance of democracy in the world is compiled and summarized in the most authoritative compilation to date. Other data sources have been used as appropriate, including national statistics and extensive Web searches. Where single sources are inconclusive, multiple sources have been consulted. The allocation of scores on the basis of information from multiple sources is sometimes unavoidably a matter of best judgment. National and international experts have been consulted. An asterisk indicates an allocated score that is by best judgment and/or with some missing data.

Strength

Strength of potential for delivery of democratic value:
(1) CON: Consolidated as measured by the timing of the final introduction of universal suffrage
1 = before 1940
0 = after 1940
Barbados is allocated a score of 1 for reasons explained in the text above. Poland is allocated a score of 0 although universal suffrage was introduced in 1918, because of weak democratic credentials pre-1989. In the case of the Czech Republic, a score of 1 is allocated on the basis of the 1920 introduction of universal suffrage and the 1918–38 strength of democratic credentials. Spain is allocated a score of 0 in spite of the introduction of universal suffrage in 1931 because of the weakness of historical democratic credentials. Australia and the United States get scores of 0 because of the late final recognition of universal suffrage (1962 and 1965 respectively). Source: UNDP 2002.
(2) PRS: Robustness of free press
1 = highly robust (score 20 or lower)
0 = less robust (score above 20)
Freedom House classifies press freedom on a scale from 0 to 100; the lower the score, the more free the press. Countries with a score between

0 and 30 are considered to have a free press. A free press exists almost by definition in a democracy; a good democracy has a press that is not only free but eminently and robustly free. A score of 20 or lower on the Freedom House scale indicates a robustly free press. That, as it happens, puts France, for example, just into the less robust category (with a score of 21), which seems appropriate considering the degree of state control in the electronic media and the top-down structure of the print media (cf. appendix B). Source: UNDP 2002; Freedom House (Freedomhouse.org).

Capacity

Capacity of governance for adequate decision making:
  (1) EFC: Government effectiveness
  1 = higher
  0 = lower
Capacity is based on the World Bank indicator of effectiveness in government, which again is based on international survey data. The score of 1 is allocated to countries with a World Bank effectiveness score above average for the democracies included in the comparison. In the case of Korea, a score of 1 is allocated in spite of a low World Bank score. This is based on my own work, with research students, on the Korean welfare state, which demonstrates a high level of government effectiveness (cf. Kwon 1998). Source: UNDP 2002; World Bank (worldbank.org/wbi/governance).

  (2) ECP: Protection against the political use of economic power
  1 = protected
  0 = unprotected
The issue being measured here, the power of money in politics, is crucial in a framework of democratic quality. But it is so far inadequately articulated in democratic theory (but see chapter 2) and as a result is not well described empirically. There might be a case for saying that all democracies are wanting in their ability to control money politics and that money has a way of infiltrating politics everywhere one way or another. While, for example, in some countries political parties are open to private donations, they have in other countries (e.g., in Scandinavia) found ways of funding themselves from the public purse. In either case, the result is a disenfranchisement of party members who no longer hold the power that would make parties financially dependent on them for their fees. This might suggest a score of 0 for all democracies on this indicator. However, there are clearly differences between the democracies in how open they are to the transgression of economic power into politics, and that should be reflected in a comparison of relative quality. There is, for want of solid

appropriate data, a high degree of subjectivity in the allocation of scores on this indicator. It is informed by country scores on the Corruption Perception Index of Transparency International and the Graft Index of the World Bank, as summarized in *Human Development Report 2002*, but those data are inconclusive for the purpose. The transgression of economic power into democratic politics is not primarily or only by corruption or graft. It is certainly also by the reliance on a high level of private donations, openly or secretly, in party and campaign funding, as seen typically in the United States and Britain. These countries are allocated a 0 score, as are Italy, France and Germany, for example, on the basis of evidence of financial scandals in political life. Source: UNDP 2002; best judgment.

Security

Security of resources for freedom:
 (1) POV: Incidence of income poverty
 1 = low level
 0 = high level
For the rich countries in the comparison, the basis is relative child income poverty, the score of 1 allocated to those with a child poverty rate of less than 10 percent in the UNICEF League Table of Child Poverty. That, for example, just pushes postunification Germany to the wrong side of the divide, although western Germany specifically has a lower than 10 percent child poverty rate, which could be seen as an appropriate sensitivity in the measurement to strains in German democracy of reunification. For the less rich countries, the score is allocated on the basis of the UNDP Human Poverty Index and other poverty indicators in the *Human Development Report 2002*.
 Source: UNICEF 2000, 2005; Luxembourg Income Study (lisproject .org/keyfigures); UNDP 2002.
 (2) HCR: Security of health care
 1 = higher
 0 = lower
This indicator is measured in public health expenditure as a percentage of GDP. The level of *public* expenditure on health is an indicator of the effort in the country's public policy to make (quality) health care available to people irrespective of their own economic ability to purchase health care or health insurance and hence of the availability of quality health care to *everyone* in the population. In estimating the indicator relative to GDP, it reflects public policy effort relative to economic capacity, which is to say differences in political effort after controlling for differences in economic ability. Private health expenditure is outside of the indicator.

Britain gets a score of 0 because of its low level of public spending on health in spite of the National Health Service, which appropriately reflects deep concerns in Britain itself over the quality of health care, and the United States gets a score of 0 because of a low level of public spending on health in spite of a high level of private spending and reflecting known inadequacies in health care coverage. (Britain might today well have scored 1 on this indicator following increases in public health expenditures from around 2002.) The score of 1 is allocated to countries with more than 6 percent of GDP in public health expenditure (the highest level being 7.9 percent, in Germany). Source: UNDP 2002.

Trust

Subjective confidence and trust

(1) GOV: Confidence in government

1 = higher

0 = lower

Based on two questions from the World Value Survey and European Value Survey about "confidence in Parliament" and "confidence in the civil service." The score of 1 is allocated to countries in which the level of confidence increased on both questions from 1990 to 2000 *and* is above the average for the countries included in the comparison on both questions in the 2000 round of surveys. Confidence is measured as the percentage responding "a great deal" or "quite a lot." The score hence depends on both *trends* and *levels* in confidence and relies on a pattern of response and not any single figure. The average 2000 confidence in Parliament is 40 percent and in the civil service is 43 percent. The United States, for example, gets a 0 score on "confidence in Parliament" because of a 38 percent response in 2000, and a 0 score on confidence in the civil service in spite of a 55 percent response in 2000 because that was down from 59 percent in 1990. Source: Inglehart et al. 2004.

(2) FRE: Experienced freedom and trust:

1 = more

0 = less

Based again on two questions from the World Value Survey and European Value Survey about "freedom of choice and control in life" and "trust in people." The score of 1 is allocated to countries in which the reported experience of freedom increased on both questions from 1990 to 2000 *and* trust was above average on both questions in the 2000 round of surveys. Experience of freedom of choice and control in life is measured as the percentage responding "a great deal" (7–10 on a 1–10 scale). Trust in people is measured as the percentage responding "most people can be trusted." The average 2000 response for freedom/control is 64 percent and for trust in people 36 percent.

Missing data for the confidence and trust questions: Barbados is allocated the same scores as Iceland (the other small island democracy in the group); Costa Rica has the same scores as Chile; and Botswana has the same scores as South Africa. Figures for 1990 are not available for Australia and New Zealand and, in the case of Switzerland, not for the confidence questions. In these cases, scores are allocated on the basis of the 2000 response rates only. Source: Inglehart et al. 2004.

CHAPTER 2

Is Economic Democracy Available?

> Genuine democracy will be economic and social as well
> as political.
> —Tomas Masaryk, 1927

ECONOMIC DEMOCRACY is an idea in need of being reinvented. While political democracy triumphed in the twentieth century, economic democracy failed. In turn, the absence of economic democracy strikes back and undermines political democracy.

THE LOGIC OF ECONOMIC DEMOCRACY

One reason to ask for economic democracy could be that it follows from the idea of democracy that economic power should be under democratic control. Although that is a logical position, there is not much to it in the end. Economic democracy, contrary to political democracy, does not appear to be something people are ready to take to the streets and fight for.

There is, however, another argument, more pragmatic and instrumental and therefore possibly more persuasive, which goes to the democratic quality of society. If we have democracy in political life but not in economic life, and if the weight of economic power grows relative to political power, then citizens might have reason to question how democratic their society really is and whether political democracy is really of much relevance. If democracy is seen to decline, citizens will rightly see their share in it to be worth less and will have reason to be indifferent and to withhold participation, whereby they would be reacting to decline in a way that produces further decline.[1]

Five trends on the meeting ground of democracy, public policy, and capitalism are adding up to a formidable shift in the balance of power. First, with economic growth, the simple weight of economic power has grown enormously. Political power is constant: each voter has one vote. Economic power grows: each holder of capital holds progressively more capital. When there is more capital, capital speaks more loudly.

This is a revised version of an essay first published in Democratization 2004, *no. 2.*
[1] For evidence of disenchantment, see, e.g., Parr et al. 2000.

Second, private wealth is not only accumulating but is increasingly concentrated in the hands of a small elite. True, more people are owners of valuable holdings but the total stock of capital is increasingly concentrated in its distribution.[2]

Third, with economic liberalization, private capital has been given (or reclaimed) access to arenas previously under direct political control. In the European welfare states, public utilities have been massively privatized, and public services—such as schools, hospitals, transportation, and prisons—are increasingly delivered by various forms of public-private partnerships.[3]

Fourth, while political power is pulling or being pushed out of market arenas, private economic power is invading political arenas. The main mechanism is the escalating cost of party and campaign politics, something that puts political power into the hands of those who are able to and interested in funding political activity.[4]

Finally, with globalization, deregulation, and new electronic technology, capital markets have gone international and increasingly escaped the nation-state.[5] This has radically strengthened the hand of capital. On the one hand, it has more or less freed itself from political control, which for all intents and purposes—the European Union notwithstanding—continues to reside in the nation-state. On the other hand, if capital should see its freedom or profitability endangered by legislation where it operates, it can threaten to pull out and move to better markets in more friendly countries. I will call this *the threat of exit*. The credibility of that threat has given capital unprecedented powers of veto in economic legislation.

WHY FAILURE?

Citizens in democratic societies value both prosperity and equality, the dilemma Arthur Okun called *the big trade-off*.[6] They want equality but not at the cost of prosperity, at least not of much prosperity. If they can have prosperity or a reasonable hope of prosperity, they will sacrifice equality, or at least some of it. There is in a democratic society no scope for economic democracy that comes at the cost of economic efficiency. I will call this *the imperative of efficiency*: no political arrangement will be

---

[2] As shown by in particular Wolff 1996.

[3] See, e.g., Commission on Private Public Partnership 2002.

[4] "The financial sector was the biggest business donor to U.S. political campaigns over the past 14 years, giving nearly $227m to candidates and parties, according to a survey released yesterday." *Financial Times*, 23 October 2002.

[5] Stiglitz 2000.

[6] Okun 1975.

democratically feasible unless it is seen to be (reasonably) compatible with economic efficiency.

Various attempts can be identified through the last century to subordinate economic resources and activities to political control, all failures. The extreme case is that of the Soviet-style command economy, in which the highest hopes of socialist "democracy" were once invested. The Yugoslav-style workers' democracy has not survived, the British-style nationalization of heavy industry has not survived, the French socialists' move under President Mitterand to nationalize major banks was but a brief experiment quickly given up with no sadness, and the Swedish idea of bringing capital under democratic control in "wage-earner funds" withered the moment it was tried.[7]

These experiments failed because they did not survive the encounter with the imperative of efficiency. The theory that political control over the economy would be conducive to economic efficiency proved wrong. By the end of the century, the domain of equality had been pushed back out of economic life and increasing income inequalities were absorbed in society with little or no political resistance.[8] The big trade-off bids us to compromise, and the compromise that has materialized is that political equality has been obtained in equal rights and the universal vote but that economic equality has been given up because it is seen not to be possible without prohibitive costs.

The lesson so far, then, is that if we were to raise again in any realistic manner the vision of extending democracy from the political to also embrace the economic, we would need to ask how that could be done without a significant economic cost. Economic democracy that is not economically sound is not democratically credible; it will not be wanted. It is not just that it will be unwanted by those who are in control of capital; it will be unwanted by ordinary citizens. The imperative of efficiency is a hard test. What made the command economy a forceful idea in its time was that it promised both equality and efficiency, and the reason it became discredited is that there is no longer any basis for upholding that hope. Yet an acceptable alternative idea of economic democracy must again make that promise. It must show that economic *power* can be democratic without economic *efficiency* being sacrificed.

WHAT ECONOMIC DEMOCRACY?

Imagine an economy that generates enough income to satisfy the consumption needs of everyone who lives in it but nothing more, and that

---

[7] Pontusson 1992.
[8] Atkinson 1995a.

distributes that income with perfect equality. Economic power would then be distributed democratically. Everyone would have a tiny fraction of it and no one would have more than anyone else. It would be equivalent to the political power contained in the vote and sit with the people in the sense that everyone has a say but no individual or small group a controlling share.

Of course, no economy looks like that. In most real economies, first, there is a surplus. More income is generated than is required for basic consumption. That surplus sits mainly with the rich in the form of cash and accumulated property.

Second, there is not equality. The distribution of income in modern capitalist economies has been described imaginatively by Jan Pen as "a parade of dwarfs (and a few giants)."[9] At the bottom of the distribution is a group of people with very low incomes, less than can reasonably be seen as adequate to their needs. They are the poor, those without the economic power to shape their own lives according to normal standards and expectations in their society. In the middle of the distribution is a large group with more or less even incomes, around or (most of them) just short of the mean income in the economy. Their income is adequate to their needs, but they have little or no surplus. At the top of the distribution is a third group whose incomes are above or (most of them) much above the mean. They are the rich: they have money for their own needs and a surplus, hence also wealth.

This is obviously a rough description. The lines between the groups are not sharp, there are distributions within groups, persons can move up or down from one group to another, and the overall distribution is not stable. But modern capitalist economies do divide by income and wealth into three classes, which we might for convenience call the upper class (or the rich), the middle class (or ordinary people), and the underclass (or the poor). The underclass is small, say 5 to 10–15 percent of the population. The upper class is also small, say 10 to 20 percent, while the middle class is the large one, comprising perhaps 70 to 80 percent of the population.[10]

Economic power is of two kinds, the power of freedom (the power to make one's own choices for one's own life) and the power of dominance (the power to shape or influence the choices others can make). The class pattern of economic power is as follows.

First, there is a deficit in the underclass. Poor people are without the economic resources necessary for effective freedom and obviously have no power of dominance.[11]

[9] Pen 1971, p. 48.

[10] For comparative statistics on the distribution of income, see Atkinson et al. 1995.

[11] Here I use the terms "poverty" and "the poor" as terminological conveniences. For more precise language, see chapter 4.

Second, there is the mixed situation of the middle class. People with middle-class incomes have the money to meet their own needs and hence some considerable power of freedom, but they have little or no surplus; pretty much what comes in goes out. They may have some wealth, typically in the form of housing property and modest savings, but not wealth that contains power of dominance. They have freedom of choice, but the economic power that decides much of the choice that is available to them is in the hands of others.

Third, there is a surplus of economic power in the upper class. The rich have economic freedom, of course, plus the additional power that comes from serious wealth. They hold an effective monopoly on the power of dominance.

If this is now the prevailing and democratically unsatisfactory distribution of economic power, we might sensibly see economic democracy as a distributional matter. That theory would then prescribe a redistribution of economic power to those who have too little from those who have too much. As political democracy has been realized by equalizing political power, economic democracy would be realized by equalizing economic power. I turn first to the problem of power: under what conditions and to what degree could we realistically see political power applied to the redistribution of economic power? Then I consider practical measures of redistribution, in part with the help of selective examples.

POLITICAL VS. ECONOMIC POWER

I start from the assumption of political democracy and take that to mean that all citizens are equal in the political power contained in the vote. I do not consider except in passing other sources of political power, such as information, organization, and the like. I assume that people have objective interests that arise from their socioeconomic conditions, that they are disposed to acting rationally to advance or protect those interests, and that both economic and political power are things people would rather have than not have. The only route towards economic democracy that I consider is the legislative one. I assume that legislation flows from the dogfight of interests and power and do not consider the intervening institutions and processes through which that happens. The context is the advanced capitalist democracies.

Political power is equal between persons, but that translates into inequality in the class pattern, although in a very different distribution to that of economic power. Here it is numbers that add up. Both the underclass and the upper class are weak and the middle class is in control, making the underclass dependent on it and the upper class threatened by it.

The first rule of economic democracy. Economic democracy depends on the mobilization of ordinary people; there will not be economic democracy unless ordinary middle-class people decide to use their voting power to make it happen. However, political power goes only so far. Its use depends on middle-class interests (what it might *want* to do) and on constraints (what it thinks it *can* do). The use of political power is constrained by other forms of power, principally the economic power that sits in the hands of the upper class. But economic power cannot override political power in any kind of coercive way. The middle class has the political power it has, and no economic power can take that away (short of a coup d'état, which is outside the context of the present discussion). Economic power must therefore work politically through *arguments* that those who hold political power accept.

The arguments that have clout are the two I have introduced: the imperative of efficiency and the threat of exit. The best arguments for the upper class are those that the middle class freely accept as persuasive. The upper class then gets its way by the force of reason. The efficiency argument is of this kind. The exit argument is of a very different kind. It works by making the middle class feel forced to concede under duress.

The reason the efficiency argument is good and the exit argument is bad (from the point of view of the upper class) lies in what we might call *moral capital*. Reputation, esteem, and honor are valuable commodities in democratic capitalism, essential for the upper class, whose position is perforce a defensive one, in their mastery of the political game. The efficiency argument is good because its use, when *sachlich*, costs nothing in moral capital. The exit argument is bad because, although effective, it often works only at the expense of moral capital. If you force others to yield to your interests against their will, you get what you want but your esteem suffers and it will be more difficult for you to have it your way next time.

The interest of the *middle class* is to attack the power surplus in the upper class; the upper class has much of what the middle class wants more of. But that is not to say that the middle class will take action in that interest. It *ought* to want to take on the rich, but that may be a rather theoretical interest. The most sophisticated experiment in economic democracy to date, that of wage-earner funds in Sweden, is illustrative. It seemed to promise the middle class everything but found it not receptive. Such funds were established and were in operation from 1984 to 1992, when they were closed down. Their establishment did without doubt eat into the economic power of private capital, but they failed to attract the support of ordinary people, who were offered voting power over the governance of the funds but did not show much interest even then. It was argued, clearly correctly, that power would shift to wage earners—that is, the middle class—collectively, but that did not move the people who constituted the class said to be gaining power. No power or other benefit came to *them*. They saw nothing in it for themselves and were mostly indifferent.[12]

The second rule of economic democracy. For the middle class to be interested in it, economic democracy must come in a form that brings tangible benefits to the members of that class—not just to the class collectively but to persons in it.

Even if the middle class should *want* to expropriate upper-class power and might see gains to itself in doing so, it will be fearful of acting because of a perceived risk that economic efficiency may suffer. The imperative of efficiency is a subjective matter; it is about middle-class *fears*. If the upper class is able to argue persuasively that it is the best manager of capital in the interest of economic efficiency and growth, its economic power will not be under threat from middle-class political power.

The third rule of economic democracy. The middle class will only be interested in forms of economic democracy it is very confident can be implemented without noticeable loss in economic efficiency.

The interest of the *upper class* is to protect its surplus in economic power, but it does not hold the political power to do so. It needs to persuade the middle class to nonaction. The efficiency argument is its most effective weapon. It suggests that it is in everyone's interest that those who happen to control capital are allowed to do so with relative liberty. If others then concede, they are doing so rationally and for their own good. This is the basis for a social contract: the middle class leaves the upper class free in economic enterprise and the upper class underwrites the prosperity of the middle class.[13]

If the efficiency argument does not persuade the middle class—and there are without doubt many forms of power surplus in the upper class that have no basis whatsoever in economic efficiency—holders of capital can resort to the threat of exit. However, raw threat is an expensive argument to use. While the imperative of efficiency enables the upper class to mobilize the moral force of a shared interest, the use of raw threat leaves it exposed in naked defense of privilege. This hands the moral argument to the middle class and forces the upper class into a very uncomfortable position. That position it wants to avoid, which is to say that it would be

---

[12] Gilljam 1988.

[13] In the case of Sweden, that contract was made explicit in a historical compromise in the Saltsjöbaden agreement between unions and employers in 1936; cf. Korpi 1983. The policy of wage earners' funds was an attempt to use political power to overturn that contract, but it soon transpired that there was not the conviction in the middle class to carry that through.

willing to pay something to avoid it. There is therefore a meeting ground between the middle class and the upper class for economic democracy—not necessarily much but some. That ground is in economic power which, first, is not persuasively rational by arguments of efficiency and which, second, cannot be defended without expending disproportionate moral capital. To put it bluntly, outrageous or outrageously used income and wealth are fair game for middle-class political power.

The fourth rule of economic democracy. There is a window of opportunity for economic democracy in forms of economic power that cannot be defended rationally by the imperative of efficiency.

The interest of the *underclass* is to obtain economic freedom, but it does not have the political power to claim it. It needs to persuade the middle class to act in its behalf. The middle class in turn has an interest in helping the poor. Poverty threatens the social order that serves the majority well and is a disturbing nuisance in otherwise pleasant middle-class life. Here the middle and the upper classes are allies.

However, this interest is only to contain poverty, not to eradicate it. Rampant poverty is dangerous and unpleasant, but some poverty—not too many people who are too poor—is not. Furthermore, the interest of the middle class in helping the poor is tempered by the awareness that it would also have to pay the brunt of the cost of antipoverty policies. It could theoretically pass on that bill to the upper class, but that avenue is constrained by the imperative of efficiency (as will be explained in more detail below). The numbers are with the middle class, and most of the tax burden will fall there.

The fifth rule of economic democracy. A policy to effectively lift the poor to economic freedom rests on a magic whereby the middle class makes itself interested in doing more for the poor than is in its interest to do.

In capitalist democracies, we now see, the facts on the ground in the joint arena of political and economic power limit very severely the space for economic democracy. But the constraints are not so severe as to leave no space at all. The way to reinvent economic democracy is not to devise a new big scheme but to identify the narrow openings that realistically exist for the use of political power to redistribute economic power.

TAXATION

If the middle class could use its political power freely in taxation, it could massively redistribute income and wealth. But that is not possible. The middle class is itself interested in holding taxes down and is not (knowingly) going to impose on itself a (much) heavier tax burden than it is able to impose on the upper class. The upper class in turn has the power to resist taxation and therefore holds veto power in tax policy.[14]

In direct taxation, the upper class can control the *level* with the threat of exit. When capital is movable, a tax regime that looks unreasonably harsh in comparison with other countries is not within possibility. This is seen as so obvious—and is on display daily in the financial pages—that the argument works on its own without the rich having to expend any moral capital.[15] Economic democracy in one country by way of noticeably higher taxes than in other (comparable) countries is therefore not a viable option.

No longer a viable option, I should say: This option has been closed down thanks to the increasing credibility of the threat of exit following the globalization of finance markets. Until recently, even highly developed capitalist economies maintained very different levels of taxation. Today, they no longer do. From 1960 to 1980, the average level of public spending (which is a measure of the real tax level) in OECD countries increased from 28 percent to 43 percent of GDP, and the difference between these countries in that measure *increased* (the coefficient of variance between twenty-one OECD countries increased from 22 to 25). From 1980 to 1998, government spending in the same countries stabilized (it was still at 43 percent in 1998). In that period, the difference between them *decreased* strongly (the coefficient of variance dropped from 25 to 17). There is still difference but much less so. The Scandinavian countries remain at the top of the range but much less ahead of the others than previously. Their public spending in 1998 was at 51 percent of GDP, compared with, for example, 43 percent in the southern European countries. In 1980, the difference between those two groups of countries was 49 and 30 percent. The tax level has remained high in the Scandinavian countries but is now only moderately higher than elsewhere.[16] Furthermore, it is moderately higher than elsewhere not because the "real" tax level is noticeably higher

---

[14] In fact, the middle class does accept a heavier tax burden than it imposes on the upper class in today's reliance on indirect taxes. This is because it also has an interest in public services and sees no other way of funding them, and possibly because indirect taxes are less visible than direct taxes.

[15] A case study: On 20 June 2003, Peter Hain, a long-standing member of the British Labour cabinet, gave a public lecture on various policy issues. On the morning of that day, it became known that his manuscript included a call for a debate on taxation, including the possibility of ensuring "that hard-working middle income families and the low-paid get a better deal" and for "those at the very top of the pay scale contributing more." That resulted in what Hain called "an absolute frenzy" in government circles, and by the time he delivered his lecture in the evening, the intended call for debate was dropped in favor of "We will not raise the top rate of tax, and there is no going back to the old days of punitive tax rates to fund reckless spending." (As reported in the *Guardian*, 21 June 2003.)

[16] These data are from Castles 2004, tab. 2.2.

but because more of social security contributions are included in the tax account.[17] Even Scandinavian exceptionalism in taxation is now pretty much a thing of the past.

It is also able to hold the *distribution* to what is considered reasonable, now on the efficiency argument. Strongly progressive tax rates simply are inefficient.[18] The only way to make them politically acceptable is to make concessions on the tax base to the rich by opening up exemptions and deductions, whereby the actual tax distribution becomes both arbitrary and less progressive than the formal rates. An attempt to tax the rich in a way they see as confiscatory may lead holders of capital away from economically productive investments and into speculative ventures or to exit.

These arguments, strong as they are against a high tax level and sharply progressive rates, have very little force against a regime of moderately high taxes and in particular of moderately progressive rates. In resisting a harsh regime, the rich have the facts of how taxation works on their side. In a more moderate regime, the facts do not work for the rich. These taxes, far from being thought unreasonable, are necessary for the good cause of providing adequate public services. Moderately progressive rates are neither self-defeating nor economically distorting, and are fair to boot. While a harsh tax regime can be resisted on the basis of objective facts, a moderate regime could only be resisted at the cost of expending moral capital. Since there is little to be gained, that resistance is not cost-effective for the upper class. Hence its veto power in taxation is not absolute, and the middle class *can* push the upper class to concessions on taxation. It cannot push it very far, but it does have something to go on.

The conclusion that it is possible to maintain a moderately progressive regime of direct taxation, although seemingly weak, is of great significance in the present discussion. Such a tax regime will have but a limited effect in redistributing income, but it will have a considerable effect on tax psychology. As long as taxes are progressive, even if only moderately, the middle class will be able to believe, rightly, that the rich pay more to the funding of public policies than they themselves have to pay.[19] Those policies are under the political control of the middle class: public services are things the middle class give-away, including to the poor. The middle class is therefore able to give away more than it itself has to pay for. That opens up the possibility that the middle class can give at least a bit more

[17] See Kangas and Palme 2005.

[18] Barr 1998.

[19] In the aggregate, the middle class pays more than the upper class, of course, but each person in the middle class will pay a bit less of his income than each person in the upper class.

to the poor than it is actually in its own narrow interest to give away—since the additional gift is paid by the rich—and produces half of the magic that could make the middle class more generous towards the poor than it actually is.

The difference between a moderately progressive tax and a flat tax might not seem to be very significant but is in fact monumental. The deceptively attractive flat-tax idea is in fact a Trojan horse that could contain a devastating attack from behind against not only any policy of economic fairness but also the very power to tax in a democratic state. (See appendix D.)

The Poor

It is established that it is possible to significantly reduce the extent of poverty with the help of welfare-state policies without a significant sacrifice in economic efficiency.[20] The most effective regimes in this respect are the northern European social-democratic ones.[21] Their success is explained historically in the emergence of broad political coalitions that reached across class divisions.[22]

The effectiveness of those regimes is contained in what has been called *the paradox of redistribution*: they have far-reaching universal policies that distribute benefits not only to the poor but also to the nonpoor.[23] Universal policies come with various benefits. They are target effective in the sense that they ensure (as far as is possible) full coverage of the poor and that no one in need is left unprotected; they are not economically distorting; and they are politically effective in that they are capable of mobilizing broader political support than that which comes from the self-interest of the middle class to contain poverty. A regime of universal policies could produce the second half of the magic to make the middle class more generous towards the poor than it is by self-interest.

Universal social policies are expensive and would therefore require strong political backing. Political backing would have to come from the middle class. Under what conditions might the middle class make itself interested in policies that go beyond its instinctive self-interest?

If antipoverty policies are shaped so as to avoid poverty traps and other work disincentives, which is possible in regimes based on universality, the imperative of efficiency does not stand in the way. The salient arguments

---

[20] Ringen 1988, 2006. In chapter 4, I discuss the possibility that this eventually will lead to the eradication of poverty.

[21] Goodin et. al. 1999.

[22] Baldwin 1990.

[23] Korpi and Palme 1998.

are then the more political ones. First, the middle class would need to see benefits to itself in the policy in addition to benefits to the poor. Second, the middle class would need to believe that the sum of what it gives to the poor and what it gets itself is (at least a bit) more than it is itself paying for. And, third, the upper class would have to be prepared to accept the necessary tax bill, since otherwise the middle class would not be willing to tax itself sufficiently.

The first two conditions are satisfied in a regime of universal social policies and moderately progressive taxes. Ordinary people get free education, health care, and so on, and the rich pay more. The third condition, however, may be difficult to satisfy. The upper class is unlikely to (have to) comply if it is able to argue that the policy imposes a heavier tax burden than in other (comparable) countries and if it can use that argument without expending much moral capital. This is so far the likely scenario and that brings us to a preliminary conclusion that it is difficult to see how an antipoverty program built on universal policies could arise spontaneously from the play of interests and power.

However, what *has* happened *can* happen. In the Scandinavian countries, a welfare state was created that was more generous to the poor than the middle class needed to make it. Could what is unlikely to happen spontaneously again be brought about deliberately? In principle, the middle class should be on board, since it could design policies that both are generous to the poor and contain benefits to itself if only the upper class could be persuaded to go along.

Where the broad coalition has not emerged, it seemingly would have to be brought about by a catalyst outside and above the class pattern of interests and power. This force would need to establish the cause of antipoverty policy so firmly that it would be morally expensive to resist or ignore it. It would be an idealistic lobby with the capacity to champion the cause of the poor persuasively and explain the kinds of policies that would be needed.

Is that a condition we can realistically see satisfied today? The historical experience in broad-coalition countries is not encouraging. Those coalitions were interest based. At a time of mass poverty, the risk of falling into poverty was so high that interest in building a tight safety net against it was broadly shared.[24] The success of the Scandinavian welfare state, then, is explained by the happy coincidence that a broad coalition emerged early enough. The Scandinavians were able to start building their expensive welfare states well before they could afford it. With poverty now more marginal, the same kind of shared interest is not there, and a broad antipoverty coalition is therefore less likely. With increasing afflu-

[24] Baldwin 1990.

ence, although effective antipoverty policies should be more affordable, it has paradoxically become too late politically.

On the other hand, broad coalitions never did arise out of interests alone and have always had to be advanced by moral persuasion.[25] However, here too the current experience is discouraging, namely, the case of Britain. Its antipoverty lobby is strong, vocal, and visible, but even this persistent, well-informed, and well-organized lobby has been unable to persuade (or shame) the majority to break with a tradition of social policy that allows high rates of poverty both among the elderly and children to persist.[26] This could be because there is insufficient commonality of interest to cement a political coalition that could turn the moral argument of the lobby into sustainable policy (or, of course, that a vocal lobby is not necessarily an effective one). The best conclusion for now is that in the absence of a moral force of exceptional persuasiveness, it can be predicted that antipoverty policy will not move beyond the narrow agenda of containment. However, even though a strong moral lobby would seem to be a necessary condition for the mobilization of antipoverty policies beyond the ambition of containment, it would still not necessarily be a sufficient condition under present social and political circumstances.

THE MIDDLE CLASS

The next challenge is to put more economic power in the hands of ordinary people. The obvious question is where that is to come from. The imperative of efficiency stands in the way of taking (much of) it from the rich. Economic democracy by way of economically empowering the middle class would seem to depend on its own magic: giving to ordinary people without taking from the rich.

There is, as it happens, a source of economic power that the middle class could exploit and seems ideally suited according to my rules of economic democracy. In the modern welfare state, vast economic resources sit in public or semipublic budgets for the purpose of providing services to citizens. The economic power that these resources carry is already removed from private hands, be they rich or not, and can be redistributed further without being taken out of anyone's ownership or out of market use.

The middle class ought to have an interest in expropriating this power. That interest may be poorly articulated, since the habit of thought may hold powerful bureaucracies to be necessary for welfare, but it cannot be

---

[25] This is explained elegantly in a history of social policy in Norway; cf. Seip 1994.
[26] Donnison 1982. See also www.cpag.org.uk.

in the interest of middle-class citizens, or of poor citizens for that matter, to be needlessly subject to bureaucratic power. We here meet a theme in social policy that goes back to Adam Smith in *Wealth of Nations*: the perils of helping people by empowering authorities.[27] The more effective way, when possible, is to empower people themselves. Democratizing bureaucratic power would satisfy my second rule of economic democracy.

There do not appear to be any strong political arguments against shifting the power that sits in welfare bureaucracies from those bureaucracies to their clients. The power of the rich would not come under attack (only that of bureaucratic elites); rather, the middle class and the upper class should be allies in this interest. There are no efficiency arguments against it. These are resources that are already under political control. Indeed, the redistribution of these resources into the hands of ordinary people would bring them closer back to market use. It would also make institutions more answerable to their users, something that should be expected to stimulate more efficient arrangements. Hence, the third and fourth rules of economic democracy are also satisfied.

THE EXAMPLE OF PENSIONS

State pensions are exposed to political risk. Earners pay some form of social-security tax today in return for a promise from the present government of a pension from a future government when they retire. The experience is that pension rights as such are usually pretty safe, but not their value.[28]

Occupational pensions are exposed to company risk. The company may be unable to meet obligations (as dramatically illustrated by the case of Enron in 2001) or the employer may defraud (as criminally done in the case of Maxwell in 1991). This risk comes on dramatic display in large bankruptcies but is also seen in gradual erosions of pension rights, as for example in the flight from final salary schemes.

When Bismarck made himself the unlikely father of the modern welfare state by introducing compulsory social security in his newly united Germany in the 1880s, he wanted a fully state-run system in order to bind workers in loyalty to the state. Employers, however, were unwilling to give up their power over workers in an insurance scheme and prevailed.[29]

[27] This understanding of Adam Smith has been re-created by Rothschild 2002.

[28] In Britain, for example, the State Earnings-Related Pension was deliberately made unattractive when opting out became available in the 1986 social-security reform to encourage earners to move into private schemes. See also Eliasson 2001.

[29] Mommsen 1981.

Since then, the debate over pensions has been about the balance of power over workers between state and employers. In most of the twentieth century, the state was the winner and pensions tilted to state systems, but employers have now reclaimed pension power. With large pension cohorts and smaller worker cohorts, taxpayers are hesitant to pay expensive state pensions for others today in the face of uncertainty about their own pensions tomorrow.

State pensions are in decline and occupational pensions on the rise. This shifts economic power sideways from government to capital but not downwards from élites to ordinary people. Earners are moved out from under political risk and back into company risk and remain powerless. A democratization of the economic power that sits in pension savings and pension capital would come about by earners taking ownership of their own pensions through their own savings.

This, however, brings on market risk. If pensions are grounded in capital investments, which owned pensions would in some way have to be, there is the risk that investments may decrease in value or fail to generate revenues. Market risk is mostly about volatility. If we go by the experience of the last century, we should expect that markets rise but with temporary, sometimes serious, setbacks. Market risk comes from the inability to bridge temporary crises. That risk can be contained through regulations. Pensions and pension funds should be managed by institutions with no other business. The mesh of pensions and other business in company schemes brings on risk and makes regulation elusive. There should be some pluralism of institutions to ensure competition and to make mutual insurance possible so that they would underwrite each other.

Pension rights would sit in personal pension accounts that would be indisputably owned by the pension holder in the same way that bank accounts are owned. Economic power of ownership would shift from paternalistic employers or government agencies to individuals, and with the additional benefit that they would be able to feel safe about their pensions, as they are already able to feel safe about their bank savings.

There would have to be state backing. All earners would need to be obliged by law to save for a pension; there would have to be a minimum state pension safety net; the pension industry would need to be strictly regulated; and the state would have to accept responsibility as insurer of last resort. (I follow up on these matters in more detail in chapter 3.)

THE EXAMPLE OF SCHOOLS

The remarkable thing about public schools—the schools available to ordinary people—is that those who matter the most have the least say. Economic and administrative power sits in bureaucratic agencies and to some degree in the schools themselves, while parents and pupils are subjects.

A system of universally available free public schools is, in most countries, in reality a system of divided schooling: free schools for the majority and for-pay schools for a minority. In a divided school system, there will be divided school loyalties. Many of the rich will give their loyalty to elite schools, while the constituency of public schools will be a residual majority. The economically resourceful will not have a strong interest in the public schools, which will therefore not have undivided support in the population and in particular of some of its most resourceful people.

Since the desired situation is that of the minority, the recommended action would seem to be to empower the disadvantaged majority rather than to disempower the advantaged minority. That could be done by giving all parents the kind of power the minority of parents already have, the power of money.

School budgets contain economic power. The democratization of this power would come about by shifting money from agency budgets and into the hands of parents. That could obviously not be a redistribution of income to parents for their discretionary use. The money would remain earmarked for schooling but allocated in such a way that all parents would control their share of the school budget.[30]

An example of a practical arrangement could be as follows: Let all schools be for-pay schools and let all parents pay for the schooling of their children. Allocate to all parents, rich and poor alike, their share of the school budget for them to use to pay for the schooling of their children. Let that be in the form of earmarked educational vouchers valid for school use only. Give parents the freedom to buy schooling for their children from the school of their choice.

The general objection against a system of for-pay schools is that if pupils could choose schools, then also schools could choose pupils, and there would be segregation again. That, however, is easily avoided. The purpose of universal for-pay schooling as argued here is to move power from authorities to parents and pupils. If schools can choose pupils, power would remain with the school. Schools that could—by virtue of reputation, for example—would cherry-pick among pupils and take the most able ones for themselves and reject the others, who would then have to be taken care of in schools that were not in a position to reject them.

However, schools need not be allowed this possibility. Freedom is by definition for persons, not for institutions. If schools have the freedom to choose pupils, pupils do not have the freedom to choose schools. Freedom

---

[30] My argument here is in terms of power and fairness. There is also an efficiency argument, whereby empowerment is likely to follow through to improved educational achievement; cf., e.g., Howell and Peterson 2002.

for institutions at the cost of freedom for persons is simply a contradiction in terms. Parental power of choice in schooling would require precisely that schools were not able to choose pupils.

All schools would in other words have a duty to take all kinds of pupils, without discrimination. No school should be able to give itself advantage by directing difficulties on to others. All would have to compete on an equal footing and be prepared to work within the reality that not all pupils are equal or have the same abilities.

What, finally, about those schools that have more pupils applying than they could take? Would they not be able to cherry-pick and make themselves special? Not if they are properly regulated. In these cases, the intake could be determined by lot. All parents and pupils have the same right to choose schools. Schools do not have a right to discriminate. Decision by lot is the fairest of all possible methods for the distribution of goods in short supply—and established as a democratic method of allocation since the early democracy in Athens.[31] This would prevent schools from undermining the freedom of parents and pupils to choose, and it would prevent parents with connections from being able to arrange for their children to get into the best schools.

THE RICH

What now to do with the rich? They have too much power but massive redistribution and wholesale nationalization can be ruled out. Is a third magic available: to rein in the economic power of the rich without taking their income or property?

Only outrageous or outrageously used income and property are subject to being challenged. A first candidate might be exceptionally large holdings of wealth. Is it plausible to argue that with the growth and accumulation of private wealth, the very largest holdings have grown beyond efficiency and decency and that at least the top of those outgrowths should be chopped off? Regrettably perhaps, it is (in the first instance) difficult to see how this argument could prevail. The middle class is constrained by the fear that capital will be used less efficiently under political control than in private hands. The fact that some holdings are very large, even if felt to be obscenely large, is not likely to eliminate that fear.

Furthermore, the holdings in question are by definition the most powerful in the land. The middle class would not sensibly choose to do battle with the most powerful possible opponent, all the less since it would not believe that it would itself have much to gain from it. These holdings,

---

[31] Manin 1997.

being exceptionally valuable, are precisely the holdings the rich would be prepared to expend moral capital to defend. Hence, property that is outrageous only by its size is not a realistic direct target of middle-class political power.[32]

What remains, then, is the targeting of income or property outrageously used. The argument in defense of economic power that is persuasive to others is, in the end, the imperative of efficiency. Ergo, the noneconomic use of economic power is without this defense. Such uses are then subject to political counterpower because their defense would be costly in moral capital.

Two uses recommend themselves for consideration: political use and inheritance. The political use of economic power has no defense at all in economic efficiency. Nor do there seem to be other moral arguments in its favor. It rests, to the degree it is argued as a matter of principle, on a rather strained view of property rights: that individual freedom contains a right for property holders to use their property in whatever way they wish. But the right to *hold* property cannot in itself contain a right to any *use* of property.

Inheritance is just a transfer of ownership, in this case within the family to the next generation, and is as such a nonuse of wealth. There are, however, efficiency arguments in favor of the institution of inheritance: the knowledge that property can be passed on within the family motivates property holders to its efficient use. No doubt it is also a strongly held norm that it is a right to be able to preserve property in the family, which is to say that there is moral force behind the institution of inheritance beyond the efficiency argument.

However, if the efficiency argument falls away, the remaining defense of inheritance becomes weaker and starts to look more ruthless than moral. This came to view in the recent debate in the United States over the inheritance tax. When President Bush in 2001 proposed the abolition of all tax on inheritance, opposition was raised by a coalition of charities and some of the very richest people in the country.[33] Their arguments were twofold. First, removing the inheritance tax would also remove from the rich, and in particular the very rich, a motivation to charitable giving. That could be detrimental to a range of social causes, from scientific research to poverty relief. Second, private holdings had in many cases become so substantial that no sensible purpose could be served by simply

---

[32] There is also the category of outrageously *acquired* holdings, e.g., from "golden goodbyes" to failed executives. These practices are now increasingly being challenged, for good moral reasons. For our argument, however, such holdings, although sometimes individually large, would not in the aggregate represent a significant stock of economic power for redistribution.

[33] Gates and Collins 2003. See also www.responsiblewealth.org and www.ufenet.org.

passing it on in the family. On the contrary, that would contribute to the emergence of a nonmeritocratic economic aristocracy with unhealthy economic power. In other words, in the view of this opposition, neither efficiency arguments nor moral arguments favored encouraging the undivided preservation of large fortunes in the family.

This now brings us back indirectly to large holdings. Nationalization may not be in the cards, but could the arguments stack up so as to put it within realistic consideration to divert the top of large fortunes to social purposes at the point of inheritance? What suggests this possibility is that this measure would not eliminate the institution of inheritance and therefore not come up against the imperative of efficiency, at least not strongly. Though this is a very considerable step towards a realistic possibility, it is not sufficient. Property-rights arguments and sheer power—the threat of exit—remain. There would be no prospect of middle-class political power touching the holdings of the very rich unless those arguments could be made politically impotent. That again would depend on the identification of a cause for the use of the diverted holdings, preferably with both efficiency and moral arguments in its favor.

The Political Use of Money

With the escalating costs of electoral politics, the power of money is transgressing into politics in such a way that fair democratic struggle is eroding from inside. Politics becomes expensive, and parties and politicians dependent on those who can fund them.[34] This is driven by varied interests. Politicians who can raise the money benefit because it eliminates competition from those who cannot. Those who have the money benefit because it gives them the possibility of buying influence. Commercial media benefit because much of the expense comes their way as revenue. A vast industry is created of consultants, publicists, pollsters, and other hangers-on.

The funding of parties and campaigns from donations is not necessary for democracy. Party budgets can be kept within boundaries by limiting

[34] For example, in the 2004 U.S. presidential elections: "The U.S. presidential contest is set to be the first billion dollar election in political history. According to the latest official figures, George Bush and John Kerry together have raised more than $500m, double the previous record set by Mr Bush and Al Gore in 2000. Allies and surrogates operating through a loophole in the campaign finance laws have amassed a further $330m and are rapidly sucking in cash, most of which will be thrown into the Bush-Kerry duel in the form of attack advertisements. Add in the $150m in federal funds provided to the candidates, and the considerable funds spent on the presidential contest by the Republican and Democratic party machines, and it is clear that the billion dollar mark is going to be passed." *Guardian*, 14 October 2004.

parties to revenues from membership fees. This would shut out the influence of money in parties and make membership the basis of party power.

Campaign spending could be held down with the help of capping rules. The control over funding could be handed over to citizens. With capping, total campaign funding would be known. That could then be allocated from the government through vouchers distributed to citizens for them to distribute on to politicians and organizations of their choice. All other funding, including from candidates' or officials' own sources, could be treated as corruption.

These simple measures would in one blow both empower ordinary citizens and kill the corrupting influence of money in democratic competition. No issue of citizenship rights arises. Full freedom of speech, expression, and participation remain. What is at stake is what should be at stake: the opportunity of the rich to remove their own interests and participation from fair competition and to buy up the apparatus of politics.

THE RATIONAL USE OF WEALTH

During the twentieth century, and in particular its last decades, economic restructuring and growth boosted the stock of private wealth. Although highly concentrated in its distribution, this wealth sits in a growing number of large fortunes. Private wealth has thereby become a rich source of potential taxation.[35]

According to my rules of economic democracy, for the middle class to use political power to control economic resources it would need to persuade itself that ordinary people would benefit and that the resources in question could be put to good economic use. Furthermore, the intended good use would have to be so morally persuasive that it would be costly for the rich to resist. Strongly progressive taxation and outright nationalization are ruled out both because the middle class would not be confident that benefits would come their way and because the upper class would be able to resist. A way would have to be found to implicitly tax the very rich without explicitly taxing them.

The future of higher education is the cause that could put both moral and efficiency arguments behind a policy of diverting the top of large fortunes from private to social use. Advanced democracy and capitalism need a highly educated citizenry and workforce. Young people want and need ever more education. The way of life is (or should be) approaching about a third of the life course spent in childhood and education (including lifelong learning), about a third in paid work, and about a third in

---

[35] Ackerman and Alstott 1999.

retirement. That means that the third in work would have to pay for the two other thirds. The relatively short period of work would then have to be highly productive, which would require a high level of education, which in turn would require the allocation of vast resources to education. We need to find a way of providing for mass participation in ever higher levels of education. That could be done as follows.

First, allow ordinary people access to higher education. This is a matter of making it affordable, which could be done by giving everyone, say at the age of eighteen, a scholarship account worth, say, six years in education beyond secondary school.

Second, it would have to be funded. Some of that could be shifted from public budgets for higher education into the hands of students, in the same way I have suggested in the case of schools. But the move from limited to mass participation in higher education would obviously require mass additional funding.

Working people would unavoidably have to pay in one way or another. Ordinary taxation would not do; the tax level would be prohibitive. Nor would it do the job to leave it to parents to pay for their children or to students to pay for their own education retrospectively. Middle-class people would incur an unbearable burden in midlife when they have the least potential for saving or paying off debt. Young people from low-income families would effectively be excluded.[36]

It seems better to allow working people to postpone payment until they are better off and to relieve them of this burden in the early part of their careers when they have better uses for their limited means, such as raising children. We could take advantage of the growth in private fortunes and go to wealth rather than to income for the funding of education. As always with taxation, it would not be painless but less painful than to take it out of income.

For this to come about, we need additional arguments that give the middle class further interests in the policy, making it for them something worth fighting for and reasonable, that is, something costly for the rich to resist.

Private wealth can be seen as earned or given. Wealth earned is the result of effort, industry, and prudence. Wealth given is the result of privilege, opportunity, and luck. Most holdings are probably a combination of these, but smaller holdings, such as standard housing property and basic savings, are likely to be predominantly wealth earned, whereas larger holdings are likely to contain more wealth given. Property rights would then seem to

---

[36] Britain is, unwisely, in the process of introducing a system of university fees to be paid by students retrospectively when they become earners. There are initial signs that this is discouraging entry into higher education.

differ: to be stronger in the case of wealth earned and weaker in the case of wealth given. Therefore, let wealth below a reasonably high threshold be protected private property and only wealth beyond this threshold be considered available for social use. The institution of inheritance is preserved, middle-class holdings are protected, and only holdings that have a weaker protection in property rights are targeted.

Let the targeted holdings then be protected from the risk of political appropriation and misuse. They should not be taxed for the benefit of the government's treasury but be strictly earmarked for education in a social contract in which those who have surplus wealth underwrite society's necessary investments in human capital.

Furthermore, let ownership remain decentralized and the capital in question remain in the market for economic use. This could be done by directing private holdings beyond the threshold at the point of inheritance sideways into earmarked funds rather than downward within the family to the next generation. Such funds we might call, for example, human-capital foundations. These foundations would hold capital for normal use and investment, as do pension funds, for example. Those who (albeit by enforcement) "invest" capital in such a foundation would have membership in it and a say in its running and would in that sense remain owners. The foundations would obviously operate under regulations and should probably have public representatives among their governors, for example, appointed by the central bank. There might be as many human-capital foundations as anyone would wish; any mega-rich person would be free to establish his or her own.

These foundations could then be taxed for the purpose of funding higher-education scholarship accounts. Foundations might be established gradually and enable a gradual shift of the funding of education from normal taxes. After a while, the allocation of new capital and the tax rate would probably be determined so that human-capital foundations in total did not grow noticeably as a share of the economy.

CONCLUSIONS

Economic democracy is achieved through measures to modify democratically damaging inequalities in the distribution of economic power. Such measures are seen as desirable in the interest of protecting the democratic quality of society.

Economic democracy has traditionally been seen as a matter of taking economic power out of private hands and putting it in one way or another under democratically accountable collective control. Attempts to democratize economic power in this way have generally failed, mainly because they have proved costly or risky in terms of economic efficiency. The approach in this treatise is more individualistic: it sees economic democracy not as a matter of collectivizing economic power but of redistributing it between persons. Economic democracy in the traditional understanding is, I have concluded, not democratically available. Democracy rests on an individualistic philosophy, it is about power to *persons*. If economic democracy is to be democratically viable, its theory must conform. The way to salvage the idea of economic democracy is to build its theory on the premise that democracy is about empowering *persons*.

How, in contemporary advanced capitalist democracies, could steps towards economic democracy come about, given the prevailing relations of political and economic power and the constraint that it would have to be done democratically? What openings realistically exist for the use of political power to redistribute economic power?

Taxation. Progressive tax rates are a necessary condition of economic democracy. This is primarily for reasons of tax psychology. The middle class is unlikely to tax itself sufficiently to fund fiscal measures towards economic democracy unless it can believe that the rich pay at least a bit more than they themselves pay. Strongly progressive rates are not possible, but moderately progressive rates can be imposed because it is not cost-effective for the upper class to resist.

Empowering the poor. All democratic countries have public policies to contain the problem of poverty. What are the conditions for moving beyond a policy of containment towards the ambition of eradicating it? The conclusion on this question is pessimistic. Antipoverty policies beyond containment are not impossible in capitalist democracies, but where that breakthrough has not been made during the early evolution of the welfare state, very demanding conditions need to be satisfied for it to happen later. The prediction is, barring the emergence of exceptionally powerful moral lobbies, that antipoverty policies will remain within the limited ambition of containment.

Empowering the middle class. The middle class could improve significantly its position of economic power by using its political power to shift the economic power contained in welfare budgets from welfare bureaucracies into its own hands, that is, to ordinary people. This is entirely possible since the middle class would be giving itself economic power without taking it from the rich. What seems to stand in the way of such democratization is a mind-set that believes powerful bureaucracies are necessary to implement welfare.

Disempowering the rich. The income and wealth of the rich is protected by their power to threaten to move capital abroad and by middle-class fears that policies that challenge capital may endanger their own prosperity or future prosperity. Middle-class political power could realistically be used against capital only in the case of income or property used "outrageously," that is, when the use is not rational by credible arguments of economic efficiency and its defense would otherwise be costly in moral capital. The political use of money is found to be in this category and so, probably, is the right of inheritance to the top ends of large private fortunes. These uses of income and property could be blocked without nationalizing the income or property in question and without removing the relevant economic resources from market use.

Power and awareness. The use of political power to redistribute economic power depends entirely on the middle class. The middle class could be (at least a bit) more generous to the poor than it is by self-interest by exploiting its power to (moderately) overtax the rich. But can it persuade itself to confront the rich for this purpose? It could very significantly increase its own economic power by expropriating the economic power that sits in welfare bureaucracies. But is it prepared to take on those bureaucracies? It could pull the teeth of at least some forms of economic power in the upper class, such as the political use of money. But is it up to confronting the rich? Very significant redistribution of economic power to ordinary people (if not to the poor) is there for the taking as far as political power is concerned, but the readiness to use political power to that end depends on overcoming middle-class awareness and fears.

CHAPTER 3

What Should Welfare States Do?

> They [social services] are part of the price we pay to some
> people for bearing part of the costs of other people's
> progress. They are the socially caused diswelfares involved
> in aggregate welfare gains.
> —Richard M. Titmuss, *Commitment to Welfare*

IN THE INTRODUCTION to the 2006 edition of my book *The Possibility of Politics*, I reviewed twenty years of welfare-state trends following its first publication. I ended up observing, or predicting, that thinking about welfare-state reform, at least in Europe, is reverting to a model akin to the one William Beveridge laid out in *Social Insurance and Allied Services* in 1942.[1] His was a more austere welfare state (a term, incidentally, he did

---

The Research Committee on Poverty, Social Welfare and Social Policy of the International Sociological Association, RC19, has been an intellectual home for me. In annual workshops, run with Protestant discipline and efficiency, we have over the last twenty years or so followed the moving research front in comparative welfare-state studies. In the present essay, I translate the capital of knowledge and ideas I have gained from cooperation with my colleagues in RC19 into a personal statement about the future of the welfare state. I draw on other experiences also, but that RC19 capital has been invaluable. I do not suggest, of course, that my colleagues necessarily agree with my analyses. I only want to celebrate the great importance of international institutions of durable academic cooperation such as RC19. I have had the opportunity to present elements of this work in lectures on welfare-state reform at the Graduate School of Public Health of Seoul National University (on 12 April 2005, at the invitation of Soonman Kwon), at the Wissenschaftszentrum Berlin (on 25 May 2005, at the invitation of Jens Alber), at the Swedish Institute for Social Research of the University of Stockholm (on 18 April 2006, at the invitation of Robert Erikson and Walter Korpi) and the Centre for Comparative Welfare Studies of Aalborg University (on 26 April 2006, at the invitation of Jørgen Goul Andersen). I have benefited greatly from helpful discussions on those occasions. I wish to thank N for allowing me to use her case story in the section on social care below.

[1] *The Possibility of Politics* was first published in 1987. In it, I pulled together years of work and reflection on social policy, including from previous publications (e.g., Ringen 1981, 1984, 1985, 1986; and Ringen and Wærness 1982). This work has continued and now again I draw on material published in the process, e.g., Ringen 1991a, 1997b, 1997d, 1998a, 1998c, 2003a, 2005c; and Ringen and Uusitalo 1992. I also draw on lectures I have given the last few years on the history of welfare states to graduate students in social policy and economic and social history at Oxford, and on excellent discussions with my students around these lectures.

not like and did not use) than those we have later come to know. It was "from the cradle to the grave," but in the form of basic social insurance. Beyond that it was a duty for everyone to work and provide for their own welfare.[2]

My observation-prediction may have an element of wishful thinking to it: I persuaded myself that what I think should happen will happen. Here I want to follow through and explain what the calling back of Beveridge from beyond the grave might practically mean. The consequences present themselves, obviously, mainly in the treatment of social security. I will conclude in favor of a new social contract, one built on the reawareness of self-reliance, and then, flowing from that idea, for substantive realignments in real social provisions. As Beveridge did, I also find that it is impossible to deal meaningfully with social security in isolation from other social policies. Beveridge got around the difficulty that everything depends on everything by focusing his attention (as was his mandate) on social security but introducing assumptions about health care, family policy, and employment as necessary conditions for his social-security blueprint to be made workable. I do much the same in my treatments of social care and family policy, except that I am not constrained by any mandate from discussing those policies in some detail. I also include an assumption that was not on the agenda in Beveridge's time, that of multicultural integration. This essay, then, is unashamedly prescriptive.[3] Reverting to old Beveridge in fact makes for radical new reform.

A modern welfare state should be universal: it should extend social protection to everyone and leave no one outside and abandoned in high risk or destitution. But universality means different things to different people. For Beveridge, the father of the idea of universality, it meant that everyone should have protection against falling into poverty. In Scandinavia, at least in Sweden and Norway, it came to mean tax-funded public provision: that state and municipalities should be the providers of all forms of social insurance and care for everyone.[4] The origins of that brand of universality are quite complex. When social security was consolidated

---

[2] In chapter 5, I demand rather aggressively that we should always say "families" and never "the family." I ought really to ask the same here: "welfare states" and not "the welfare state." I should do that all the more since I have myself long argued that welfare states should ideally be analyzed individually in light of their specific historical and national circumstances and that it is hardly even pertinent to treat them as types; cf. Ringen 1991a. However, as a matter of convenience here, I say "the welfare state" as often as I should have said "welfare states."

[3] Reflections on the welfare state now concentrate on reform. We are finished with the idea of crisis, thanks mainly to Pearson 1994 and Castles 2004. My prescriptions for reform are in my mind a dialogue particularly with Gilbert 2002, Esping-Andersen et al. 2002, and Fererra 2005.

[4] On the Scandinavian model, see Erikson et al. 1987.

into "people's pensions" in Sweden and Norway in the 1950s and 1960s, the political issue was more about public or private control over the capital from pension savings than social protection as such. If we start from the ideological position that the state should be the provider, universality may well mean state provision. But if we are more pragmatic about the arrangement of provision, we will probably see universality more as a matter of what protection is delivered to whom than of who delivers it. A political argument for universality is that social protection is not on a secure basis unless everyone is included so that everyone has an interest in supporting the system. I will argue that social security in this meaning has not been achieved anywhere and that the key to its achievement is universal insurance rather than omnipotent public provision.

Democratic governments have a surprisingly narrow range of instruments to play.[5] They can tax and spend, which means that they expropriate income from households and businesses in order to pay for the services and transfers they give back to households and others. If they are able to hold a different profile in giving than in taking, they will change the distribution of resources and well-being in society. In a way, that's the welfare state as we know it.

Or they can regulate. With taxing and spending, governments and government agencies do the doing (or at least so it looks). With regulating, governments tell private agents what to do and the doing that gets done is decentralized to persons, households, associations, and businesses.

In my future welfare state, I see relatively more being done by regulating and relatively less by taxing and spending. My recommendations add up to redirecting the welfare state from supporting consumption to supporting institutions—towards a welfare state for investment.

One reason for predicting or recommending a shift in that direction is that democratic governments in a world of global capitalism are severely constrained in their power to tax, and in this respect are more constrained now and in the future than previously (as I have discussed in chapter 2).[6] Capital has become more movable internationally. That has strengthened the hand of capital vis-à-vis governments: the credible threat to move financial or physical capital out of the country is raw veto power. Since all taxes are directly or indirectly costs on businesses, it is against taxation that capital is most likely to use its power. No government can now afford to tax noticeably more than other governments (in comparable countries). As long as taxing was more open, new policies could in large measure be funded from a growing pool of public money. Since around 1980, total

[5] I discuss the paradox of big governments with small tools under the heading "The Powerlessness of Powerful Government" in Ringen 2004d.
[6] See also Mkandawire 2004, in particular the introduction.

public spending in the advanced countries has converged towards a stable level, and new policies now have to be funded predominantly from reallocations within a pool of public money that is no longer increasing.[7] That is a very different and more difficult environment of public policy. Governments tax to their limits and have vast budgets but very little of *new* money to draw on.

There are things I believe democratic governments should do more of than they are doing that can only be done by taxing and spending. Therefore I think they should not use up their tax capacity for purposes that can be handled without taxes. My prescriptions are much about creating space within the boundaries of tax capacity for necessary government spending by not making claims on that capacity for purposes that do not require spending from government coffers.

What I think can largely (but not fully) be managed outside of taxing and spending is social security. That would be most fortunate. Social security is costly. If it could be removed from taxation, very considerable tax capacity would be freed up for other purposes. A great deal of tax capacity would still be freed up even if nontax social security would have to be subsidized to some degree from taxation. Social security is increasingly costly. Needs are running ahead of tax capacity. Social security will not be on a secure footing unless nontax forms of funding can be found.

What I think the freed-up capacity should be used for is mainly (but not only) family policy. Family productivity is in decline, including in child rearing. For reasons I explain in chapters 5 and 6, it should now be an urgent priority in the welfare state to arrest and reverse this decline. This will require new money and again depends on freeing up tax capacity.

THE AFFLUENCE ASSUMPTION

I start from two broad assumptions, or sets of assumptions, which we might call *the affluence assumption* and *the population assumption*.

In the social sciences, we have been notoriously disinclined towards the analysis or even acknowledgment of affluence. We have (for good reasons) been more concerned with the conditions of the poor than the rich. We have also (for good reasons again) been much concerned with inequality. Since inequality tends to persist through economic growth, there seems to be more continuity than change in social conditions as we study them.

It is now time to take affluence seriously. In Western Europe, North America, and elsewhere most people have become affluent. Take Britain

[7] This shift is documented in Castles 2004.

(which is far from being the most affluent of the affluent countries). Both household income and household spending have multiplied by 2.5 in no more than thirty years. Since 1990 alone, the net wealth of households has almost doubled and their marketable wealth has more than doubled. In 1970, only one in three households had a telephone; today, three of four households have one or more mobile phones, and more than half are connected to the Internet (many more, probably, since this number is changing faster than statistics can keep up with). From 1970, the number of occupier-owned dwellings has increased by 90 percent, and the number of rental dwellings declined sharply. The number of motorcars more than doubled, and by 2003 the number of passengers at U.K. airports was six times the number in 1971. In thirty years, the number of students in higher education has multiplied by about four (and for women by more than six).[8] Not everyone is affluent, obviously, and in relative terms there are as many as before, possibly more, who have less than average affluence.[9] But those people we sometimes call ordinary have become very well off indeed.

Affluence changes people. For my purpose, the change to observe is in power. In poor societies, the situation of the common man is one of low income and only basic educational resources. In the affluent society, the situation of the common man, and we must now include the common woman, is very different. He and she are now empowered, both in income and property and in competence and skills. This changes the moral foundations of the welfare state and again helps to clear the ground for resurrecting the ideology of self-reliance. The marriage of affluence and competence is the stuff of what in chapter 6 I call real freedom. Much more than before, citizens are capable of autonomy. It is a positive ethical principle that persons who have competence should be free to arrange their own lives. It is a good moral principle that people who *can* pay their own way *should* pay their own way. The consequence of affluence is that the common man and the common woman graduate to this status. Beveridge may have overestimated the capacity for autonomy in his time; at least his philosophy was not heeded when the democracies started to build new welfare states after World War II. But today that philosophy should have more resonance. In the preaffluent society, many people were in need of much help; the welfare state of that society would be a paternalistic one. In the affluent society, more people have the resources and skills to fend for themselves; the welfare state of that society will and should be less

---

[8] These examples are from *Social Trends* 2005 (www.statistics.gov.uk/socialtrends).

[9] In Britain, income inequality was steadily lowered from around 1950 to 1975 but then increased again so that the distribution is now more unequal than it was half a century ago; cf. Atkinson 1995a; *Social Trends* 2005(www.statistics.gov.uk/socialtrends).

paternalistic. *Less* paternalistic, as we will see, not nonpaternalistic: a welfare state without paternalism is a contradiction in terms.

Affluence also comes with changes in society. There is only one way to achieve affluence, and that is through work.[10] And there is only one way to produce affluence from work, and that is to make work more productive. It is not by *more* work we become affluent but by *better* work. The society of affluence presents itself to women and men, and to children, as escalating expectations on competence, skills, education, organization, planning, discipline—on performance in all shapes and forms. Its economy is a high-tech and rapidly moving knowledge economy. People are made better off, but also more is asked of them. They are empowered but also are made to live in ways that require more power. The affluent society claws back what it gives: it gives people the tools to live well but also makes the achievement of good lives more demanding.

Social expectations in an economy of affluence come together in an expectation to live and work productively—hence in being prepared for productivity and therefore in education, hence in being a good worker and citizen and therefore in plan and discipline, hence in being up-to-date and therefore in acquiring new skills. For those who can meet its expectations, this economy is good. It rewards them with a high standard of living. But there are two qualifications.

First, to benefit, you must be able to manage rising expectations. People must be in a position to deliver performance and to cope with the strains. This means investment and reinvestment of capacity in those people.

Second, not everyone will be able to cope. An affluent society is inevitably a society of social exclusion. This means social care.

The first effect of affluence in the welfare state is that nothing happens. Even when affluence becomes the widespread condition, it does not become the condition of everyone. Many will remain in need of care. It may even be that the need for social care increases with increasing affluence. The display of exclusion amid affluence in, for example, beggars in the streets or angry yobs who rage against society in antisocial behavior is not paradoxical but expected. Advances in affluence to the benefit of the mainstream may simultaneously cause more people to fall outside of the mainstream. There may be less poverty, but we should not necessarily expect that to follow through to less need for basic social support. This may help explain why still in the Scandinavian countries—with their high income levels, even income distributions, and solid safety

---

[10] Some individuals come to affluence in other ways—for example, by inheritance or by winning the lottery—but even inherited or given wealth does not come out of thin air and must first be created.

nets—between 5 and 10 percent of families receive in any year poverty relief in its modern form.[11]

Most great welfare-state reforms through the twentieth century were inspired more or less strongly by an ambition to make poverty relief obsolete. The idea has been to build safety nets of social insurance so secure that no one would fall through and be in need of relief. That was also Beveridge's idea. He assumed that with universal social insurance supported by free health care, child allowances, and full employment, the need for relief would be absorbed in insurance arrangements. This is a beautiful dream but regrettably only a dream. The need for last-resort relief has never been superseded, and there is no secure safety net without it. About this, Beveridge was too optimistic. To follow in his spirit of universal protection today from what we have subsequently learned we must start with, and not neglect, the need for social care in addition to social insurance.

The second effect of affluence is to boost the demand for education, more education, and continuous education. Today's affluent economies run on human capital. If we think back to conveyor-belt production systems or further back to the early phases of the industrial revolution, persons were tools for the exploitation of physical capital (as they are today in transition economies). Growth was driven by innovations in physical capital without much need for investment in workers. In the knowledge economy, the total stock of capital is increasingly made up of human capital and physical capital is devalued to becoming the tool.[12] Better productivity now depends much more on better workers. In one generation, the very meaning of work has been redefined and is now for almost everyone a matter of data manipulation in some form, including mobile telephony. In less than a generation, the source of value in information technology itself has shifted from hardware to software.[13]

An economy that runs on human capital must invest in people. For reasons of both productivity and international competitiveness, this economy needs a high level of education in most of its workers and it needs

[11] Gustafsson 1999.

[12] In Norway, to counterbalance the misunderstanding that the country is rich because of its access to natural resources, in particular petroleum, the government commissioned the Central Bureau of Statistics to estimate the value of the national wealth and its components. It was found that oil and gas reserves make up 13 percent of the country's wealth and that the wealth that sits in people in the form of human capital (defined as future earning power in the present population) accounts for 76 percent. (NOU 2005:05, *Enkle signaler i en kompleks verden*, Oslo: Official Government Publications, estimated for 2001.)

[13] Which is why IBM declined and Microsoft grew and why an intended hardware revolution in India failed but progress was rescued by an unanticipated software revolution. On technology and globalization, see T. Friedman 2005.

those workers to upgrade, improve, and expand their skills continuously. Its workers need to qualify themselves, and to requalify, for participation in that economy. Individual workers need to qualify as much as or more than others in order to compete and keep up. The drive for increasing and expanding education and training is inescapable.

THE POPULATION ASSUMPTION

Improvements in health and health care have resulted in increased longevity. The second demographic transition has carried through to low and ultralow fertility. Together these effects present themselves to the welfare state as aging and as lower-than-replacement birthrates. Aging changes the *dependency ratio*. In Britain, for example, the number of people older than sixty-five relative to those aged twenty to sixty-four stayed at about 27 percent during the last two decades of the twentieth century but is now on the rise and set to reach 50 percent well before 2050.[14] Low birthrates change population trends. Europe is set to lose 100 million to 125 million people by 2050, from 725 million today. Population numbers are now in decline in most countries in Eastern Europe, and they are expected to start declining in southern Europe and Germany from around 2010. On the edge of Europe, the Russian population is set to fall from 145 million today to about 100 million by 2050.[15]

This new demographic scenario represents a new setting for the welfare state, radically so. In response, we are led to different ways of thinking about the welfare state and to new ideologies and mind-sets, and we are led to reshaping its constituent social policies.

Post-1945 welfare states were built on an assumption of demographic stability. It was thought that successive generations would be more or less of the same size, so that each generation would in the course of life contribute to and draw on the welfare state in about equal measure. That assumption has now collapsed spectacularly.

[14] For an excellent overview of European population trends, see Coleman 2005. See also Ringen 2003b.

[15] United Nations Population Division, *World Population Prospects: The 2002 Revisions*, un.org/esa/population/publications/WPP2002). See also UNPF 2002. Population decline is looming also in Japan and Korea, for example. In Australia and Canada, population numbers are set to continue to increase in spite of low birthrates because of high rates of immigration. In the United States, the population will continue to grow because of both high birthrates and high immigration, the former stimulated by the latter. The economic problem with low birthrates is that the inflow of new human capital slows down. That problem is to some degree disguised in total population trends, which are influenced upward by increasing longevity.

Under the assumption of demographic stability, intergenerational fairness was seen to be built in and delivered automatically. This perceived fairness made it possible to trust in the durability of the welfare state. We would pay for our parents' pensions and care today and our children for ours tomorrow.

With the collapse of demographic stability, so has intergenerational fairness collapsed. When generations are of shifting size, they contribute and benefit inequitably. The members of large generations pay less and probably benefit more; those of small generations pay more and probably benefit less. What finally collapses is the basis of trust. The young can no longer feel secure that they will themselves in due course benefit fairly from what they are now contributing.

The rebuilding of trust under new conditions is enforcing radical changes in a welfare state inherited from a different society. These changes come through a new story of the welfare state and in the form of substantive policy shifts. The new story is one of self-reliance. The main reorientations in policy go under the names "pension reform" and "workfare."

We used to be told that we pay for each other, that the young were paying for their elders' needs. Now we are being told that we pay for ourselves, that the young are paying into their own future standard of living. The real political economy of pensions and retirement is exactly the same; it is about the ability to share and the continued ability to share. At any point in time, a society has a pool of consumption available to it, and that pool has to be shared between the young, the old, the economically active, the dependent, and so on. Most of the elderly and other dependents will get pretty much their share one way or other whether they are many or few. The young have to see to it that they are productive enough to provide sufficiently for both themselves and their dependents. That is a wonderful incentive for work and productivity. With the kind of economic growth we are now accustomed to and can expect, this is and will remain manageable.

But not *easily* manageable. Hence reform. And to ease reform, the story of social security needs to be told differently to start creating now the culture that will tomorrow enable sharing under more difficult circumstances. To teach us to share when sharing will ask more of us, the story of the welfare state is tilting towards telling us that what we are sacrificing today we are setting aside for our own retirement tomorrow.

Pension reform today means incentives and propaganda to get us to set aside more for retirement, to start setting aside earlier, to work in preference to claiming welfare, and to work longer and delay retirement. Although pension systems are different and are being changed differently, this is everywhere the crux of the matter.

If those who are economically active do not save, they will be confiscating so much consumption that not enough is left over for others. This may look like a problem of bookkeeping in social-security accounts over time but is in fact a matter of how much we produce *now* and how we share it *now*, and then of how much we will produce *tomorrow* and how we will share that production *then*. It's about perceived fairness over time.

Pension reform comes in as many varieties as there are pension systems, but the general thrust is to encourage earners to save. This is being done by telling them and making them believe that their own future pensions depend on their own present savings. That is not strictly true. Future pensions depend on future production and political decisions *then* about the sharing of that production. But it is indirectly true in that future production may depend on present savings and that future sharing certainly depends on a culture and habit of saving having become established. If earners are not encouraged to increase their saving enough to balance the demands of the growing ranks of elderly, there may not be enough economic growth to manage future distributions without conflict, and there may not be a social culture capable of generous sharing.

Workfare started as an eccentric idea in the United States. Too many people were reliant on poverty relief, in particular too many lone mothers. The system was both ineffective and expensive. There would be gains all around, both to social budgets and social clients, if more of those who were on welfare could be brought into work and self-reliance. That strategy proved unexpectedly successful in diminishing the welfare rolls. It did not prove to be a soft option for governments. Success depended both on heavy investments in personal social assistance and on governments accepting a responsibility as employer of last resort. But work proved in large measure to be an alternative to welfare.[16]

American workfare was not inspired by demographics but by inefficient policies. The experience of its success, however, came just in time for it to be incorporated into the new social contract that was in turn the child of demographic necessity. Hence, to great surprise, an idea that was first reviled as a ruthless neoliberal attack on welfare in certain remote areas of the American heartland became a universal theme in the modernization of the welfare state in Europe, under the labels "welfare to work" (in Britain) and "activation" (on the Continent).[17]

There is nothing new in the idea of helping dependents to work. Unemployment support is generally shaped to that end. Rehabilitation from illness or injury back into work is a long-established pillar of social care. But there is something more to workfare. It is, again, a story as much as

[16] Wolfe 2001.
[17] See, e.g., Saunders 2005.

a policy. That story is told to everyone—to the man in the street as much as to those on the margins of dependency. The story is, behind the usual rhetoric of welfare, a simple one: work and self-reliance are *good*, dependency and welfare are *bad*. It is about shaping mind-sets, expectations, habits, and behavior, about how we see ourselves and each other, in short about the new social contract of self-reliance.

The meaning of population decline in Europe is contested. It may not come to pass, or at least not on the scale now anticipated. Demographics have a way of changing in unexpected ways. If it does come to pass, it is not clear whether the consequences would be mainly benign—for example, less population pressure on resources and environment—or mainly malign, be it economically or socially.

However, in political and government circles in OECD countries and in the European Union, for example, the prospect of population decline is starting to spread a concern that is bordering on deep fear.[18] Rightly or wrongly (rightly in my opinion) the view is silently taking hold that population decline would be costly, in particular that the decline in birthrates to much below replacement levels is likely to lead to economic decline—that it already is, in fact. Much of Europe is stuck in sluggish growth and high unemployment. An economy that does not reproduce its labor force will suffer a deficit of new human capital and find it difficult to maintain growth and vitality. Fewer children today means fewer new workers tomorrow, as well as fewer consumers, fewer students, fewer investors, fewer innovators, fewer capitalists, and so on. We could try to compensate by investing more in each person but it would seem safer to have more people to invest in.[19]

Therefore, the population question is returning to center stage of European public policy. This influence is seen in the welfare state first and most

---

[18] Population issues are increasingly prominent in European Union social documents (see, e.g., *The Social Situation of the European Union 2004*, ec.europa.eu/employment_social/ publications/2004/keap04001). There is an emerging awareness of immigration as an instrument of economic policy (see, e.g., OECD, *Trends in International Migration 2003*, oecd .org/document/37/0). A silent subtheme in the question of Turkish membership in the European Union, for example, is the benefit of incorporating the large and young Turkish population into the economy of the Union.

[19] One shrewd observer who shares this analysis is the former Irish prime minister Garret FitzGerald. He explains the "Irish economic miracle" in part by demographic good luck: "[B]ecause our birth rate peaked in 1980, several decades later than in the rest of Europe, we have been able in recent years to increase our work force far more rapidly than anywhere else in the industrialized world. . . . Unfortunately, much of this advantage is now about to disappear because between 1980 and 1995 our birth rate fell by over one third. The bulk of this decline in our young working population is going to hit us during the first decade of the twenty-first century, eventually reducing by almost 30% the number of Irish-born entrants into the labour force" (FitzGerald 2003, p. 107).

directly in family policy. From having been a good and kind concern on the edge of the architecture in which the hard stuff has been social security and health care, family policy is capturing the center of attention. For my part, I think there are other very good reasons for upgrading family policy in addition to the demographic ones, as I explain in chapters 5 and 6, but demography seems to be the driving force politically. This is now strongly audible in social policy discourse.[20] Whether it also is or will become strongly visible in durable changes in real policies is possibly too early to tell. There seems to be an awareness that there are compelling reasons to invest more strongly in family policy, but that *is* a matter of investing and therefore of finding the means. This could prove difficult because there are competing needs, notably those created by aging, because it is not clear that new family policies will pay off in higher birthrates, which is what the political concern is mainly about, and because family policy could suffer relegation to the category of old-fashioned nanny-statism, which might not fit snugly with the new ideology of self-reliance.

The second great influence following from concern over the population question is in immigration and related matters. If we in the leading industrial countries are fearful that the decline in birthrates will lead to further decline economically and otherwise, there are good reasons to try to get birthrates up again with the help of family-friendly policies. But there are two problems: it may not work, and even if it works it will take a long time. Even successful pro-natalist policies today would not noticeably start to carry additional human capital into the economy until towards midcentury. Therefore, European governments are hesitantly turning to immigration and, to their surprise, finding themselves competing with each other over immigration and for immigrants.[21]

Systematic immigration means immigration policy. Immigration policy is invariably a brutal affair. It may be packaged attractively but is, when all is said and done, about attracting desired immigrants and shutting out undesirable ones. This kind of policy, however it is presented and however it is organized, is difficult to present and get accepted in liberal political cultures with little or no experience of immigration.[22]

Immigration policy will need legitimacy and will need to be made acceptble with the help of provisions for immigrants and immigrant families. For such legitimizing provisions, European and other governments

[20] See, e.g., Commaille and de Singly 1997; Esping-Andersen et al. 2002; Mason et al. 2003.

[21] See Ringen 2004c, which is a think-tank pamphlet on European population trends, immigration, and multiculturalism.

[22] Only in the United States does the political culture allow a high level of immigration, including tacit acceptance of illegal immigration, without the guidance of an explicit immigration policy. Australia and Canada are the pioneering countries in immigration policy.

will mobilize the apparatus of their welfare states. Social policies have always been for purposes beyond themselves. Poverty relief was for social control. Bonapartism was invented after the European revolutions of 1848 as a method of appeasement through concession. Bismarck's innovation in social insurance was for the management of "the worker question" and the building of his German state. The post-1945 universal welfare state was to prevent the kinds of social disintegration that had followed the First World War. Governments will obviously use their welfare states to manage their problems of the day; that's why they hold themselves with welfare states.

SOCIAL CARE

An exercise in welfare reform is well advised to start with a warning. And then a plea. The warning is to stay clear of any idea that the welfare state can be made obsolete. It has evolved out of necessity and does not become unnecessary just because we grow rich. Nor is any magic formula available that will solve all or most social problems in one go. I confront one such false promise in appendix E, the undeservedly successful idea of a basic minimum income. The welfare state will persist because it will remain necessary. It will take the form it has always had: a patchwork of policies that respond, imperfectly, to needs and aspirations and that come together, imperfectly, in a civilizing influence in capitalism.

The plea is to preserve social care. Theoreticians have always been tempted to think away the need for last-resort help. Now the temptation is to think that affluence eliminates the need, but it doesn't. Universal protection depends, finally, on mechanisms that are able to catch individuals and families who are in danger of falling into helplessness. There is and will be social exclusion; social exclusion is another name for being in need of help. Some people, for a variety of reasons, fall through the safety net of general provisions or are otherwise unable to cope with social expectations. Some people who are neither in precariousness nor in dependency may find themselves temporarily in situations of needing help beyond what they can find in their own networks. If we want to encourage welfare-to-work programs, those on the margins of the labor market will need help to get established inside them. This argument needs to be stressed. "Welfare to work" is sometimes seen as a matter of enforcing work in order to free governments from responsibility for welfare. The last part of that assumption is certainly false. Full employment that embraces those on the margins of employment and employability depends more on social care than on labor markets.

The Scandinavian welfare states have been much admired for their comprehensive universality. I agree, and I have again added my voice to that admiration in chapter 2. What is less recognized, however, is that they are also remarkable for having retained poverty relief in its old-fashioned form. It is no longer called poverty relief, of course—it has been renamed social assistance—but the structure is the old one: administered locally through municipal social-assistance offices under strong, or at least some, local political control and dispensed on a more or less discretionary case-by-case basis. Social assistance has not been retained because it has been explicitly wanted but rather in spite of being seen as an embarrassing remnant from a more primitive age. It has been retained because it has remained necessary for adequate social care.[23] It has, however, been modernized. What was once deliberately mean has been made generous. As a result, most of the stigma has been removed from receiving social assistance. The tightness of social safety nets in the Scandinavian systems owes much to universality but also more than is often known or acknowledged to the continuation of poverty relief.

Social care is the most underdeveloped and undervalued branch of social policy. Those who think about social policy prefer to think about the big systems and give less attention to such mundane matters as how to organize personal help for the helpless. As always, there is the temptation to think that if we only get the system right, the rest will fall into place on its own. But it never does.

No system is available for social care. For example, to see means-tested income support as *the* right formula for *the* poor is mistaken. Means-tested benefits can look good on paper but are in practice never target efficient. A year after the introduction of tax credits in Britain, "a third of all tax credit awards (1,879,000) had been overpaid. In all, the overpayments amounted to £1,931 million. More than half a million awards (630,000) had been overpaid £1,000 or more—including 40,000 awards where the overpayment amounted to more than £5,000." In the next round, this shows up as often severe problems for clients when overpaid awards are clawed back.[24] Furthermore, some of those who are at risk need service support more than income support, or in addition to income support. When income support gets established as the system, service support tends to be neglected. The French political scientist Pierre Rosanvallon has given it a name: *salarier l'exclusion*—pay them and be finished with it.[25]

[23] The unlikely story of the failure to abolish old-fashioned poverty relief in Norway after 1945 is told perceptively by Terum 1996.

[24] Parliamentary Ombudsman, *Tax Credits: Putting Things Right*, June 2005, publications.parliament.uk/pa/cm200506.

[25] Rosanvallon 1995.

It is almost correct, although a bit strong, to describe the history of social policy thinking as a quest for a system with no loose ends. Some have looked to markets, some to social networks, and others to universal rights. The very idea is an illusion, and experience has always disproved it. It is almost correct, although a bit strong, to say that the quest for systems has been at the cost of the needs of those who fall outside of any system. In social assistance, the attempt to substitute rights for discretion has left those in precariousness pretty much abandoned—often with a bit of cash, which often is not what they need, and often without services, which is often what they do need. In personal social services, outside of health care and education, the general state of affairs in the modern welfare state, from one country to another, is chaos, mess, scandal, abuse, and inefficiency.

Behind systems there must be *help*—pragmatic, practical, down-to-earth help for those who are helpless. Help for those who fall through. Help for those who have bad luck. Help for some of the unemployed who need more than income support. Help for some of those on the welfare-to-work route. Help for young people who need assistance with training and to get started in work. Help for families in trouble. Help for lone parents who struggle to cope. Help to persons and families, not just to categories—the old, the disabled, the lone mothers, the poor—but to the real persons and families who are in need of help.

Social care comes in various forms. The need may be for cash assistance; people do fall on hard times. Or it may be for service support, say help to vulnerable families in the form of respite child care. Or for a combination. For example, in discretionary social assistance of the Scandinavian brand, the social-assistance office may decide to give a couple who is expecting their first child economic assistance to equip their kitchen and to do that by sending a social worker with them to make the purchase and ensure that the cash is used to best effect and for the intended purpose. This is paternalism, or perhaps maternalism, but it is also flexibility in help.

In social care, the right help is what is right in each case. What is right in each case can only be determined on a case-by-case basis. It is a matter, first, of establishing the need and then of prescribing the right kind of help. Since the needs and circumstances of those on the edge of exclusion change often and rapidly, the mechanisms for responding to their needs must be flexible. Since the right kind of help is often, perhaps usually, some combination of different kinds of help, some kind of coordination is usually involved in the effective delivery of help. The recipe for effective social care is not a monolithic system but case-by-case flexibility and coordination.

This is very similar to the delivery of health care. But there are differences in how it is done. In health care, in the ideal case, the assessment of need is professional, help is prescribed according to the needs of the patient, and there is a frontline service—the family doctor, the general practitioner—who is charged with the job of coordination. In social care, in the typical post-poverty-relief case, the assessment of need is bureaucratic, help is prescribed according to rules, and administration is by one agency for each kind of help with coordination being either absent or chaotic.

A bureaucratic system may well, with luck, be fair and objective but will tend to be ineffective when the clients are among those who are the most resourceless, when clients are clients *because* they are resourceless. Those difficulties present themselves both to clients and to providers. For the client, one difficulty is the need to be in control of complicated bureaucratic rules and procedures when interacting with officials having often inadequate professional competence and capacity. Another difficulty is to keep track of coordination in a system in which each agency is responsible for its own turf and rules and no one is in charge of the overall picture. Mistakes are inevitably made in the application of bureaucratic rules, and bureaucratic mistakes are compounded in problems of coordination between agencies of interacting and often competing responsibilities.

On the side of caregivers, there are problems of inflexibility. Bureaucratic rules that allow little attention to the particular circumstances of each client may result in irrelevant help given and relevant help denied. The absence of coordinating capacity makes it difficult or impossible to prescribe the right combination of different kinds of help.

Bureaucratic social care is typically managed, to use a health-care analogy, as if the patient would start by making his way to a doctor in charge of pills and find that her competence and authority was limited to looking in a rule book that tells her all cancer patients have the right to an allocation of red pills. Whether the patient is also in need of surgery would not be for her to consider. If the patient were to find a surgeon, he would again find someone trained in the reading of a rule book for the allocation of surgery with little or no detailed diagnosis. The pill doctor would not know about the surgery and the surgeon would probably not know about the pills previously prescribed, except what the patient might tell her.

In the absence of professional competence, the job of quality control falls on the clients. Clients who are in social care because of some inability to cope must make themselves the overseers of bureaucratic rules and their application. In the absence of coordinating capacity in the system of delivery, coordination also lands with the clients. It is for them to ensure that one agency delivers what enters as an assumption in another agency's delivery. For example, in the great 2005 tax-credit debacle in Britain, one reason for overpayment was that a tax credit was often paid out without adequate knowledge of other incomes or payments that the tax credit in principle is conditional on, or without capacity to take into consideration often rapidly changing circumstances. That, according to the parliamentary ombudsman, was partly the result of rigidities in the tax-credit system—awards are annual and are inadequately adjusted for changing circumstances during the year—and "the delivery of tax credits has been designed to be wholly IT based and does not take proper account of the needs of customers."

In health care, ideally, patients get three things: help, professional quality control, and coordinated care. In social care, typically, the fortunate clients get help, but quality control and coordination are outsourced back to the clients themselves. They may get useful help, but claiming and administering it becomes a job, sometimes near full-time, in which the helpless are asked to take charge of what it is they need help for.

These problems are easily visible in Britain's regime of social care. Britain has had exceptionally high rates of child income poverty. It has been an aim of recent governments to reduce those rates and eventually to eliminate child poverty completely. To that end, various forms of income support have been introduced and refined for low-income parents, including tax credits. These reforms work: they have had the effect of significantly bringing down child poverty rates.[26] This is of course very good news. But the downside is that support comes in various streams and presents itself to the recipients as something of an administrative nightmare.

Here is a case study in how it works and does not work: N is a lone mother in London with a two-year-old son. She has a full-time job at or near the minimum wage. The father mostly looks after the son one day and night a week but contributes little or no financial support.

N and the son (this is midyear 2005) live in a flat they have been allocated permanently by the local council. The flat is owned by a housing association, and N pays rent. She receives a housing benefit from the council, which in theory is paid directly to the housing association and is subtracted from her rent, but mistakes get made. She must herself make sure that this benefit actually gets transferred and that no underpayment builds up in her rent. She needs to keep in touch with the housing association about this, for which purpose it has a help telephone number. Calling that number puts her in touch with an official who may or may not be someone she has been in touch with previously and who may or may not know the circumstances of her case.

The housing association has outsourced its maintenance function. If there is a maintenance need, N cannot use the housing association help

---

[26] Hills and Stewart 2005.

number but must contact "maintenance" directly. That may result in maintenance being undertaken, or N may have to contact the housing association to sort out that the matter is indeed a case of maintenance.

The housing benefit comes from the local council. It is determined according to other incomes and circumstances and can change when incomes and circumstances change. Those are complex calculations and mistakes get made. It falls on N to ensure that the council gets the calculations right and pays the right housing benefit to the housing association: the full benefit so that she does not fall into arrears with the housing association and not more than the benefit she is entitled to so that she does not later have to repay the council. For this purpose, she needs to stay in touch with the housing-benefit office. Contact by mail is useless; to ensure action or get information, contact needs to be by telephone or preferably in person and often involve lengthy periods of waiting. N has no allocated official to contact and will speak with different officials on different occasions. Her details are supposed to be in a computer log, but this depends on her data being logged and updated correctly which sometimes happens and sometimes not.

The son attends nursery school three days a week. N pays a nursery fee, about two-thirds of which is compensated as part of her child tax credit.

N receives two forms of tax credit, the child tax credit and a working tax credit. The child tax credit is determined by the number and age of children, earnings, and nursery fees. The working tax credit is determined by earnings and age. Whether the child tax credit and working tax credit are mutually interdependent is not clear to N.

On matters that have to do with both the child and the working tax credit, N needs to stay in touch with the agency she knows as "tax credit." That contact is only by telephone via help lines to call centers. There is one help line for new claims and another help line for existing claims. The experience is typical of all call centers: waiting, waiting again, and then misunderstandings.

N pays a council tax that is partly offset by a council tax benefit. That benefit comes from the local council and is managed by the same office as the housing benefit. As with the housing benefit, N feels that she must stay in touch with the benefit office to check against underpayments or overpayments. Contact by mail, again, is ineffective and her experience is that she must go in person. That usually means queuing and waiting, sometimes from one queue to another, sometimes for up to two or three hours.

A half year after getting her permanent flat, N was informed that she had for a while been receiving a council tax benefit (of £26 a week) that she was not entitled to. This information comes in a letter along with a claim to repay £230, giving her seven days' notice to start repaying or making contact.

N also receives a child benefit, as do all parents. This benefit is managed by yet another office but with no hassle. "This is the one I like," says N. "It works."

Before N secured the permanent job she now holds, she also had to deal with both the job center and the local Department of Social Security office about looking for work, about the job seekers' allowance, and about income support in interactions that are, after the fact, just too complicated to explain. That experience N now describes simply as "bloody chaos."

Before she was allocated her permanent flat, N was in temporary council housing. For about six months of that period, her housing benefit was unresolved. Getting it resolved took a stream of correspondence and endless, sometimes daily, visits by N to the benefit office. She, in council housing, was required to provide the council with documentation on housing outlays such as electricity, gas, water, and even the council tax. She had to provide pay slips, bank statements, and on one occasion documentation confirming that a small deposit into her bank account was a gift and not payment for work. Her housing benefit was underpaid for that period, resulting in her rent also being underpaid and arrears in the rent building up. Those arrears have subsequently been claimed back, a year after the fact, a claim N has contested. This is all processed through a different office than her housing-benefit office.

From N's point of view, she receives valuable help through these arrangements, and without them she would not have been able to cope financially. That's how it works out in the end. During the process, however, the management and practicalities of getting help are described with words such as mess, mistakes, waiting, queuing, wasting time, endless phone calls, waiting again, mistakes again. N has to make herself a technical expert and, for all intents and purposes, the case manager of her own case. She has to ensure that she does not cause mistakes by giving faulty or inadequate information about her circumstances and that she fills out complicated forms correctly, and she has to be on guard against mistakes made in the system, such as computer mistakes, which may come back to her in the form of repayment penalties later.

Controlling and coordinating is a job N had to learn and then work on and spend time on. It is a difficult job to learn. Mistakes are likely to be made or not discovered in the client's initial period as a client. Many clients get off to a bad start and carry the consequences of mistakes with them for months or years.

One reason this is a difficult learning process is that there is nowhere for N to go in this myriad of agencies for general information about rights, dues, and procedures. For that, N and others in her situation must go to yet another office, the Citizens' Advice Bureau. That is an excellent institution, but it is also another office for N to call on, travel to, and spend time with.

Once in receipt of help, N has to keep on top of her own case in order to reduce as much as possible the inevitability of mistakes and to sort out the mistakes when they are made. This involves direct costs in addition to time and hassle. One cost is for telephone calls. N cannot afford both a land line and a mobile phone and has only a mobile phone. Another cost is for transportation to and from necessary visits to the various benefit offices. These costs are considerable and make it financially difficult for N to be able to undertake necessary controls and coordination.

We know from government statistics that the help that N benefits from works. It is protecting her and many others in her situation against poverty and is contributing to bringing down Britain's disgraceful rates of child poverty. But those statistics do not show the price N and others pay for this assistance in sheer work, time, and outlays—and in the humiliation of being treated mistakenly, punished for having been treated mistakenly, and pushed around by those who have the power to help them.

This is a very British system, made up of rights, rules, and bureaucracy. (Although social care is not a system, per se, I cannot explain what it is without the convenience of the word.) The Poor Law was repealed in the 1948 National Assistance Bill. Since then, it has been a principle in British social policy to make do as much as possible without discretionary provisions and to manage social care on the basis of objective rights. This has been seen as a way of protecting those in need from the humiliation of having to ask for help and the risk of being harassed by officials with the power to give or deny.

The Scandinavian countries' experience is different. Instead of abolishing poverty relief, they have kept it but renamed it and made it generous. For many of the purposes N in Britain has to wander between offices, she would there have been able to deal with a single office, the local social-assistance office. This office does have in its power to give or deny help and to determine the kind and extent of help in the poverty-relief tradition, but now also has a good deal of help to offer.

These two ways of administering social care are in practice not as different as they may look. Discretionary poverty relief has not been abolished in Britain but persists, albeit on a low level, since 1988 in the Social Fund. In the Scandinavian welfare states, there is means-tested income support in addition to social assistance—for example, housing support.

Both models, the British one based on rights and the Scandinavian one based on discretion, are capable of delivering help. One is not necessarily more or less generous than the other. Both have, by and large, eliminated the old stigma of poverty relief. Help is considered a right, and there is not much shame involved in accepting it, at least not profound social shame. It is no doubt always humiliating to have to ask for help and to be at the mercy of officials; whether that is more so in one or the other model is not easily said. The theoretical logic in favor of a rights-based system would predict humiliation to be a particular cost of discretionary social assistance. But humiliation does not seem to be prevalent in the Scandinavian brand of renamed poverty relief, nor has the abolishing (or practically reducing to a minimum) of poverty-relief-type care in Britain done away with humiliation. N's wanderings between offices and officials who heap on her compounded mistakes and anxieties and her waiting and queuing at offices that do not act or respond unless she shows up in person, are both practically burdensome and emotionally humiliating.

In some respects, however, these are clearly different models. In the Scandinavian one, there is more flexibility of care. Indeed, it is precisely that flexibility that has been a main argument for preserving poverty relief. The British system is rigidly bureaucratic, with an emphasis on income support and with service support being either absent or, since income support and social services are totally separated, uncoordinated. A rights-based system runs on very specific rules about eligibility and thereby invites cheating in a way that is to some degree avoided in a discretionary system that by definition has fewer rules to cheat against. In the Scandinavian system, there is a frontline service, the social-assistance office, which in principle is in charge of information, quality control, and coordination. This office has both income support and service support under its authority, and it may well offer help in, for example, sorting out difficulties in means-tested housing support even though that is administered by another agency. At least to some degree, quality control and coordination is taken care of for the clients and not left to fall on them. The social-assistance office has a general duty of care, and clients experience less of being shuttled between agencies and offices. In that respect, at least, the discretionary system produces less humiliation.

This comparison is probably kinder to the Scandinavian system than it deserves. There, too, social care remains disorganized, haphazard, and burdensome for clients. But in the administration of social assistance, it is possible to see the outline of a model of something that has never been achieved anywhere: an administrative arrangement for responding to the needs of the most vulnerable of citizens without extracting from them a price of gratitude in the form of unfreedom, bureaucratic hassle, and administrative humiliation. Adam Smith, 250 years ago, introduced a criticism of what he saw as a form of tyranny: the power of officials in posts of authority, including officials in charge of helping the poor, to deny individuals practical liberty and infuse their lives with fear.[27] There has subsequently been much liberalization, but we are still in search of the solution of dignity for those who cannot cope without the help of officials in offices of authority. It is, however, within reach. It is not a big-budget problem. It is not rocket science. It is a matter of organization. Two simple administrative arrangements could do the job.

There would be a one-stop frontline service as the one and only point of call for information and help. This service would be local and would be both the information center and the care center. It would have the power and authority to assess needs and prescribe help on a case-by-case basis and then the responsibility to coordinate the relevant package of help as appropriate in each case. No doubt, there would still be different agencies for the administration of different kinds of help but they would be behind the front line and not burden clients with the job of coordination.

The frontline office would operate on a high level of competence and trust. It is conspicuous in Britain that this is so well understood in health care—an understanding that is embodied in the National Health Service in the core institution of the general practitioner—but that there is no similar understanding in social care. The key to competence and trust is professionalism. For the frontline service to function with trust, it would need to be in the charge of professionals with a similar competence in social care that medical doctors have in medical care. We would, in other words, need to elevate advanced social-work training to a level that would make it trustful to invest in officials the delicate authority that is required for effective care.[28] Doctors are allowed very far-reaching powers over patients without (except in exceptional instances) abusing it. The same could be the case in social care, with the right model of administration and the necessary degree of professionalism.

It ought to be as obvious to ask for help in social care as it is in medical care. We should recognize that modern social expectations are often harrowing. If information and assistance were no-nonsense available, we would experience, as in medical care, that the help needed in most cases would be very limited: a bit of information, some guidance or reassurance, perhaps a bit of money. We might experience that people were able to ask for help before their need had become acute. Bureaucratic rigidities would not stand in the way of prescribing what is right in each case, or of following up and modifying flexibly to changing circumstances. It

---

[27] See Rothschild 2001.

[28] That would take a very considerable amount of elevation, as I know from my frustrating time in charge of postgraduate social-work training at Oxford University.

would be possible to deal with the needy as people and not just as cases of clients.

Of course, it is not necessary to do anything at all with social care. Those in need of care are a resourceless minority. It might be politically expedient to do just what is necessary and no more. But there are powerful rejoinders against that complacency. People will be in need of help, and it is impossible in a civilized society to not deal with them. Being in need of help does not disqualify one from citizenship and from the right to dignity. We cannot have an effective safety net against poverty without effective social care, hence no universal welfare state without it. Family policy, as we will see below, will be incomplete without a capacity for care. Finally and basically, the quality of justice in a society should be judged by how it deals with those who are the worst off. This is the moral meaning of the *difference principle* formulated by John Rawls in *A Theory of Justice*. By this argument a society would not qualify to be considered just unless it dealt justly with those most in need.[29]

FAMILY POLICY

Families need support in the form of money, time, and social care. The purpose of that support should be to stop or reverse the decline in family productivity (which I explain in chapter 5), to help and encourage parents and prospective parents in their aspirations to have and raise children, and to enable parents to make their own choices in their various trade-offs between family and work.

The easiest and most effective way to channel economic support to families is through a universal child allowance, paid to all mothers at a standard rate depending on the number and age of children. The level of the allowance should be high so as to compensate for the opportunity cost of having

---

[29] The difference principle, in its strict interpretation, stipulates that inequalities need to be justified as being to "the greatest benefit of the least advantaged" (Rawls 1971, p. 83). But this contains a logical short circuit. It can never be to the benefit of the least advantaged today to be disadvantaged today, and it could not be necessary today that they are disadvantaged today since there is then by definition someone who is advantaged who could give something to the less advantaged. It could be to the benefit of someone tomorrow that someone else is disadvantaged today, and that could make the least advantaged tomorrow less disadvantaged than they would otherwise be. The difficulty, however, is that a reasonable time perspective could be so long that the disadvantage of the least advantaged today would be justified in the interest of those who would be the least advantaged in the next generation. That could be bad news, indeed, for those who are the least advantaged today and might give them no protection against avoidable destitution here and now. Also, the justification of disadvantage to some for the benefit of others seems contrary to the spirit of the difference principle.

and rearing children. This is to give parents the freedom to make their own arrangements in family life and child rearing. It would make it affordable for parents to work at home, part-time or full-time, if they should want to. No disincentive is created against both parents having paid work. (I explain the underlying family-economy assumptions in chapter 5, drawing on my previous work in *Citizens, Families, and Reform.*)

The allowance should be given for the first child to encourage child rearing, and for subsequent children to encourage more than one or two. The amount should be at the maximum level while children are young, which is when they are most costly, and then reduced as the children grow older, up to the age of, say, sixteen.

The child allowance makes child rearing affordable, contributes to a sound financial basis for families with children and thereby to family stability, and redistributes income internally in families to the benefit of children. When paid to the mother, more of family income is brought under the control of mothers; mothers are more likely than fathers to spend for the benefit of their children. In the case of lone fathers, the allowance would obviously be paid to the father.

Time support should come primarily through access to day care for small children. Governments may well choose to subsidize day care, but the easiest way is to make the child allowance sufficient to cover the costs of day care. Parents can then make their own choices in the trade-off between paid work, child care at home, and day care. Provisions will emerge to the degree parents want them. In addition, working parents should be entitled to paid leave around the time of births, up to, say, a year, possibly shared between the parents.

This adds up to a generous package for parents of small children. There are reasons of fairness and of efficiency. Child rearing is a job parents do for society and we, society, should support them. The raising of children is important to the economy and the polity. It makes sense for an affluent society not to shoot itself in the foot through careless preparation of the next generation. For parents and potential parents in an age of freedom and choice, other priorities compete against having children. Young people want to have children but will be unable to give child rearing priority if economic conditions are against it.

If there is now an understanding, as I think there is, at least in theory, that it is entirely normal that normal families need support in the form of money and time resources, the same is possibly not true when it comes to practical help. Here I think a postmodern belief that families are private, that they should manage family matters themselves and on their own, and that it is a weakness or a defeat to be in need of help is crowding out an ancient wisdom that parents should not be expected always to be able to cope with the strains of child rearing.

A godparent is a relative or friend who participates at the baptism of a child. We perhaps think of godparenting as a religious institution but in the Christian churches, where godparents are required or strongly expected, that is not laid down in the Gospel. It is something the church has invented, a convention that emerged sometime in the history of the church.

Godparents take it upon themselves to follow the upbringing of the child, in particular that it is raised in the faith. They commit themselves to a duty for the child, and this commitment is formalized in a pact at the baptism. They obviously do not take on a responsibility in place of the parents, but they do have an independent duty of care. If the parents are unable to raise or take care of the child, they have the godparents for support. If the parents neglect the child, the godparents have a right, and perhaps an obligation, to intervene for the child.

The responsibility of godparents has now become pretty symbolic, but that was not always the case. In the rural Lutheran Norwegian culture from which I originate, at least, it was imposed in earnest by the church and accepted in earnest by both parents and godparents. The reason, I think, was an understanding that children and parents were vulnerable and that the good rearing of children was difficult. It was a matter of raising them in the faith, but faith was in a sense beside the point since at the time it was obvious that the difference between good and bad child care was precisely about faith. It was in giving support to good child rearing, as that was understood, that godparenting was seen to be useful.

Behind this there was, no doubt, also the understanding that children were in danger because of poverty and mortality. Families were fragile. Parental responsibility was heavy. Wisdom and experience said that normal families in their normal undertakings could easily find themselves in need of support. The godparent convention would reflect an understanding that it was not to be expected that families could always manage on their own to take care of their children and give them a good upbringing.

Although the risk of family collapse because of mortality is greatly diminished, it has been replaced by an even greater risk of divorce and dissolution. It has not become easier to raise children. There is not much reality left in godparenting in secular societies, but the need in families for practical support and help has not diminished.

In my opinion, we should try to resurrect the simple idea that families need support. Although families today do have much support, including from the state, the idea of practical family support remains controversial. "The nanny state," they say in Britain. The controversy is visible in the question of sex education in schools, which many see as objectionable to the privacy of parents and families. Although family life has in many ways become more regulated, the idea of family privacy is nevertheless *the* modern idea of the family. If we believe that family life is only about emotional needs, we obviously want the family to be left in peace and privacy since we do not want anyone to regulate our emotional lives. But that is not the state of the family. Families do much more. They do jobs. They need support. They need, as a matter of routine, access to social care.

In chapter 5, I recommend that we encourage togetherness as a basis of family formation, certainly between parents in the raising of children. Should togetherness then be encouraged with economic incentives? Should formal togetherness, marriage, be encouraged? There is a long tradition for so doing via tax deductions for married couples. There are good reasons for maintaining that tradition, since economic productivity gains result from people living together rather than on their own and separately and from unions being formalized. This being so, the best way is to give a tax deduction for each parent (which could come as a negative tax to parents who are not working and earning). That would give an equal benefit to each parent. Tax deductions, as compared with income deductions before tax, are of more relative value to low-income families.

My recommendation to encourage togetherness is based on economic considerations more than moral prescriptions. If parents increasingly live apart, or together without formalizing the union, costs devolve on others. It is therefore fair to use economic incentives to encourage the alternative. Since informal cohabitation is more or less strongly motivated by economic considerations, we should expect at least some effectiveness in the use of economic incentives to encourage marriage.

The difficulty is that parents who do not live together may feel that they are being penalized. This could be compensated by other forms of economic support to lone parents.

The "problem" of lone parenthood is mainly a problem of lone motherhood. While there are many lone mothers, there are fewer lone fathers; and while lone mothers are predominantly young and poor, lone fathers are likely to be older and well off. Lone motherhood is seen by some as a provocation. There is fear that helping lone mothers encourages lone motherhood. The social acceptability and practical possibility of having children outside of marriage or a permanent partnership may help to increase total birthrates. The problem is a tangled web of instrumental practicability and muddled moralism, to be disentangled with a warm heart and a cool head.

Although the mother is single—setting aside lone fathers for the moment—there is usually a father. Fathers have responsibility for their children, including financial responsibility. This responsibility stems from fatherhood and does not depend on marriage or living arrangements.

If the parents do not live together, for whatever reason, the normal expectation should be that they sort matters out between themselves to provide for their children, including provisions for the mother to help her raise the children. Parents should be stimulated, encouraged, and helped to reach their own accommodation. The father has a clear duty to contribute adequately to this, as he would have had had they lived together. Not living with the mother, he is not there to contribute to the work, at least not as much as he could have, and might be expected to contribute all the more in money.

Only when parents are unable to sort matters out themselves is there a financial problem that lands with someone else, usually the government. This is the case if the father is unable or unwilling to contribute financially. He is unable if poor (or, obviously, if deceased). If unwilling, there is the all-too-common and often brutal parental fight. Some lone mothers have adequate incomes of their own, but many do not.

For many lone mothers and some lone fathers, some kind of public income support needs to be available. The difficulty is, first, to determine the need. This depends on whether there is a settlement with the absent parent, and what kind of settlement, and on what other sources of income the parents have. Furthermore, there are inevitable poverty traps to deal with. One is against work. If taking work causes a loss of income support, work is discouraged. Another one is against entering into a new partnership. If the new partner has an income and that causes a loss of income support, the reestablishment of partnership is discouraged or cheating encouraged.

These matters, from help to reach an accommodation between parents who do not reside together to economic and practical support for lone parents, are in my analysis typical matters of social care. They are not resolvable by blanket rules but should be dealt with on a case-by-case basis. The poverty-trap problems, for example, are unavoidable but can be mitigated with the help of practical and flexible transition arrangements whereby taking work or entering into a new partnership is not irreversible and not made to cause a sudden loss of income support. This reflection on family policy provides additional support for the logic of social care that I have laid out above.

Social Security

The welfare state's story of social security has been that we pay for each other: the young pay for the old, employers for workers, husbands for wives, and the state for everyone. The truth is that it is workers who pay for everyone, themselves included, but the books have been kept as if social security were a pyramid game that you pay a bit into now and get more out of later.[30]

A by-product of that bookkeeping is that the status of social-security property has been utterly ambiguous. Earners pay taxes during work-active years, including social-security taxes, in the belief that they thereby earn entitlements. But the value of their entitlements are determined politically year by year and may change in ways that have little or no relation to what earners have paid for them, or entitlements may simply be annulled. Workers contribute to occupational pensions in the belief that they have entitlements in those pensions, but the capital is owned by employers, who may maintain a solid financial base for future pension payments but may also fail to do so, in which case workers may in due course find their entitlements to be worth less than they had thought, or worth nothing at all. Employers may redefine entitlements by cancelling retrospectively final salary formulas, for example, or may plunder their own pension funds. Companies may go bankrupt and pull occupational pensions with them into the abyss. Workers may find they are locked into company pension schemes in ways that make it difficult for them to change jobs. On death, social-security entitlements may or may not be inheritable property. On divorce, wives may or may not have rights in their husbands' pensions, or husbands in their wives'. Social security is supposed to protect people against the loss of income in contingencies such as old age, illness, disability, and unemployment, but this security is and remains precarious for all who do not own their entitlements.

Demographic necessity is changing the story of social security. Now we are being told that we pay for ourselves. This reinvention of the legend is a prelude for changes in the substance. Social security is always insurance, even if not always in name. It is a deal among those included to cooperate in a manner that gives them all security. For social security to be universal, everyone must be included. For it to be secure, the insured should have ownership.

Assume that we start from a tax-funded social-security model. There are many such models that differ in many ways, but what is common is that the state in some way takes in taxes with one hand and distributes pensions and other transfers with the other one. This model is now unsustainable because demography is driving demand up and globalization is pulling tax capacity down. The lack of sustainability is in some cases

---

[30] In the Scandinavian model of consolidated "peoples' pensions," the consolidated systems were in the beginning genuine pyramids, in that transition arrangements gave the first generation mature entitlements for nonmature contributions. That was supposed to settle down to mature entitlements for mature contributions, but a demographic shift intervened so that the systems started to look like an inverted pyramid in which mature contributions would produce nonmature entitlements.

already visible. For example, in England and Wales (but not in Scotland), free long-term care has in recent years been gradually removed from availability in the National Health Service because it is deemed no longer to be affordable. This is a case of assumed entitlements being quietly annulled and an insecurity that was thought eliminated thus re-created. It is not yet visible everywhere. In the Scandinavian countries, the tax model still looks sustainable because the tax level appears to be staying higher than the OECD average.[31] But that statistic is deceptive. General taxation is on a downward slope, converging towards the OECD mean, while rising social-security taxes are holding that convergence back in total taxation.[32]

The solution is to turn to insurance or—remember Beveridge—*revert* to insurance. In insurance, you get what you pay for and what you buy becomes your property. There is no social-security tax, only premiums that come out of the household budget. If you believe social security is a pyramid scheme that by magic produces more value than is invested in it, at least for yourself, insurance may look like a bad deal. But if you stay in touch with reality and recognize that everyone cannot be better off by a trick of paying for each other, buying property should be attractive compared with giving away your saving capital to others who promise to take care of you down the road. For example, workers may be tempted to believe that it is somehow to their advantage that employers pay a social-security tax on their behalf (in the form of employers' social-security contributions), but this is an illusion. They are paying it themselves through lower wages but in part are handing their savings over to their employers and not getting the security of property in return. It is in the interest of the insured that the books are kept so as to show that they are paying for their own insurance; that is what gives them ownership in the resulting entitlements.

In principle, most forms of social security could be converted to social insurance, and in due course that may happen. Health care, for example, could be and in many countries is claimed and distributed by way of health insurance. Even unemployment or illness could be insurable, at least with a little help from state subvention and regulation.

But a big-bang revolution of converting all forms of social security into social insurance would not be practicable or advisable: not practicable because one cannot turn complex systems upside down overnight; not advisable because it is not clear that insurance is in fact the best arrangement across the board. Health insurance in the United States, for example, has proved utterly ineffective in controlling health-care costs. When the

---

[31] About 25 percent higher; cf. Castles 2004.
[32] As documented in Kangas and Palme 2005.

problem you start from is escalating costs, you might not want to turn to arrangements that have driven up costs.[33]

Pension reform today means adapting to demographic necessities that will be defining the political playground for the next decades. Pension reform is a slow affair and the process has just started.[34] The ground has been cleared by the retelling of the story. Now the question is of following through to substance. There are, in the first instance, two main candidates for conversion to insurance: old-age pensions and long-term care. In remaining tax-funded services, reform would then continue, at least for a while, to take the shape of workfare and other means of cost control.

Old-age pensions and long-term care are ripe for conversion to insurance because there is enough recognition of a crisis and because the conversion would be relatively easy. With current trends in demography and tax capacity, trust is ebbing away under these two pillars of social security, a trust that needs to be re-created to secure the entire edifice of social security. The re-creation of trust rests on a re-creation of intergenerational fairness. The key to intergenerational fairness under demographic fluctuation is that generations insure themselves instead of paying for each other.

Pension reform is an unholy alliance of changing stories and changing substance, of pedagogics and conditions, of appearances and realities. Much is about bookkeeping. Social-security contributions are thought of as taxes because they are packaged into the overall tax bill and entered in national accounts under the heading of taxes. Separating the stories, pedagogics, and appearances from substance, conditions, and realities is never straightforward or probably even possible. In large measure, the purpose of social security is to give people the comfort of feeling secure.

On old-age pensions, Sweden has shown the way (as it has so often). In 1999, pensions in Sweden were redesigned into an insurance framework. Before that redesign, earners paid a social-security tax (in Sweden nominally paid in full by employers) in return for a promise from the state of generous future pensions. When politicians and citizens, with the helpful influence of economic crisis, resolved that that promise could not be kept or trusted, pensions were redesigned into a demographically flexible system and presented to earners and others as their own insurance of them-

---

[33] Still, health insurance has much to recommend it. The British National Health Service is the model tax-funded system. The ambition has been to make high-quality health care universally available and free at use, but that ambition has been frustrated. Patient experience in the NHS ranges from the sublime to the disastrous. When it is disastrous, the experience is also that the patient is completely powerless. In theory, it should be in the interest of patients to be buyers of health care, since that would give them power and and turn the tables on the providers by making them dependent on their "customers."

[34] See Immergut et al. 2006.

selves. Earners still pay a social-security tax but get in return not an abstract promise of a pension but annual statements that show (by modified actuarialism) what their tax contributions are worth in likely future pensions, much as if they were dealing with a private pension insurance.

The great invention in the Swedish reform was the introduction of a pension insurance that was universal, state-owned, and run on a pay-as-you-go basis. It had previously been thought that insurance would require the building up of pension funds and that therefore the transition from a tax-based pay-as-you-go system to one driven by the logic of insurance would be prohibitively costly and difficult. Swedish ingenuity invented insurance-based pay-as-you-go and made a near-painless transition. There was a loss in pension generosity but gains in sustainability and trust, the latter clearly being seen to be worth the former.

On long-term care insurance, Germany has shown the way. In 1995 and 1996, a separate long-term care insurance was introduced that aimed to provide basic security against the costs of long-term care, both institutionalized and outpatient care. Almost the entire domestic population is subsequently covered by this insurance. The reform grew out of the existing health-care insurance and was essentially a matter of changing the appearance of health insurance by dividing a single insurance into a dual one consisting of a general health-insurance account and a separate account for long-term care. The idea was to make health insurance all-inclusive and sustainable by showing separately the cost of long-term care.

Sweden and Germany have shown the way. The achievement is impressive but not necessarily to their advantage. The price of being on the vanguard of innovation is that you must carry the burden of invention, must implement without experience, and may be held back by appearing radical. The benefit of being a late starter is that you can be more radical without appearing radical, and you have the benefit of the experience of the pioneers and the incentive to catch up and do better than those who took the first fumbling steps.[35]

The Swedish and German reforms were essentially pedagogical devices to make palatable a loss of generosity (the Swedish case) or an additional extraction of social-security taxes (the German case). Pedagogics is an essential part of pension reform: it is about creating a culture of sharing under more difficult circumstances. But it should not stop there, it should also be about substance and go on to creating increased security through entitlement property. The need now to back off from what was previously promised, or as in the German case to raise additional taxes, is evidence that social-security entitlements in the welfare state have been less secure than they were thought to be. Even after Swedish- or German-type re-

[35] For the theory of advantageous backwardness, see Gershenkron 1962.

forms, this insecurity persists. There may be less insecurity if the reforms have improved the financial sustainability of social security, but it is still "we" who are paying taxes that "they" decide on. In ten years, a new political generation may cut back our entitlements yet again. In the German case, the reform made social security yet more tax dependent, which we can already now see was the wrong direction of reform. Nor are these reforms pedagogically radical; they do not teach us much that is new about saving and sharing.

In principle, if social security is to be a matter of insurance, the state could withdraw and leave it to citizens individually to make their own provisions. The affluence assumption might be seen as an argument for that view. But only theorists with no sense of the vagaries of human nature would think this might result in security, never mind universal security. In a "free" system, there would be various temptations not to take out insurance or for insurers to refuse insurance. The result would be a safety net full of holes through which some would fall into precariousness or dependency on the charity of others. By historical experience, state involvement is indispensable to the security of social insurance. The German case shows this dramatically. There, the state-backed system of social insurance that Bismarck introduced in the 1880s has in essence survived the collapse of Bismarck's state, the collapse of monarchy, the collapse of democracy, economic collapse and hyperinflation, horrendous defeats in two world wars, Nazism, the reemergence of democracy in West Germany, and the reunification of the two Germanys. The paternalistic hand of the welfare state is indispensable to security: to guide us, to protect the careless among us against our own carelessness, and to protect all of us against the selfishness of some. The regulating and contributing hand of the state is equally indispensable to making insurance fair and complete and to backing up insurance itself with reinsurance in the last resort.

To create entitlement property, we need insurance. Workers should, for example, not be dependent for their pension security on the goodwill of employers who hold the workers' pension savings in schemes or funds in their ownership. Pensioners should not be dependent on the will and ability of politicians of the day to tax workers enough to give those no longer working adequate pensions. For universality, we need to include everyone. Nonworking wives should, for example, not be dependent on the goodwill of their husbands to give them a share in their pensions on divorce. For the creation of a culture of saving and sharing, we need to start early and teach everyone the habit of setting aside. For workability, we need state regulations to make social insurance obligatory, state subventions to make universality practicable, and state backup to reinsure the insurance entitlements.

The nature of state involvement would depend on the organization of provision. The state might well be the provider of insurance, in much the same way that the state may own banks in which people can hold savings accounts. An alternative would be to use private providers but place them under appropriate state regulation, oversight, and last-resort reinsurance. The advantage of the state being the provider is an element of security in the duty of delivery being vested in institutions owned by a state that is responsible to voters. The disadvantage of state monopoly is the usual disadvantage of monopolies—the risk of inefficiency—and also that it would undermine the perception that entitlements are property. In the Swedish example above, for example, the power to change the value of entitlements continues to sit in the political institutions of the state. The advantage of private provision would be competition, efficiency, and a real appearance and sense of ownership. The disadvantage is that fairness and security would all rest on complex state regulations and subventions which it could prove difficult to get right.

For my purpose, it is not necessary to make any absolute recommendation on how best to arrange provision. Social insurance is not exactly the same under state and private provision but is still possible in either case. I happen to think a mixed model could combine some of the advantages of both—for example, an element of subjecting state providers to private competition—but I see no reason to think or recommend that all countries would arrange social insurance in exactly the same way. My recommendation below is limited to the outlines of an insurance model that could be implemented practically in different ways. This includes also different transition arrangements for going from a tax model to an insurance model.

I start with the hand of the state and with the imposition of a duty on all citizens to insure themselves against social contingencies, in this case, economic hardship in old age and the risk of needing long-term care. When everyone has that duty, everyone is insured and everyone knows that everyone else is insured and paying their way. There is fairness, security, and trust.

I would impose this duty on all citizens from an early age, say eighteen. The early start would be mostly for pedagogical reasons and to get the spirit of saving and setting aside established as early as possible. Most people at that age would not be in a position to save. Therefore the hand of the state would come in to initially do their saving for them. This initial saving would be on a low level, and this would therefore be a cheap way for the state to guide everyone to the habit of saving.

If the state is to force everyone to save, it must also ensure that there are appropriate institutions for them to save in. It is possible that private providers could do the job, but it is difficult for me to see how a fully universal social insurance could function without the help of state provision. I therefore assume a state social-insurance institution.

At age eighteen, three social insurance accounts would be opened by the state social-insurance program for all individuals. Those accounts would be the property of the individuals and would be held by them for the rest of their lives. Deposits into those accounts would be unambiguously theirs.

Account no. 1 would be for a basic old-age pension. Into this account all persons would have a duty to deposit an annual premium according to a schedule over the life course so that those premiums would add up to an adequate basic pension at a prescribed age, say seventy.

Account no. 2 would be for an earnings-related old-age pension. Into this account all persons would, from the day they start earning, have a duty to deposit a premium set at a minimum fraction of earnings according to a schedule over the life course that would make up an additional pension on a reasonable level relative to lifetime earnings.

Account no. 3 would be for long-term care. Into this account all persons would have a duty to deposit an annual premium up to the age of, say seventy, again according to a schedule over the life course that would add up to the anticipated cost-risk of long-term care.

The detailed terms and rules of insurance would be regulated by law at intervals, for example, in response to demographic change, possibly annually. At any time, the existing terms would represent the offer of the state social-insurance program, and those terms would be guaranteed in the program for those eighteen-year-olds then entering the system for the rest of their lives.

Accounts nos. 1 and 3 would, in the Beveridgean spirit, be flat-rate premiums for flat-rate entitlements, the same for everyone. Premiums would as the main rule be paid continuously up to the age of say seventy. In account no. 1, premiums would cease in the case of retirement before seventy. Anyone should be free to retire when they want and to take out their pension entitlements as they have accumulated up to their chosen age of retirement. In account no. 3, premiums would cease when the long-term care insurance is activated.

From age eighteen to, say, age thirty, the state would pay the premiums in these accounts. Many young people (e.g., students) would not be in a position to pay, young workers often earn low wages and would be more employable for not having to cover social insurance, and many would be in transition and family establishment. At about age thirty, however, probably in a transition over a few years, the duty of insurance would practically transfer to the insured.

From then on, that duty would, in principle, be absolute. For example, if a couple makes the choice that one of them works at home, the partner who works for pay would have to be able to pay the basic social insurance for both, just as he or she would in other ways have to support both. If a worker decides to take a year off, for example, to travel around the world, he would have to save up for his sustenance, which would now include the payment of social insurance.

There would, however, be some exceptions. These would be for persons who are not earning because they are unable to earn (as opposed to having chosen not to earn). This would include, by relevant rules, periods of child rearing, of unemployment, of illness, and of continuing education. In those periods, the insurance would again be paid by the state.

Premiums into account no. 2 would be strictly earnings-related. They would start when earnings start and cease when earnings cease. The duty to save would apply equally to employees and the self-employed. If an earner does not have earnings in a period for whatever reason, no premiums would accrue to this account.

The accumulated and unused entitlements in accounts nos. 1 and 2 would be property and as such inheritable and divisible, for example, in certain circumstances at divorce.

This is what would be offered in the state social-insurance program. It could be run as a state monopoly but it could also be subjected to private competition. The way to open up the competition would be to give insurance holders the option to move their insurance accounts, with the value that sits in them and the duty to continue to maintain the accounts, to private insurers. Under the terms outlined above, an opportunity to opt out should probably come in at a certain age after the insurance obligation has fallen unambiguously to the person, say, at age thirty-five.

State monopoly or not is a matter of political preference. A possible argument in favor of monopoly is that opting out from a partially state-subsidized system would represent a state subvention of private insurers, but that is probably not a strong argument. The state is not an interested party in social insurance but only an instrument of its citizens. If they think social insurance is improved by competition, they have no reason to be concerned that this improvement might come via "imbalanced" transactions between the state and private providers. Another argument could be that allowing in private providers could create a messy field in which insurers might find it difficult to maneuver and impose an extra duty of regulation and oversight on the state, but this should be no different in social insurance from other insurance markets or, for example, banking. The principle argument against state monopoly is that while the enforcement of a duty of insurance is a reasonable expression of solidarity, it might be considered oppressive to force people against their will to take their insurance from the state. A further argument in favor of competition is that it would put pressure on the state social-insurance program to perform. To keep insurers, it would have to offer insurance that is as good as insurers could buy elsewhere. With monopoly protection, the state social-insurance program would be shielded against such pressure, and insurers might have reason to suspect that their insurance savings were being maintained with less efficiency than possible.

EDUCATION

Ever more young people continue ever longer in education. Ever more middle-aged workers engage ever more in lifelong learning. We are approaching something very astonishing: workers spending nearly as much of their careers being invested in at different levels of schooling and education as making use of that investment in productive work.

This investment is calling on vast and increasing resources of labor for teaching and physical capital in the form of buildings and equipment. Students must be supported while not in the workforce and supporting themselves. Already now, in a typical European population, more than a fourth of the population is occupied day-by-day in the business of learning and teaching in the formal institutions of education.[36] And this number is a moving target. The future need is massive. If there are to be nearly as many people being trained for work as there are workers at any time, we will have to allocate nearly half of the national product to training.

We are not there yet, but we are on our way. The challenge of funding the educational needs of an affluent society is now presenting itself visibly in the funding of expanding higher education. Where higher education has been free, which is to say funded from general taxation, it is becoming increasingly difficult to underwrite future expansion in higher education in that way. There simply is not enough tax capacity, at least without using up so much that not enough would be left over for other necessary purposes.

We might think we should stop the expansion of higher education at a tax-affordable level—today as always, there is no shortage of warning that too many people are taking too much education they are not competent to absorb and will have no use for—but this is wholly unrealistic. Education is in demand and investments in human capital are necessary. Education is expanding and will continue to expand.

Therefore, funding must be found. If tax funding is unavailable, we need to invent a new way of allocating resources to education to ensure

[36] E.g., in the case of Norway, with 4.3 million people, there are 500,000 pupils and 40,000 teachers in primary schools, 200,000 pupils and 20,000 teachers in secondary schools, and 180,000 students and 12,000 teachers in universities and colleges. In preschools and kindergartens, there are 200,000 children and 50,000 teachers and caregivers (many part-time).

our ability to meet future needs for additional investment in human capital. In chapter 2, I introduced a concept of nontax taxing and applied that concept to the funding of education.

I suggest that mass higher education be funded from wealth rather than from income. This is not painless, but it is infinitely less painful than the alternative. I further suggest that this be arranged without confiscating or nationalizing wealth but by allocating a top slice of large fortunes into *human-capital foundations*, the proceeds of which would be earmarked for education. Furthermore, those proceeds would go into giving everyone, say at age eighteen, a scholarship account worth, say six years of education beyond secondary school which they could draw on at any point in the careers, but for educational purposes only.

My reasoning is that funding must be found and that someone must pay for it. The money must be found where money is available. The way to make that palatable is to use the money to empower students and workers without shifting economic power from private owners and households to the state.

IMMIGRATION AND INTEGRATION

Nothing is new about immigration, of course, but in Europe the deliberate use of immigration as an instrument of economic policy (or population policy) is an innovation in the process of being embraced. Immigrants are not "guest workers"; immigration is about larger numbers and more permanence.

The provisions under the auspices of the welfare state to make immigration policy manageable go under the name of *integration*. I predict that evolutions in European welfare states in the next two or three decades will be strongly influenced by the need to respond to immigration.

The theory of integration remains underdeveloped. The relevant instruments are socioeconomic services and cultural accommodation, but while the need for services is recognized, the importance of the cultural dimension remains to be articulated. Immigration to Europe on a new scale will be predominantly by people who are from "elsewhere" not only geographically but also culturally, including in religion, ethnicity, and race. European societies are metamorphosing into multicultural ones.

This is a difficult transition, often painful and riven by conflict. The outcome may be societies of new culturally defined divisions or harmonious coexistence. It is possible to prescribe a simple theory of integration in the interest of social harmony:

- Services to allow immigrants a modicum of socioeconomic equity are a necessary but not sufficient condition of integration.

- True and secure integration would not be achieved even if socio-economic integration were to succeed.

- Successful integration in a multicultural society rests crucially on cultural accommodation.

This theory is based on the premise that we live in democracies and on the assumption that we take the ideals of democracy seriously. That being where we stand, we believe that *everyone* who lives in these democracies has a right to an equal stake in and co-ownership of community, society, and systems of governance. That must include newer populations, whom older populations invite and accept to their countries. If immigrants were allowed to constitute an underclass in the countries they migrate to, that would be a serious blemish on the democratic quality of those countries and raise questions about the legitimacy not only of immigration policy but of the democratic polity as such. In fact, that is what is happening, of course, which is another way of saying how short we have come towards a robust understanding, never mind implementation, of integration.[37]

Integration, at least democratic integration, depends finally on the minority being able to feel that the country they live in is their home in the same way it is the home of the majority. It is not enough that the members of the minority are paid adequately in socioeconomic rewards and services. They must also have the full range of civil, cultural, and religious rights on an equitable basis and a status of respect that is not inferior to that of the majority.

Socioeconomic integration rests on services, education, health care, income support, and such matters for which there is ample experience in the welfare state. There is not necessarily much experience in extending social services to people from other cultures, and this is no doubt an extra challenge, but it is still known territory for welfare-state workers.

Cultural integration is something else. It is a matter of assuring respectful coexistence. That comes about not through services "we" give "them," but through a continuous process of dialogue in which "they" and "we" participate on an equal footing and educate each other mutually. "We" must ask as much of ourselves as of "them."

---

[37] Evidence of this shortcoming came dramatically on display in France in late 2005 and early 2006 in social revolts of near-revolutionary proportions. One is reminded of the essential influence of the "February revolutions" in Europe in 1848 on kick-starting the modern welfare state in France and Germany in the second half of that century. See also appendix B.

Dialogue may seem innocent and banal, but it is far from it. Although it is a nasty expression, there *is* a clash of civilizations in today's world. In the older democracies, this clash expresses itself in the strains of their multicultural metamorphosis, from the national scene to the remotest village. The way to cushion and overcome this clash is through dialogue. This is desperately needed globally, regionally, nationally, and so on down to the neighborhood. Dialogue means continuous interaction and exchange to build bridges over gulfs of ignorance, prejudice, separation, and fear. Not just the occasional meeting once problems have occurred, but continuous exchange to create mutual knowledge and understanding. Not just high-level and high-visibility encounters among elites (although that, too) but on all levels and woven into the ordinary business of life. Continuous means in institutions, not just that some people get together now and then and talk about religion or language, but in permanent arrangements that enforce permanent contact and exchange. The institutionalization of multicultural dialogue for integration is something we so far hardly have even the most elementary language of concepts to grapple with.

CHAPTER 4

Can We Eradicate Poverty?

> . . . whether there need be large numbers of people doomed
> from their birth to hard work in order to provide for others
> the requisites of a refined and cultured life; while they
> themselves are prevented by their poverty and toil from
> having any share or part in that life.
> —Alfred Marshall: *Principles of Economics*

"THE GOVERNMENT of Barbados is resolutely committed to the eradication of poverty from our social landscape." So wrote the Barbados Ministry of Social Transformation in its 2003 *National Strategy Plan*.[1] So write many governments today in similar documents and programs. And so they write when they write together. In the Millennium Development Goals adopted by the UN General Assembly in 2000, the overall aim is the eradication of poverty.

These bold statements contain a philosophy of the problem. Poverty is not just one of several social issues, it is a very special one; it is a problem

This study started with a lecture on poverty measurement methods at the Pobreza y Dignidad Humana *conference in Ciudad Victoria, Mexico (23–26 September 2003), convened by the governor of Tamaulipas, Tomás Yarrington Ruvalcaba, and the Colegio de Mexico. Subsequently, theoretical and empirical developments have been presented and discussed in the form of lectures and seminar presentations at the Institute of Sociology of the Academy of Sciences of the Czech Republic (Prague, 27 November 2003), at the Sir Arthur Lewis Institute for Social and Economic Studies of the University of the West Indies (Cave Hill, Barbados, 2 June 2004), at the annual conference of the Research Committee on Poverty, Inequality and Social Welfare of the International Sociological Association (Paris, 2 September 2004), at the 2004 ESPAnet conference (Oxford, 10 September 2004), and at the New Approaches to Poverty seminar convened by the United Nations Research Institute for Social Development (Geneva, 4 November 2004). I am grateful for helpful insights and suggestions on these and other occasions from Julio Boltvinik, Araceli Damián, Fernando Cortés, Rosa María Rubalcava, Meghnad Desai, Dave Gordon, Jiří Večerník, Marek Skovajsa, Andrew Downes, Jonathan Lashley, Elsie Le Franc, Olli Kangas, Peter Saunders, Bruno Palier, Bea Cantillon, Björn Halleröd, John Veit-Wilson, Thandika Mkandawire, Huck-ju Kwon, José Figueiredo, Alex Peyre, and Tony Atkinson. The study has evolved in a process of dialogue with my friend and colleague Axel West Pedersen of NOVA Norwegian Social Research. Laurie Blome Jacobsen of Fafo Institute for Applied International Studies did indicator tests and estimated the international statistics, and Arne S. Andersen of the Norwegian Central Bureau of Statistics estimated the Norwegian statistics.*

[1] Barbados Ministry of Social Transformation 2003, p. 51.

that should be *eradicated*. We cannot meaningfully say that of most social problems. For example, we would not say of social inequality that it should be eradicated. Inequality, if there is too much of it, should be reduced or modified. One reason we would not aim for more is that inequality, when not extreme, is in some ways a good thing that reflects freedom, social diversity, and economic energy. But not so poverty. It is an unqualified bad of the worst kind. It is (next to slavery) the ultimate social ill. Therefore it should not just be reduced or modified or brought under control; it should be eradicated. This is why we single out certain conditions with the heavy name of poverty. The conditions we justly call poverty are not simply unfair or unfortunate; they are unacceptable. It is because they are unacceptable that we have reason to call them poverty.[2]

The idea that poverty should be brought to an end is a modern one. It was invented in Europe about two hundred years ago, in the wake of the American and French revolutions. The inventors were Tom Paine in England and the Marquis de Condorcet in France, both inspired by Adam Smith. Their invention was a double one. First was the leap in mind-set that transformed poverty from a normal, natural, and inevitable thing into an aberration that should be eliminated. Second was a plan for how to go about eliminating it. The first condition was prosperity, so that there would be enough for all to live well. When a society is prosperous, there is no need for anyone in it to be poor. The second condition was that prosperity be managed so that everyone would be assured of having enough. Both Paine and Condorcet drew up detailed plans for what we today call the welfare state.[3]

Their invention in the first instance did not survive politically, but it did philosophically. When Alfred Marshall ushered in neoclassical economics, in *Principles of Economics* (1890), he tied from page one the whole rationale of economics, both its practice and its science, to overcoming the problem of poverty. His successor, A.C. Pigou, in *The Economics of Welfare* (1920), went on to prove the usefulness to society of redistributing income from the rich to the poor. Regrettably, his proof was ahead of its time and was refuted by Lionell Robbins in *An Essay on the Nature and Significance of Economic Science* (1932). Robbins argued that economics can measure income but not its usefulness to those who

[2] Of course, eradicating poverty may or may not be a realistic goal of public policy. The government of Barbados, for example, sees that as its long-term goal. Its operational goal as expressed in 2003 is to reduce the incidence of poverty by 40 percent by 2012. The operational Millennium Development Goal on poverty is to reduce by half by 2015 the number of people in the world in "extreme" poverty, defined as living on less than one dollar a day.

[3] The story of the idea of societies without poverty is told by Stedman Jones 2004. On Adam Smith and Condorcet, see also Rothschild 2001.

hold and use it. His objection was technically correct but morally faulty and has now in turn itself been refuted, first by Amartya Sen, who has shifted the foundations of economics from utility to freedom, and recently by Richard Layard, who has demonstrated that we can now measure the usefulness of income even on the welfare economists' narrow terms.[4] The result of these advances is that now even economists know what everyone else has always known, that additional income is more useful to the poor than to the rich. As it was once obvious that poverty was a natural thing, it has become obvious that it is something that should be ended.[5]

In due course, Paine and Condorcet's invention was also accepted politically. The welfare state was first designed as an instrument of social order; for its unlikely father, Count Bismarck in Germany, it was a tool of state building and for managing *die Arbeiterfrage*. In the twentieth century, however, it became accepted as politically realistic that prosperity should be used so that everyone would be assured of having enough. This acceptance was put to words by William Beveridge during the Second World War in his important plan for postwar social insurance. At war's end, the democracies set about building welfare states on the principle of universal security.

If poverty can be eradicated, and if this depends on the double act of prosperity and redistribution, we should expect it to have happened by now. If Paine and Condorcet thought there was prosperity enough two hundred years ago, that was nothing compared with what we have subsequently achieved. If redistribution is a matter of, in the historian Asa Briggs' words, "the deliberate use of organised power through politics and administration in an effort to modify the play of market forces," that we now have.[6]

Poverty is obviously not eradicated in the world, but if it were to be eradicated anywhere, it should be where there is ample prosperity and effective redistribution. To test if what *should* be brought to an end *can* be ended, we would look to the Scandinavian countries. We will be able to do this below; in fact we will be able to look to where it would be most likely to have been overcome, to Norway. That little country has more prosperity than probably any other, a more even distribution of economic resources than in probably any affluent country, and an excellent welfare state of social security and safety nets.[7] As it happens, it is data availability

---

[4] See, e.g., Sen 2002; Layard 2005.

[5] See Sachs 2005.

[6] Briggs 1961.

[7] Norway became a mega-affluent country in the last decades of the twentieth century thanks to the exploitation of North Sea petroleum. Much of that wealth is held as savings by the government in the form of financial capital in international markets, as of 2006 at a value in excess of $100,000 per household (norges-bank.no/nbim/pension_fund). Shifting

that will lead us to observing Norway, but fortunately that leads us to look where we would want to go anyway.

The State of the Art

Scientific poverty measurement started just over a hundred years ago with Benjamin Seebohm Rowntree and his *Poverty: A Study of Town Life* (1901). His ambition was to answer a very simple question: how much poverty is there? With the use of a precise instrument for counting the poor, Rowntree was able to show persuasively that there were at the time more people living in poverty in Britain than had generally been thought to be the case.

In the century following Rowntree's breakthrough, and particularly in the last two or three decades, we have seen a colossal growth in the volume of research on the measurement of poverty, vast improvements in the quality of comparative data, and impressive advances in the technology of analysis.[8] However, if we now take stock of where one hundred years of research has taken us, we see a rather perplexing combination of progress and lack of progress.

On the side of progress, we must count the refinement of poverty measurement as initiated by Rowntree into an established mainstream approach. Poverty measurement rests on solving three problems: the problem of identification (how to identify the poor), the problem of aggregation (how to aggregate the poverty of the poor into a measure of poverty in their society), and the problem of data (what kind of information to use to solve the problems of identification and aggregation). In the Rowntree tradition, the relevant data are income data (or, as for Rowntree himself, wage data), identification is by some variant of the income poverty line, and aggregation is by some variant of the head-count method. This tradition I call *the income approach*.

But there is also a conspicuous absence of progress, in rather surprising ways. In spite of unquestionable advances in the quantity and quality of research, economists and sociologists working within the mainstream have made little if any headway in their ability to answer their own core

---

governments run huge budget surpluses. Social provisions and services are excellent and generally to the population's satisfaction (as confirmed in a 2005 survey; cf. www.dep.no/krd/norsk/tema/kommune). Norway has in recent years led the UNDP's human-development league table.

[8] On the history of poverty research see, e.g., Glennerster et al. 2004; on improvements in the quality of comparative data, see *The Luxembourg Income Study*, www.lisproject.org); on advances in the technology of analysis see, e.g., Sen and Foster 1997.

question. If anything, we are now, paradoxically, less able to report on the magnitude of poverty than Rowntree was in his day.

The inconclusiveness of the income approach is visible in its inability to compare poverty across the divide between poor and rich countries. The whole problem is for the most part swept under the carpet in a tacit pretense that poverty in poor countries is one thing and in rich countries is something else. For example, the *Human Development Report* uses one kind of poverty statistics for OECD countries and another kind for the poorer countries of the world and does not attempt to relate measured poverty in these two categories of countries. Although that may be convenient, it is neither theoretically nor methodologically satisfactory. We generally believe there is or may be poverty in both poor and rich countries, and we usually think it is meaningful to discuss this problem in the language of poverty whether we are considering high-income or low-income countries. That being so, we must believe we are at least on one level speaking about the same kind of thing irrespective of economic environment. If we think there is poverty in China, which no doubt there is, and poverty in the United States, which no doubt there is, and if we think that in both cases it is a matter of *poverty*, we should be able to compare it.

Methodologically, too, this subdivision of the world makes little sense. A country at the top of the range among poor countries would display a relatively low measure of poverty, but if it jumped up on the economic ladder and into the group of rich countries, and hence into a different measurement regime, it would for its progress most likely display a higher measure of poverty, a shift that would be totally unconnected from any real change in real poverty. Empirical measures that change in ways that are not connected to changes in the thing they are said to measure—or may perversely change for, say, the worse when the thing changes for the better—are of course not of much validity.

It may be difficult in practice to compare poverty in rich and poor countries, but skirting around that difficulty with the help of an escape clause that says there are different kinds of poverty is just a way of conjuring away the problem we should take on. Rather than avoiding the difficulty, we should take it as a test of the robustness of an approach that it is able to generate meaningful comparisons not only among economically and otherwise similar countries but also between countries on different levels of economic development.

Nor is determinacy much better in comparisons between countries on a more level economic pegging. That has been strikingly demonstrated by Tony Atkinson in an exploration of poverty in Europe. He starts with "two cautionary tales." The first one is presented in a range of poverty estimates for two countries, France and the United Kingdom (using data

TABLE 4.1
Estimated Percentage Size of the Poverty
Population in Two Countries

France			United Kingdom		
5.3	9.6	16.8	1.7	4.1	9.9
7.0	13.5	22.5	3.1	9.2	20.9
6.4	12.5	22.0	3.8	10.3	21.0
6.6	11.9	20.1	2.6	8.6	19.9
7.4	13.0	21.2	5.3	13.6	25.0

Source: Atkinson 1998.

for 1984–85). These results are summarized in table 4.1 (in which I give only the estimates in order to show the range, without including methodological details). The second tale is about trends in one country (Ireland, using data for 1987 and 1994). Six different trajectories are shown, three with poverty increasing over the period and three with poverty decreasing, all at different rates.

The estimates included in these tales all make good sense, and all are based on solid data and derived from sound definitions and methodological choices. But their divergence shows that even good statistics on poverty do not enable us to help those who only want to know the most elementary things: How much poverty is there in my country? More or less than there used to be? More or less than in a neighboring country? From the extensive research summarized in Atkinson's tales, we can hardly say more than that there is some poverty in these countries (and the skeptical reader may doubt even that), but we can say next to nothing with authority about its extent and how it compares between countries and changes over time.

Poverty *is* a difficult concept to define, and any effort to measure it is fraught with problems of judgment. No single, final, and objective measure is to be found. But the range of statistical measures now on offer, as laid out in Atkinson's tales, is too wide and random to be believable. The problem is not so much that different projects give different answers (although that, too, considering how different the answers are) as that there is no consistent sensitivity in income statistics on poverty to elementary differences in time and space. Reasonable variations in definitions and statistical specifications will necessarily give a certain variation in empirical results. But some variations are such that if they result from reasonable procedures within a scientific paradigm, they must be taken as evidence that something is wrong in the paradigm itself. If we take it that poverty is a real thing that can be measured, there cannot at the same time be both more of it in France than in Britain and more in Britain than in France. It has to be one way or the other. Nor can there in Ireland, or anywhere else, be both more of it and less of it today than earlier. We may not be able to establish a single trajectory as the only true one, but if impossibly inconsistent trajectories emerge from the data, there must be something amiss in how we have been led to read those data.

One reason for persistent indeterminacy in measurement may be that there has also been very little advancement towards a genuine theory of poverty, towards an understanding of what poverty *is*. Poverty research has mainly worked from operational rather than theoretical definitions.

Rowntree solved the problem of identification by drawing the poverty line at the level of wages needed for a family to purchase a specified list of "necessities" for "physical efficiency," and solved the problem of aggregation by the head-count method. These solutions made good sense and were first seen to be persuasive, but they did not fully stand the test of time. Using the same procedures, with only some minor modifications in the list of necessities, he continued his work for another half century, publishing a second report in 1941 and a third one in 1951. These studies found a very considerable reduction in the number of people in poverty and pointed towards a not-distant future when the problem might be conquered and poverty eradicated.

Shortly after Rowntree's final report, however, poverty was surprisingly "rediscovered" in rich countries such as the United States and Britain.[9] His methodology therefore started to look biased downward; there seemed to be more poverty than Rowntree's "measured poverty." If that was the case, it would seem that there could be poverty even where necessities were satisfied. But if so, what is poverty? In Rowntree's work there was really no theory to fall back on behind his operational definition.

A revival of research was stimulated, informed by relative deprivation theory.[10] That, in turn, led to a different kind of operational definition under what came to be known as *the relative theory of poverty*. While Rowntree had identified poverty in an index of commodities, prices, and wages, relative theory now identified it as starting at a point on the income distribution below which people would be deemed unable to live in a minimally acceptable way, it being understood that the "minimally acceptable way" was a moving target depending on what was "the usual way" in the society and at the time in question.

These different operational definitions clearly reflect different ideas about what poverty *is*, but those ideas remain poorly articulated. If there

---

[9] In the United States by Harrington 1962; in Britain by Abel-Smith and Townsend 1965.

[10] Culminating in Townsend 1979. On relative deprivation, see Stouffer et al. 1949, Runciman 1966.

is such a thing as a relative theory of poverty behind the new operational income definitions, we have been given no more to resort to than some very general statements. Peter Townsend, for example, in his break-through study of relative deprivation poverty, defined poverty as lacking in "the resources to obtain the types of diet, participate in the activities and have the living conditions and amenities which are customary, or are at least widely encouraged or approved, in the societies to which they belong."[11] And according to the European Union, poverty is recognized in "individuals and families whose resources are so small as to exclude them from the minimum acceptable way of life in the Member State in which they live." This is not much to go on for an understanding of what poverty is. If it is a lack of resources, which resources—income, property, education, social capital? Or perhaps it is not resources at all that defines what poverty *is*. Resources may be what explains a problem that is finally identified in participation, exclusion, and way of life. On these matters, no clarity has emerged.

This leaves us with theoretical and methodological conventions, in what has become a very sophisticated field of research, which are such that no reasonably authoritative answer is forthcoming to that old core question: how much poverty is there? As a result, we simply do not have the research tools we need in order to establish in say Norway whether or not poverty has been eradicated. As things stand, we just don't know.

The road out of this impasse does not go through further statistical sophistication under prevailing conventions. Mainstream poverty research can in this respect hardly become better and more sophisticated than it already is, and further improvements in its technology is not going to do us much good. Although one might think that all the groundwork that could be done would have been done in one hundred years of effort, that is not so. We need yet again to go back to first principles and re-investigate the very meanings of poverty and measurement.

I suggest two subtle shifts in perspective and language. I will have a good deal to say about poverty, but as we go along I will show that what we should really want to be told about is *the problem of poverty*. I will have a good deal to say about measurement but will argue that the better way to go about it is by *social reporting*. The core question we should address, I think, is not how much poverty there is but what the problem looks like. What we should want to do is to inform societies about their problem of poverty as truthfully and believably as good scientific craft will allow. That is an ambition for applied social research on a par with, for example, the monitoring of population trends or economic growth. It is an ambition that asks more of us than that we go out and count the

---

[11] Townsend 1979, p. 31.

poor. We need tools that enable us to produce robust and consistent comparisons over time and between societies and countries. We are still in search of those tools, and we are not going to find them by honing yet again the tried tools of the income approach.

THE INCOME ASSUMPTION

Rowntree built his work on two assumptions that were so obvious at the time that they did not even need to be spelled out. One was that the job at hand was to measure poverty, and the other was that the main tool for so doing was income (or wage) analysis. The first of these assumptions—the measurement assumption—is still maintained unquestioningly in almost all branches of poverty research and has hardly even been recognized as an assumption. The second one—the income assumption—remains the approach of mainstream poverty research but has gradually become questioned and has lost its status of being universally seen as the obvious way to do it. The opening up of poverty research to approaches other than the income approach has, however, not fed back into a recognition that even the measurement assumption may not be as obvious as it looks.

Given procedures of identification and aggregation, and good data, the income approach displays the correct trends and differences in whatever is thereby measured. This leaves a great deal of scope for the useful application of the income approach. For example, UNICEF produces important and informative comparative data on child poverty in this way (which I myself make use of in chapter 1).[12] In the United States, the Census Bureau publishes annual official statistics on poverty that are generally accepted to be authoritative, using an operational definition very similar to the one Rowntree used.[13]

However, there are two problems. First, no agreement has emerged on procedures of identification and aggregation. Individual projects may produce reliable results, but there is no consistency across projects. For example, what has emerged as a European relative income approach flatly rejects the procedures used by the US Census Bureau. It is because of this lack of methodological agreement that different projects generate the range of estimates displayed by Atkinson.

Poverty measurement by the income approach has failed to produce results that could reasonably be accepted as reliable. Rather, the experience is an entirely dismal one:

[12] UNICEF 2000, 2005.
[13] Pioneered by Orshansky 1969.

· Income measures are not persuasively sensitive to differences or changes in poverty. This we have seen in Atkinson's tales above.

· Income measures are not robust as to the magnitude of poverty. Experiments show that minor variations in the specification and processing of income data often result in major variations in measurement results.[14]

· Income measures do not produce stable results that stand up when tested against other evidence. The moment income data is supplemented with consumption or social-indicators data, if only cautiously, measurement results tend to change strongly.[15]

These problems of reliability *could* be overcome in the income approach, but this would require a high level of agreement on very detailed methodological procedures and specifications. Such agreement in not in sight.

Second, beyond reliability, there is the more fundamental problem of validity. Validity in the income approach depends on poverty being defined as low income but as we have seen, that way of defining poverty has now mostly been given up. This has opened the field to alternative operational definitions. For example, the UN Development Programme, in its *Human Development Reports*, compares poverty in developing countries in terms of deprivation in three dimensions of human development: healthy life expectancy, knowledge, and access to economic provisionings. That makes good sense, but so did Rowntree's definition and so do various relative-income definitions. The question is why these definitions make good sense, and how can we decide which ones make more sense than others—again, in other words, what poverty *is*?

There is no reason to think that the income approach should not continue to be used in poverty research. In spite of theoretical difficulties, there are practical arguments in its favor, notably the usefulness of income data. The income approach does enable us to pin down poverty unambiguously (if not reliably) using information that everyone (thinks they) can grasp and understand. This may have political and pedagogical advantages. There are also advantages for further research in identifying poverty on a single scale that lends itself to use as a variable in causal analyses. (But a single scale is not necessarily what we should be looking for, as I argue in appendix F.)

[14] See, e.g., Kangas and Ritakallio 1998.
[15] See, e.g., Ringen 1988; Mayer and Jencks 1988; Travers and Richardson 1993; Halleröd 1995; Nolan and Whelan 1996; Whiteford 1997; van den Bosch 2001.

For some purposes, it may not matter that the income indicator may not display "real" poverty. As long as we use consistent definitions and standards, we can take it that the income indicator reveals real and relevant differences and trends. For example, when UNICEF compiles league tables of child poverty in rich countries, using the percentage of children living in households with incomes below 50 percent of the national median, and finds differences between Denmark and the United States of 2.4 and 21.9 percent, this clearly tells us important things about differences in living standards and vulnerability in these two countries and it does not really matter all that much whether we call that poverty or not.

But practical expediency is not enough. We have a range of tried approaches that all seem sensible but give wildly different results and have no agreed-upon way of mediating between them. That lack of agreement is, of course, a devastating verdict on the approach itself. If there were a persuasive way to do it, we would by now have agreed on that way.

Ultimately, what we need to be able to do is to test for the *eradication* of poverty. This is the modern understanding of the problem. Relative-income approaches are, however, by definition (almost) incapable of performing that test. For example, the most recent UNICEF table on child poverty gives a rate of 3.4 percent for Norway. This represents the proportion of children living in households with an income below half of the median income in that population. On the face of it, poverty has not been eradicated in that country. However, this statistic is estimated directly from the distribution of income. If that distribution in Norway was about as equal as it could be in a mixed capitalist economy (which may or may not be the case), then by mathematical logic measured poverty could not get much lower. (The Norwegian rate is nearly the lowest in the UNICEF comparison, only in Denmark and Finland is it slightly lower.) If it were to get lower the next time UNICEF compared child poverty, that would be *only* because the income distribution had changed (and could theoretically happen even if the real standard of living of those at the bottom of the distribution had declined). It is not unconceivable that even Norway could equalize its income distribution yet further, but I would be willing to bet a very good sum of money that UNICEF will never encounter a zero rate of child poverty by its operational definition. The relative theory of poverty is strangely archaic. It harks back to what was obvious before the great revolutions and at least from the time of Jesus: "ye have the poor with you always."[16] It is a theory that pretty much sets aside by a priori definition the vision of Paine, Condorcet, Marshall, and others that poverty is an ill that can be overcome and a problem that can be brought to an end.

[16] Mark 14:7.

The Measurement Assumption

To want to measure something is to believe that the thing in question is something that exists objectively and that the facts of it can be teased out with the help of an appropriate definition and an instrument of measurement that yields a valid recording of the thing as defined. Hence, Townsend, in the very first sentence of *Poverty in the United Kingdom*, promises that it will prove possible, with the help of relative-deprivation theory, to define poverty "consistently" and measure it "objectively."

However, no consistent definition has been found and, as a result, no objective measure. This may seem a bit of a mystery after one hundred years of effort, but there is a good reason: there simply is nothing out there to define. There is no such thing as poverty in any objective understanding. Poverty is not a fact, it is a moral problem. The nature of that problem has been alluded to in various ways above. Poverty is what should be eradicated, and the reason it should be eradicated is that it is *unacceptable*. That code word has followed us all the way through to the definition of the European Union: the minimum *acceptable* way of life. This is what poverty *is*: it is what is unacceptable. The search for the meaning of poverty must go through this understanding of *unacceptability*.

Poverty, then, is not something people have or have not or are or are not and that can therefore be counted up. That's just not the kind of thing it is. The problem of poverty is about the existence of social conditions that are unacceptable. Something that is defined by unacceptability, and in that meaning subjectively, is not objectively measurable. The effort to define poverty, in the interest of making it measurable, has been an exercise in overspecification. The need to find a way to separate "the poor" from "the nonpoor," which is the key to the measurement of poverty, has created an artificial need for something that does not exist, namely poverty as a badge that can be attached to some people and not to others. We have been chasing a ghost on the trail of, in David Piachaud's words, the Holy Grail.

Since there is no such thing as objective poverty, the idea of measurement is not really the one we should be pursuing. There may be many good reasons for imposing an operational definition on a set of data—for example, to single out those in an income distribution who are below half of the median income, and possibly even to call them "the poor"—but if we have no other information to go on than where people sit on a distribution curve, we have no basis for saying that these people really live in poverty and that this is really a measure of poverty in this or that society.

We should probably have listened more to the way people, ourselves included, speak about poverty when we do not speak scientifically. The problem is then usually not framed as lacking this or that item of consumption or even being without money; it is about dignity, the ability to make choices and live one's own life, the risk to children, the feeling of exclusion. We know that poverty is an obscure and ambiguous thing; why then, we should have asked ourselves, are we hell-bent on making it an object of unambiguous measurement? We have defined and defined again and measured and measured again only to see definitions multiply and measures spread out. Is it then not more likely, we should have asked, that we are on the wrong road than that we have not yet traveled the right road far enough? Had we asked such questions and taken on more doubt, we might have seen that what society needs to be informed about is something more complex than an objective fact that can be pinned down in a simple statistic. We might then have been encouraged to find a way of displaying a problem rather than to pursue with futile energy the measurement of the unmeasurable.

From Income to Social Indicators

Setting aside other purposes in poverty research for which the income approach may be well suitable, it would seem that for our purpose—to inform societies about their problem of poverty—the experience recommends that we look for another way of doing it. The alternative to the income approach is some kind of direct approach in which the problem is displayed through social indicators of the experience of poverty.[17]

It is not easy today to argue the case for social indicators in preference to income measurement. What was once, in the 1960s and 1970s, a "social indicators movement" largely ran out of steam and was discredited for having promised more than could be delivered. That was the destiny of, for example, the inflated social indicators program at the Organisation for Economic Co-operation and Development.[18] It is also difficult because income analysis often looks methodologically advanced while social indicators analysis may have an appearance of naïveté. However, if what looks sophisticated is unable to answer its own question, it can hardly be the right methodology. The social indicators approach is, I will argue, for all its apparent simplicity, capable of delivering the consistent sensitivity that has eluded the income approach.

[17] As I have argued previously in Ringen 1988.
[18] OECD 1982.

We might think of social indicators as an alternative way of solving the problems of identification and aggregation, but I believe it is more fruitful to see the step from income to social indicators as a change in philosophy more than just in data. One consequence is that we should no longer see the end result to be a single measure of poverty. The problem is better displayed in a battery of indicators, and there is no compelling reason to pull those indicators together into a single measure or index. (This matter, the index problem, is the one considered further in appendix F.)

Turning to social indicators obviously opens up new methodological questions, finally about what a robust set of indicators should look like. One way to approach the choice of indicators is to see it as a matter of political demand and supply. Society is in demand of information about itself; the scientists are the suppliers of that information. In a democracy, society resolves through the democratic process the kind of information that is needed for democratic politics to run efficiently, and the scientists work out the details of how to provide that information objectively. In the early social-indicators movement, this was seen as a matter of identifying politically a relevant list of social concerns and then sorting out scientifically the indicators to inform on those concerns.[19] A recent study of social exclusion in the European Union follows this tradition. The meaning of social exclusion is determined in the political apparatus of the European Union and exclusion thus defined is then explored scientifically with appropriate social indicators.[20]

This has much in common with one way of solving the problem of identification in the income approach. If one can identify in the social policy regime the minimum income support needy citizens have a right to, one can take that to be an implicit political consensus about the poverty line and use that as a basis for measurement.

The advantage of this way of doing it is that normative questions that cannot easily be answered scientifically are taken to be answered democratically and that politicians can be held to account by standards they have themselves committed to. But there are also serious disadvantages. One is a bias in favor of power. To ask society what its social concerns are, is to ask those in power. Those in power are not poor, and the poor are not in power. The purpose of informing society about poverty is finally to speak on behalf of the powerless and to contribute to creating the concern society should have for poverty. It is not satisfactory to assume that concern will be there waiting to be acted upon if only the facts are made known.

---

[19] See, e.g., Erikson et al. 1987; OECD 1982.
[20] Atkinson et al. 2002.

Furthermore, the policy-definition method skirts around and avoids the question of what poverty or the problem of poverty *is*. It enables the scientist to proceed from yet another operational definition without much of an underlying theoretical definition of the concept. This, in turn, gives society little persuasive reason to believe necessarily that those identified as poor really *are* poor.

The lesson, then, turning now again to social indicators, is that to find more robustness than has emerged by way of the income approach, we need some more theory on which to build the empirical exercise. In the operational definition, I will suggest, we should look for simplicity and transparency, but this should be grounded in a careful reflection both on the concept of poverty and on what it means to inform society about it.

THE PROBLEM OF POVERTY

As long as there is inequality, there is deprivation, at least relative deprivation. Since everywhere some level and form of inequality is acceptable and sometimes desirable, there are deprivations that are by definition not unacceptable. To understand the problem of poverty is to understand not deprivation but the unacceptable face of deprivation.

Everyone wants to live well. For the individuals, well-being is in the way they live and how they experience and feel their life to be. But the social meaning of well-being is that people have the *freedom* to live in the way they themselves see to be a good life. (I develop this in detail in chapter 6.)

One of the necessary conditions for a life that is in any meaning free is to have security against enforced deprivation in material resources of such severity that it denies one any real power to enter into a life of one's own making. There is much more to freedom than poverty or not, and freedom from poverty does not on its own make one's life free. But it removes the bottom barrier in material resources that makes it impossible to have a life that can start to be free. It is this lack of elementary freedom that is at the heart of the moral problem of poverty. The problem of poverty manifests itself in the lives of persons and families as an enforced lack of basic material power to live as one wants or as reasoned fear that one might fall into that situation. It is to live under the dictatorship of material necessity without choice and control in one's daily life. That's what poverty *is* (at least as a starting point), it's about freedom and power and the lack thereof.

The linking of poverty and freedom is today entirely conventional. It grows out of the recognition that human rights include social rights and then, centrally, freedom from the fear of poverty. It is recognized in modern theories of development.[21] It can be found in any policy statement or document from the World Bank or the UNDP. It is contained in the language of freedom from want, hunger, and poverty.

This form of unfreedom comes to people in two ways. First, obviously, it comes from actual deprivation, from living wretchedly. Escaping poverty means entering into the domain in which, as far as material resources go, you can start to shape your life by your own choices. But in addition it comes from the *fear* of deprivation. Since a life in poverty is a paralyzed life, the danger that poverty may be around the corner is terrifying. If you have reason to think that you are in real and imminent danger of falling into poverty—for example, of losing your livelihood and finding yourself utterly unable to make ends meet or to properly feed your family and you may have to go without or to take on debt that you know you are without the means to repay—the need to avoid that destitution will take hold of your mind and life and make you as near to being as unfree as if you were already deep in poverty. Here we start to see some of the difference between *poverty* and *the problem of poverty*. A society's problem of poverty contains more than a certain incidence of people being poor. It also expresses itself in the fear of becoming poor.

We have words available in everyday language to describe degrees of poverty. There is *destitution*—being without what is indisputably needed. There is *want*—being without what everyone should have access to. There is *vulnerability*—living in conditions so fragile that circumstances might easily cause you to fall into destitution or want.

These words reflect an ordinary commonsense understanding of poverty as a problem in several dimensions. Destitution, want, and vulnerability—these are time-honored words that reflect a sound understanding of what kind of social problem we are up against. This vocabulary has all but disappeared from the scientific language of poverty, which reflects how, under the relative theory, the reality of poverty also has been defined away. Poverty has been made intangible; it is anything that is relative to a range of unspecified standards. It is the understanding that poverty is a real, tangible problem I am trying to rebuild here. The rehabilitation of the classical language of poverty is for that purpose. This language reflects an idea of poverty as a social problem that is complex and needs a battery of words and terms for its explanation.

There are many kinds of deprivation: deprivation of love, companionship, happiness, enjoyment, leisure, rest, and other good things. Poverty is *material* deprivation. In material terms, freedom grows out of holdings. If you *have* nothing, you are without any power to do and live as you wish. If you hold capital, even if not much, you have a platform to stand

---

[21] See, e.g., Sen 1999b.

on in society. Holdings are in the form of physical and human capital. These are the kinds of resources people use when they live by shaping their own lives. For our purpose, physical capital consists of monetary savings and real property, and human capital of skills and knowledge.

To be in or near poverty is to have no or next to no holdings to fall back on and to be unable to maintain even what little you have. It is to have inadequate monetary resources to meet consumption needs and to be without reserves, wherein force and necessity expose you to the danger of destitution or falling into debt. It is to be denied human capacities, or to see those capacities being worn down so that you cannot obtain or maintain such resources that you need to function with any measure of autonomy in your society.

The inclusion of human capital in a concept of holdings and resources is today not controversial and needs no further justification. That given, I apply a narrow understanding, as is appropriate in a context of poverty. I do not include, for example, health resources in the concept of human capital, since that would bring us beyond what is safely contained in a demanding concept of poverty. I see physical capital as a matter of consumption capacity and human capital as a matter of earnings capacity. There are, no doubt, arguments for being more inclusive, but it is a sound rule in any theorizing about poverty to keep things as basic as possible.[22]

Most people live in deprivation in some meaning, such as having less than others or less than they want or feel they should have, and even some pretty well-off people can, no doubt, feel miserably deprived. It is neither being nor feeling deprived in itself that constitutes poverty. We put some forms of deprivation into the reserved category of "poverty" when there is something special about it. Poverty is *severe* deprivation.

Deprivation is so bad as to be called poverty when it is so severe that it is unacceptable. We have reason to censure the quality of a society in the name of poverty when people are forced to live, or at risk of living, in a way that is so inadequate that no one should have to live like that.

Everyone needs to subsist and hence needs the means to avoid destitution.[23] The criterion of destitution is personal efficiency, the ability to function as an individual person (physical efficiency, Rowntree called it). This is the kind of visible hardship described by Amartya Sen as "an irreducible core of absolute deprivation in our idea of poverty, which translates re-

---

[22] There might be an argument for including in some way *social capital* in the form of social relationships that mediate between the individual and her resources and advance or impede her ability to use them effectively, but I have found no practical way of doing that while keeping the concept of poverty safely down to earth. On social capital see, e.g., Berger and Neuhaus 1977; Coleman 1990; Bourdieu and Wacquant 1992; Putnam and Goss 2002. See also appendix G.

[23] On needs, see Doyal and Gough 1991.

ports of starvation, malnutrition and visible hardship into a diagnosis of poverty without having to ascertain first the relative picture."[24] Beyond destitution there is want—being without what the society you happen to live in makes necessary. The criterion of want is social efficiency, the ability to function as a social animal. Everyone depends on being able to call on the respect of others. This is what Adam Smith referred to in *Wealth of Nations* as "whatever . . . creditable people, even of the lowest order . . . would be ashamed to appear in public without." The examples he used were a linen shirt ("in the present times, through a greater part of Europe") and leather shoes ("rendered . . . by custom . . . a necessary of life in England").

These criteria are universal. Anyone who is to work or play or read a newspaper, to be a husband or wife or lover, or to raise a family or help friends needs some power to be able to *do* that, to possess some personal efficiency. Everyone—except those who have chosen to live as hermits—lives in a community and needs to be able to hold his ground against others with the help of some social efficiency. There is no freedom for those who cannot go into society and take on normal doings, or who are forced by want or shame to avoid engaging with their fellows, or who do not have the means to engage with them on a minimally equitable basis. If you are paralyzed for want of means, or for that reason have to excuse your existence in encounters with your betters or stand with cap in hand, you are not your own man. You are without the raw material basics of a free life.

People must have enough of food and such shelter and clothing that they can get up in the morning and get on with the ordinary business of life. This is a requirement of living and the stepping-stone for being able to enter into social relations. Those who cannot protect themselves against the elements with clothing, who do not have shelter for rest, and who do not have enough nutrition to move about and work are indisputably poor. Everywhere and in any kind of society, that situation is unacceptable. It is unacceptable even if the resources available in the society are such that destitution is unavoidable. That kind of deprivation may be explainable but is always humanly unacceptable.

But destitution goes beyond deprivation in food, shelter, and clothing. Destitution means that people have to make do without what they need for personal efficiency. Basic material needs are not only for physical capital but also for human capital. Those who cannot build up and maintain a minimal basis of functional skills are destitute. They are for those reasons as unable to *do* things as if they were unable for want of cash.

---

[24] Sen 1981, p. 17.

While destitution is in each person's own efficiency, want beyond destitution is in people's relations to others. People suffer destitution when they cannot do things because they do not have necessary material resources. They suffer want when, following Adam Smith, shame stands in their way, when their material conditions are such that they have good reason to fear that others may think that they can or should be treated with indifference or as an inferior or that they will be shunned because others do not trust them to be able to reciprocate if called upon.

What *poverty* is, I have said above, is a lack of basic power to start getting into a life of one's own making. I can now add that what constitutes that lack of basic power is destitution and want. Wherever and whenever we speak of poverty, be it in the United States or China or in Britain today or a hundred years ago, it is the identification of destitution or want that gives us reason to name and shame that society with the disgraceful label of poverty.

In addition, as established above, the *problem of poverty* includes the risk of destitution and want. Theoretically, anyone is at risk, but in the spirit of taking poverty to be a matter of severe deprivation, it follows that the risk of destitution and want that we should observe as a part of the problem of poverty is severe risk, or vulnerability in the classical terminology.

When we observe people living in poverty, we observe something that should not be. It is the denial that makes poverty a moral problem. It is a matter of *enforced* deprivation.

There are several ways in which people can live on a low material level without it constituting the kind of problem that should cause us to call it poverty. The monk who has chosen a life without property and renounced all material desires except the bare necessities of food, clothing, and shelter is poor by a mechanical definition but not in a moral meaning. His situation is not evidence of any shortcoming in his society. But if outside of the monk's monastery a peasant is toiling in order to support his family and obtaining no better a standard of living than that of the monk, we see poverty. His situation is proof that this is a society in which people are denied decent material living conditions. The monk and the peasant have the same low standard of living, but the correct poverty count would be one and not two.

The monk is not poor in the moral meaning of the term because his situation is his chosen lifestyle. Others may make other lifestyle choices that also include a low standard of living. Being a student may be a choice of that kind. Another example is young people who take "gap years." A gap year is time off, typically between finishing secondary school and starting further education or during college or university studies or between completing education and starting a serious career, typically spent traveling or hanging out and having a good time. Young people can do this because they live in a culture of affluence that makes it possible, affordable, and neither shameful nor too risky for them to opt out in periods and live on a low budget for the sake of experience. By a technical income measure, they may live below a poverty line during the gap period, but their situation does not reflect poverty in the problem meaning of the term. Rather the opposite. This is a society that allows and enables (young) people even the freedom to live from hand to mouth in periods.[25]

Various other lifestyle choices may include more or less of material sacrifice. There are eccentrics who strongly prefer leisure to income, idealists who sacrifice for the sake of duty, misers who save endlessly for the sake of saving, lovers of nature who prefer a simple life in the outdoors, travelers who value a particular kind of freedom so highly that they are prepared to suffer for it materially. What the incidence of voluntary material sacrifice may be is not easily said, but it may well be quite high, at least in certain periods of the life course and at least in societies of general affluence. Where poverty is widespread and the struggle for existence raw and brutish, a notion of voluntary sacrifice is likely to be rather academic. But if that is so, it is all the more necessary to be aware of it in comparisons between societies on different levels of economic development.

Dues and Duties

We now hopefully know a bit more about poverty: a freedom-denying severity of enforced deprivation in material resources. And hopefully something about the problem of poverty: destitution, want, and vulnerability. But we need to get deeper into the moral meaning of it.

Those who are in or in the vicinity of poverty are in desert of the help and protection of others. They have a just claim on the special consideration of others, and those others have a duty of special care for them. What is due to some is a duty on others. This is all good circular logic: desert is defined by severity of deprivation and severity of deprivation by desert. What that circular logic circulates around is the idea of the *unacceptable*. It is from the unacceptability of the social conditions in question that dues and duties arise.

But just what is it that makes certain conditions unacceptable? The idea of unacceptability depends on an assumption that it is possible to find

---

[25] Recent explorations of poverty in Scandinavia show relatively high incidences of income poverty among young people in their twenties (Gustafsson 1999). It has been suggested that this is spurious, in our terminology that what is reflected in gap year affluence rather than poverty. The interpretation is contested but the examples show that the main

some rationally shared understanding of what makes deprivation *that* severe, but finding that common ground is clearly not easy.

One way might be to think that people have not been able to form a reasoned opinion about poverty because they do not know the facts. That is the thinking that lies behind the measurement assumption. If we can produce an objective measure of poverty, we can present indisputable facts to society about unacceptable deprivation and a decent society will have to act on it. This is a sound idea. We, as a society, need to know the facts. But knowing the facts is not sufficient for anything more to happen. If there is one thing we must now have learned from a century of experience, it is that facts do not on their own produce consensus. Even Rowntree's original facts, as carefully defined and construed as they were, were contested, and as we know, relative facts grounded in the relative theory of poverty are easily and painlessly dismissible.[26]

The reason facts alone do not speak is that consensus escapes us not only because of ignorance but also because of disagreement. The reason again is that people have different interests in the matter. To find common ground we need not only to clear away ignorance but to resolve a power struggle. Once we agree that poverty is unacceptable, we also, if we are reasonably rational in our opinions, agree about dues and duties. We then in effect have a social contract between disputing parties, in this case principally between the haves and the have-nots. Those who stand to acquire dues have an interest in maximizing what they can get out of it. Those who take on duties have an interest in minimizing what they have to put into it. The have-nots have a reluctant interest in being seen to be poor. They thereby acquire a call on the duty of others to help them. The haves recognize a duty to help those who are poor but are reluctant to accept a definition that turns their recognized duty into a heavy burden. Under fortunate circumstances, democratic institutions should be able to carry that power struggle forward to a reasonably fair consensus.

If the problem were ignorance, we should measure. But that is not the problem, and therefore measurement will not do the job. What society is in need of is not a statistic but a way of resolving its own confrontation

---

finding in a significant body of research hinges on the issue of lifestyle choices versus enforced deprivation.

[26] The nearest we are to a shared understanding of the extent of poverty in rich countries based on statistical facts is the situation in the United States and the use of the Census Bureau's official statistics. I, for one, think it is a very considerable achievement to have obtained this degree of authority in statistics on a matter so controversial as poverty. On the other hand, it is not easy to see just what that shared understanding is an understanding about. It is hardly a shared understanding about unacceptable deprivation, since a constant flow of hard facts showing poverty to be widespread has not resulted in concerted action to eradicate the unacceptable.

over the thorny question of unacceptability. This is where social reporting comes in as an alternative to measurement. Social reporting is not so much about laying down the facts, although that too, as about displaying the problem of poverty to society in such as way as to help the competing interests in the politics of poverty towards a rational view of the extent of unacceptable deprivation. That is a matter of providing solid factual information but, beyond that, of helping society to agree with itself on (to return to Smith) what custom has rendered necessary. The idea is not to instruct society about certain objective facts but to hold up to it a mirror in which it can see itself as it is. Social consensus is obviously not something science can produce, but it can help society to find it by informing the political process.[27] The job of informing society about its problem of poverty is about helping it to understand itself and to resolve what Walter Korpi has called *the democratic class struggle*. It is to both enable and force people to resolve whether what they see in the mirror that is held up to them, with reasonable adherence to the facts and out of respect for the interest of others, should be deemed unacceptable.

THE POLITICS OF SOCIAL REPORTING

Information about poverty is often bad news. It reveals to citizens that something is lacking in their society and tells policy makers off for not doing better. It sends out a message of shame. It distributes dues and duties. Questions about poverty are asked because they are unavoidable in any context of social justice, but experience shows that the answers then given are often resisted or avoided: the message is often one that neither citizens nor policy makers truly want to hear. A theme that runs through the history of poverty research is the need to persuade a reluctant public to accept facts it finds it necessary to ask for but unpleasant to acknowledge. The challenge is to be able to tell people what they know they should know but are inclined to disbelieve in such a way that they have reason to accept it to be true.

Social reporting takes place in a political battlefield. There are two debates running side by side: an academic debate on the meaning of poverty and how to approach its study and a political debate in which citizens and policy makers (reluctantly) look for satisfactory facts around which they can form a view about the problem. Both scientists and politicians would probably want these discussions to be intertwined and mutually

---

[27] I have discussed this idea of applied social research as a matter of informing the political process in more detail in *Democracy, Science and the Civic Spirit* (1993), reprinted in Ringen 2005a.

informing of each other but that partnership has proved difficult. When scientists offer up their methodologies and statistics, they enter political life and encounter interests. The Right, the Treasury, and various coalitions of taxpayers may well want to be told that the extent of poverty is low, whereas the Left, the Ministry of Social Welfare, and various coalitions of activists may suspect the problem to be widespread and look for that to be confirmed.

There is no clear demarcation between the academic and political debates, nor do most of those who are motivated to explore the problem of poverty wish there to be. Some are political warriors who use research as an instrument of politics, but even those who stand back from direct activism usually want to influence politics indirectly by telling the political contestants the true story of poverty in their society. A methodology that is to achieve that status must sit firmly on sound scientific procedure and in this sense be as objective as possible. But it also needs to be guided by a sensitivity to the inescapable fact that social reporting is political. A practicable methodology must tell the story of poverty in a way that is believable. The first condition is a solid scientific base, but that is not the only condition. The methodology must be transparent to those who are asked to believe what it says so they can be comfortable that they know what it means, and the information provided must be understandable to those who are asked to believe it. It must speak to them in a way that enables them to overcome their inclination to disbelieve and to accept, against their reluctance, that what is displayed is indeed the problem.

There is a way for the scientist to preserve his integrity when his work unavoidably becomes embroiled in the politics of poverty. I call this *the cautionary principle*. Applied poverty research is motivated by a desire to uncover problems that many in the political community are inclined to think are not there. The scientist is being scientific on a political battlefield in which he knows power is asymmetrical. Those who need society to recognize its problem of poverty are the powerless. To succeed in the job of informing society it is not enough to uncover a problem, what is uncovered must be believed—and it must be believed in particular by those who may have an interest in disbelieving it and the power to suppress or brush aside unpleasant information. The way to tell a nasty story so that it will be believed is to tell it so that it cannot be disbelieved, so that nothing in the way it is told will give those who wish to disbelieve it the opportunity to do so. The way to do this is obviously first to avoid anything that could cause the message to be seen as biased but also—since it is a message about a shameful state of affairs—to avoid anything that could cause it to appear exaggerated. If those who wish to disbelieve the story find in it any excuse to discredit it as overtold they will, and the message will be dismissed because it does not force those who are inclined to disbelieve it to accept it. If this side in the political debate cannot be persuaded—those who are on the other side are already in the poverty lobby and do not need persuasion—there will be no consensus, no social contract, and no unacceptability. There is not much use in preaching to the believers. Unless the infidels can be converted, there will be no agreed-upon facts on the ground from which to move forward to rational deliberation and effective public policies. The disbelievers need to be forced to accept that the story they are being told is the true story; they need to be put in a situation of being unable to dismiss what they are told. Others may feel that the full extent of poverty is not displayed, but this does not matter for the story's power to be accepted. What matters is that what is displayed cannot be dismissed. What is displayed must obviously be the scientific truth and nothing but the truth, but the benefit of doubt should be seen to lean towards undertelling the truth and away from overtelling it.

The cautionary principle was established (although not given the name) by Rowntree himself. His measure of poverty was extremely parsimonious and deliberately designed so that it could not reasonably be dismissed as exaggerating the true extent of poverty and therefore as unbelievable.[28] The cautionary principle is strategic: it is the scientist visibly imposing restraining rules on his own work in the interest of being believed. But it is more than strategic. It is a solid scientific principle to frame the test of one's hypothesis so that the expected outcome is made difficult to prove. When it is then proved, it is thereby all the more solidly proved. Scientists err if they frame their tests in favor of the anticipated or desired outcome. When scientists strategically apply the cautionary principle, they infuse their work with the believability that comes from a procedure transparently based on good scientific craft.

The recommended strategy now is to stay carefully in touch with what the problem of poverty is made of—destitution, want, and vulnerability— and to shape the design transparently and understandably in application of the cautionary principle. The instinct of the scientists is to tell the true story by telling it fully, but therein lies the temptation to overtell it. Their inclination is to want to show how complicated the story is and what masses of data are needed to tell it, but therein lies the danger of telling it so that only they themselves can understand it. As always, if you want to be believed: keep it short, keep it simple, and keep it straight. The challenge is not to draw the picture in its full complexity, but quite the opposite: to show how a complicated picture can be drawn truthfully

---

[28] He may not have succeeded perfectly in this, but in retrospect he did pretty well. When the relative theory caused the cautionary principle to be abandoned in British poverty research, believability declined. The reason the U.S. Census Bureau statistics are seen to be more believable is that they obey the cautionary principle.

with the help of few and simple images. That is a challenge many artists will recognize, and any poet. It is also the challenge in the art of social reporting on complex matters such as the problem of poverty.

THE INDICATORS APPROACH

The annual *Human Development Report* of the United Nations Development Programme is today probably the world's most influential publication on standards of living and poverty. What is striking in that report is that it just drops not only the income approach but the whole idea of measuring poverty. It reports on human development with the help of select and simple indicators, with no pretense that it is telling the full story—and thereby succeeds in answering the questions it poses more persuasively than had it tried to answer it more fully.

The reason the *Human Development Report* succeeds in a way that is seen to be believable is not only because of its brazenness and good luck in the choice of indicators. There is more to it; it tells the story it has to tell with the right tools for the telling of that story.

The idea of the indicators approach is to communicate a message with the simplest and sparsest possible use of information. It is not to measure anything or to tell how anything is in its full complexity. It is to indicate—to indicate relevantly, of course, but still to indicate.

An indicator is a small piece of information that is recognized to be far less than a full measure of the underlying thing but there are good reasons to accept as indicative of it. An indicator is relevantly indicative of a thing when

- it reasonably portrays the size or extent of the thing;

- it is correctly sensitive to differences: if there is more of the thing here than there, the indicator reflects that difference;

- it is correctly sensitive to change: if the thing changes, the indicator changes accordingly; and

- it is insensitive to irrelevant differences and changes.

A fortunate advantage of moving from measurement to social reporting is that we no longer need a precise operational definition of poverty. We need a theory of the problem, as I have tried to lay it out in this essay, but there is no need to move from there to a specific definition. That would only be needed if we wanted to measure the thing, but since that is not our intention we can dispense with the futility of imposing on the unmeasurable a definition for the purpose of its measurement. No one has been able to meaningfully define poverty precisely enough for its measurement. The beauty of social reporting is that we do not need more by way of definition than it is possible to find.

THE POVERTY MATRIX

At the heart of the indicators approach is a simple but powerful idea. We are concerned with a problem that is endlessly complex. Some of us know something about it from our own and other research. In our broader community, others—such as citizens and policy makers—ask us to use what we know to tell them how things stand. If we try to tell them all we know, we will fail to enlighten them. Although we know much, there is also much we do not know, and even what we know is only qualified knowledge. If we try to tell the story using as much as possible of the knowledge we have, it will inevitably get bogged down in endless details, caveats, qualifications, and reservations. Those whom we are addressing will not be able to understand what we are trying to say. As far as they are concerned, their question remains unanswered.

The alternative to answering the question fully, which is impossible, is to answer it selectively. It is to use our knowledge to extract essential and strategic information that is selected and designed to enlighten those who ask us what the problem looks like. We do not know enough about the problem to say exactly how big or severe it is. But it leaves footprints in the lives of people and we should know enough to understand what footprints to look for and how to display the evidence they contain. This is an odd job for scientists. Their instinct is to amass information and still warn about the uncertainty of it all. The logic of indicators is to cut to the bone and select information ruthlessly, and then to be assertive about the big story that is told with the small images.

We look not for a single footprint, then, but for patterns of footprints. Before turning to specific indicators, we need an instrument to give order to the pattern of indicators we are looking for. For that purpose, I propose a *poverty matrix*, the logic of which follows from the discussions above. The matrix as given in table 4.2 shows the categories of information for which we will need empirical indicators.

In cells 1 and 2, we need indicators of the degree to which people suffer severe deprivation in personal efficiency. In cells 3 and 4 follow indicators of severe deprivation in social efficiency, and in cells 5 and 6 are indicators of risk.

TABLE 4.2
The Poverty Matrix

| | Forms of Deprivation | |
	Physical Capital	*Human Capital*
Degrees of deprivation		
Destitution	Cell 1	Cell 2
Want	Cell 3	Cell 4
Vulnerability	Cell 5	Cell 6

AN EMPIRICAL EXPERIMENT

In 1972, an extensive survey of living conditions was conducted in Norway for the purpose of compiling a comprehensive set of social indicators on styles and quality of life in that population.[29] That was subsequently followed up by the Central Bureau of Statistics in surveys in later years using the same framework.[30] From these surveys we can extract time series of social-indicator data covering a period of about thirty years. Those time series allow us to follow changes in living conditions in one of the world's richest countries over a period of rapid economic growth.

Around 1990, the Fafo Institute for Applied International Studies in Oslo launched a program of applying the framework of the Norwegian surveys to poor trouble-ridden countries in the world. This started in the Palestinian Occupied Territories on the West Bank and the Gaza Strip, in a research project (funded by the Norwegian Ministry of Foreign Affairs and the Ford Foundation) that contributed to bringing about the "Oslo process" of talks between the Israelis and Palestinians, which led to the 1993 Oslo Accords that were sealed in a meeting between the Israeli Prime Minister Yitzhak Rabin, PLO Chairman Yasser Arafat, and U.S. President Bill Clinton on the lawn of the White House on 13 September 1993.[31] Fafo subsequently obtained the support of the Norwegian Ministry of Foreign Affairs and others to conduct similar surveys in a range of countries and regions, from post-Soviet Latvia to most recently post-Saddam Iraq. These surveys have used some questions identical to those used in the Norwegian surveys. From this material we can therefore extract cross-sectional comparisons of countries that range from the moderately poor

---

[29] Rødseth et al. 1976.
[30] www.ssb.no/emner/00/02/.
[31] The project is described in Heiberg and Øvensen 1994.

to the very poor using the same social indicators as those in the time series for Norway.[32]

These data are unique in the world as a source of comparative social indicators on poverty. They make it possible to compile cross-sectional comparisons between pretty much the richest and best-organized country in the world to pretty much the poorest and most disorganized one and a time series over thirty years for the richest country in that comparison, all with an identical battery of social indicators. The available surveys are, in addition to Norway, for Latvia, 1994; Jordan, 1997; Palestinian refugee settlements in Jordan, 1999; Palestinian refugee settlements in Syria, 2001; Haiti, 2001–2; and Iraq, 2004.

The comparisons I am able to make here are determined by where the relevant surveys were conducted and by what is contained in the data generated by those surveys. The sample of countries and territories is therefore a bit eccentric but certainly not uninteresting. The data sets contain indicators that are eminently pertinent and relevant for the present purpose but the indicators are nevertheless chosen from those available in surveys that were designed for purposes other than the present one. Not many questions are shared among all the surveys I have needed to draw on. Some other available indicators were discarded for this purpose after tests showed they were not relevantly sensitive—for example, indicators of functional health—but the choice of indicators has in large measure been dictated by availability. In the end, I use one indicator for each of the six cells in the matrix, and for each indicator I disaggregate by gender and age.

The logic of the indicators approach is that the indicators should be read as being indicative of their underlying thing, not as measures of themselves. Hence, when I use "living without stable, piped drinking water" as the indicator of destitution in physical capital, I read the incidence on that indicator as evidence of destitution rather than of water deprivation specifically.

The indicators of destitution are "absolute": they have the same operational definition in all countries. The indicator of destitution in physical capital is living without piped drinking water. That is a sign of raw destitution and, we can safely assume, one of the first things anyone would want to improve if one could.[33] The indicator of destitution in human capital is elementary functional illiteracy.

---

[32] The first Fafo survey, that in the Palestinian areas, is not available for the present purpose.

[33] Of course, there are people who would freely choose a lifestyle in which they sacrifice even this elementary level of comfort, for example, hermit monks in certain religious groups.

The indicators of want are "relative": the operational definition changes with circumstances. The indicator of want in physical capital is reported inability to afford adequate food and clothing on a regular basis. We must assume that respondents answer this question in the context of their experience of consumption and spending expectations in their society. The indicator of want in human capital is lack of education beyond the compulsory level in the particular society. That level of education varies between countries in a way that reflects differences in the social understanding of necessary minimum education.[34]

The indicators of vulnerability are meant to capture the risks of falling into destitution or want. Vulnerability in physical capital is indicated by fear among those who are in the labour force of losing their livelihood. Vulnerability in human capital is indicated by being neither in the workforce nor in school among those who are at the age of entering into independent social lives.

The statistics in tables 4.3 to 4.5, at the end of the chapter, are an extract of the full set of estimates made. The data are from ten separate surveys: six international ones and four for Norway. This is compressed into three condensed tables, but behind these tables are more extensive underlying data that help the information in the tables to be read with confidence.

FINDINGS

There are two substantive questions: what does the problem of poverty look like, and has poverty been eradicated where that should have happened? And one methodological question: does the indicators approach work?

On the problem of poverty, observe first the poorest country in the comparison in table 4.3, Haiti. No doubt, any way of estimating poverty would show it to be widespread in this population. However, if poverty is estimated as relative-income poverty, it would be identified in a level of income below some definition of the average and therefore probably to a proportion of the population around or below one-half. Fafo did produce estimates of this kind, from the same survey data used here, and found the incidence of income poverty to be 48 percent and of extreme income

---

[34] I use the terms "absolute" and "relative" with displeasure. It is a misunderstanding that has caused much confusion in poverty research that absolute and relative definitions of poverty represent competing theories. As I have shown elsewhere (Ringen 1988), poverty has always been seen to be relative, and there never was such a thing as an absolute theory.

poverty to be 31 percent.[35] That clearly understates the true problem of poverty in that country and understates it severely.

In the social indicators profile for Haiti, destitution is near universal. That is the case in physical capital irrespective of age and gender, and in human capital for the elderly. In the nonelderly group, human capital destitution does not afflict nearly everyone but still afflicts well above half the population. This is a truly devastating picture of overwhelming, raw, and desperate misery. It is a level of misery the relative income measure does not and cannot communicate.

Destitution being near universal, the subsequent statistics for Haiti might be of less practical interest. In theory, when almost everyone lives in destitution, almost no one should be in want or be vulnerable. However, these indicators are not defined in this hierarchical manner. In this population, want, like destitution, describes the way the vast majority of the population live. Under vulnerability, the majority of those who are in the labor force (which should include most of those not in destitution or want) are in fear of losing their job. Here, then, the problem of poverty touches almost everyone, including those who have a livelihood as a very high risk of losing it. The lower frequency of vulnerability in human capital is not easy to interpret but could suggest that this indicator, although the best one available for the purpose, may not be as reliably sensitive as it should be.

At the other extreme, the case of Norway, the picture is *totally* different. There, destitution is nonexistent. (I do not have actual data on the human-capital indicator, but we can safely take it that elementary functional illiteracy is near nonexistent; it is something it has not been considered worth asking in the surveys. The comparison with Latvia, where the question has been asked, bears that out.)

The comparison between Haiti and Norway shows the enormity of difference in the world in the experience of poverty, from national populations in which poverty in its most desperate manifestation is near universal to populations that are spared raw material degradation. This total schism in the world between those who are at the top and those at the bottom fails to come through in relative income comparisons. Those comparisons do not display poverty by what it *is*. They reduce it to abstract relativities and therefore do not tell us what the problem looks like. The incidence of relative-income poverty in Haiti in these data is, as mentioned above, about between 30 and 50 percent. In Norway, relative-income poverty is typically estimated to be about between 2 and 10 percent, and sometimes up towards 20 percent.[36] This is still different, but these relativ-

---

[35] Direct communication from Jon Pedersen of Fafo.
[36] www.ssb.no/emner/05/01. See also www.fami.no.

ities also reduce the difference between top and bottom in the world to a relative one.

Even in the Norwegian case, deprivation in the form of want is reported, but as it is near universal in Haiti, here it is near nonexistent. A mere 2 to 3 percent reported that they, in the context of other social expectations on spending, are not in the position that they can afford new clothing or fish or meat regularly. Those in want of human capital are about as many (or few) among the young but are more numerous among the elderly, who obviously have a lower level of education. Hence, the only figures of any significance to indicate a real incidence of want in this population are figures that survive in the elderly from previous social conditions that no longer afflict those who are now growing up in this society.

Between the two extremes in table 4.3, the indicators display patterns that make good sense. The social indicators approach appears capable of reporting on the problem of poverty in a way that is relevantly sensitive to the real experience of poverty in the world. That is supported further in table 4.4, which compares Jordan, Palestinian refugee settlements in Jordan, and Palestinian refugee settlements in Syria. These are populations living side by side in the same part of the world, yet are obviously very different populations. The refugee populations live under different political regimes and have origins different from the Jordanian national population, and the two refugee populations are again of different origins. In this comparison we should expect sensitive indicators to display different profiles of poverty, which indeed they do. The more detailed interpretation of just what those differences mean is beyond the scope of this experiment; here I take this display as further evidence of the sensitivity of the indicators approach, even when operationalized in a simple battery of indicators, as here.

Does Norway display a case of poverty having been eradicated? The portrait we can hold up to the Norwegians about the experience of poverty in their country at the beginning of the twenty-first century shows no destitution, very low and diminishing levels of want, and some frequency of vulnerability. How should they interpret that portrait? On destitution there is nothing to interpret: destitution is eradicated.[37] What about the remains of want? That which is age-specific is disappearing year by year. What is recorded as want in human capital looks like this: Compulsory

---

[37] No doubt there are people who live in destitute circumstances, for example, those who are homeless. All we can say about them statistically is that they number fewer than to be recorded as a survey statistic. Whether homelessness or, for example, begging manifests a problem of poverty in the circumstances of that country is a matter of judgment. It is probably right to say that social assistance and services are such that no one is homeless or begging by inescapable necessity.

education is nine years of schooling. Only 4 to 5 percent of the relatively young are without *more* than what is defined as the minimum necessity in this country. Is that a basis to censure this society in the name of poverty? That's for the Norwegians to decide when they observe themselves through this mirror.

Two to three percent reported that they cannot afford basic necessities. What does that mean in moral terms? If we look to the comparison, we see that these frequencies are much lower than even in the nearest country of comparison, Latvia. Could they conceivably be lower? We know a bit more about who reported this nonaffordability. There were 3,892 respondents aged thirty to sixty-nine. Of those, 108 were "poor" by an income definition (equivalent income less than 50 percent of the median), or 2.8 percent. Of those again, 13 percent reported that they could not afford new clothing or fish and meat regularly, which is only a slightly higher frequency than in the population average. More than nine out of ten of those who reported nonaffordability are above poverty level by the income definition. The Norwegians need to decide if what they see here is poverty in the sense of unacceptable deprivation. In the last couple of years, the terminology of poverty has again come into use in political language in that country. Outside observers, say officials in the Barbados Ministry of Social Transformation, who are at work to eradicate what is really poverty from their social landscape, might be excused for finding that somewhat odd.

If we were to conclude from what we now know about destitution and want this to be a case of poverty having been eradicated, we might find the data on vulnerability rather irrelevant. One cannot be vulnerable to poverty where poverty has been eradicated. Still, a relatively high number of people who are in the workforce feel that they are at risk of losing their jobs, and a fair number of young people are without a foothold in either education or work.

Table 4.5 gives some additional evidence on the Norwegian case. Only in 2003 was destitution eradicated. Up until then, there were still remains of destitution in the Norwegian population—not much, but some. Want in physical capital appears stable, which may support the view that this indicator has gotten about as low as it can get. In human capital the trend is downward, which suggests also that if we discount the age effect, this indicator may be about as low as it can get. From what we have seen above about the sensitivity of these indicators, we have reason to trust these trends and nontrends to be real. This table, I think, may support a recommendation that the Norwegians might, on this evidence, declare poverty to have been eradicated in their country. Vulnerability persists, however, although it is not entirely clear what the vulnerability is to.

Some further conclusions can be drawn from these tables. First, even in countries that are comparatively advanced in the world economically and politically, the problem of poverty typically persists on a shocking scale. Compare Latvia in 1994 and Norway in 1995: these are socially very different worlds.

Second, there are countries in the world whose populations are utterly and shamefully neglected and unprotected against raw poverty. What is by any standard unacceptable is allowed to exist in a way that can have no moral excuse.

Third, there may be a pattern in these data that may suggest some regularities on the road towards the eradication of poverty. Destitution may be less widespread and less difficult to eradicate in human capital than physical capital, but want may linger more stubbornly in human capital than in physical capital. If life chances that are free from destitution and want are a possibility, though a distant one for most people of the world, life without some fear that there is a risk of economic unfreedom does not seem to be within reach.

Fourth, there may be a pattern in these data to suggest some regularities in the social distribution of poverty. The elderly are not more subject to deprivation in physical capital than younger people, nor women more than men. In human capital, however, the old are more exposed than the young, and women more than men. If there is a gender distribution in poverty, these social indicators suggest that it manifests itself particularly in human capital deprivation.

CONCLUSION

Two centuries ago, the dream was born that people could live together without the blight of poverty. For those who have harbored that dream, there is some good news and some bad news. The good news is that poverty is demonstrably something that *can* be eradicated. That is a very notable conclusion, as poverty research until now has been inconclusive on this question.

The bad news is that although eradicable, poverty is very difficult to eradicate. Even in the test case of Norway, which is unique in the world in terms of wealth, equality, and welfare state provisions, remains of even destitution have lingered until the very last observation in our time series.

If we are bold enough to suggest, from these simple data, that it happened at the beginning of the present century, for the first time in human history, that poverty was eradicated from a social landscape, we also have to note that this is observed only in a tiny corner of the entire social landscape of humanity, that this corner of prosperity is beyond the reach of the majority of mankind, and that poverty was not eradicated until two hundred years after the idea was born, one hundred years after the welfare state started to take shape, and sixty years after it started to be made universal. It should have happened much earlier and much more widely, and it is an embarrassment that it has not. The United Nations now wants it to be achieved in the rest of the world. That is a glorious ambition but one that has history against it.[38]

I deliberately described the present empirical exercise as an experiment. It is an experiment in the rehabilitation of social indicators. The criterion against which I have tested that approach is its ability to produce comparative results with a consistent sensitivity that has eluded the income approach. I test this by using a battery of indicators that are pertinent according to a theory of the problem of poverty and by applying that battery to the kinds of cross-sectional and over-time comparisons in which income approach results are indeterminate. In particular, I test it by its ability to generate meaningful comparisons across the divide between poor and rich countries.

This experiment is, I think, successful. It is obvious to anyone—including myself, of course—that what I have to go by is no more than a handful of elementary indicators. What is surprising, however, at least to me, is how sensitive that battery of indicators has proved to be. These indicators tell stories of differences and trends in poverty in the world that are entirely believable. They bring to the surface facts about world poverty that have been concealed in relative income comparisons. And they bring to the surface precisely such facts that have made relative income comparisons difficult to believe. The experience is the same here as with the indicators of democratic quality in chapter 1. Social indicators, when sensibly selected and compiled, are a powerful instrument for the display and comparison of complex social phenomena.

From this, I draw the conclusion that there is a capacity in the social indicators approach for social reporting on the problem of poverty with a robustness that the income approach has not been able to deliver and that we are here on the way towards finding the apparatus to inform the world about the problem of poverty not as an abstract theoretical relativity but as it really is experienced in the lives of women, men, children, and families.

However, what I have offered is in no way a final recipe for social reporting on poverty. There is more work to do on the theoretical founda-

---

[38] The operational goal of reducing "extreme poverty" in the world by half by 2015 is possibly achievable as extreme poverty is defined in the Millennium Development Goals framework (less than one dollar a day). If it is accomplished, that is likely to be mainly thanks to progress in China and India and in spite of no or much less progress in other

tion and on the politics of social reporting. It remains to be explained inescapably that poverty is unacceptable and to establish the earnestness of the idea that what this means is that poverty should be eradicated. The poverty matrix is sound, in my opinion, but the specifics of the matrix applied are not necessarily the final ones. The idea of using a battery of indicators that are reported in raw form and without being pulled into a final index is sound, in my opinion, but there may be arguments for doing both (which I discuss in appendix F). The indicators I have been able to use are good and pertinent, but are not necessarily the ones I would have used had it been possible to design indicators specifically for the purpose. With richer data, it might have been possible to draw on more, and more detailed, indicators and to display the experience of deprivation and risk more precisely. Destitution, want, and vulnerability are, in principle, hierarchical levels of deprivation, but I have here not been able to treat them in this way empirically. Hence much work remains. While this experiment does, I think, give some new answers to old questions and should help us towards a better understanding of poverty and unacceptability, it also sets an agenda for further research.

---

areas, notably Africa south of the Sahara. See World Bank, *Global Monitoring Report 2005*, worldbank.org/global-monitoring.

TABLE 4.3
Comparative Indicators of Deprivation in Selected Countries

	Haiti 2001–2	Iraq 2004	Jordan 1997	Latvia 1994	Norway 2003
Destitution					
Physical capital					
Men 0–9	95	49	23	22	0
Men 30–39	93	45	23	16	0
Men 60–69	96	42	23	21	0
Women 0–9	95	49	22	23	0
Women 30–39	93	45	21	14	0
Women 60–69	93	41	24	21	0
Human capital					
Men 30–39	54	16	26	—	—
Men 60–69	84	57	30	2	—
Women 30–39	67	34	33	—	—
Women 60–69	90	87	47	2	—
Want					
Physical capital					
Men 0–9	72	25	na	13	3
Men 30–39	66	24	na	10	3
Men 60–69	73	24	na	15	1
Women 0–9	70	24	na	14	3
Women 30–39	66	25	na	11	4
Women 60–69	71	25	na	19	2
Human capital					
Men 30–39	75	61	51	14	5
Men 60–69	91	82	91	55	24
Women 30–39	82	74	61	9	4
Women 60–69	93	94	97	54	33
Vulnerability					
Physical capital					
Men 30–39	60	na	69	51	19
Men 50–59	na	na	80	59	19
Women 30–39	78	na	88	51	21
Women 50–59	na	na	56	64	20
Human capital					
Men 15–19	21	24	15	10	7
Men 20–24	29	25	24	20	9
Women 15–19	29	62	28	9	7
Women 20–24	51	79	76	26	9
N (respondents)	33,004	130,861	35,593	8,900	5,872

— = negligible; na = not available

Indicators

Destitution

Physical capital: % not living in a residence with stable piped drinking water (Norway, hot water).
Human capital: % who cannot, without difficulty, write a letter to a friend.

Want

Physical capital: % who cannot afford either new clothing or fish/meat three times a week.
Human capital: % with no education beyond the compulsory level in the country.

Vulnerability

Physical capital: % in fear of losing their job (persons in the labor force).
Human capital: % not in education and not in employment.

TABLE 4.4
Comparative Indicators Of Deprivation In Selected Countries

	Jordan 1997	Jordan, Settlements 1999	Syria, Settlements 2001
Destitution			
Physical Capital			
Men 0–9	23	59	23
Men 30–39	23	61	24
Men 60–69	23	63	15
Women 0–9	22	60	23
Women 30–39	21	62	24
Women 60–69	24	68	16
Human Capital			
Men 30–39	26	12	8
Men 60–69	30	56	20
Women 30–39	33	20	9
Women 60–69	47	97	43
Want			
Physical Capital			
Men 0–9	na	48	39
Men 30–39	na	42	35
Men 60–69	na	51	35
Women 0–9	na	48	38
Women 30–39	na	49	35
Women 60–69	na	56	37
Human Capital			
Men 30–39	51	65	47
Men 60–69	91	96	60
Women 30–39	61	63	40
Women 60–69	97	99	71
Vulnerability			
Physical Capital			
Men 30–39	69	47	49
Men 50–59	80	na	21
Women 30–39	88	25	27
Women 50–59	56	na	18
Human Capital			
Men 15–19	15	18	19
Men 20–24	24	24	19
Women 15–19	28	40	43
Women 20–24	76	78	69
N (Respondents)	35,593	16,347	27,030

— = negligible; na = not available

Indicators

Destitution
Physical capital: % not living in a residence with stable piped drinking water (Norway, hot water).
Human capital: % who cannot, without difficulty, write a letter to a friend.
Want
Physical capital: % who cannot afford either new clothing or fish/meat three times a week.
Human capital: % with no education beyond the compulsory level in the country.
Vulnerability
Physical capital: % in fear of losing their job (persons in the labor force).
Human capital: % not in education and not in employment.

TABLE 4.5
Comparative Indicators of Deprivation in Norway

	1973	1987	1995	2003
Destitution				
Physical Capital				
Men 0–9	na	0	0	0
Men 30–39	1	2	1	0
Men 60–69	3	1	2	0
Women 0–9	na	1	0	0
Women 30–39	1	1	0	0
Women 60–69	3	2	0	0
Human Capital				
Men 30–39	na	na	na	—
Men 60–69	na	na	na	—
Women 30–39	na	na	na	—
Women 60–69	na	na	na	—
Want				
Physical Capital				
Men 0–9	na	na	2	3
Men 30–39	na	2	2	3
Men 60–69	na	0	1	1
Women 0–9	na	na	1	3
Women 30–39	na	4	2	4
Women 60–69	na	2	1	2
Human Capital				
Men 30–39	17	17	9	5
Men 60–69	59	37	34	24
Women 30–39	23	19	13	4
Women 60–69	58	52	49	33
Vulnerability				
Physical Capital				
Men 30–39	7	9	17	19
Men 50–59	9	11	12	18
Women 30–39	10	10	14	21
Women 50–59	8	8	14	20
Human Capital				
Men 15–19	19	10	8	7
Men 20–24	7	10	15	9
Women 15–19	18	4	7	7
Women 20–24	45	11	14	9
N (Respondents)	2,966	3,952	3,720	5,872

— = negligible; na = not available

Indicators

Destitution

Physical capital: % not living in a residence with piped water (from 1995, hot water).

Human capital: % who cannot, without difficulty, write a letter to a friend.

Want

Physical capital: % who cannot afford either new clothing or fish/meat three times a week (1987, not meat or fish at least every second day).

Human capital: % with no education beyond the compulsory level in the country.

Vulnerability

Physical capital: % in fear of losing their job (persons in the labor force).

Human capital: % not in education and not in employment.

CHAPTER 5

What Do Families Do?

> The greatest, however, of all the means we have mentioned
> for assuring the stability of constitutions—but one which is
> nowadays generally neglected—is the education of citizens in
> the spirit of their constitution. There is no advantage in the
> best of laws, even when they are sanctioned by general civic
> consent, if citizens themselves have not been attuned, by the
> force of habit and the influence of teaching, to the right
> constitutional temper.
> —Aristotle, *The Politics*

THERE IS A VIEW—let us call it the postmodern theory—that the family is
an old-fashioned institution and ill-suited for survival in a modern society.
This view owes much to a premodern inspiration, Friedrich Engels's unfortunate but influential analysis in *The Origin of the Family, Private
Property, and the State* (1884). He thought that the family takes its form
by what is historically necessary and that there is therefore a particular
kind of family that emerges with industrial capitalism. This is the family
that is best suited to the reproduction and daily re-creation of industrial
labor and that specializes in that task. By extension, if the industrial age
created a kind of family that was functional to its needs, we would expect
that family to fall into obsolescence with the passing of industrialism.

The family of the industrial age came to be called the *nuclear family*—
the small family of mother and father and children—private, withdrawn

*Family analysis is, in my experience, the most difficult of any social analysis and one that
one never really gets completely right. This essay pulls together years of work on my part
on family demography, family economics, and family policy. I have during those years benefited from a long dialogue with Norwegian demographers, in particular Turid Noack and
Lars Østby of the Norwegian Central Bureau of Statistics, and on family policy with my
friend and colleague Kari Wærness. I am no less grateful to David Coleman of Oxford
for his always generous help on matters demographic. For the important discussion of the
cohabitation convention, I have included the main elements of a lecture titled "Marriage
and Cohabitation—What's the Difference?" I gave at the Max Planck Institute for Demographic Research in Rostock at the invitation of Jan Hoëm. For that lecture, in turn, I drew
on a consensus meeting on cohabitation of the Norwegian Demographic Society, for which
I drafted and subsequently revised a consensus document. A previous essay on which I build
here is from a book in Norwegian,* Veien til det gode liv, *and I am grateful for support*

from economy and polity, and dedicated to itself. We now know that Engels was mistaken about the origins of the modern family, indeed about the very existence of any type of family peculiar to the industrial age. Much changed with the industrial revolution, including in families, but the overriding experience in family organization was continuity. Engels thought the industrial revolution would have to result in family revolution and went on to say that it did, but those who have observed the matter have seen no such revolution. Yet somehow, when it comes to family history there is a temptation to believe presupposition more than evidence. Peter Laslett, the historical demographer, has summed it up forcefully: "The delusion about marriageable age is, perhaps, the most conspicuous of all the errors we seem to want to make about everyday life in the old world, but is not the only one. More far reaching in its consequences for the view we take of ourselves, and the plans we make for our society and its welfare, is the supposition that the family group in the pre-industrial world was large. It is erroneously believed that it was large because it contained whole groups of kinsfolk living together. . . . In any case, and this seems to be the most deep-seated and important generalisation of all, in the familial, patriarchal world the family was seen as the source of welfare. Sickness, unemployment, bereavement were all the responsibility of the family, and so to a large extent was education. To fulfil all these functions the family in the old world would have to be large. Something like this seems to be the general impression of family life among our ancestors. But their families were *not* large, at least the average family was relatively small. In fact the evidence we now have suggests that household size was remarkably constant in England at all times from the late sixteenth until the early twentieth century."[1]

Still, the idea persists that modernization gave birth to the small nuclear family, that the nuclear family is the family of its age, and that we are now entering a new age and that the nuclear family's time is up. Modernization, we often believe, means an increasingly sophisticated division of labor between increasingly specialized institutions. While the traditional family—so the story goes—did both production and private life, the industrial age did not need families for productive purposes. The economy had become a market economy and production was lifted out of families, leaving them to concentrate on what remained and hence reduced to satisfying social and emotional needs only. The family was "marginalised" because it had fewer functions to perform.

---

in that round from Erling Kagge and Kristin Johansen. The context of this essay is the contemporary European demographic regime of low fertility and low immigration.

[1] Laslett 1971, p. 93.

However, the family as an exclusively social institution is a myth. The emergence of the nuclear family was a myth, and so is its passing. In fact, any story that is told in the language of *the* family is likely to be mythology. It is true that families today are on average smaller than, say, a century ago, but that is not because they are no longer "extended"; it's just that there are fewer children. Families remain what they have been: versatile and relevant for the satisfaction of a range of human needs.

How We Live Now

A family is a household of at least two people who live together on a more or less permanent basis.[2] A person who lives alone is a household but not a family. A lone parent and a child are a family. Two adults who live together in marriage or cohabitation, with or without children, are a family. If there are three adults, for example if grandmother moves in, it is still a family. "Family" is obviously more: it extends to kin (and sometimes to friends as when children call their parents' close friends "auntie" and "uncle"), but it is not kinship and the like I am concerned with here; it is the meaning of living together that interests me. (For convenience I use the term *families* although I should probably use *family households*.)

Most people live most of their lives in families. This is as true in modern affluent industrial and postindustrial societies as it has ever been. Almost all children grow up in a family. Now as previously, the family in which a child grows up may change during his or her childhood, sometimes radically—previously, for example, often as the result of the death of a parent, now more often as a result of separation or divorce—but nonfamily childhoods are extremely rare.

Adults, too, generally live in families. Most of them live with someone else and most of those who live alone are either young adults who are not yet in a family or older adults who have family life behind them. In many European countries, adults living alone are a growing (if still small) proportion in the population but that is a snapshot statistic resulting from many demographic trends, including longevity and thereby more widowers and, in particular, widows living alone; rising numbers of students and of young people moving out of the parental home earlier or before marrying and therefore more young people living alone for a while; and more

---

[2] This is a broader definition than some might find palatable, but I think it is good: it makes "togetherness" the defining principle. Some family sociologists may object, but then family sociology is a science that has not defined or even wanted to define its object. As a result, family sociology suffers from an excess of discourse and a shortage of forceful analysis. That void is then filled by others who have at least instruments of analysis to bring in, notably by economic demography as pioneered by Becker 1981, a tradition I follow here.

divorce and separation, followed by more middle-aged people living alone, often temporarily. If an ideal of singlehood is emerging, it is not something that at least yet adds up to significant numbers. Many adults experience family disruption during the course of their lives, typically as a result of divorce or separation, but that does not seem to discourage their attraction to family life: increasing rates of separation and divorce are followed by increasing rates of re-cohabitation and remarriage.

In a more or less typical European population, modern living arrangements are as follows:

· About one person in four lives with a spouse and children under the age of eighteen.

· About one in five is a child who lives with both parents.

· About one in six lives with a spouse, but not with children.

· About one in seven lives alone.

These four groups make up 75 percent of the population. The rest divide about equally between single-parent families and cohabitants with or without children—families again in other words. Only one in seven in the entire population lives alone at any point in time, and that includes people who have previously lived with others and some who will later on.

The children (under age eighteen) in this population live as follows:

· Two out of three live with married parents.

· One in nine lives with cohabiting parents.

· One in six lives with a lone mother; one in sixty with a lone father.

· Almost eight in ten children who live at home live with both parents.

· Fewer than two in ten children do not have siblings in the family.

If there is anything atypical in this tableau, it would be that the frequency of informal cohabitation is on the high side.[3]

---

[3] This is the present Norwegian population. I owe this illuminating arrangement of the data to Turid Noack. These statistics may be slightly deceptive. Much is in rapid change in family arrangements and statistics lag behind. Almost all partnerships in Norway now start in cohabitation rather than marriage. Social trends suggest that possibly a third of all women and four in ten men will remain unmarried. Two generations ago, this proportion was about 5 percent. More new marriages and cohabitations are likely to be dissolved than to last the life. About half of all children are born outside of wedlock.

So if we ask how people today arrange their lives and life courses, one firm answer must be that life is usually lived in families.

The Productivity of Families

What do all those people, who in their many ways live family lives, do? Do they retreat to their families every now and then, say, in the evenings and for the purpose of re-creation so that they can be ready to go back into society next day and engage in the real business of life? That is perhaps one way of seeing it, but it would better represent the facts to turn it around: families are where people live, except every now and then when some family members go off for work or education in order to re-create family life. Full-time workers will be out for work no more than forty to forty-five hours a week, and fewer than that on average if we calculate in holidays and vacations. If they sleep eight hours a night, that still leaves seventy to eighty hours of the week. For those who do not work or go to school, or who do so part-time, there is all the more time left over. Over the life course, full-time workers clock up more free time, particularly in typically twenty to thirty years of retirement. What may look like time left over in fact makes up the bulk of our living time. And the bulk of that time again is used for family life. This is not to say that it is free time; much of it is work, although not paid work in the market. Nor is all family time spent in the family home or with all family members together. Family life is also spent with kin and friends, or away on holidays, sometimes the family as a group and sometimes not.

These little communities of two, three, four, and very occasionally five or more persons, in which people are engaged in nothing more dramatic than going about the business of daily life together, and some in periods of having and raising children, are in fact remarkably productive institutions. The story is about that this is no longer true, that the family that in olden times had many functions to fulfill has now become marginal because it is bereft of functions. But that is a fairy tale.

The Engels-inspired postmodern theory predicts that modern families are not engaged in economic production. They may be sites of all manner of social and emotional life, but institutions of economic production they are not. The way to confront this theory is not to go on about the social significance of families but to investigate their economics. If it should turn out that modern families are economic institutions, the whole theory of the marginalized modern family simply falls and no reason would remain to listen to it. This theory is built on the assumption that it is specifically economic functions that families no longer perform. Testing the veracity of that assumption puts the theory to its decisive test.

In a study of within-family economies in contemporary Britain, I have done just that.[4] What I found is that modern families continue to be extraordinarily important as economic institutions. By economic institutions, I mean institutions that contribute to people's economic standard of living. That includes farms, fisheries, manufacturing plants, stores and supermarkets, service organizations, and the like. But also families. People get access to the standard of living that is generated in the economy in various ways, importantly of course by buying goods and services in the market, and also through rights to public services. But since they generally live in families and spend much of their time in family life and engage in various activities there, it is unlikely that their standard of living is something they get exclusively from outside of the family. We would hardly have invented the idea of living together unless that contributed to our well-being, and that is likely to include economic as well as social benefits.

Once we start to think systematically about it, it is easy enough to see that togetherness in family life does indeed contribute to our economic standard of living. First, families produce goods and services. The things we buy in markets are, by and large, raw materials that we process further at home. We do this with the help of labor, now called housework, and capital, such as stoves and tools—straightforward production in other words. A meal produced at home, for example, obviously has more value than the groceries from the supermarket that go into it. We do this kind of work all the time. Even if you buy a chocolate bar, it takes a tiny bit of additional work to remove the wrapping before you can enjoy it. That's work. Make no mistake about it: some people pay servants to do it for them. The Prince of Wales is said to have a servant to squeeze out toothpaste for him onto his toothbrush. We usually do not pay each other for family housework, at least not directly, but what is being done is no less production for that.

Second, family members cooperate. They cooperate in production. Two people can usually produce a meal more efficiently together than one alone, provided they are able to cooperate and do not get in each other's way too much. This is the same as in any other enterprise of production: cooperative division of labor adds to productivity. Families, furthermore, are, economically speaking, also institutions of consumption—most of what is produced in a family is also consumed in that family (although some may be given away to others or exchanged or sold)—and family cooperation extends to consumption. If I live in a house, what I consume is not the house but the housing I get out of it. If a second person moves into the same house, he or she will also have housing from that same

---

[4] Ringen 2005a.

house without taking away from me the housing I already have from it (at least not much until the family grows to the point that the house starts to get crowded). As by magic, two people have housing for the price of one house. We share many things in families: furniture, books, newspapers, cars, tools, TV sets, stereos, computers, and so on endlessly. It makes a great deal of economic sense for people to live together as compared with everyone living on their own.

Families themselves therefore, in what we usually do not think of as anything else than perfectly ordinary daily life, create value through production and cooperation. That's the way family life adds to the economic standard of living of family members. There is value added in family life. Note value *added*. We cannot be rich, or hardly even live, by family production alone. Families need raw materials to work on, and the primary source of affluence lies in the productivity we are able to mobilize in mainly market work in the production of goods that families subsequently process further into consumption goods for family members.

This value can be estimated. My estimates show that the value of consumption that comes from production and co-operation within families is equal to, or actually a bit more than equal to, the value of goods and services those families can buy in the market for their income. The standard of living is usually measured by the value of goods and services available in the market, with possibly some adjustments for free public services, but that is severely wrong. Goods and services brought into the family home are processed further there before they reemerge as consumption for family members. This further processing more than doubles their value. The most recent estimates I was able to make (with access to the complicated data sets needed for this kind of exercise) were for 1986, where I found that the family economy added 113 percent to the value per person of goods and services available in the market.

This was an astonishing finding, at least for me. My experiments were entirely conventional economic analysis, relying on straight and narrow concepts of production and consumption and not conjured forth by any kind of expanded definition of the economic. They were designed so as to understate rather than overstate the economic size of the family sector. For example, I included only the production of such goods and services as could have been bought in the market and imputed no value for the production of emotional goods or the consumption of leisure. The values I did estimate were cautiously on the low side. In this modern economy, then, it turns out that families today do what families have always done: they produce material goods. And they do that on a massive scale. If this finding is unexpected, it is unexpected only because we are no longer used to thinking about family life in this way. But it should probably not be surprising when we consider, again, that most people live most of their lives in family life.

From these analyses, I drew the conclusion that in a modern economy such as the British one, half of the nation's economy is family economy. So much for the family that is only social and not economic.

But even that is not the full story. The argument needs to be expanded. Families produce not only consumption narrowly understood but also another important if elusive commodity: care.

My colleague Kari Wærness, of the University of Bergen, did early and pioneering work to estimate the value of family care for children, the elderly, and the ill. The simple idea was to see care as a matter of production and then to use the very same concepts and methods that are used to estimate production in the money economy. She found, in Norway in the early 1970s, that nonpaid care work in families was on about the same magnitude as total labor input in manufacturing industry.[5] Again, once we observe carefully and estimate and measure with the tools and language of economics, what we see in family life is production and productivity.

I concluded above that half of the nation's economy is family economy. In that conclusion, I did not take into consideration the production of care. I should have said that *more* than half of the nation's consumption output comes from economic activities in families.

These findings matter for two reasons. First, they prove that modern families are economic institutions and that they are institutions of great significance in the economy. They produce things, including economic goods and values. If a small firm added as much value to its raw materials as an ordinary family does, we would say that it was outstandingly productive. Families are *not* marginal institutions in modern societies.

Furthermore, the findings matter because they explain what it is that makes family life productive. The creation of value in families comes from work, which is to say from *resources*. Families acquire capital for the purpose of production—tools and household equipment—and they use that capital in combination with their own time and labor power. In addition, family productivity comes from *cooperation*; we would call it division of labor if it were in a firm. Family members create value through their cooperation.[6] If everyone lived on their own with the same money

---

[5] Wærness 1978, 1981.

[6] Of course, by co-operation I am not suggesting that family life is always harmonious. Social relations in families can be destructive as well as constructive and can destroy as well as create value. In the film *The War of the Roses*, the couple (played by Kathleen Turner and Michael Douglas) cooperate in the first half to create a beautiful family home and turn to fighting in the second half so that eventually the home they built is "debuilt" and destroyed. A methodologist like myself might say that this was a film about equivalence scales, although it is doubtful that the filmmaker would have been aware of that.

income and did the same amount of housework each on his or her own, the output in consumption value would have been much less.[7]

More Production

We now know quite a bit about modern families. We know they are important institutions in society because they are economically important. We know they are capable of being highly productive because they are productive economically. We know what makes them productive: family members command resources and engage in cooperation. In families, as in any other institution that is in any way in the business of making something, the ability to do it well comes down to resources and cooperation.

I've gone on a bit about these economic matters in order to clear the ground. It is now established, I think, that families are significant institutions in the fabric of modern societies. They contribute. In families, things are created and made to happen; value flows from the ordinary business of family life. There is nothing to suggest that families have become marginal institutions in economic life, hence not generally in society. Families are what families have been, they are where people live their lives and where things they value are created. They are institutions to be taken seriously.

However, my present concern is not with the economic life of families as such but rather with their social life, more precisely with the social life of families and children. Democracy depends on a democratic culture. In chapter 6, I argue that democratic culture depends on citizens being able to live with liberty in a spirit of reason. That ability must be learned, and much of that learning takes place in childhood and while children grow up. This is my entry into family analysis here. Families are political institutions. They are where children come from and grow up and where tomorrow's citizens are created. "The mainspring of people's life chances lies in the family conditions of their childhoods," Gösta Esping-Andersen wrote correctly.[8] That, even more than their economic importance, is reason to take to take families seriously.

The economic analysis is nevertheless relevant. As always in social relations, the economy is the backdrop. The economic approach tells us something useful about how to get a grip on family analysis. The discussion so far has given an indication of how the real business of family life is often more or less invisible because it is shrouded in layers of ignorance

---

[7] In my estimates, about one-third of the value added to the economic standard of living from within-family economies was accounted for by cooperation in consumption. The value of cooperation specifically in production I was unable to estimate separately.

[8] Esping-Andersen et al. 2002, p. 29.

and myth. We may not know very much with certainty about the social life of families, but we must still try to reflect on family life from a frame of mind that enables us to ask what family life actually and practically consists in, what families *do*. Everyone has a stake in their own construction of "the family": postmodernists and functionalists, who see it as marginalized; feminists, who see it as a bastion of male power; gay activists, who see it as anti-same-sex ideology in disguise; religious fundamentalists, who see it as a containment of sexual freedom and women's rights; social engineers, who see it as an erratic small-scale cog in their rationally planned social machinery. The economic analysis shows us a way to cut through this fog and get around our biases. Families, it says, are institutions which *do* things. They are useful, not holy or unholy. It is because value is produced in families that we are and should be concerned with them. What makes family life important in society, outside of the private concerns of each family, is that it is *production*. This directs us to a hard analysis of soft values that takes us around the myriad mythologies of the family to seeing what is actually *done* in families as they actually are and away from fanciful constructions of the family as we think it should be.

This applies as well to families as sites of children's lives. Here, no less than in economic life, families are institutions that produce value. First of all, they produce the children themselves. It is in the nation's families that the population is reproduced and the life of the tribe is perpetuated. Where there are children there are families. Two people obviously do not need to be a family to conceive but most are, and many women and men will often not feel able to take on having children without the support of a family arrangement and without confidence in the durability of that support.

Then families provide for those children. They feed, clothe, and give them a place to live. They give them a home, a place where they can usually be safe and protected.

Families tell children who they are: where they come from, who their grandparents and ancestors are, of what kind they are, where they belong, and what their identity is.

Families teach children values and norms. From parents and in the experience of family cooperation, children learn about the difference between good and bad and right and wrong and acquire the ability to believe in that knowledge.

Families teach children to learn. They teach them how to work and how to be social. The family experience is the basis for success in schooling and formal education. It is in the family that children first learn about discussions, negotiations, and shrewdness; about give-and-take, cooperating and fighting; about what it takes to get on with others; about the combined ability to be flexible and to stand one's ground. Each family is a political academy where children get their grounding experiences of citizenship, of rights and duties, of freedom and responsibility. It is in the family that children learn the elementary virtues of manners, politeness, civility, and charm (or do not learn it, as the case may be).

Families educate children. They teach them to walk and speak, to dress and eat, to wash and brush their teeth, to behave—the thousand and one skills that make up daily life and that all who have learned them perform with intuition and obviousness (and make those who do not know them intolerable people).

All these things these ordinary little institutions provide for. Different families do it in different ways, some do it better than others. They are not alone in these jobs. Families share the raising of children with kin and friends and the training of children with schools and nurseries. But to the question of what families *are*, one answer, also when we see families from the point of view of children, is that they are institutions of production.

Families obviously do more than what they do with and for children. They do economic production, as we now know. They are also sites of private, intimate, and emotional life; of people living close to one another, sharing meals, beds, bathrooms, and tools; of joys and sorrows; of love, resentment, and sometimes hate; of the human condition in its raw form. Families offer people a setting of genuine intimacy with others, for giving and receiving a life of serious and lasting commitment and for living out the basic human experiences of love and the raising of children. They are sites of social anchorage. They provide their members with a basis for their activities in work, community, and polity. The family is a place to regenerate and recharge, to escape out of public space and be oneself, and to find intimacy, comfort, solace, and encouragement. Families contribute over the whole spectrum of social and economic production in a modern society. A productive society depends on productive families. Importantly, it depends on them to produce and raise children.

LESS PRODUCTIVITY

Society sits on a capital of family enterprise. However, families are not static institutions; they are always changing and probably more now than ever. The stock of capital is immense, whichever way you see it, but by all accounts the *trend* is that this capital is declining in value. Not dramatically, not so as to deplete it, and not necessarily irreversibly; there is no crisis or collapse of the family. Families are not bereft of functions or marginalized, there is no revolution, and no new type of family is emerging. In families, much is the same, only slightly less. Families continue to produce ferociously, but the trend is that they do so with less productivity.

It is easy to see how that happens economically. Families buy raw materials and process them further at home. The more raw those raw materials are, the more of the processing for ready consumption is done at home. One trend in consumer markets is that goods offered in shops and supermarkets are more processed. We buy washed potatoes, mixed salads, and ready-made meals that can be finished in a few minutes in the microwave. Even these goods are raw materials that require further work at home before they can be consumed. Heating up a ready-made meal may not take much time, but that saving of labor has been made possible by investing in more home capital—in this case, a microwave oven. We continue to depend on family production, only slightly less.

One reason is that families are smaller. There are thus fewer people in each family to pitch in to production and share in consumption. Families are smaller because there are fewer children, but that is of less significance for family productivity since children are mainly (but not only) consumers and not producers in their families. But families are also smaller because there are fewer adults. This is because there are more lone-parent families. This trend matters *very significantly* for family productivity. A family with two adults has forty-eight adult hours available a day for family and non-family activities and can use those forty-eight hours efficiently with the help of productive divisions of labor. A family with one adult has twenty-four hours to draw on and no resort to divisions of labor.[9] This is a monumental difference.[10]

A second reason there is less cooperation in families is that they have become more prosperous. When we get richer, we can afford to cooperate less. If a family has one car, all family members perforce cooperate to satisfy their transportation needs from that shared vehicle. If the family

[9] As always in family analysis, generalizations get it slightly wrong and need to be qualified. A lone parent may get help from the absent parent, and in fortunate cases, the two of them may cooperate well even if not living together. There may also be productive cooperation between parent and child, possibly more so in lone-parent than in two-parent families since the lone parent needs the cooperation of the child more.

[10] The difference in resources is obvious. Here is a story of the difference in cooperative capacity: A lone mother comes home at 7 p.m. on a wintry day. Two hours earlier she had left work, picked up her one-and-a-half-year-old son from nursery and stopped by the local supermarket to shop, all by public transport. Her flat is one flight of stairs up. She gets herself, her son, the buggy, and the shopping in. The boy is now seriously tired and hungry (as is she). She gets his heavy clothes and shoes off and sets him to play. Then after unpacking the shopping, she discovers that there is no milk. The boy will need milk that evening and in the morning. She cannot leave him alone in the flat to go back to the store for milk. He wants food now and is unwilling to get dressed up and go out again with his mom. That is an example of what the absence of access to cooperation means in practice. Lone parents live with it every day. That they cope is heroic, but heroism does not change the facts of resources and cooperation.

gets a second car, there is less family cooperation involved in the family production of transportation services. Pater and Mater have each theirs. He takes his to drive to the football club, and she takes hers to visit her mother-in-law. When they had only one car, Pater might have dropped Mater off and gone on to the football club after having agreed to pick her up again on his way home. With affluence, our homes are increasingly full of things—TVs, radios, stereos, computers—and we gradually depend less on cooperating with each other.

The result is that family economies contribute relatively less to our final standard of living and market economies relatively more. This is visible in the estimates of the value of family production and cooperation I have mentioned above. The value added as I estimated it was 113 percent in 1986, but that was down from 126 percent ten years earlier. That still leaves a family sector of imposing size but nevertheless a markedly shrinking family sector.

The relative shift in the economy from families to markets could be considered a good thing. It could simply be that we can afford to free ourselves from the burden of family work, in particular that women can be more free from family work. But it is not necessarily as good a thing as it may look. The economic effects of the growing number of lone-parent families is clearly not for the good. It may also be that what we think is more affluence is a bit of an illusion. We may think we are richer because we buy more things in the market but in fact be no better off in standard of living because of what we sacrifice in family production and cooperation. Be the goodness of it all as it may, however, the facts of the matter are that while family economies continue to contribute greatly to our standard of living, this contribution is nevertheless on a downward slope.

This trend in family productivity is a small piece in a larger puzzle that has been called the *second demographic transition*, a transition in the entire demographic regime that occurred in Europe and elsewhere towards the end of the twentieth century (and is possibly still going on). The main elements in this transition are birthrates falling to a new low after the post-1945 baby boom, increasing rates of divorce, more children born outside of marriage, more partners living together in cohabitation and fewer in marriage, and rising numbers of lone-parent families. Related trends are more married women and mothers working outside of the family and also a rise in the numbers of people living alone, including in middle age groups (mainly urbanites). These trends in living arrangements possibly coincide with, and may be driven by, ideological shifts in values and attitudes that go under names such as individualization or postmaterialism and that may include a weakening sense of family and of men's responsibility for children and a generally stronger belief in individual autonomy and a weaker acceptance of norms of authority.[11]

The new demographic regime is clearly new but still only moderately new. It is not that all families are now of a new type. Far from it. Most families with children are still "traditional" families of a married couple who are and see themselves as traditional parents. Most marriages (observed Coleman) are still ended by the death of one of the partners rather than divorce. But it describes a trend. Families on average are smaller, less likely to be constituted by a married couple and more likely by a cohabiting couple or a lone mother, and when constituted by a couple more likely to experience separation and divorce.

One fallout is less economic productivity. A second consequence is a decline in social productivity as well. That decline is dramatically visible on the account of fertility: posttransition families produce fewer children.

Throughout the rich world, the production of children is now much below what is needed to maintain these populations at their present size.[12] In Europe, population decline has started. The continent is set to lose 100 to 125 million people by 2050, from a population of 750 million now.[13]

Why we really have fewer children and what that really means is a bit of a mystery, which I am not in a position to resolve here. However, two striking observations can take us some way towards making sense of the trend towards ultralow fertility.

First, not only are birthrates low, they are lower than parents wish them to be. In surveys, young adult Europeans, both women and men, continue to express a desire for having children. The optimal number is usually considered to be two or three. If they were to go on and have the number of children they say they want, the resulting fertility would be at or above the replacement level. The number of children considered optimal is about the same in all European countries, so the difference between actual and optimal fertility is greatest in the countries where actual fertility is lowest.[14] The reason actual fertility is as low as it is, is not that parents and

[11] On the demographic transition and its causes and consequences, I draw in particular on Mason and Jensen 1995; McRae 1999; and Coleman 2005. I have discussed some aspects of the new demographic regime in Europe in more detail in Ringen 2004c.

[12] Notably in Europe but including also, e.g., Japan and Korea. The exceptions in the rich world are the United States, where population growth is set to continue as a result of both relatively high immigration and high fertility (the former contributing to the latter), and probably Australia and Canada, which are set to maintain population growth through high immigration and in spite of low fertility.

[13] See, e.g., UNPF 2002; United Nations Population Division, *World Population Prospects*, un.org/esa/population/publications/WPP. "Europe" here refers to countries to the west of the former Soviet Union.

[14] As documented in Esping-Andersen et al. 2002. Some demographers believe that the desired family size may be adjusting downwards nearer to actual family size, at least in some European populations.

other young people want so few children but that for some reason, they do not have the number of children they want.

There is every reason to take this survey evidence at face value as a realistic expression of the real desire for children. What is reported is the logical number of desired children under the demands and constraints of the second demographic transition and conforms to what should be expected. I return to that logic under the discussion of resources below.

There is also reason to take this evidence very seriously. Since more children are wanted than produced, ultralow fertility is not unavoidable and the process of declining fertility not irreversible. It is just a matter of making it possible for parents to achieve the number of children they want to have.

This observation helps us to get around the question of whether low fertility is a good or a bad thing. I happen to think that ultralow fertility is, for many good reasons, a cause for serious concern, but the question is controversial. However, since parents and prospective parents want more children than they are having, it would seem obviously desirable to find ways that would enable them to realize their family ambitions and have more children. It is not necessary to get bogged down in a discussion of how people should live. We know how they, in this respect, want to live.

The second observation is that low overall fertility is the result of declining fertility in particular in those families we should expect to be most able and geared to having children: families of married couples. Outside-of-wedlock fertility has increased, so much so that differences between European countries in overall fertility are less the result of differences in fertility in families of married couples—which is remarkably stable throughout Europe—than of differences in fertility in cohabiting couples and single women. By and large, overall fertility is higher in countries where it is more acceptable and practically possible to have children outside of marriage or by mothers on their own.[15]

This observation, combined with the first one, suggests that the problem of low fertility is a result of organizational difficulties. When parents and prospective parents continue to want "enough" children, the reason they have fewer than that cannot be a shift in values, at least not about the desirability of having children and the optimal number. When, within that framework of stable values about having children, those who establish their lives in the most family-friendly way are having fewer children, then it must be safe to assume that something is standing in people's way and making it difficult for them to live as they wish. Ultralow fertility is therefore a *problem* and that problem can be expressed as one of low productivity, of not managing what is wanted. People are unable, it seems,

---

[15] This observation I owe to Coleman 2005.

to get their lives together in the way they want. Something is discouraging them away from their persistent inclination to have "enough" children. The demand for children is not falling away. That's not where the problem is, and there is no issue of harassing people about having children. They want children. The way to put the question is to ask what are the conditions that would encourage or help parents and prospective parents to have the kinds of family lives they hold to be desirable. The way to help parents to achieve the number of children they want is to remove what is preventing them from realizing their intentions.

Whether or not the decline in the social productivity of families carries through from the production of children to the raising of children is less clear. We should think this productivity ought to be on the increase. Today's parents are more affluent and knowledgeable than their parents and grandparents were, and that ought to translate into better care for children. Most parents have fewer children to care for and should be able to give each more attention. We know from surveys of time use that parents do spend more time with and on their children.[16]

On the other hand, there is evidence to suggest that the productivity of not only childbearing but also child rearing may in some ways be in decline. Some such evidence is anecdotal. It is often said that more children and young people have become more bad-mannered and badly behaved, less respectful and less aware of norms of proper and improper comportment, more prone to using bad language, less socially skillful and cooperative, and less socially prepared for schooling and more disruptive as pupils.[17] But it is not all anecdotal. There is solid evidence from research that family matters for children's transition into adulthood.[18] If one aspect of family change is less family stability, we might expect that to show up again as new or increasing difficulties for some children who grow up in less stable family circumstances on their way into adulthood. One indication from Britain is births to teenage mothers (which is significantly more frequent there that in most other European countries): daughters from pretransition families—those having grown up in a family with both parents—are significantly less likely to become teenage mothers than daughters from lone-parent families or of parents who divorced or separated.[19]

[16] See, e.g., Gershuny 2000.

[17] For example, at the 2004 annual conference of the British National Association of Head Teachers, the general secretary, David Hart, issued a stark warning about increasing problems in parenting resulting in children coming to school without necessary social skills and parents refusing to support school behavioral policies. See *Financial Times*, 4 May 2004.

[18] See, e.g., Kiernan 1992; Ermish and Francesconi 2001a, 2001b. For a summary of evidence, see Coleman 2005.

[19] See, e.g., Wellings and Wadsworth 1999.

On this, we can hardly claim firm knowledge. We know that families are less productive economically and also socially in the basic matter of producing children. We may suspect a similar trend in the productivity of child rearing, not at all that family productivity in the raising of children is falling away, but that here as elsewhere, there is a trend towards some lower capacity. Parents are no doubt as capable of raising their children as ever, probably more, but parents raise children in an institutional setting, in families. Families are in identifiable ways on a curve of slowly declining productivity. If that means that the support parents have from their institutional setting is weakening, even if not dramatically, the job of parenting may be getting more difficult. Add to that the possibility of new demands in raising and training children for lives in complicated societies built around cultures of rights and liberty, knowledge economies, and democratic polities. If parents are in a better situation to undertake that job, more is also demanded of them. Being a parent today is a demanding job, to put it carefully. Ask any parent of teenage children. We do not have to start from any postulate of crisis in child rearing, and certainly not in parenthood, to be concerned for the capacity of today's parents to meet the requirements of modern child rearing.

RESOURCES

Families do things, I have said—but of course they don't. Family *members*, persons, do things. How well they do what they do, I have argued, comes down resources and cooperation. If I am right, something must be happening in the second demographic transition to the resources family members can draw on and their conditions of cooperation that explains the trend towards declining productivity.

The resources parents bring to the job of parenting are basically money and time. Skills come into it too, but not as an issue in the analysis of trends. I prefer to go by the all-but-radical assumption that parental ability for parenting is not in decline.

Simple logic would suggest that parents and prospective parents are more resourceful than ever. Most of us, including young people and parents, are more affluent and better educated than our predecessors a generation or two ago, and we might expect that young people today would be better set to have and raise children than ever before. Strangely enough, however, that is not the case, at least not economically. In spite of increasing affluence—or actually because of it—children have become more expensive and less affordable.

The distribution of income in modern capitalism is such that families with children, taken as a group, find themselves on the lower ranks of the income ladder. This is clearly not the situation for all families with children, but occurs often enough to pull the whole group down. During the last two or three decades, in most European countries, the distribution of income has shifted towards increasing inequality. The bulk of families with children find themselves on the losing end of that redistribution. The second demographic transition has coincided with a deterioration in the relative economic standard of families with children.[20]

The effect of low income is that parents are unable to provide adequately for their children, or they are able to do so only by sacrificing seriously in their own standard of living so that they cannot provide adequately for themselves. Most European parents are hardly poor, but many have fewer economic resources than they need to maintain expected standards in their own societies. This is a deprivation in economic resources that puts parents at risk of being unable to bring up their children in a way they feel they should and ought be able to.

This discourages parents and prospective parents from having children. Those who already have children and who experience economic hardship are likely to be reluctant to have more children. Those thinking about having children will be discouraged by seeing that those who have taken the plunge find themselves in economic strain. Of course, this is not the only consideration that comes into decisions about having children, but it is unavoidably among those considerations. Economic hardship will, other things being equal, discourage parenthood.

This is all the more so since the risk of low income in families with children is directly related to the fact that they have children. In an economy of affluence, child rearing is very expensive. Children need what the general standard of their society says they need, and parents have to be able to provide that standard or else feel that they and their children live in want. Rising affluence means rising expectations also on the part of children, and parents have to provide.

The rising cost of raising children is no doubt a deterrent to parents, but is not the only deterrent and probably not the main one. Children cost what parents on average spend on them, and that is what parents on average can afford to spend. Parents who want children want to spend on them. Spending for the benefit of children is not so much a sacrifice for most parents as their preferred lifestyle and what they want to spend their money for. Of course, it is a difficulty if they have to spend ever more on their children, but their real problem may nevertheless not be spending so much as being able to spend. Outlays discourage parents from having more children and prospective parents from having children at all, but even more decisive in their minds may be affordability. Having children

---

[20] www.lisproject.org/keyfigures.htm. See also Moynihan et al. 2004.

is costly for parents long before they come to the point of spending. It costs them by disabling them from earning some of the income they could otherwise have had.

Parents have become more affluent but nevertheless more economically vulnerable to the costs of raising children. One reason, again, is that more parents are lone parents. Most lone parents are seriously deprived in their capacity to earn income, again for the simple reason that they do not have time and do not have resort to divisions of labor. The issue here is resources, not skills. A lone parent may be as skillful as any other parent but is unavoidably at a disadvantage in resources.

Not only lone parents, however, but joint parents also are victims to their income-earning capacity being partly eroded when they have children. This follows in their case from their lifestyle. Joint parents now typically build their lives and economic expectations on two jobs. The psychologically expected family income is from two earnings. When two earners have children, at least one of those earnings must be given up, fully or in part, for longer or shorter periods. This may subsequently delay promotions and hold back career prospects, particularly for mothers.[21] Children come with a price tag in the form of present and future income forgone. Economists call this an *opportunity cost*—the cost of doing one thing over doing something else that is more profitable.

The reality of an opportunity cost now stands forcefully in front of young couples who are contemplating having children (or more children). The force of the opportunity cost is new. In the course of two or three generations, the economic circumstances around decisions about entering into parenthood have in this respect been drastically redefined. The ideal has shifted from the one-earner family being the desirable lifestyle to two earners having become the norm, a shift that combines behavioral and psychological changes in a complex pattern to which I return in more detail in the next section. If previously both parents had to work and earn, as frequently true for working class families, that was of necessity and not of choice. Now the lifestyle of choice is two jobs and two incomes. This has its own reasons, including the emancipation of women, but a result is that young couples have adapted their expectations and consumption habits to two incomes. When the family income was (ideally) from one earner, there was little or no experience of an opportunity cost. Either Mater was not earning or she would expect or hope to stop earning on entry into marriage or at least on having children. Or she was earning out of necessity and would have to continue to earn. Or she was earning out of choice, in which case the family would most likely have paid help. As status is now associated with two earnings, then status was in the one-

---

[21] As shown by, e.g., Joshi and Davies 1993.

earner family. The psychological family income was from one earner. No opportunity cost and no loss of status was perceived in giving up the second income. As more families become more prosperous thanks to two incomes and female earnings become more important in family incomes, the trend is that the opportunity cost *increases*. Furthermore, the full opportunity cost is in the sacrifice of status as well as of income. Not only have many families with children been losing out from an inegalitarian redistribution of income, they have also seen a rise in the economic and social price they pay for the pleasure and privilege of rearing children.

For British families, the income terms work out like this: (1) As a general rule, families do indeed sacrifice income when they have children. This is universally the case for young families, and it is universally the case for families with young children. (2) The first child has the greatest impact on income. Young families (head of household under age thirty) with a single child under age five sacrifice about a third of their potential income. The momentous decision, as far as income goes, is the decision to move from not having children to having them. (3) After the first child there is an additional, although modest, income sacrifice associated with additional children. (4) As families and children grow older, the opportunity cost goes down. For example, for families in the age group thirty to thirty-nine (head of household) who have a single child under age five, the opportunity cost is about 20 percent (as compared with about 30 percent in the younger age group). In the same head-of-household age group with a single child between ages five and nine, the opportunity cost is short of 10 percent. (5) Over a ten-year period of observation (1976 to 1986), the opportunity cost of children has *increased* for example from 22–27 percent to around 30–37 percent for young families with the youngest child under age five.[22]

If money is a constraint on parenting, time is another one. This is obviously the case for lone parents: the twenty-four hours again. In whatever way we look at it, the resources available to lone parents for the raising of children are infinitely less than those available to couples. There are deep difficulties in society in dealing with the fact of lone motherhood because of moral hangups. It would clarify matters a great deal in social policy if we just set moral concerns aside, assumed equal moral virtue in all parents, and brought the matter down to earth as an issue of resources.

Couples have more time available to them and have the benefit of being able to make their time go further by cooperation, but time is a constraint for them, too. In their case, it is less a result of an absolute deprivation in time resources than one of socially determined demands on their time.

---

[22] This is a summary of estimates in Ringen 2005a, ch. 3.

Parents and prospective parents today face two great demands on their time: on the one hand finding the time to produce and raise children, and on the other hand finding the time for paid work outside of the family. All parents, both lone parents and those living together, now face strong social expectation to participate in paid work. Those expectations come from generally accepted norms that all parents should, if at all possible, work in paid jobs outside of the family. It comes from governments that want to control social budgets by encouraging parents, including lone mothers, to work and earn for their own needs. It comes from a new ideology of paid work, in which working is seen as a good thing in itself rather than as a sacrifice for the necessity of earning an income. And it comes from economic adjustments to the experience and expectation of having two incomes. For example, when many couples on the housing market are two-earner couples, house prices adjust upwards to what they can pay and housing becomes prohibitively expensive for single earners. Parents, including those living together, are pretty much caught up in a two-earner regime that is, for most of them, simply impossible to opt out of.

This particular brand of the work ethic is discouraging parenthood and is eating into the resources of parents for the raising of children. For all intents and purposes, society is now telling prospective parents that no one should expect to be able to devote their time fully or primarily to raising children. That is obviously not a dictatorial message. It comes from norms that again come from what most people see as right and desirable for them. Nevertheless, the time parents feel they must devote to paid work is time they cannot devote to having and raising children.

I concluded above that the declining productivity of families in having and possibly in rearing children comes from a difficulty for many parents to fashion their lives in the way they want. That difficulty is largely about clearing competing demands on time. We want to have children as much as we did before, but we also want paid work more than we did before. What is changing is not the desire to have children but the strength of the competing demands on our time. They make it more difficult to live out the desire for having children, even if that desire itself is not waning.

This time effect, I believe, is sufficient to explain the discrepancy between the desired and actual number of children in European populations. Couples start from the norm that both expect to work. They must then ask themselves how many children they can have and still be able to manage both family and work. Once couples have decided that they want children, very few want only one. For most couples, more than two is difficult to manage when both see themselves as working parents, and only a few will think they can manage three or more. That adds up to what we know is the overall desired number of children at or a bit above replacement-level fertility. This is the logic that gives credence to survey evidence on the desired number of children.

However, if most couples see two or three children as the desired number, many of them will not be able to achieve the number they want. That would only happen if many of them were prepared to "risk" having more children than they want, which is something most parents will not see themselves able to do. The combination of the two-earner work ethic and the ideal of having two children causes many prospective parents to delay entry into parenthood until they are quite old. This has the effect of reducing final fertility because many simply run out of time. Hence, the desired number of children resulting from the new ideology of paid work logically leads to the actual number of children inadvertently falling short of that desired number.[23]

Once we think about the business of having and raising children as a matter of resources, and then about money and time, we see that parents are seriously constrained in the resources they are able to devote to parenthood and that those resources have, paradoxically, become *more* constrained with increasing prosperity. This is the case whether we consider parents' productivity in having children or in raising children they have, and whether we look to the situation of lone parents or of parents living together.

The social policy conclusion is now obvious. Given that we think parents should be able to live the kinds of family lives they hold to be desirable, we need to find ways of making money available to parents and of making time available to them. It needs to be a bit easier and more attractive for parents and prospective parents to have children so that more of them could be a bit bolder in going for the number they want.

COOPERATION

The productivity of families depends first on resources, as we have seen, but then in addition on the ability of family members to cooperate in the use of their resources. That tells us first, when we consider parenting, that we should encourage togetherness. This may sound like moral posturing but is nothing of the kind. It is a statement of fact and not of morality that there is productivity in togetherness and that productivity is lost with

---

[23] There is a parallel between the logic of "too low" fertility in rich communities and "too high" fertility in poor ones. In many poor communities, parents cannot risk not ending up with enough children and compensate by having more than they want. In many rich communities, parents cannot risk ending up with more than enough children and compensate by having fewer than they want.

the loss of togetherness. When one person on her or his own has to do a job that requires the cooperation of two to do well, productivity is lost.

However, efficiency does not come from just living together; it comes from the ability of those living together to cooperate productively. That ability, again, depends on its own conditions. Those conditions, once we have dealt with resources, are in the social relations of the partners and can be considered under the headings "purpose" and "trust."[24]

Partners who enter into a joint enterprise of parenting need a shared understanding of their enterprise to succeed in the job they set out for themselves. That is no different in families than from any other setting of cooperation. Families, to repeat yet again, *do* things, they produce value. A family is a setting in which resources are put to cooperative use. Families are *organizations*. In all organizations, efficiency depends on an understanding of what the organization is about—on what, in business organizations, for example, is often referred to as *mission* or, in the words of President Bush the elder, "the vision thing." An organization that is able to establish its mission in such a way that the members of the organization take it to be their shared purpose is on its way to creating an internal culture of efficient cooperation.

The second demographic transition is often assumed to contain, or in part to be driven by, changes in values and ideologies.[25] The significance of new values is contested, and ideological shifts are not easy to observe and to prove or disprove. I lean towards skepticism and to the view that the demographic transition has more to do with changing economic conditions. Even so, attitudes towards family life are clearly on the move, and changing attitudes are an element in the greater transition, although possibly more as intervening variables between changing economics and demographics than as ultimate causes.

At the core of the second demographic transition is a shift is in gender relations: the emancipation, independence, and assertiveness of women. Most reflective commentators would now take this shift to be for the better, and there is no need to dispute that here. However, the fact that a social trend is generally for the good does not necessarily mean there may not also be costs. A consequence of gender equity on the cost side could be an increasing uncertainty about the organization of family life and less of a shared understanding of the family mission.

---

[24] My method of analysis now shifts to one of *conventions*. When people live in community with each other, they together create conventions in the form of shared norms, beliefs, and habits that work back on them as individuals and exercise a powerful influence on mind-sets and behaviors. This perspective of conventions I owe to the inspiration of one of the greatest European sociologists ever, Eilert Sundt (1817–1875). See Sundt 1980, 1993; and, e.g., Rogoff and Ringen 2005.

[25] See, e.g., Lestaeghe 1995.

There are many misunderstandings about the feminist revolution, often stimulated by some outreach of postmodern theory. One such misunderstanding is that married women, prerevolution, were only housewives. For example, Esping-Andersen wrote that "everywhere the post-war social contract was built on the realistic assumption that women, once married, withdraw into housewifery."[26] But that was never the case. There is nothing new about working wives and mothers. Many working-class and other more or less poor families, and families in farming and other primary industries, were by necessity two-worker families (although not necessarily families of two *employed* workers). Nor is there anything new about middle-class working mothers and wives; certainly in middle-class families in which Mater had the capacity to command an attractive job. What is new in behavior is found in families in which there is choice. Previously, choice most often resulted in a sharp gender division of labor in which Pater decided and Mater obeyed; Pater was citizen and Mater homemaker. Since this was the common arrangement of choice and of the upper classes, it also became the norm for how things ought ideally to be. Not all families, probably not even most of them, lived according to that norm, but this was very much the picture people had in their minds about the kind of family organization they should aspire to.

This has all changed. First, choice no longer produces the old gender division of labor. Now wives and mothers choose to work even when they do not have to, at least mostly. That's the main change in behavior, a radical change but probably less so than is often assumed. In addition, and probably more radically, social norms have changed. The paternalistic organization of family life is simply dead as a cultural norm. While the change in behavior has come in degrees, the change of norms has been absolute. It used to be a good thing in most people's minds that Pater worked and supported the family and that Mater was supported and did not have to work. Now, what we tell each other to aspire to is equity in work outside of the family (and, hesitantly, inside the family, too).

Whether this is a shift in values is not altogether clear. It is perhaps better seen as a shift in power. The vision of the paternalistic family rested on the power of the husband to define the family project, and the choice to live according to that vision, when choice was available, was pretty much *his* choice. The passing of this inequity in power is clearly something that should be celebrated and now mostly is celebrated. But that notwithstanding, the vision of the paternalistic family did exert a powerful influence in people's minds—including, no doubt, the minds of women—and was able to create in society and in families a shared understanding of

[26] Esping-Andersen et al. 2002, p. 20.

family projects. Family was *vision* and individual projects were about finding one's place in the pursuit of that vision.

That prerevolutionary vision was not fair but it was efficient. It represented a division of labor which it was in the interest of both Pater and Mater to make work, in his interest because it was to his advantage and in her interest because she had no better alternative. When it was in Pater's power to define Mater's role, it was in her interest to make the most out of the role available to her and to build for herself a power base in the management of the family. This was a vision that created order—the wrong kind of order with our eyes, but order nevertheless.

Now that vision has evaporated, deservedly so. The question then is whether an alternative and modern vision has evolved to take its place and guide partners to productive family cooperation. This has probably not happened. Instead we are left with something of a void in our understanding of family and its mission. With the collapse of paternalistic power, the power behind the vision of family as a joint project has eroded. What we have in its place is less an alternative vision of the family project than individual visions of individual projects. A mind-set that told people to adjust individually to the joint project has been defeated by a modern mind-set in which the real projects are individual and joint projects, such as family, are what now must adapt.

Of course, this is a crude caricature of real evolutions (as always when we generalize about families). People continue to feel very strongly about their families and are as always prepared to sacrifice individually for the joint endeavor. But there is nevertheless a subtle drift in priorities, following from a radical shift in norms and power relations. It is not that we have become indifferent to making families work, clearly not. But again there is a trend: family is a weaker priority and self a stronger one. Partners continue to cooperate and to do so, as we have seen, with great productivity. But the productivity of cooperation *is* weakening. This may in part be a result of a weaker and less clear sense of mission in those organizations we call families.

The second condition of cooperation is trust. Cooperation is a matter of give-and-take. If people, be it two or many, are to be able to cooperate efficiently, each must be prepared and able to renounce self-interest for the benefit of the joint interest. The ability of people to enter into cooperation in that spirit depends on their ability to trust that those they enter into cooperation with will respond in kind and not exploit their willingness to let the joint interest prevail for their own self-serving purposes. Trust here means having reasons to believe that those I cooperate with will cooperate with me in return, now and in the future.

Two alternative partnership arrangements are now available: formal marriage and informal cohabitation. Marriage is still the most-used basis of family formation but is in the process of being outcompeted by cohabitation. In Scandinavia, which is at the lead in this trend, more than nine out of ten new unions are now cohabitations. Many subsequently marry but about half of all unions remain informal. Cohabitation has gone from being eccentric to ordinary in no more than a single generation.

As usual in family discourse there are moral concerns, and as usual family analysis is best served by setting those concerns aside. I will take it that if the coming of cohabitation matters as an issue in family policy, it would be for its consequences for families as institutions that produce value.

Why people who want to form families have suddenly started to prefer doing that on the basis of informality is not easily said. One possible explanation could again be new values and ideologies. It could be an aspect of modernity that young people see a commitment to each other that is not "trivialized" by the formalities of a contract as in some way more personal and genuine. But that does not seem to be the case. Cohabitation is chosen over marriage mainly for practical and prosaic reasons. In surveys, cohabiting couples give as reasons for choosing informality that they wish to try things out, that they are uncertain about the durability of the union and wish to retain an easy way out, and that the practical process of marriage itself is time-consuming, tedious, and expensive.

Rather than being deliberate, it may seem that the growth of cohabitation is a bit of a coincidence and something that just rolls on by its own force once it has started, not so much because it is seen to be superior but just because it is convenient.

One argument in favor of that explanation is this: once socially acceptable, cohabitation will tend to be preferred to marriage in two out of three situations: if both partners are uncertain about the firmness of the union, wherefore cohabitation is in the interest of both, and if one partner is uncertain, since in love the partner who loves the least has the most power. Only if both are equally certain and firmly committed would it be in the interest of both to choose formal marriage.

A further argument is that the convention of cohabiting before marriage contributes to changing the meaning of marriage itself. Marriage comes later. It becomes more a matter of formalizing an already established fact than of being a life-changing moment. The act of getting married is in a sense devalued as a statement, both in the eyes of the partners and of their family and friends. A secondary effect is that yet another useful convention has had to bite the dust: it seems to be on its way out that parents, usually and mainly those of the bride, pay for their children's wedding. It then becomes more expensive for young people to get married, and that works back to further encouraging cohabitation.

These arguments suggest that once social pressures for marriage are relaxed, a self-perpetuating process of cohabitation starts moving and takes on force. That's where we probably are. The next question is whether it matters.

From the short experience of increasing cohabitation in its modern form, we now know there are very considerable differences between living together in cohabitation and living together in marriage. It may seem a trivial matter of formality whether two people who decide to form a union chose to formalize it or to commit to it informally, but if so this is a small difference with large consequences.

First, unions of cohabitation are less stable than unions of marriage; among couples with children, the likelihood of breakup is two or three times greater in cohabitations than in marriages. The risk of divorce is greater in marriages that start in cohabitation than in those that start directly in marriage; "trying it out" does not increase the likelihood of long term success.[27] The patterns of custody and care for children after breakup are different depending on marriage or cohabitation; in particular, the involvement of previously cohabiting fathers in the life of their children is weaker. Breakups in cohabitations with children occur earlier in the children's lives than breakups in marriages. In a culture of cohabitation compared with a culture of marriage, more children will have experienced family instability and breakup and may grow up themselves more hesitant about committed family life.

Second, cohabiting couples do not see themselves as a union as strongly as do married couples and have a different sense of joint rights and duties. They have less joint management of money and finance. There is more legal uncertainty. Cohabitation does not have the same disciplining influence on the partners' lifestyles as does marriage; cohabitation does not bring with it the same degree of change towards a family lifestyle.

These differences between cohabitation and marriage are genuine and not spurious. Some of the differences probably result from selection. Unions that are uncertain at the outset are more likely to become and remain cohabitations, therefore cohabitations are more likely to break up. This, however, does not fully explain the difference; in addition there is a "marriage effect." While cohabitation may result from a drift of non-decisions, the decision to live together in marriage is perforce more explicit and formal. The process of marriage and the wedding itself delays the decision to start living together and may enforce more careful reflec-

---

[27] This specifically is the experience in Scandinavia, where cohabitation is the more prevalent. It is not necessarily the experience in societies where cohabitation is less prevalent. That again could be because of different selection effects, depending on whether cohabitation is usual or unusual.

tion. Couples signal strong commitment to others that they wish not to fail, and the prospect of breakup is seen more unambiguously as a failure. With marriage, the process of divorce is at least somewhat time-consuming and cumbersome; with cohabitation not so much as a concept of divorce remains.

Marriage and cohabitation, then, are subtly different kinds of conventions—and that is a difference is of consequence. Cohabiting unions are less stable than marriages; with more cohabitation, there is less stability in families altogether, including less stability for children. Cohabiting couples think differently about their union than do married couples; with more cohabitation there is less "we-thinking" and more "me-thinking" in families altogether. They cooperate differently; with more cohabitation there is less joint management in families altogether.

As always we must qualify. Unions of cohabitation are not always and hardly ever dramatically different from unions of marriage. The differences are only marginal. But many marginal differences that pull in the same direction add up to a significant total effect in the aggregate.

Partners obviously know the nature of the union they live in. They hardly sit around comparing their own to the alternative, but they know what they have. If their union is informal, whether they have made that choice because of uncertainty or they are just following the convention, they experience its balance between we-thinking and me-thinking as it is and its level of joint management as it is. They may not be explicitly aware that their union is, in these respects, probably different from what it might have been had they been married, but they of course experience the union as it is. Compared with marriage, cohabitation is, in the terminology of appendix G, a union of loser social anchorage. It binds people less to each other. Hardly dramatically so, but often perceptively so.

Partners who live together with relatively weaker bonds to each other know what those bonds are. They know the degree of anchorage that is built into their union and its degree of uncertainty. They know the degree of predictability in their union. Their joint life happens to be less predictable that it could have been had they chosen to formalize it. They may have no awareness of that difference, but they know what they have. The predictability they consider is the predictability they have.

Compared with a union of stronger anchorage, cohabitants live with more uncertainty. They know their union as it is. Their knowledge tells them how it is prudent to live and think in the union they have and such as it is. It tells them it is prudent to plan and invest with caution for and in the joint life, which they know is uncertain. It tells them to be cautious with taking the continuation of the joint life as their assumption. They may be as determined and committed to the continuation of their joint life as anyone could be, but they cannot avoid knowing that the foundations of that joint life are as they are. Those foundations contain a good deal of uncertainty. Uncertainty enforces caution. It makes the partners hold back and secure, not necessarily because they have chosen cohabitation in order to be able to hold back on their commitment but because there is something in an informal partnership that makes it risky to commit fully. This feeds back into the psychology of cohabitation. Cohabiting partners are perforce just a little bit uncertain about each other. Partners are clearly always uncertain about each other, but a formal partnership gives some protection against that uncertainty, which is absent in an informal union. Their uncertainty therefore tends to be a little bit more than had they tied themselves together in a formal bond. The partners have not formed their partnership in such a way as to help them to trust each other. They do trust each other, at least enough to have formed a union, but their bonds of trust will unavoidably be just a touch less tenuous. With the same degree of commitment in a partnership of cohabitation and a partnership of marriage, the cohabiting partners are forced to think a bit more of *me* and less of *us*. This is not because they are different kinds of people, but because they live under the influence of a different convention.

FAMILY POLICY

I started this essay by dismissing the postmodern theory of the family. That in itself is something worth getting done. I wish I would never again find myself in a discussion of family matters and have to suffer the mythology of the nuclear family being served up as insight and obvious fact (a hope utterly in vain, no doubt). Ideas matter. The idea that the family is a marginalized and therefore insignificant institution is one that has done and continues to do harm to social rationality. Instead of spreading rumors about the marginalized family, we ought to speak to each other about the manifold things families *do* and of their productive power.

That established, I have gone on to identify a trend towards a decline of productivity in family life, a trend that is observable in hard economic and demographic statistics. This decline is incremental and gradual and not of crisis proportions. It does not change the fact that families are massively productive institutions, and it does not marginalize them. But it is steady and significant and means that family life, although still a good investment of time and effort, is becoming a less good investment. There are still very good reasons for people to live their lives in families, and it is therefore not surprising that that is how we by and large continue to arrange our lives, but those reasons are slowly becoming incrementally less persuasive. There is less economy in family life. The individual sacrifices that go into the building of joint family projects are marginally less worth making. Family members and those thinking of forming a family may be marginally less inclined towards joint family efforts and lean marginally more towards giving individual efforts more priority. These diseconomies in the next round eat into the social productivity of families—for example, the ability and readiness of parents and prospective parents to accept the trials and tribulations involved in having and raising children. Parents, including those who arrange their lives in the most family-friendly way, *are* having fewer children. The reason is not, we know, that they want fewer children. It could be because the effort is subtly less worthwhile.

The declining productivity of family life is, I have suggested, associated with or caused by various well-known trends in the second demographic transition. One such trend is the redefinition of the economic circumstances around entry into parenthood whereby greater prosperity has strangely made children less affordable and child rearing more expensive. Another trend is the increasing prevalence of lone-parent families. Lone-parent families by definition have fewer resources to put into the job of child rearing. When more families are lone-parent families, the aggregate pool of resources in families for child rearing is smaller. A third trend is gender equity. That has changed power relations in families, with the effect that the definition of family projects may have become more contested. And a final trend is the substitution of cohabitation for marriage, with the effect that cooperative trust in partnerships has become more elusive.

That is what it looks like to me. The story is one of new demographic and economic constellations that work by changing social and power relations inside families to produce the unfortunate result that families, compared with markets, are becoming less productive.

If this is a good analysis, it is also a paradoxical one. The social trends that make up the second demographic transition are, for the most part, positive. They reflect a new freedom for people to live their lives by their own choices. The reason additional prosperity has made children less affordable is that it is based on two family incomes, whereby more income is likely to be sacrificed with the having and rearing of children. The two-earner lifestyle is something we have because we want it. Cohabitation may make trust a scarcer commodity, but many couples want it. Gender equity may sharpen the power struggle in the family home, but no one wants to revert to paternalism. Lone motherhood is often involuntary but it is certainly progress that it is acceptable and affordable.

The paradox is that these are good things that nevertheless add up to the bad effect of undermining the productivity of family life. The world is unfortunately not so wisely arranged that good causes cannot produce bad effects. That's the drama of the second demographic transition. More freedom in family life, which is desirable, comes at the price of less productivity in family life, which is undesirable.

The demographic transition is a fact on the ground. There is no way back. There is no "golden age" of traditional family life to revert to. We are where we are and must make the most of it. Family policy cannot undo what has come and gone. We must work with the consequences of the demographic transition and, as far as possible, try to unlock its paradox.

We are, on the cost side of the account, in a regime in which something is standing in people's way and making it difficult for them to get their lives together as they want. This is in one way an encouraging finding. It means that if people were free and able to arrange their family lives in the way they wish, they would arrange their lives more efficiently.

Family policy should help parents to combine parenthood with other life priorities. What stands in their way and, for example, prevents them from building the kinds of families they want with the number of children they want, is the difficulty of combining that with what is now seen as a full life outside of the family. Bluntly, it is too difficult for women to be wives, mothers, and workers.

No doubt, something could be done by fine-tuning taxes and transfers to create family-friendly incentives. Those matters I have dealt with in Chapter 3. There is, however, an intriguing detail that bears being added here. One of the strange consequences of the rise of cohabitation is that it is killing the convention that parents pay for their children's wedding. This is making it more expensive for young people to get married and is possibly the main reason they do not. A useful convention has gone lost. That is sad; it is a bit like a language that dies because there are no longer enough people to use it or a species of animal or plant that goes extinct.

Conventions are strange things. They are of our own making, and if they vanish it is because we no longer believe in or make use of them. But also, the conventions we make for ourselves are in return the making of us. The human animal is social; we live in communities. We do not make our lives alone; we do it, when we do it rationally, with others—which is to say by conventions, by what we say and signal to each other about how to do it. Conventions are man-made, if not always made by intent and deliberately; they do not fall out of thin air. What is man-made can be created by plan and purpose.

Social policy is in large measure a business of creating conventions. It supports ways of life that are seen to be desirable or productive and discourages what is seen to be undesirable or wasteful. Family policy supports the family way of organizing joint lives because that way is seen to be useful. Should we use social policy to try to reverse the unfortunate demise of the convention that enabled young people to marry without having to think about the cost of the wedding? A strange idea, you may think, but no stranger than this, for example: It has long been considered in cultures such as ours a matter of honor to be able to give deceased family members a decent funeral. Since that is expensive, one of the early social demands was for funeral support. A rationalist may object: why not just cut the cost and put the support to something more utilitarian? But the convention was there and people wanted help to obey and maintain a convention they were attached to. If young people do not feel honorably able to hold a wedding except on some (expensive) scale and therefore prefer not to if parents are disinclined to pay, why not find another way?

If I were a pure moralist and said that young people should marry out of decency, I might be tilting against the windmills. But that is not what I am saying. I am saying that it is *useful* for two young people who start out to make a life together to do so on the basis of a formal contract. It is economically useful. That being the case, it seems to me to be just ordinary social policy to see if something could be done. Since what is behind the decline of marriage is the loss of a convention that helped young people to arrange their joint lives in a way that was supportive towards its success, why not use social policy to re-create the convention in a new way? It would be simply another case of social policy substituting for what families used to do but are no longer able to: a case of, in Richard Titmuss's words "partial compensations for disservices, for social costs and social insecurities which are the product of a rapidly changing industrial-urban society."[28] Entirely standard social policy, in other words.

This useful convention could be re-created easily and cheaply with the help of a public subsidy of weddings (possibly limited to first weddings), which is no stranger than, for example, banks in Britain giving first-time buyers mortgages at a favorable rate. What is expensive individually is cheap collectively. It is likely to be an effective policy—with possibly more effect than we can usually count on in social policy—since it is in fact cost that is holding some young people back from getting married. The elimination of the cost would eliminate the barrier. It would also represent a signal of encouragement. And it would most likely be cost-effective since it would contribute to preventing some of the future costs that come from the instability of unions of cohabitation.

However, tinkering with taxes and subsidies is still not where to start. Where we are is really in an ideological battle between, as I interpret it, an idea of "families" that are useful and an idea of "the family" that is

[28] Titmuss 1968, p. 133.

holy. Before we get down to the practicalities of family policy, we need practicable ideas to work from.

Towards this end, some recommendations flow from the analysis above. First, we need more factual knowledge about the life of families. The mythology of the nuclear family has been able to survive and prosper because it has met very little resistance from factual accounts of what families are and how they work and evolve. In mere economic terms, the family sector is as large as or larger than the abstraction that is usually called the economy or the market but, by comparison, almost no research is invested in it.

Better knowledge ought to result in a better understanding of the significance of family life, but we may need to assist the translation of knowledge into a culture of understanding. Being a family member and parent is an important office in life. In no other position do others depend on you as directly as in family and parenthood, and in no other post do you matter as much for the well-being of others. I am an advocate for seeing the disposition to and readiness for family life as something to be learned. Education for family life and parenting should be given in schools, for all pupils, from primary school. This should include knowledge of family and society, family economics and law, child and parent psychology, gender relations, the ethics and practice of love and sex, and the ethics and practice of parenting and child rearing.

Boys and men in particular need better understanding. As a result of the feminist revolution, girls and women know what they want and are no longer obliged to be satisfied if they cannot have what they see as a full life. There has been no similar masculine revolution of consciousness; therefore boys and men are in confusion about themselves in a world of gender equity. If they cling to the notion of superior status and power, women will simply turn their backs on them—which is already happening, we can see, from the fact that a rising majority of divorces are initiated by women. Modern women want men who are useful, faithful, and good fun, and they have the power to say "No, thank you!" if their men do not meet their expectations. The idea of families as equitable partnerships is already there with the women, who will take it if it offered but will not make do with second-best. It is for boys and men to understand and adopt the inevitability of accepting their women as their equals and to give as careful thought to modern masculinity as women have to modern femininity—or to be rejected as useless.

A second recommendation is that we should encourage togetherness. All children have a father and a mother; we should encourage parents to raise their children together. In togetherness there are resources—the forty-eight versus twenty-four hours again—and in togetherness there is the possibility of cooperation. Lone parenthood is costly, and not because the lone parent is a bad parent; that is unlikely and is anyway something of which we know nothing. It is costly because the lone parent, whether she or he, has fewer resources and less resort to cooperation.

Once we recommend togetherness, we should also recommend that partnerships be formally institutionalized. The convention of informal cohabitation has brought massive change into family life, much more and radically than we are usually aware of, changes that contribute to less durability, productivity, and trust in family partnerships.

Of course, encouraging togetherness and formal togetherness may be more easily said than done. The question of incentives will no doubt present itself, but before that we must yet again go back to the battle-ground of ideas. We need knowledge and the communication of knowledge. We need to respect the facts. We should get away from evasive nonopinions that intimidate that all family arrangements are equally good. When it comes to the child rearing they are not; those that bring more resources to the job are better. Lone parenthood is costly. It is excessively burdensome for the parent and it does not channel enough resources to the job of parenting. We need not and should not speak negatively about lone motherhood; most lone mothers perform miracles of heroism in their lives. But we should speak positively about the productivity of togetherness.

We need sound and truthful ideas about families and family life, ideas based on facts, and we need to give those ideas life by speaking about them repeatedly and forcefully. A little bit of encouragement goes a long way. The fact-based story of families and children that I recommend we tell each other is this:

- It is usually better for parents to cooperate in raising their children than to have this job rest with only one parent.

- It is usually better for parents who cooperate in raising their children to live together than for them to live apart.

- It is usually better for parents who live together to keep their union together than to dissolve it.

- A union that is formalized in a pact usually has a better chance of lasting than one that is based on informal cohabitation.

Usually—not always and for everyone, but usually.

Finally, we need to back up the ideological battle for the well-being of families with, as always, hard economics. We should relax the new and harsh work ethic that is denying parents the choice of giving the raising of children priority over paid work. In particular, it is counterproductive to force lone mothers into working. They should, as others, have the choice; yet increasingly, they are being compelled. It is often just too hard. It leaves them too little time to raise their children. One suspects there is a long-term idea, fully intended or not, to discourage lone motherhood by making it burdensome. But that is to punish the children for the sins of their parents. There will be lone mothers and fathers and there will be children growing up in lone-parent families. The contribution that many lone mothers can make to society by raising their children is immeasurably more valuable than what they can contribute in often low-yield jobs.

Families need more resources. Parents need more money so that children become more affordable and they need more time so that child rearing can be compatible with the freedom to work outside of the family. This is a matter of child and family economic support; of nursery schools, day care, and kindergartens; and of schools that offer children a place to be for the duration of their parents' working days.

Some may here see an issue of socialization of child rearing, but if so it's that or nothing. The social productivity of families is essential for the future of economy, society, and democracy. That efficiency, including family productivity in the raising of children and the reproduction of the population, is not going to be regained without more resources in money and time. The alternative would be to ask parents to give up what has been gained, in particular in gender equity, and that alternative is simply no longer on offer.

CHAPTER 6

Where Does Freedom Come From?

> For I do not do the good I want, but the evil I do not want is
> what I do. Now if I do what I do not want, it is no longer I
> that do it, but sin which dwells within me.
> —Saint Paul, Romans 7:15–16

THAT FREEDOM is a good thing is obvious and needs no elaboration here. But it is also a difficult thing that makes claims on those who have it for its productive husbandry. If it liberates, it also comes with burdens. In the language I will be using below, liberty is trivial unless combined with reason.

But just how does reason come into it? A first possible answer is that reason goes to the good use of liberty once you have it. If that is right, we could deal with reason in one of two ways. We could either, in the rational-choice tradition, simply assume rationality and say no more about it. It would then be sufficient in the theory to investigate the conditions of liberty because its good use could be taken for given or to be exogenous. Or we could take it that reason comes into a full understanding of the problem of freedom, but *afterwards*, once we get down to the use of the thing.

The rational-choice solution is the easy one, but it has come to be seen as unsatisfactory. John Rawls, for example, first tried to ground his theory of justice in a rational-choice account but soon found that did not work: "it was an error . . . (and a very misleading one) to describe a theory of justice as part of a theory of rational choice. What I should have said is

This essay was first presented as the inaugural lecture at the Green College Seminar on Human Values and Social Policy, Oxford University, on 17 February 2005, titled "Isaiah Berlin's Liberty Today." Extracts of that lecture were published in two installments in Society *(March/April and May/June 2005). An early essay on the first part was used as an academic radio lecture on the Norwegian Broadcasting Corporation in 2004 and subsequently published in Norwegian in a collection of lectures. A short version of the second part was presented to the symposium "Is Freedon a Daughter of Knowledge?" at the* Kulturwissenschaftliches Institut *in Essen on 10–12 April 2006, at the invitation of Nico Stehr. Reflections on these matters started for my part at a seminar in Paris in October 1996 with the astonishing (as I saw it then) title "La rationalité des valeurs." I am grateful to Raymond Boudon for the invitation to that seminar and for many conversations on* la raison, les croyances *and related matters and to Knut Erik Tranøy, Michael Lockwood, Kenwyn Smith, Siep Steuerman, Henry Hardy, Avner Offer, Jerry Cohen, Irving Horowitz, Jonathan Imber, Margareta Bertilsson, and Steve Fuller for helpful comments and suggestions.*

that the conception of justice as fairness uses an account of rational choice subject to reasonable conditions . . . within a political conception of justice, which is, of course, a moral conception. There is no thought of trying to derive the content of justice within a framework that uses an idea of the rational as the sole normative idea."[1] It is now pretty much common sense, as indeed it has traditionally been before the rational-choice diversion, that understanding freedom is a matter of also understanding its use.[2]

Another way of thinking about it is to see reason not only as a condition for the prudent use of liberty but as part and parcel of the thing itself, as for example in Joseph Raz's concept of freedom as autonomy.[3] Having liberty is then not a sufficient condition of freedom; you must also have it in your power to control the difficulties the gift of liberty comes with. That is a condition not only of the good use of liberty, it is part of what it means to be free. Reason now comes in *before* the fact, as an argument in the definition of freedom.

These two approaches to freedom—with or without reason—I have called *the real-freedom school* and *the liberty school*, respectively.[4] In this chapter, I intend to defend the real freedom school as the proper moral underpinning of a theory of democracy that puts the promotion and protection of freedom at its core.

My attraction to the real-freedom school goes back to an early work on social anchorage (in Norwegian under the heading *sosial forankring* which rings infinitely eleganter than the stodgy English translation). Out of that work came, for me, a conviction that what is important in the human condition is how people are connected more than how they are "liberated" from one another. That conviction became an outlook on social life that has later influenced me in many ways, including now in this exploration of freedom. I include a short extract of some of that early work in appendix G.

The Liberty School

The classical liberal concept of freedom is simple and powerful: to have the right to do as one likes. This was the position of John Stuart Mill in *On Liberty* (1859): "Over himself, over his own body and mind, the individual is sovereign. . . . A person should be free to do as he likes in

---

[1] Rawls 1985, n. 20.

[2] John Stuart Mill was certainly of that understanding (cf. Capaldi 2004), as was before him Adam Smith for whom "prudence" was "of all the virtues that which is most useful to the individual," prudence being defined as the union of reason and self-command. (Smith 1759, 4:2).

[3] In Raz 1986.

[4] In Ringen 2005b.

his own concerns."[5] There is much more to say about what to do with freedom when you have it—for example, how to translate a free life into a happy life—but that's a discussion not about what freedom is but about how to use it. What freedom *is*, is to have the right to do as one likes. If you have the right to choose, you are free. Freedom comes from *rights*, and rights are a sufficient condition of freedom. It is one thing and one thing only.[6]

A century later, Isaiah Berlin set out to defend that position against, as he saw it, a long line of philosophers who spoke for freedom in such a way as to endanger freedom itself and the then current challenge of more or less Marxist inspiration that freedom depends on social security instead of on rights and liberty. His target was (a version) of the real freedom school and he branded philosophers of this ilk "enemies of human liberty."[7]

Berlin defended the classical position against that view with the help of the concept of negative liberty: to be free to do as one might wish without interference or coercion by others. Freedom is liberty and liberty is to be not prevented from making one's own choices, end of story. (He used the terms *liberty* and *freedom* synonymously).

With the recent publication of his collected papers on liberty, we can now see how strongly Berlin first held to that position. A long letter he wrote to George Kennan in 1951, although offering no definition of freedom and going off in many directions, is very much in the spirit of one thing, and one thing only: "This [when the desire for choice is broken] is the ultimate horror because in such a situation there are no worthwhile motives left: nothing is worth doing or avoiding, the reasons for existing are gone." And further: "[U]pon one's attitude to this issue . . . depends one's entire moral outlook, i.e. everything one believes."[8]

But this collection also enables us to see that Berlin departed from the strict view once he got down to more systematic work. In "Two Concepts of Liberty" (1958), he defends negative liberty as the bastion of freedom and warns against the dangers of ideas associated with a concept of positive liberty—freedom *to* as opposed to freedom *from*—but positive liberty, although raged against, is not thrown out. This is certainly the case in the introduction to his *Four Essays on Liberty* (1969) in which he replies to critics. Negative and positive liberty are both attractive ideas. The primacy of one does not lead to the rejection of the other. They "start

---

[5] Mill 1859/1991, pp.14, 116.

[6] As we shall see, this does not exhaust the modern liberal theory of freedom, but it is worth being reminded that a strong subschool has emerged of libertarian dogmatism, finding its perhaps clearest expression in Milton and Rose Friedman's *Free to Choose* (1979).

[7] In a remarkable series of radio lectures on the BBC in 1952, now published in Berlin 2002b.

[8] Berlin 2002a, pp. 340, 336–37.

at no great logical distance [but] the fundamental sense of freedom is freedom from chains. . . . The rest is extension."[9]

Freedom is now complex—what is extension is not nothing—and it is not easy to say just what it is. In a retrospective essay written in 1996, freedom has come to rest on negative and positive liberty in pretty equal measure, but with the provision that the danger of "frightful perversions" is greater in positive liberty than in negative.[10]

The story line in these works is that the point in separating out negative liberty is that something in the broader complexity of freedom is *fundamental*. There is no alternative theory that is valid instead of the negative one. Negative liberty is not everything there is to freedom, but it is where freedom starts. The way to protect against "perversion" is to insist on the *primacy* of negative liberty. Rights are not only a necessary condition of freedom but the first and most basic condition. Freedom understood as positive liberty is a dangerous idea when turned into policy because it has proved to be particularly susceptible to being perverted. But if freedom is perforce seen to contain an element of positive liberty, the insistence on the primacy of negative liberty serves to insure against the dangers contained in the idea of positive liberty.

The classical view, then, that rights are sufficient for freedom, did not survive. A fair reading of Berlin's work is that he started with the classical liberal view as his hypothesis but in the course of his project, the hypothesis falls.

The classical theory, however, is not rejected outright. It survives in the form of an insistence on the primacy of rights. This clear sense of where things start and what comes first is, in my opinion, the lasting and important result of Berlin's work on liberty. Freedom *is* a concept that can be perverted. We know well enough from experience that practices that may render people unfree can be defended with philosophically attractive ideas about freedom. To be politically safe, the concept needs to be tied down. Something in the thing freedom is basic, necessary, and nonnegotiable. Freedom depends on more than rights, but without rights there is no freedom. It goes to the individual's ability to promote his interests, but not *instead of* the protection of interests. Any notion of freedom without rights is dismissed, as is any idea of freedom based on positive *instead of* negative liberty. Rights are where freedom starts.

It is a pity that the classical view has had to be given up. Had we been able to stay with it, we would have had a simple, straightforward, and

---

[9] Berlin 2002a, pp. 35, 48. See also, e.g., Jahanbegloo 1992, in which Berlin is challenged to clarify his view on negative and positive liberty and refuses to discard positive liberty as such.

[10] Berlin 2002a, pp. 322–28.

operational concept of freedom—freedom would be something one has or does not have—and an eminently attractive one politically. This concept has the strength of modesty; it makes of the claim to freedom no more than the obvious claim to live by one's own will. That is an idea of freedom that is easy for its friends to demand with conviction and costly for its foes to oppose.

But it was finally not defensible. After Berlin's reexamination, the liberty school was no longer the same. Freedom simply is not one thing and one thing only. There is more to it.

FROM LIBERTY TO FREEDOM

The reason rights are not a sufficient condition of freedom is that to not be denied the right to make one's own choices is not to have the ability. One can have the right to choose without being in a position to make choice.

This proposition that freedom consists of something more than rights, and hence that rights are not a sufficient condition of freedom and freedom therefore is not one thing and one thing only, is provable. If what infuses rights with value is that they can be used for something, say to be drawn on in case one is in danger or need, there is no value in just *having* rights. For his rights to matter to a person, he must at least be aware of and have knowledge of them. Awareness and knowledge are not contained in rights, they are faculties or competences in the individual (or in someone else who has been delegated authority on the part of the individual, say a custodian of some kind). A person who has a right without knowing of it (or without the protection of someone else who knows of it for him) does not have the freedom it is the purpose of the right to give him. Hence, the proposition that freedom depends on rights, which is true, presupposes something more on top of and outside of rights, at least some knowledge or awareness. What is worthy of debate, then, is not whether rights are at the core of freedom, which is established, but what is contained in the "something more" that comes on top of rights.

What more there is to it, as far as the liberty school goes, can be found in subsequent developments in liberal thinking. First, from the modern theory of justice as formulated by Rawls in *A Theory of Justice* (1971): a just society is one in which everyone enjoys basic rights and commands basic goods. Applied to freedom (which was not the concept Rawls addressed himself to) we would say that to be free, a person needs to have the right to make her own choices, but in addition that she must also have the power to make use of her rights. Freedom depends, on top of rights, on also *resources*.

As soon as the strict classical view is given up, the inclusion of resources follows logically. In a market economy, for example, everyone usually has the right to partake of whatever goods are in the market, but you can only make claims on goods and be a free consumer if you have money to buy. Rights open up choice for you but do not on their own give you choice. Cohen has defended the inclusion of money as a condition of freedom against Berlin, and van Parijs has defined real freedom as depending on an assured minimum income.[11]

Rights are now rejected as the exclusive criterion of freedom, but the Rawlsian theory is consistent with the primacy of rights. It is not resources *instead* of rights, but in addition to rights once rights are given.

However, no more than that rights alone are a sufficient condition of freedom, are rights plus resources sufficient. We are still not in a position of necessarily being able to make choices. I may have rights as a consumer in a supermarket, for example, and resources, in this case money in my pocket, but will still not have choice if it should happen that there is nothing to choose from. Just that situation came, as I happened to experience it, shockingly on display in Warsaw in the autumn of 1981, when a deep economic and political crisis resulted in ordinary grocery stores suddenly running out of goods and consumers with money finding nothing to buy. (I, coming from the rich West, had never experienced the strangeness of stores just not getting filled up with goods.) Money is a resource that normally enables its holder to make claims on goods, but here that normality broke down and no amount of ztoty had any power to procure anything. (That power had shifted exclusively to hard currencies in currency stores.) This was not because of discrimination or rights being otherwise denied. The stores were open and no one was denied access. Nor was it a result of a lack of resources. Consumers had money and wanted to buy. But unfreedom it was—mothers were unable to get milk for their children! It was a case of choice being denied to people with rights and resources because there was nothing for them to choose from. The freedom of choice comes to people not only through the rights and resources they themselves hold but also from how social and economic options are laid out in the world around them.

People with rights and resources are still not free unless *arenas* are open to them in which relevant choice is available.[12] Freedom depends on there being schools, jobs, and shops with goods. If there are no books, newspapers, cinemas, and theaters, cultural experience is not available. If there are no competing parties and associations, political participation is not

[11] Cohen 2001; van Parijs 1997.

[12] On the resources-arenas model, see Coleman 1971; Rødseth et al. 1976; Erikson et al. 1987; Ringen 1995.

an expression of freedom. And those arenas must be open to *you*. For example, if the best private schools in the country discriminate against minorities and you are among those discriminated against, that education is not available to you however clever you are and however much money your parents have to pay the fees. And what they offer must be relevant to you. If you are a Muslim in a predominantly Protestant European country that offers your children schooling, but only in Protestant schools and you want your children to have a Muslim education, the availability of Protestant schools does not give you choice and freedom.

The possibility of exercising choice, we now see, depends on the individual's resources, on the availability of arenas with a relevant array of options for choice, and on those resources and options being linked by rights.

The step from rights and resources to including arenas as well has been argued (although not in that language) by Amartya Sen and Martha Nussbaum in *the capabilities approach*.[13] This approach is not dogmatically defined (which in part accounts for its flexible fruitfulness). It may not be explained in identical terms by both authors; Nussbaum, perhaps under the influence of Aristotelian philosophy, taking perhaps a slightly broader view than Sen and including more explicitly elements of reason as will be discussed below. However, the crux of it is that freedom lies in the linkage of rights, resources and options.[14] Resources sit with individuals and options in their environment, while rights infuse those resources with the power to make claims on those options.

That brings us to where the liberty school stands today. Freedom sits on rights. The rights that constitute liberty make up the first and basic condition of freedom. But people need more than rights in order to be free; they need first the right to make their own choices but then also the power to do so. The power of choice comes from a combination of resources with individuals and options in arenas. People who have rights, resources to make use of rights, and a social environment that offers them relevant options to choose from have real power of real choice.

The Politics of Freedom, I

The liberty school tells us a good deal about the specifics of basic government responsibility in a democracy.

---

[13] Based on research on famine and gender inequality, see Sen 1981, 1999b; Nussbaum 1999.

[14] For that interpretation in more detail, see Ringen 2005a.

It starts with rights. Most of us would probably insist that we own our rights and that they are not given us by any government. We have, for example, human rights by virtue of the simple fact of being humans. If these rights are denied us, that is an abuse of power. If we have them, it is not because they have been given us by our government but because what is ours has not been taken away. However, the rights that are ours by right are exposed. There are powers out there that may have an interest in curtailing them and be able to do so. We need to protect these rights, and for that we must turn to the government. Under democratic governance, the politics of freedom start with the protection of basic rights.

That recommendation follows from both the classical and revised versions of the liberty school, but from the revised version follow further recommendations. Freedom now depends also on resources. Most people get most of the resources they need to live freely from their own efforts and arrangements. For example, the money we need to be able to operate in consumer markets we mostly get from work and through family. But not everyone can do that all the time. We are at risk of illness, unemployment, abandonment, incapacity in old age and of finding family obligations unmanageable and so on. Unless there is a backup of security against contingencies and misfortune, some people will sometimes fall into poverty and, in that sense, unfreedom. That backup could be private, such as a system of voluntary charity, but by experience that has never been enough and is not enough today. A free society is one in which *everyone* is free, including those who fall victim to misfortune.[15] In the same way that we must turn to our government for the protection of rights, that is also where we must go for ultimate social security. It must be a responsibility of democratic governments to give all citizens last-resort protection against poverty.

Furthermore, a free life is possible only with access to arenas that generate relevant options of choice. That depends on there being arenas of action and on *something* being generated in those arenas, which is to say on a certain level of abundance (e.g., labor markets with jobs and stores with goods), on arenas being open to everyone, and on relevant things being on offer.

The question of abundance I move around by assuming that I am dealing with societies in which there is sufficient abundance for freedom. That is a reasonably safe assumption. Although a society of freedom probably must have some abundance, what restricts or enables freedom on this level is less what collective means add up to than the way they are managed. With the exception of economies in utter destitution, poverty is

---

[15] Except, of course, those who are legitimately denied some of their freedoms, notably in punishment for crimes.

usually the result of mismanagement (or plunder) more than of pure scarcity, even in countries where poverty is widespread.[16]

The question of arenas being open is already dealt with; if citizens have rights they have access to the arenas they want access to. That leaves the question of the relevance of the things they can expect to find in those arenas.

Citizens are in demand of things they want. When they have resources, they can put power behind that demand. The supply, however, is in the hands of others who are in it because they want a share of the resources citizens can give them or deny them. If that game is played straight, a supply will usually emerge that pretty much reflects what citizens demand. For games to be played straight, the arenas in which they are played are not rigged. If consumers have money, providers who want a share of their money must offer them goods they are willing to give up money for. If citizens hold the power of the vote, politicians who want votes will have to supply policies or put up parties that offer voters what they want. Or so providers will have to do if consumer markets and political arenas are not rigged. Since citizens want the goods providers offer as much as providers want the resources citizens bring to the exchange, providers can gain the upper hand if they can control the demand so that citizens will have to make do with what they elect to offer them, for example, goods at inflated prices or a more limited choice of policy options than is in demand in the citizenry. That will be the situation if arenas are rigged, which is to say, if power sits with those who should not have it (providers) and not with those who should (citizens).

Providers will usually have an interest in rigging the arenas in which they operate and, if they can, will do so with the help of monopoly or oligopoly arrangements.[17] Citizens are in control in unrigged arenas but cannot without help prevent others from rigging them. Again, they need to turn to their government for protection. A final recommendation from the liberty school is that democratic governments accept a duty to regulate consumer markets, the game of politics, and other arenas so as to protect them against being rigged.

If we call government activities to protect citizens against poverty and arenas against rigging *the welfare state*, we can conclude that it follows from the teaching of the liberty school in its late twentieth-century incar-

---

[16] See Dasgupta 1993. Even governments in very poor countries, often *particularly* in poor countries, tend to spend on military purposes that are not justified by national defense what could contribute decisively to, e.g. education and health care, which is to say that destitution in their populations is a result of political priorities and not shortages.

[17] As Adam Smith famously observed: "People of the same trade seldom meet together, even for merriment and diversion, but the conversation ends in a conspiracy against the public, or in some contrivance to raise prices." Smith 1776, 1:10:2.

nation that a well-functioning welfare state is a necessary ingredient in the politics of freedom. The arguments in favor of the welfare state, then, are not only in terms of welfare but also of freedom. This has not always been clear in liberal theory, but that dispute can now be laid to rest as a result of the Berlin and post-Berlin revisions of that theory which say that freedom depends on things to choose with and from in addition to the right of choice.

THE REAL-FREEDOM SCHOOL

Although the liberty school has refined and improved itself, the *definition* of freedom remains the same. Freedom is to be free to do as one wishes. Finding out more about what that takes does not change the meaning of what it *is*. The real-freedom school does not quibble with the liberty school on these matters. It objects more fundamentally about the meaning of freedom. That objection goes back at least to Aristotle, who almost 2,500 years ago not only rejected the concept of what I now call the liberty school but also suggested an alternative understanding. "The reason for this [that people live contrary to their real interests] is a false conception of liberty. . . . liberty is assumed to consist in 'doing what one likes'. The result of such a view is that. . . . each individual lives as he likes—or, as Euripides says, For any end he chances to desire. This is a mean conception [of liberty]. To live by the rule of the constitution ought not to be regarded as slavery, but rather as salvation."[18]

Doing what one likes is a mean conception because it may be something one just happens to want. What we should live by is not likes or even interests, but interests that have more to them than just being wants. The way to do that is to obey the constitution. That sounds like a contradiction; it is as if to say that freedom comes from obeying.

The liberty school's theory of freedom is attractive, but its beautiful simplicity is too good to be true. There is too much it does not say. It says rights, but what rights? Basic rights, I have said, but that qualification is taken from common sense and not from the theory. It says resources, but what resources? The resources that are needed to avoid poverty, I have said, but that again is found nowhere in the theory. It says abundance, but not how much. If we were to listen only to the theory, we would have to say that the more rights and the more resources and the more abundance, the more freedom. But anyone must know that he is on the wrong path if he is led to equating the quality of freedom with the quantity of abundance.

[18] *The Politics* 1310a12.

There is also too much it does say that is implausible. If freedom is the freedom to do as one wishes, it would seem to be freedom for whatever one wishes. One writer who has taken in earnest the ideas of the liberty school and followed them where they logically go is Philippe van Parijs in *Real Freedom for All*. If freedom is for whatever one wishes, that might include for example to live as a surfer on Malibu Beach. If we truly believe the liberal theory, we would believe that someone who has that wish has a right to live in that way. From this van Parijs suggests that governments should have a duty to give everyone a basic income so that everyone is assured the means to actually do as they wish, including to live as a beach bum if that is what they want.[19]

Now, we all know that we are not free to live as surfers on Malibu Beach. We may have some theoretical right to it but very few of us have the means to do so, however strongly we might wish it. That, van Parijs seems to say, means that we are denied real freedom, but most of us shrug it off as obvious that freedom does not mean being free to chuck it all in for a life on the beach just because we might wish to and do not for that reason cry foul about not being free to live as we want.

In fact, if we reflect practically on it, we do most of the things in daily life we do because we must, not because we want. We get out of bed in the morning because we have to. The worker takes the bus to work although he would rather go for a walk in the park. The housewife cleans and cooks although she would prefer to read poetry. I'm in my car and want to go into the street to my left, but it is a one-way street and I have to drive around the block and wait at two red lights. We are all prevented all the time from doing as we like.

The classical liberal might perhaps respond something along the line that as long as you have a right, you are free even if practicalities lead you to doing what is not on the top of your wish list. The modern liberal (as well as the libertarian, the Marxist, and van Parijs, who tries to be all three) might say that it is proof that working women and men are not free that they lack the means to actually do as they actually want. But most of us know that much of what we do we must do, that much of what we want we cannot have, and that those of us who live in free countries can still live more or less free lives. If we are unfree, it is not because from time to time or even often we must do what we do not want. That, we know, is just life.

Although it is an attractive idea, freedom may not *really* or fundamentally or finally be about doing as one wishes. Aristotle was a wise man. We should probably trust that he had good reasons for brushing aside

---

[19] On the basic-minumum-income issue, see appendix E.

"doing what one likes" and that he said it was about something more because he had understood something that is not immediately obvious.

One reason to think there might be something wanting in the liberty school's theory is that most liberal thinkers do not seem to fully believe it. Van Parijs wants to, but that gets him into a position others are inclined to see as outlandish: a theoretical proof of something that is obviously false. The theory seems to make more out of choice itself, choice for whatever anyone might wish, than most of its followers are willing to swallow. The business of making choice, after all, is pretty trivial and as much a burden as a boon in life.

Having choice is clearly a good thing that has a central role to play in any story of freedom, but everyone knows that if choice is a good thing, it is not for the goodness of choice itself but only in force of some purpose there is something to. Berlin knew it. In his 1951 letter, what is the total horror is to have no worthwhile *motives*. Choice is not for the sake of choice and not for the purpose of being able to follow any motive or desire. Freedom is valuable because it makes it relevant to reflect on how to live. The blessing in being free is not that you can run around and make choices all the time but that you can relevantly ask yourself what to want.

Joseph Raz knows it. In *The Morality of Freedom*, freedom is autonomy and autonomy is being able to exercise choice insofar as the choices are worth making. A free person is not someone who just follows desires such as they are but someone who is "the author of his own life." That is to use one's opportunities effectively but also to be in control of the purposes one uses opportunities for.

Amartya Sen knows it. The capabilities approach is about functionings, and functionings are valuable beings and doings. It is not just being and doing what one wishes but about beings and doings that make one's life good. So does Martha Nussbaum. What makes sense of choice is having valuable purposes to make choice for. She identifies such purposes in a list of "central human capabilities," which includes being able to imagine, think, and reason; being able to have attachments to things and persons outside of oneself; and being able to form a conception of the good and to engage in critical reflection about the planning of one's life.

And ordinary people know it. In a recent radio conversation, a former drug addict who had managed to kick a heavy habit explained the benefit: "I am free now to do as I want—to be a decent person, really."

What is lacking in the liberty school is a sense of what choice is for. Having a right to do something is not in itself a reason to do it. On German motorways you have the right to drive as fast as you want, but that is not a reason to drive as fast as your car will take you; you still have to decide. To desire something is not much of a purpose. Things are not valuable because they are wanted, they are wanted because they are valuable—or so we should insist. We are all burdened with desires we do not want to satisfy; nothing could be more humanly normal: the desire to punch someone in the nose, to steal someone's money, to take gruesome revenge, to seduce one's colleague's wife, to cheat at cards (even to cheat at solitaire), to seek advantage by lying, to smash up the neighbor's car with a sledgehammer when its alarm goes off in the middle of the night. In Venice, wrote Montesquieu in a letter in 1728, "only debauchery there has the name of liberty."[20] Doing what one likes is indeed what Aristotle saw it to be: for any end one might chance to desire.

There are good reasons to listen carefully to the liberty school. We know about the priority of rights not only from philosophy but also from experience. Where freedom has to be fought for, it is fought first as a battle over rights, as in civil-rights movements from the United States to South Africa and elsewhere. Martin Luther King's "dream" in his great speech in Washington DC on 28 August 1963 was one of equal rights, and it was by equal rights he would recognize the land of freedom. When on 12 March 2004, millions of people congregated in the cities and towns of Spain to protest the terrorist atrocity in Madrid the day before that had killed more than two hundred people and injured and maimed thousands, it was the basic values of human rights, liberty, and democracy they rallied around, no doubt feeling that what had been attacked was their yet young democracy. If we look back fifty years, civil and political rights were established in Western Europe and elsewhere as general rights, but were credibly challenged by an alternative set of ideas that promised a particular kind of real freedom in a system of planning, equality, and security but without rights. The effective defense of freedom was then to speak about liberty in its most elementary meaning. Berlin's arguments in favor of negative over positive liberty are seen against that backdrop as basically political and strategic.

We also know from experience that freedom depends on means. If you are poor, you live by needs and not wants and do not have much choice. Poor people are entitled to say that some of the rights they have are for them only formal rights because their poverty prevents them from doing what their rights say they can.

But the liberty school's theory of freedom is in the end still unsatisfactory. It is philosophically unsatisfactory in that it is open-ended, it stops nowhere, and it makes freedom depend on everything and ever more of it. The theory is unfinished; it is in need of being closed.

It is also politically unsatisfactory in that it carries too little persuasion on the battlefield of ideas. Freedom in the world today, as always, is something some have and others do not, some enjoy and others want, some

[20] Quoted in Venturi 1979.

are for and others are against. The cause of freedom needs ideas that arm its defenders and disarm its detractors. A theory that can be criticized for equating freedom with abundance and does not contain a powerful riposte against that criticism is a godsend for the enemies of freedom and an embarrassment to its friends. Politically, too, it is unfinished; it needs to be brought down to earth with a touch of modesty. The theory just does not speak to us about freedom in a way we know it should. It speaks about freedom more as a good than as a value.

What Aristotle may have seen, or so we can imagine, is that free choice is in fact a matter of obedience. Any choice must be for a purpose and is, when rational, an act of obedience to the purpose it is for. The liberty school defines freedom as being able to obey one's own wishes. For Aristotle, that is the mean conception because it may be just any wish. His alternative seems to be that we link up the idea of freedom with some notion of meaningful choice. He happens to call it the rule of the constitution, but that is semantics and means much the same as worthwhile motives, choices worth making, and valuable beings and doings according to Berlin, Raz, Sen, and Nussbaum.

Being unfree does not mean that you do not make choices. You still get up in the morning, get on the bus, wash the house, drive around the block, and so on. It means that in the larger scheme of things, you are not yourself the master of your life and not able to live by your own will. It means that someone or something says to you that *this* is the way you must live, whether you like it or not, and circumstances conspire so that you must obey as you are told. The problem of freedom, said Berlin, is finally about the question of who is to be master.

There are two ways that your choices may not be according to your own will. One way is that they are dictated to you by someone else who has the power to oblige you to obey. The other way is that choices, although not imposed on you or forbidden you by an outside dictator, emerge through psychological processes that are a mystery to you so that what you do in life is to satisfy desires you just happen to *have*. In the first case, you live in a visible dictatorship: you are forced to obey what others order. In the second case, you live under an invisible dictatorship of forces: if you just obey wants, you are not making a life by your own will; you are the slave of desires of unknown provenance.

I think it is fruitful to treat the inability to be in control as a kind of dictatorship, at least under certain conditions. A political dictatorship removes from you the ability to act freely. A psychological dictatorship removes from you the ability to decide freely why to act. That is real unfreedom. If forces take hold of your mind and drive you to a life that is not of your own choosing, you are not free. These forces may include political propaganda, commercial advertisement, peer pressure, and the like, or inadequate education relative to social expectations in the complexity of modern societies, for example. That kind of perverted freedom is a real and present danger. Materialism and consumerism, for example, are forms of addiction that can deceive anyone into a lifestyle of futility.

Liberals have for good reasons been concerned with freedom from visible dictatorship, the freedom from interference or coercion that is contained in Berlin's negative liberty. Others have been more aware of the freedom from dangers in one's inner self. Any psychologist will be aware of that. The unreflected life, said Socrates, is a life not worth living. The Stoic tradition in philosophy is directed to the wisdom of liberating oneself from one's desires rather than indulging them. So is Buddhist thinking.[21]

Those of us who have the good fortune to live in affluent democracies, say in Western Europe or North America, live in freedom as the liberty school defines it, at least by and large. Even so, or perhaps even therefore, we are up against a crisis of freedom. The freedom we have is not assured and always threatened. One of the ways it is threatened is from the danger that we ourselves pervert it. One of the ways we are in danger of doing that is by taking liberty to be license, that we translate freedom from coercion into freedom to whatever, for example, to greed, ruthlessness, selfishness, and hubris. This is a real and present danger, that we who happen to live on the top of the world use an idea of unrestrained freedom so that others in that world have reason to see it as an ideological smokescreen for power and privilege.

Nor does the combination of freedom of choice and abundance seem to do for us what we should expect of it. In terms of being able to do as we like, we have never had it so good; but for all the choice that has become available to us, we do not seem to experience life as better or to find more happiness in it.[22] Moving up from a life without freedom to one of freedom from poverty, for example, is also to move up in happiness. But moving further from there to yet more choice does not seem to be followed by yet more satisfaction. There is happiness in being able to graduate from a life dominated by needs to one that allows wants but not much in moving from there to being able to satisfy ever more wants. The reason is that we adjust our expectations so that the more we have, the more we want. It seems that it is not we who have wishes but they us, and that we are enslaved on a treadmill running after wishes that run before us and keep their distance.

[21] See, e.g., Mishra 2004.
[22] For excellent summaries of evidence, see Layard 2005; Offer 2006.

FROM FREEDOM TO REAL FREEDOM

Ever since Emile Durkheim mapped the social correlates of suicide and developed his theory of solidarity and anomie more than a century ago, sociologists have known that the individual who lives in a state of unrestrained liberty lives in mortal danger. This person, far from being the master of his destiny, is likely to be lost in a social universe he cannot comprehend, without the anchorage he needs for purpose, decisiveness, and power of action. That is possibly what Aristotle had long understood, that the person who does as he likes is likely to become lost and in danger of living contrary to his interests. And it is possibly what others see today in a decline of social capital that deprives people of the intangible communal resources they need to make sense of their lives and societies.[23]

Freedom consists in freedom of choice, says the liberty school, but the real-freedom school disagrees: it rests on that but only as a start. In addition, we depend on competences and skills for a free life. Choice is not a matter of just being at liberty to do as we want, it is *difficult*. We humans are fallible. When we can do as we want, we are in danger of getting it wrong. Nothing of value in life is cost-free but liberty is unlikely to help us to recognize costly choices as the right ones. Real interests are more often long-term than immediate, but short-term gratification is usually more likable. Well-being, argues Avner Offer (in a rich theory of the probability of fallible choice), comes not from choice but from self-control. And so, I argue, does real freedom. If liberty seduces you to choices that are not in your own best interest, you are being led around by the nose and hence are not free. A choice governed by a wish is just a choice. What makes it *your* choice is that it is something you have decided is worth having or doing. Amartya Sen wrote in a summary comment on much of his own reflection on freedom: "Even though the idea of freedom is sometimes formulated independently of values, preferences and reasons, freedom cannot be fully appraised without some idea of what a person prefers and has reason to prefer. . . . Rationality as the use of reasoned scrutiny cannot but be central to the idea and assessment of freedom. . . . To deny that accommodation. . . . would involve, in effect, a basic denial of freedom of thought [and have] the effect of arbitrarily narrowing permissible 'reasons for choice', and this certainly can be the source of a substantial 'unfreedom'. . . . The 'rational fool' is, in this sense, also a victim of repression."[24]

---

[23] On Durkheim see, e.g., Horowitz 1999. On social capital see, e.g., Putnam 2000. On social anchorage, see appendix G.

[24] Sen 2002, pp. 5–7.

Those who seek happiness in the liberty to do as they want will never find it. To chase choices is to allow wants to be master and to condemn yourself to pursuing something that cannot be satisfied. If you do not get a grip on what to obey, you are obeying something that, whatever it is, is not your own will. The liberty school may say that freedom is one thing, the purpose you use it for something else. The real-freedom school does not accept that division. If you are free to do as you wish and are more or less in control of your senses, we know something about what you would do. You would do something you know is worthwhile. If you do something you know to be wrong or destructive to yourself—say you take a spirit of sexual freedom as a license to promiscuity and sexual exploitation in spite of your own knowledge that sexual irresponsibility and exploitation is wrong—then something has gone wrong for you. When Saint Paul does what he does not want, it is no longer he who is the agent but something else that has made itself master. He calls it sin— we might say "forces." Someone who is driven by fixed ideas, inflexible ambitions, obsessions, or fanaticism is not his own master; he is, precisely, driven. Jon Elster has explained the shortcoming of the notion of doing what one wants with the story of Ulysses, who tied himself to the mast of his ship to prevent himself from steering it on ground in obedience to the overpowering desires he knew he would feel when he heard the song of the sirens.

The freedom of the liberty school is formal freedom; real freedom is something more, it is the freedom that enables you to shape your own life and to do so with good sense. The philosophers must no doubt investigate whether reason is contained in freedom or is something that comes in (or not) after the fact when you have freedom and go on to make use of it.[25] But more down-to-earth people might well find it difficult to recognize a counterfactual to the view that someone who lives irrationally is not living freely. Having liberty is where it starts but not where it ends, it is *being* free we should aspire to.

We have now stepped off the safe platform of liberal theory and onto an unsafe knife's edge of speaking of freedom and discipline in the same breath. That is precisely the kind of language that Berlin warned contains dangers to freedom. My wishes, such as they are, are at least *my* wishes. If real freedom depends on my wishes being worthwhile, worth pursuing, valuable, or reflective of real interests, then somehow someone must de-

---

[25] Although the need to do so is created more or less artificially by a needlessly restrictive concept of rationality that would have us think that the only thing people care about is utility, that desires (then usually called preferences) are exogenous, and that behavior is explained by anticipated utility relative to those desires, whatever they are. Such standard rational-choice theory is built on the peculiar idea that people do not reflect on their desires but just pursue the satisfaction of desires they just have.

cide what is worthwhile, valuable, real, and so on. If that is someone else, then coercion may be creeping in by the back door. Berlin (in "Two Concepts of Liberty" again) did not speak against positive liberty as such but warned of a slippery slope: once we start entertaining ideas in the direction that freedom is more than freedom *from*, it is "no very great distance" to the idea that finally someone else must decide what it is for. The final question is, who is to be master? If it is not I and my wants, will it be someone else?

Wants cannot be master because then there is no freedom. Not only am I not free if I just obey wants, that notion of freedom is self-defeating. Were we, in daily life, to go by the maxim that we as free women and men in the name of freedom have the right to do as we want, there would be no basis for cooperation, no basis for trust, and no community. This would be the freedom of stupidity, the freedom to insist that any want is a right and any right absolute, the freedom that makes it sufficient for me, when asked why I insist on doing what is offensive to you, to say "Because! And it's none of your business!" That's stupidity because in the community of people with that inclination, freedom is doomed. Community *is* cooperation and trust. If we do not by prudence invite cooperation and contribute to a climate of trust, rules of cooperation will be imposed, as will safeguards and controls, so that we can trust the untrustworthy. The more stubbornly we insist on rights, the more rules and controls will be imposed—and before we know it, we will live by ever more rigid rules and controls wherever we go and freedom will disintegrate imperceptible step by imperceptible step. I, for one, believe that we who live in the affluent democracies, for all the good fortune that comes with it, are long since deep into this creeping erosion of freedom. From the idea that freedom comes from rights and abundance, although itself basically correct, it is no very great distance (to use Berlin's words) to the illusion that freedom is license. From this we demand ever more abundance and ever more rights in an upward spiral of expectations that is insatiable. Unless we ourselves stop that spiral, someone else will step in and do it for us and we will find ourselves—probably *are* finding ourselves—living under constitutions of liberty but in societies of stiflingly regulated social and economic life. In the land of freedom, there are many slippery slopes. A society dedicated to both order and freedom will strike back and smother the freedom it allows you if you run with it to undermine order, and again someone else will be master.[26] We persuade our-

---

[26] For example, this is how it could happen: In Britain, we enjoy extensive press freedom. Some of the press is, in a market-driven frenzy, exploiting that freedom to ruthlessness without purpose. That has resulted in strong demands to impose a regulatory regime on the press, something that may well happen and, if so, would represent a curtailment of press

selves to believe that we are free because we have the choice of abundance while not noticing that we are sinking into the morass Tocqueville called "soft despotism."

Berlin was no doubt right to warn against the dangers of perversion that may be contained in the idea of positive liberty. He also warned of the same danger in negative liberty, but thought positive liberty particularly susceptible to perversion. That may be right or wrong depending on time and place. Where freedom is absent or rights challenged, the way to speak for it is to speak about where it starts and what is at its core. Where the liberty of rights and abundance has been obtained, the way to speak in its defense is to speak about how it is to be used. Freedom is exposed and has enemies. The way to protect it is to let others see that it is worth protecting.

Learned exchange on freedom is not an exercise in pure theory, it is a mesh of philosophical truth and strategic expediency. It is about defending something those of us who care about want others to care about or at least respect. What we say freedom *is* should be both what we believe to be true and what we think will work. That muddies the waters—read Berlin again and see how—but it is in those waters we swim. There is no point in talking to one's times about freedom if what one says is not believable in those times.

Once we come to terms with the impossibility of wants being master, we have to sort out which wants are to count. One way to do that could be to call on a higher authority, say a democratic government or a philosopher-king. To some considerable degree, that's what we do. We democratically ask democratic governments to limit our freedom of choice by imposing regulations on us. For example, we want governments to force us to save what we know we need to save for our pensions. But unless we are cautious in what we ask and allow our governments to order us to do, we fall right into Berlin's trap and allow our freedom to be perverted by undue interference or coercion.

Therefore it is fortunate that there is another way. There is no need to wait for someone else to come in and close the liberal theory by drawing a line in the sand and declaring that so much of rights, resources, and abundance is allowed but no more or deciding by fiat that A, B, and C

---

freedom. If editors had been better able to restrain themselves against ruthlessness without purpose, they would have protected the freedom they want to have without sacrificing anything of value under press freedom, akin to following the editorial rule of *The New York Times*: all the news that's fit to print. Editors who refrain from printing what is unfit to print are exercising free choice and, in the process, protecting press freedom. When they print what is unfit, they are not exercising free choice but obeying forces, in this case market forces. It is not because they are ruthless that they are endangering press freedom but because they are *purposelessly* ruthless. See appendix C.

are worthwhile purposes but D, E, and F not. Much to be preferred is that we as free agents do it ourselves, that we mobilize self-control and make ourselves masters over our wants. You want the freedom to do as you wish. You know that if what you wish is without sense and purpose you're a fool, and that you are endangering your freedom by insisting on the freedom of greed or stupidity. You know that the way to protect your freedom is to not abuse it. You know that the way to talk persuasively to others about freedom is to purge its idea of greed and hubris and to infuse it with modesty. You know that these things must be done one way or another and that if you do not impose discipline on yourself, others will do it for you. Therefore you talk firmly but softly about the right to do as you want, you speak about purpose as much as about choice and you start by sorting out with yourself what is worth investing rights and resources in and fighting for.

Berlin might have seen here another "enemy of human liberty"—or perhaps not: he was after all himself unable to stay faithful to the orthodoxy he set out to defend. There is a reason he was not. Page after page, in "Two Concepts of Liberty," against self-emancipation and self-realization; against Kant, Rousseau, and the early utilitarians; against Marx, Spinoza, Locke, Montesquieu, Burke, Fichte, and others—that rich essay is also one that becomes ever more peculiar the more one reads it!—does not do away with what is evident, that if your will is not your own, you are not by your choices living by your own will. You may have liberty, but you are not yourself master and you are not freely shaping a life.

FREEDOM AND REASON

Isaiah Berlin made the case for negative liberty and against positive liberty by arguing that the former concept was the less dangerous one. My argument for real freedom and against the liberty school is the same. I believe that the idea that freedom means to be able to do as one wishes is a dangerous idea. It is dangerous to the individual because it easily encourages the delusion that the quality of freedom can be reduced to the quantity of abundance and from there stimulates a life of frivolous and futile pursuit of more of everything irrespective of value and purpose. It is dangerous to community because it discourages decency, cooperation, and trust. It is dangerous to the standing of freedom in the world because it is an idea that will for good reasons be seen as perverse against the backdrop of mass poverty, environmental decay, and cultural confrontations. Unless we rein in our understanding of freedom, we endanger the free life and undermine the cause of freedom.

It is also a dangerous idea in the world. Ideas matter; the ideas we cultivate collectively strike back on us individually and influence our minds and actions. If the rich and powerful minority in a world of mass poverty and environmental abuse makes freedom its supreme value and associates that with ever more rights and abundance, it will set itself on a path of greed, widening differences in standards of living, exploitation, and provocation—and towards a world in which freedom either ceases or becomes meaningless.

As luck will have it, we can pull the concept of freedom down to earth without doing violence to the meaning of freedom. The idea that freedom is just a matter of being able to do as we like is too simple to be credible, and we need have no fear about rejecting it. The idea that freedom is being our own master bids us to ask for something more in freedom than the liberty to do as we like. This idea tells us that the meaning of freedom is to be in control not only of choice but also of the purpose of choice. Our debate about what more there is to it has taken us from rights to also include means, and now moves on from there to also include purpose.

It is not enough that someone else is not master for you yourself to be master. It is necessary but not sufficient. You are not your own master if you let passions reign and just obey wishes, desires, preferences, or whatever we might call such commanding sentiments. The real-freedom school defines freedom as being able to live a life of one's own making. Freedom in this meaning comes not from being able to do whatever but from knowing something about what it is worth doing and then being able to do that.

This, I think, is common sense and something most people, if not all philosophers, know. But just what is it they know? What exactly is it that is worthwhile and valuable and worth doing? We are always up against wishes we know are no good. We can then either dispose of those wishes and do what we know we should do and not what there is nothing more to than that it is wanted. But if so, how do we do that? Or we can mess things up for ourselves and, in the name of liberty or some other confusion, obey wishes that are contrary to our interests. Avner Offer believes that the capacity for self-control declines with affluence and uses the striking example of increasing obesity, which he calls an epidemic of affluence: people massively using their liberty of affluence to eat themselves to ill health and death.[27] If so, what is it that goes wrong? How can free women and men take control not only over their choices but also over the will that directs those choices?

Free agents subject their wants and desires to investigation: they do not do what wants say just because they are wants; they make decisions. They

[27] Offer 2006.

decide what it is sensible to do in the pursuit of sensible purposes. What finally makes a life free, once the agent has rights and other necessary conditions of free choice, is that he whose desire for choice has not been broken (to paraphrase Berlin again) uses his freedom of choice to reflect on worthwhile motives and thus makes his life a reflective one. That's what makes it *his* life.

A reflective life is a life governed by reason, a life in which the agent wants what he has reason to want and does what there are reasons to do. What is valuable is what there is reason to want. What is worth doing is what there is reason to do. What is worth wishing is what there is reason to aspire to. *Reason* is what gets us from the freedom of the liberty school to that of the real-freedom school.

Reason is the ability to make reasoned choices about ends and means. That includes and combines the two forms of rationality suggested by Max Weber: *Zweckrationalität* and *Wertrationalität*, rationality in ends and rationality in means. Raymond Boudon has proposed a way of giving meaning to the Weberian idea. Deliberate opinions and actions are grounded in reasons, that is, they are not arbitrary to the person. Reasoned opinions and actions are grounded in *good* reasons, that is, in not just any reasons but in reasons that make good sense.[28]

Reasoned choice can be defined more precisely as choice governed by three kinds of sensitivity. The most elementary condition is *effectiveness* in the choice of means. If we want to achieve something and some choice of means is available, it is a sign of reason that we choose effective means.

That satisfies a narrow concept of rationality, which takes desires as given and then sees rationality as the inclination and ability to make choices that contribute to the satisfaction of those desires, Weber's *Zweckrationalität* in other words. Here, obviously, since we have abandoned desires as given, it is too restrictive on its own.[29] It is not wrong, but insufficient.

The second condition is *propriety*. That again goes to means, but now to the ability to decide what means it is proper to use. Although there is no reason unless there is effectiveness, competence for effective action is not enough. We admire people who are effective, but it is not for their effectiveness that we respect them. Reason implies an understanding of what it is proper to do or not to do. People of good sense know that some effective means are for good reasons unacceptable or dubious to others and that there are means the use of which would be wrong by their own standards. Ends do not always justify means. Reasonable people look for

---

[28] See Boudon 1995, 2003, and other works by the same author. On good reasons, see also Scanlon 1998.

[29] As it now is in much theory of rationality; see, e.g., Elster 2000.

means that are effective and proper and that balance these qualities with good sense; they use appropriate means.[30]

The third condition is *worthiness*. This goes to ends, to the ability to discriminate between ends that are worth effort and ends that are trivial, frivolous, mistaken, or bad. With good sense comes a critical awareness of one's goals. Reasonable persons are not egoists who pursue only their own good, they are not hedonists who seek only pleasure, they are not fools who run like headless hens after desires that have dropped on them from they know not where. They use their faculties to set themselves sensible goals. Persons of good sense choose goals that are in their own interest—challenging, stimulating, creative, potentially rewarding, compatible with abilities, fun, interesting, not outlandishly unrealistic, conducive to joy and pleasure, useful towards further goals, sensible in the quest for a good life—and they choose goals they see as worthy, good, decent, acceptable, faithful to duty.

The choosing of ends is not very different from the choosing of means. Alternative goals are in front of us and we perforce decide which ones to make ours. Goals today are also means towards further goals tomorrow. An idea that there is in this respect a sharp divide between "positive" means and "normative" goals would not stand up, never mind that ends are given and that what we choose are means to their satisfaction. Reason includes *la rationalité des valeurs*.[31] To revert to my previous concepts of rights, resources, and options, I am here arguing that reason contains more than effective choice. It includes also the sorting out of proper resort to rights and proper use of resources as well as the thorny problem of making sense of what, among available options, is relevant and valuable to your real interests.

Reason springs from an inner competence—an ability to understand, contemplate, and discriminate and from there to make decisions and choices—from a disposition to ask about and listen to reasons, and from a capacity to be touched and moved by reasons. It rests on an ability to consider goals and decide that one is better than the other and more worthy to strive for, to compare means in terms of both effectiveness and propriety, and to make choices and take actions in accordance with what you see to make good sense.

We can take self-interest as a given in the choice of goals and means. That is where sound choice starts. Self-interested effectiveness is obviously essential and entirely proper to someone who sets out to make his or her own life, but, again, not sufficient. Reason goes beyond instinct and includes the ability to temper self-interest in the choice of goals so as

[30] A notion of rationality argued in particular by Simon 1983.
[31] Mesure 1996.

to avoid blind egoism and to temper effectiveness in the choice of means so as to avoid unbridled ruthlessness. "To solve that problem [overcoming my own insistent primitive self-interest], we need to put before people's minds considerations that will sometimes, without coercion, get them listening to their self-concern less and to their concern for others more."[32]

If constraint is what others impose on us, freedom means living without (too much) constraint. Restraint, on the other hand, comes from the person himself or herself, from a sensitivity in the individual that some ambitions are better than others and some means are right and others wrong, and from a willingness and ability to abide by such sentiments. Reason depends on the ability to restrain self-interest.

The ability to live by reason may well be socially determined, for example by living in a society of orderly regulation and a culture of trust. For a culture of trust to emerge, however, there must first be an inclination towards respect for propriety and worthiness in the individuals who constitute that society. It is this prior inclination in the individual I am concerned with understanding here. I have discussed social conditions in previous chapters; now I go behind that and look inside individuals to a part of their psychological makeup.

Restraint is grounded in values and norms. People who live by reason hold to beliefs that they have faith in and that they let themselves be guided by without necessarily doing so only for prudent reasons or for fear that others will sanction them. When we act out of restraint we are, without coercion, paying attention to others, to decency, to charity, or, for example, to the environment or future generations. We are exercising the ability to act from an understanding of right and wrong. With values and norms come an awareness of the fact of difference between good and bad and right and wrong and a disposition to reflect on worthiness and propriety in our decision making. My values and norms are some of the instruments in my toolbox for forging reasoned choice out of the liberty to do as I like. They are no assurance against mistakes, but there is a world of difference between reflecting and failing and just drifting. If I reflect I am a free person; I am doing what I decide to do. If I just drift, I am unfree; I am acting from reasons I am not aware of.

For individuals, values and norms are among the building blocks that make up their inner competence (along with knowledge of the facts of the world). They are principles or maxims on a general level or higher-order rules that make themselves felt from the background of our awareness and inform more specific opinions and decisions. Only beliefs that have the capacity to be seen as particularly important and to stand above and more or less direct other beliefs or practices are eligible, so to speak. Our

[32] Griffin 1996, p. 76.

values and norms are our superbeliefs which enable us to discriminate in more practical matters. Values are superbeliefs about what is good, they help us to decide on good and bad goals and intentions. Norms are superbeliefs about what is right, they help us to decide on right and wrong means and actions. For example, if we believe that equality is a good thing, then the desire to protect or advance equality is one of our values. That superbelief helps us to make more specific choices, for example to see it worth our while to vote in elections and to decide which party to vote for.[33]

To form a belief about anything at all, I must be aware of the object of belief. That may sound obvious but is in the case of values and norms not at all trivial. To say that values and norms are beliefs is not to say that they grow spontaneously from inner sources in the soul. They come from somewhere. I cannot form the belief that equality is a good thing unless I am aware that there is such a thing to consider as equality. If I am to live by the Golden Rule—do unto others as you want others to do unto you—I must know of it.

But for a belief to become a value or norm for me there must be something more to it than simply knowing about it. I must believe in the belief. The goodness of equality becomes a value for me if I make the belief that equality is a good thing *my* belief. The beliefs that I make mine are those

---

[33] That's what values and norms are for the individual. What they are or may be more objectively is another question, which I fortunately do not have to resolve here. But I *think* it works like this: A value is a belief in the goodness of something, for example, the goodness of equality. If I believe equality is a good thing, the goodness of equality is for me a value. I may be the only one in my society to hold to that belief, but even so it remains a value for me (as long as I'm able to hold on to it against what everyone else says). If (many) others share that belief, it becomes what we could call a social value. What it is that gives certain beliefs the power that makes them social beliefs is not clear. Scanlon 1998 suggests that it should depend on the reasons that are offered to recommend them, and in particular on those reasons being such that sensible people could not reasonably reject them—that we have good reasons to accept principles that have this property as values. Social values, in my meaning, still reside ultimately in the beliefs of individuals, but once a value becomes a social value it also appears, from the point of view of individuals, to exist "out there" and to impose itself on them. That is all the more true if social values have durability, for example, if they are successfully passed on from one generation to the next. We might hope it is the strength of reasons in their favor that makes certain beliefs social values, but I would not think that is necessarily the case. A group of people may well come to hold values that are wrong in the sense that they are not grounded in good reasons, for example, beliefs about racial superiority. A social value may impose itself on individuals, such as on a new generation, in the form of conventions—values that we are aware of floating in the air, so to speak—or in a more institutionalized manner, for example, written down as laws. None of this is of course stable; values and norms, both individually and in the social meaning, come and go.

that have some power for me. My values and norms are those beliefs about good and right in which I have faith. If the Golden Rule is to be a norm that guides my life, it is not enough that I am aware of it; I could just ignore what I know it says. I must have faith in what I know.

I call that *faith*. There is something intangible about values and norms. When a value is established as a value in your mind, it has some force for you that cannot be fully pinned down. You *know* it to express what is good, right or true. You *know* you should live by it. You *know* that others, too, should share that value and live by it.

Where does awareness come from? The answer is that it is learned. If I am to know of the Golden Rule, I must be made aware of it. It may be— I rather doubt it but I do not exclude it—that (some) values or norms exist "out there" in some objective meaning (for example, that they are given by God), but even so the awareness of them must, for the purpose of our present discussion, make its way to the mind of the individual who struggles with choice.[34]

What does faith do? Faith infuses beliefs with power. If you have faith in a belief, that belief presents itself to you as a reason by which you make decisions. Your awareness of a norm makes of it a reason for you to think or do as it says. Your faith in it starts to make it a good reason.

In respect to values and norms, faith first of all separates those that you make yours from those that you discard. You live in society. In various ways—from parents, from teachers, from politicians, from leaders, from conventions, from laws—society offers you a menu of values and norms to consider. Some recommend to you the belief that equality is a good thing; others that it's each man for himself. Even values and norms are things people have to choose, if in complicated ways. The values and norms you make yours are those you attach faith to.

In addition, faith enables you to actually live by those values and norms you make yours. It is what enables you to do in fact as your superbeliefs recommend in theory, including when that costs something. For example, a speed limit of seventy miles per hour on motorways tells you how fast to drive. The law makes the rule clear to you so that you cannot be un-aware of it, but as we all know it still takes something more to actually do as the rule says when on the road. It takes the backing of a belief that I accept as authoritative, such as "it is wrong to disobey the law." What

---

[34] But it may be, possibly, that some values or norms are somehow instinctive in human beings. For example, small children seem to have a keen sense of fairness before apparently having been taught about it. People may also be differently disposed to restraint and to being guided by values and norms, possibly even by inheritance (but to inherit a disposition is still hardly to inherit specific beliefs).

makes me accept that superbelief as authoritative is that it is one I have faith in.

The inner competence to reason rests ultimately in this elusive faculty I call faith, a faculty in the soul, so to speak, that enables us to actually believe in our beliefs and practically make them authoritative signposts for our opinions and choices. For example, most of us today accept that it is wrong to treat people differently based on the color of their skin, but the awareness of that norm needs to be backed up by faith in order for us to steer clear of racial prejudice and discriminatory action. We need something to resort to in order to find the strength of conviction to really accept principles of right and wrong as practically authoritative and get beyond only paying lip service to laudable ideals.

To say that values and norms need to be backed up by faith is to say that the adherence to values and norms is a battle, or simply that restraint is difficult. Faith, then, is a quality of character, an ability to listen to arguments about right and wrong and to be moved by the outcome of such arguments. Where character comes from is not easily said, but a part of the answer must be, again, that it is learned. We need to be taught and explained about good and bad and to be guided to the ability to understand and know that there is sense and authority in such beliefs. Learning cannot be limited to mere awareness; it is also about the ability to believe and to abide by beliefs.

The awareness of values and norms must be learned. The ability to have faith in what you have learned must be learned. The capacity to reason must be learned. Freedom in the meaning of being able to live a life that is your own life rests on learning, on what the Germans call *Bildung* (for which there is, strangely, no proper English translation). Citizens who have liberty owe it to themselves to acquire the competence to live freely. By so doing they also do their community a service because they are more likely to live in a way that invites cooperation and contributes to a climate of trust.

Learning goes on all through life, but what is learned or not in childhood and youth is basic, certainly in respect to values, norms, and character. Freedom is grounded on one side in rights and on the other side in *Bildung*. It grows out of laws that protect rights and out of families and schools that foster learning.

Faith infuses beliefs with power, but how can you know that what faith puts to you as a good reason really *is* a good reason, and how can you know the difference between good and bad values and norms? Blind faith is not the stuff of free women and men. Blind faith is obeying what is dictated to you.

The alternative to blind faith is evidence-based faith. You may be so fortunate as to possess the ability to take your own beliefs about right and wrong seriously and to live more or less as you learn, but as a rational person you still want to discriminate in your use of that ability. You want to invest faith in such values and norms that there are good reasons to have faith in. That's what evidence enables you to do. With evidence, faith becomes reasoned faith. While faith starts to transform values and norms into good reasons, it is evidence that clinches it. You need more than awareness of a norm to obey it; you need to have faith in it. But you could be wrong in what you invest faith in. You might really believe, for example, that ends always justify means or that white people should rule the world. Resort to evidence is the rational way to decide which, in the larger menu of potential values and norms, to make yours.

Evidence is what makes an answer to the "why" question persuasive. Why should I tell myself that I should drive no faster than seventy miles per hour? As a rational person I do not just believe; I want to know *why* I should accept a rule in the sense that I should consider myself bound by it.

For persuasive evidence we might in a scientific age want to trust science, but scientific evidence about issues of human passion is thin on the ground. The law tells us about right and wrong, but the law can be mistaken. The Bible tells us about good and bad, but the holy texts are mysterious even to the believers. The philosophers offer guidance but are usually too circumspect to be understood. Prime ministers and archbishops tell us what to do and how to live, but trust is thin. There is evidence out there but it is not complete, not objective, and not clear and easy to make sense of; it is of many kinds and from many sources, scattered and often contradictory, always ambiguous. Different peoples and times accept different things as evidence.[35] People who want to know what they should have faith in and why seek in this mass of evidence a way to that which they have reason to take as persuasive.

Rational people want to go by beliefs that are supported by good evidence, but that is not just a matter of reading evidence as it presents itself. It is a matter of interpretation. Take, for example, "traditional family

---

[35] Garry Wills, in a discussion of the devotion to relics in Middle Age Europe, makes a brilliant comparison: "This odd black market in white magic worked somewhat as the underground trade in artworks does in the modern times. The same concern for the authenticity of the object that we witness now was exercised with regard to relics. . . . The modern purchaser submits the work to scientific tests by radiography or chemical analysis. The late-antique bishop performed his own experiments, putting the relic to an empirical test: Can it work miraculous cures? That is how Helen had established the authenticity of the True Cross, and how Ambrose, the bishop of Milan, proved that he had found the bodies of Saints Gervasius and Protasius" (Wills 2001, p. 237).

values" in the meaning that the nuclear family is the best family form. I ask why and am told that experience has shown the nuclear family to be the most stable basis for raising children. Is that persuasive? How am I to judge and know?

Persuasive evidence is tested evidence. Is it true that the nuclear family is the best basis for raising children? I can try to find the answer in my own experience, but I know that to be a flimsy basis. I am better off by asking others: "This is how I'm inclined to see it, but what is your experience and what do you know that is relevant to the question?" If I ask several others and keep an open mind, I am on my way to finding a safe opinion—or so I have reason to hope. I may ask experts or people I trust. Or I may say, "Let's sit down and discuss and explore this difficult question carefully."

In the end, evidence is tested by conversation, exchange of information and opinions, and discussion: by *deliberation*. This is no foolproof method. Its quality depends on what information is available and on our inclination and ability to deliberate openly and honestly. It may be that we use deliberation to confirm prejudices we already hold or that those who are better informed are able to manipulate those who have less knowledge. But it is the best we have. Tested evidence is evidence that has survived rational deliberation.

Reason comes from an inner competence. Values and norms are beliefs that sit in the individual. Restraint is something free people must find in themselves, as they must make up their own minds about trust in evidence. Once we ask where such beliefs and competences come from, we find that they come to each of us from our interaction with others, from deliberation. Reason originates, finally, in what Jürgen Habermas calls "deliberative rationality."[36]

Let me be clear about my argument here. Deliberation is a social condition for people to live with each other in a spirit of reason, but that is not what I am raising here. I do not deny that, of course, but what I'm presently concerned to get across is that deliberation is also a condition for individuals to be able to cultivate in themselves that all-important inclination to reason.

There is a vast difference in understanding between the liberty school and the real-freedom school. That difference goes to the meaning of freedom, between the freedom that consists in doing as one likes and the freedom that comes from being one's own master. It also goes to the question of where freedom comes from. While liberal freedom comes to individuals by their being detached from others, real freedom comes from the way they are connected with others.

---

[36] See, e.g., Habermas 1984/87, 1990.

THE POLITICS OF FREEDOM, II

Reason is a social competence: I'll be reasonable if you are. What enables me to be reasonable is trust that you will be reasonable in return. There is not much use in preaching to individuals about being reasonable in all things unless they live in an environment in which reason reasonably prevails.

But reason is not *only* a social competence. It is also a competence in the individual. For a social environment to be created in which reason prevails, the individuals who make up that environment must be capable of and inclined to reason. That's not enough for a culture of reason to emerge and persist; for that to happen individual inclinations must come together and be institutionalized so that each of us is able to live as we preach. But it is still necessary that individuals enter the social game with a willingness to reason. No convention can become institutionalized unless people bring with them those attitudes and beliefs that are the building blocks of conventions.

In this chapter I have wanted to go behind conventions and social skills and put individuals under the microscope and ask about their abilities and inclinations prior to social exchange. That is to start where I think a treatise on democracy should start, with the atom of the edifice I have called *the polity*. I have wanted to know what people need in order to live a free life. Obviously, they need many things, including, I have found, various skills and competences. Political theory has had a great deal to say about external conditions of freedom—for example, in laws and constitutional arrangements—but less about internal conditions. I'm sure it has always been recognized that the relationship between freedom and reason is something that needs to be sorted out. But how? Is reason included in freedom, or is it something else—and where does it come from? Not only have I lifted individuals out of their social context, I have tried to look inside them and to understand something about what makes them tick in the use of favorable external conditions of freedom.

The liberty school of freedom tells us much about what responsibilities democratic governments should take on, from the protection of rights under legislation to the protection of security and fair exchange under the provisions of the welfare state. The real-freedom school teaches us more about freedom than we find in the liberty school, and that again leads to further recommendations.

The politics of freedom starts from protections: protection of rights, protection against poverty, the protection of free exchange in unrigged arenas. But real freedom—the ability to live a life of one's own making—depends on more than external conditions; it rests also on the ability to reason. Reason is a peculiar competence, not so much a resource for choice as one that enables control and restraint in choice. That kind of competence needs to be nurtured more than simply protected.

The way to nurture reason is through the institutions in which people learn about values, norms, and evidence-based faith—through families, through schools and through arenas of deliberation.

The child is the father of the citizen; in particular, the child who has learned is the father of the citizen who possesses the capacity for reason. The child is taught particularly in the family he grows up in. Families are the domain of parents and parents are the best people to raise children. No government can take on the responsibility of raising children but again there is an issue of protection. Parents have children for the human experience of it, but they are nevertheless doing a job for society, including preparing the ground for the next generation's freedoms. From the real-freedom school follows the recommendation that governments should have a responsibility to protect parents' capacities to raise their children. Family policy is hence integral to the politics of freedom.

The young go to schools to learn and many continue on to colleges and universities. That democratic governments have a responsibility for the education of the young is, of course, not contested. But from the real-freedom school follows the recommendation that this is a duty also in the name of freedom.

A pessimistic line of thought is that liberty is self-defeating. Once people have the liberty of abundance on top of rights, so goes this thinking, they are beyond what it is in their power of self-control to master in their own best interest.[37] That, however, is to suggest that the ability to exercise self-control is linked directly to affluence. I think that self-control is nurtured in institutions, particularly in families and schools. There is a danger that families and schools are not up to educating the young properly towards lives of reason, and that this becomes even more difficult with affluence. If so, the enemy is not affluence but possible adverse consequences for institutions. Such consequences are avoidable. If we take care of our institutions and invest money and support in families and schools, it should be possible to extract real freedom from the promise of liberty. It is the temptation to be careless with institutions that is the enemy.

There is nothing new in including children, families, and schools in a reflection on freedom, governance, and democracy, but you would not know it from the books you are likely to read in modern political theory. For the most part, they tell you about people who seem never to have been children, about citizens and workers who have not gone to school, and about societies whose institutions are laws, rules, and conventions

[37] See Offer 2006.

but certainly not families. The people who inhabit the world of these books are often very strange creatures, indeed—for example, "utility-maximizing rational actors." What a loss it is to move so far from speaking about the world as it is, about people as social animals and societies as built up of real institutions such as families and schools. And so far from where it all started. Go back again to Aristotle and to his *Politics* and you will find in that slim book on constitutional politics long sections on children, family formation and schooling, down to such constitutionally important questions as whether all schoolchildren should learn to play the flute.

From the real-freedom school comes the understanding that the free citizen is someone who lives in bonds of deliberation with his fellows. There is more to freedom than, on the one side, citizens who make choice and, on the other side, governments that may or may not afford them adequate protection of their liberty to do so. There is something between. Citizens rely on each other for the living of lives as free agents. We must be able to *talk* to each other and listen to each other and understand each other—young and old, women and men, rich and poor, majorities and minorities, Christians and Muslims, those settled and those immigrating.[38] Democratic governments have a duty to protect citizens and their rights and security, and in addition to protect their infrastructure of deliberation.

In the half century of reflection on freedom that I have explored here, something very peculiar has happened. It started in a spirit of modesty: the claim to be free to live by one's own will. Freedom was on the defensive and its theory restrained. As reflection evolved, however, the theory was unbound and the idea of liberty shed its modesty. It came to include means on top of rights while finding no way to say what would be enough. Simultaneously, the world evolved. The competition collapsed—with the fall of the Iron Curtain in Europe in 1989. Freedom was no longer on the defensive and, for that reason, no longer in need of modesty. Nor was modesty any longer contained in its theory. The freedom of the liberty school has become a freedom capable of promoting itself in a style, assertiveness, and loudness of voice that can border on aggressiveness. It has become a voice with a potential of righteousness that is potentially dangerous to the cause of freedom. That, I think, is because we in the free world may have fallen prey to what Aristotle saw long before our time to be a false conception of liberty.

---

[38] I am here back to the end of chapter 3 and the call for dialogue. I despair at not being able to articulate this idea more forcefully. I see around me a world disintegrating into confrontation and distrust. To respond with a message of individualistic rationality is to stoke the flames. Our message *must* now be to cultivate reason, to understand ourselves as

In that conception, we are mistaken about what freedom is. We are mistaken because by our ideas we are building cultures of mistrust and soft despotism. We need to pull the theory back down to earth and find our way back to a spirit of modesty. The way to do that is to move on from the liberty school, which I think we should consider the primary school of freedom, and enter the real-freedom school, its secondary school, where teaching goes beyond the technology of choice to also embrace the wisdom of choice. That should enable us to go out into the world with a more mature understanding of freedom. In turn, that level of better education and knowledge gives us the confidence to argue the cause of freedom everywhere and to do that with more modesty and less aggression than is currently on display in Western democratic leadership, and therefore more persuasively.

---

social animals, to talk with each other rather than shout at each other, to interact, to create bonds and links and interdependence, to deliberate—to engage in *dialogue*.

> In many countries the task is to achieve democratisation up
> to the level of polyarchal democracy. But the challenge to citi-
> zens in the older democracies is to discover how they might
> achieve a level of democracy *beyond* polyarchal democracy.
> —Robert A. Dahl, *On Democracy*

THE WAY TO PROTECT democracy is not to cheer it, which we do too much, but to reform it, which we do too little. But how?

I have tried to analyze democracy by putting performance above procedure. Democracy (said Abraham Lincoln at Gettysburg) is government for the people (and of and by the people). What people want is to live good lives. For everyone to be able to live well, we all must be free to arrange our lives according to our own will. The free life comes from being our own master, which again rests on a unity of liberty and reason. That freedom is the yardstick of moral value that has guided these reflections on democracy and its quality.

FREEDOM AGAIN

Liberty is having options in front of you and the rights and means to partake of them. That is obviously essential for a free life, but, I have argued, not sufficient. Free choice is a slippery concept. Liberal theory has had much to say about *free*, meaning the absence of interference and coercion, but has concerned itself less with the nature of *choice*. What is choice? It is, it seems to me, being able to *do* things. Being at liberty to do things is a start, but the point must be to put that opportunity to use. When you have liberty, you are free from coercion; when you make use of your liberty, you start living a free life.

It is no small step from having liberty to living freely. It takes, first, some power of action. Choice can be paralyzing. In *Anna Karenina*, Leo Tolstoy's great love story from Russia at the end of the nineteenth century, Anna dithers between her husband, whom she does not love, and Vronsky, whom she does love. She is long unable to choose and is driven to the edge of insanity. When she is finally able to see that she must choose Vronsky and love, she finds that she no longer has the liberty to choose—and perishes, probably by her own doing.

Then it takes a grasp of what to want. Acting on wants you just *have* is a kind of dictatorship. A choice is only *your* choice if you have yourself decided its purpose. To invoke Saint Paul again: If I do what I do not want, it is not I that do it.

Those of us who are at home in the school of sociology that follows Emile Durkheim believe that power of action and command over meaning come from *togetherness*. We humans are social animals. We are what we are by virtue of our anchorage in community with others. "Creativity works only in groups," said Daniel Barenboim in the first of his 2006 Reith Lectures on the BBC, explaining some of what he had learned from a life in music.

Since my very first serious venture into sociology, which I gave the name *social anchorage* and some of which I reproduce in appendix G, I have followed the persuasion that in human life there is a positive association between well-being and togetherness, that it is through and thanks to our bonds with others that we can find good lives. Presently I have explored the association between freedom and togetherness. In the tradition of tragic romanticism, these are antagonistic values. In Bizet's *Carmen*, the heroine insists on both love and freedom and dies for it, like Karenina possibly by her own hand. The liberty school of freedom belongs to this tradition: freedom hails from being liberated from bonds.

No doubt togetherness limits choice but I conclude that togetherness is still a friend of freedom and not its foe—the right kind and amount of togetherness of course, as always, but togetherness nevertheless. Freedom needs liberty but liberty is not a quantity the more of which you have the more you are free. It is the platform from which freedom starts but nothing comes of it if you are not able to *do*. Ibsen, in *An Enemy of the People*, joined the liberty school and would have it that the strongest man is he who stands alone, but in this the master was wrong. He who stands alone is lost; strong is he who has the support of others. Anchorage is not without sacrifice, but what is gained is the capability I have called reason, the ability to *do* and to do sensibly.

I already know that togetherness contributes positively to well-being. Now I find in addition that it contributes positively also to freedom. That enables me in this work to celebrate togetherness and to put distance between myself and the Ibsenesque liberty-school celebration of solitude. My method of analysis is individualistic, but my conclusions are fortunately social. In the introduction, I start from a postulate that it matters enormously for people to be living in reasonably well-functioning democracies. It matters for their freedom, security, and well-being. I am justified, I believe, in lumping those values together. They come in a bundle and do not trade off against each other.

The Good Democracy

When authoritarian rationality was still a credible idea, a great schism was recognized between socialism in principle and *real existierender Sozialismus*, and it was a challenge for the believers to reconcile fact and vision. With democracy I am not sure we acknowledge the distance between what it should be and what it is. Democracy's victory has waylaid the conventional wisdom towards the belief that democracy has made it and even that we have come to the end of political history.

We know what democracy should be: a system of collective decision making where the common good prevails through the mechanism by which citizens together hold the ultimate power of control. In fact, however, citizens are not in control. More than forty years ago, the political scientist Stein Rokkan nailed it down eloquently: votes count but resources decide. That has since become ever more true. Resources trump votes. That matters. As Arthur Okun has explained, when economic power transgresses into democratic politics, public policy distorts away from the true balance of values and preferences in the citizenry.

By and large, *real existierende Demokratie* performs pretty badly. The big model democracies of the U.S. Constitution and the Westminster model are of only mediocre quality. Some are much better—the best ones are probably found in small countries with relatively egalitarian traditions, such as in Scandinavia—but even they turn out to be of poor cloth if scrutinized critically. Strangely enough, there is encouragement in these findings: the difference in quality is proof that most democracies could do better. But the current state of democracy is still that it underperforms compared with what we should reasonably expect.

I do not recommend that we start theorizing about how to implement the perfect democracy. With Isaiah Berlin, I think we should celebrate "the crooked timber of humanity" and be always reminded that "the search for perfection is a recipe for bloodshed." But to recognize imperfection is not to disparage. There are suggestions—the critic Gore Vidal comes to mind—that democracy is but a smoke screen to conceal the reality of corporate dictatorship, but that line of thinking is as wrong and damaging as the perfectionist temptation. We should now graduate from the democracy-or-not mind-set, and certainly avoid the temptation to triumphalism, and start to think seriously about the good democracy and how to make democracy better. Democracies evolve; above all we should see to it that the direction of evolution is for the better.

It is a tragedy that many enough of us are becoming less confident about democratic rule for it to add up to a trend of disenchantment. Some commentators believe this to be a result of new values, such as individualism or postmodernism, but that is not credible. Where the matter has been investigated, from Costa Rica to Norway, it has been found that citizens are as interested as ever in political and social issues but that they are losing confidence in "politics." As usual the best explanation is the simplest one. If interested and informed citizens become disinterested in politics, it is probably because they have less reason to be interested.

ECONOMIC DEMOCRACY

In working democracies, citizens hold majority control in political decision making. In economic decision making, however, citizenship control or even participation is near nonexistent. Consequences follow. Working women and men lose jobs they thought were secure and pensions they thought were entitlements as a result of decisions in which they have no say. Those who need to call on the help of social authorities are in risk of being treated as nobodies and of being harassed and hassled. The holders of wealth and capital are allowed to use their minority economic power to undermine majority political power.

The old theory of economic democracy—subjecting economic activity to political command—is defunct and should be laid to rest. But the use of political power to redistribute economic power from those who have too much to some of those who have too little is still possible. The scope for doing so is limited by what I have called *the imperative of efficiency*, but that imperative does not stand in the way of democratizing the noneconomic use of economic power. There is ample space for the political majority to decide in favor of more economic democracy at no cost to economic efficiency. That is not to predict that the extension of democracy from the political to the economic is about to happen, but it is within the range of what is possible.

THE WELFARE STATE

The demise of the welfare state has been predicted more often than anyone can count and was given official approval when the OECD, the rich nations' economic think tank, published its report titled *The Welfare State in Crisis* in 1981. But it never happened. The welfare state emerged because it was needed, has persisted because it has been useful, and has been preserved because democratic governance has been effective enough to modify it in response to the strains of demographic change and economic globalization. In chapter 6, I conclude that the case for the welfare state is built on arguments of freedom in addition to welfare and equality, and

I therefore dismiss the libertarian view that it represents a compromise with freedom.

The first job of the welfare state is to protect citizens against poverty. Of course, what really protects people against poverty is work and economic production, but beyond that there needs, as is known from experience, to be a safety net of social policy. For the welfare state to be capable of offering last-resort protection against poverty, it needs provisions that are universal and extend to *everyone*. Universal arrangements are politically demanding and are unlikely to be implemented unless circumstances conspire so that it can happen early in a country's economic development. The risk of poverty is then still so widespread that a broad coalition in favor of effective antipoverty policies *can* emerge. Later, when economic growth has contained the risk of poverty, a broad antipoverty coalition is unlikely and social policies will be limited to containing rather than eradicating poverty. In Europe, the Scandinavians had the good fortune that historical class compromises emerged to enable the building of universal welfare states to get started early. That has subsequently paid off in the eradication of poverty. Where this foundation is missing, antipoverty policies continue to falter. In Britain, for example, government determination to deal with persistent poverty among children and the elderly follows through to a complicated web of means-tested policies. That has to some extent brought poverty rates down and is containing the problem, but it has not been and will not be capable of eradicating it. Regrettably, the prospects are now bleak in, for example, Britain for upgrading the welfare state to a poverty-eradication force. From this follows a paradoxical recommendation to new democracies: you should start to build welfare states before you can afford it; if you wait until it becomes affordable, it will be too late.

Welfare states are in perpetual change. My purpose here is to contribute to the analysis of how mature welfare states can and should change. What is driving change, certainly on the European scene, is mainly prosperity and demographic instability. Within that context, I have offered a blueprint for "a welfare state for investment," which takes its inspiration for new reform from William Beveridge's old Second World War plan. With the coming of mass prosperity, we can have more confidence in people's capacity for autonomy and less need for paternalism in the welfare state. With the end of demographic stability, we need new mechanisms for the creation and preservation of intergenerational fairness. I follow on from the previous discussion of economic democracy and consider how social care, family policy, social security, and education can be organized so as to empower citizens. Welfare states are, by necessity, complex patchworks of policies that serve many and often contrasting purposes; no magic formula is available to solve all social problems in one go, no matter how intensely the theoreticians have dreamed of finding it. However, it is not necessary that welfare-state provisions systematically disempower the needy and empower official authorities, a problem in social policy that was observed by Adam Smith and that inspired his way of thinking about freedom but one that we have yet to come to terms with.

POVERTY

The modern understanding of poverty is captured in an idea of unacceptability. The conditions we justly call poverty are not simply unfair or unfortunate, they are *unacceptable*. From that follows another idea: that poverty should be eradicated. These ideas are distinctly modern. They were invented by men such as Tom Paine in England and Condorcet in France, inspired intellectually by Adam Smith and politically by the great revolutions in America and France, and carried forward by moral economists such as Alfred Marshall and his followers on to Amartya Sen today.

I now conclude that the eradication of poverty is *possible*. I take this to be a statement of fact on the logic that it is something that has observably been achieved. It has been achieved only recently and only in some small countries in a small corner of the world, in Scandinavia again. But that is enough to conclude that it is *possible*.

Two hundred years ago, Paine and Condorcet looked forward to the eradication of poverty by the double act of prosperity and welfare states. They proved right: that is how it has happened. Prosperity is necessary but not enough. The necessity of prosperity is evident from the fact that it is only in today's mega-prosperity that eradication has been achieved. The insufficiency of prosperity is evident from the persistence of poverty in some of the world's richest countries. If the eradication of poverty is possible, it is also demanding. It comes down to the effective political management of prosperity.

The political tools are those I have already dealt with: social care, family policy, social security, education, and the redistribution of economic power. In addition, we need some other tools on the level of ideas. We need, above all, a theory of poverty that is grounded in and incorporates the idea of unacceptability. To that end it is now urgent time to put the relative theory of poverty to rest in the historical file for interesting but failed theories.

"Relative poverty" is a theoretical failure because it is a concept without a counterfactual. There is no alternative to it. From Adam Smith and forward, *everyone* who has had anything sensible to say about poverty has explained it as a problem that is relative to the circumstances of time and place, and no one has suggested anything like an absolute theory of poverty. There is no such thing in social theory as "absolute poverty." Of course, the recognition that poverty is perforce relative is not to say that any degree of relativity is meaningful, but that poverty is relative is 100 percent obvious.

It is also a political failure. Although it is a red herring, much use has been made of the relative theory and the use that has been made of it is to relativize the problem so that it has become unobservable. The consequences are that, by and large, the problem of poverty in poor countries has been underestimated and in rich ones overestimated, and that therefore both the extent of and difference in poverty in the world has been concealed. Furthermore, the insistence on boundless relativity in the understanding of poverty has distorted thinking about the problem away from poverty as a real and tangible fact. If there is relative poverty everywhere, poverty is normal. What is normal cannot be unacceptable. What is everywhere cannot be eradicated, and what is not unacceptable should not be eradicated. The problem of poverty in the world is of horrendous proportions, as is the difference between the destinies of the poor and the rich. To be able to move towards the eradication of this ultimate social ill, we need the idea to be incorporated in political mind-sets that poverty is *unacceptable*. We are not there. The prevailing idea about poverty is that it is normal. The prevailing idea about policy stops at containment. The modern understanding that poverty is unacceptable and therefore should be eradicated is one that has been articulated but not accepted. Sadly, the relative theory of poverty, which is inspired by strong and genuine concern, has stood in the way of our ability to get the problem of poverty recognized as it is in all its horror and has in this way proved self-defeating. It is a well-meaning idea that has done damage to it own cause.

FAMILIES

Modern life is lived in families: on average people spend more time in family life than in any other activity, including work. Nowhere is the magic of togetherness more recognizable than in family life. In time spent together, there is production, division of labor, sharing, and cooperation. That makes families productive institutions, very productive ones. They are economically productive: our standard of living would be nowhere near what we have achieved without family production. They are socially productive, notably in the rearing of children or, if you will, in the reproduction of the tribe and the perpetual preparation of the next generations.

But, although families are and remain immensely productive even within high-speed capitalism, family productivity is on a slow but relentless downwards slide. Less economic value is produced in families and, in at least one way, also less social value: modern families produce fewer children. It may sound surprising to have low birthrates presented as a case of low productivity, but that is exactly what it is. Today's parents and prospective parents want to have more children than they end up having, which is to say that they are unable to reproduce to the level they could and would. Something in the way they live or have to live stands in their way and prevents them from creating the kinds of families they want.

In my idea of freedom as a fusion of liberty and reason, certain skills play a decisive role. They are the skills the individual needs to handle the blessings and temptations of liberty. These skills include such human capabilities, following Martha Nussbaum, as for example, empathy, care for others, the ability to love, and the ability to form a conception of the good. I sum it up as a matter of values and norms and that elusive competence I call *faith*: to be reasonably able to live practically according to what one believes to be right and good.

All skills are learned, and learning takes place in many settings and goes on all through life. But for the skills that make up reason, what is learned or not in childhood is basic and essential. This, I conclude, is the strongest of many arguments why we should be deeply concerned about the declining productivity of families. It goes to our capacity as a community to prepare successive generations for ordered joint lives—for living, in Aristotle's words, "by the rule of the constitution."

THE LIBERAL VISION AGAIN

Can we trust progress to be genuine? If things get better for society en masse, do they also get better for ordinary people? That is not necessarily the case. A minority with power could run away with the gains and leave the majority to rot.

In the liberal vision, progress is not itself genuine but can be made genuine with the help of democracy and the cautiously benevolent government it stimulates. From my previous work, I am satisfied that effective government within the constraints of democracy is *possible*. It is not necessary to resort to government by unchecked power.

The benefit of democratically constrained power is that it may enjoy authority and by authority be effective. Authority comes from trust, from citizens who believe that the system of rule they live under is one of governance with acceptable means to make progress genuine for them. The authority of democratic governance is, however, in question. The trend is for citizens to trust democracy and democratic government less. I have argued that there is less trust not because citizens have become less trusting but because they have reason to trust less.

For many of us, certainly myself, the liberal vision matters desperately. It would be just too awful if the human experience of life together in society, in particular democratic life, were not one of betterment when there is potential for progress. When I started my inquiry into the liberal vision, the crucial question was that of governance. Critics from the Right believed that benevolent government might be well-meaning but inevitably destructive, and critics from the Left believed it would be ineffectual because it was denied real power. When I now look back from what I have subsequently learned, I believe on the one hand that this question has been settled in favor of the liberal vision but on the other hand that it is not the most basic question to ask. The liberal vision rests on a unity of democracy and good government. There is potency enough in democratic rule to deliver the governance part of the deal. The more fundamental question goes to democracy itself, and then not only to its power to hold rule under control but rather to its capacity to deliver authority.

Democracy is a wonderful invention for human good, but real democracies are not good enough. Fortunately, they are in movement and are evolving. We need to get control over the direction of movement and make democracies *better*. Beyond reform governance, democracy itself needs reforming.

REFORM

British democracy is a spectacle of magical realism. Elected leaders perform a weekly shouting ritual at the prime minister's question time in the House of Commons as if they were roosters in a cockfight. Stuffy peers give lofty speeches to the milords in the House of Lords, sometimes dressed up in ermine. Judges and bishops double as legislators and sometimes treble as cabinet ministers. The monarch presides ostentatiously over a bygone class hierarchy and a nonexistent empire. The ways of British democracy are so peculiar that it is sometimes beyond comprehension in a modern age. When in 2000 the House of Commons elected a new speaker to succeed Betty Boothroyd, the event was recorded in Parliament's official *Votes and Proceedings* as follows:

> Message to attend the Lords Commissioners,—A message was received from the Lords Commissioners, by the Gentleman Usher of the Black Rod:
> Mr Speaker Elect,
> The Lords, authorised by virtue of Her Majesty's Commission, desire the immediate attendance of this Honourable House in the House of Peers.
> Accordingly the Speaker Elect, with the House, went up to the House of Peers, where he was presented to the said Lords Commissioners for Her Majesty's

Royal Approbation.

Then the Lord Chancellor, one of the said Lords Commissioners, signified Her Majesty's Approbation of the Speaker Elect.

The House having returned;

The Speaker reported, That the House had been in the House of Peers, where Her Majesty was pleased by Her Majesty's Commissioners to approve the choice the House had made of him to be its Speaker.

And then the Speaker repeated his very respectful acknowledgements and grateful thanks to the House for the great honour it had conferred upon him, and renewed the assurance of his entire devotion to the service of the House.

Madam Speaker Boothroyd's Retirement,—Resolved, nimine contradicente, That an humble Address be presented to Her Majesty, praying Her Majesty that she will be most graciously pleased to confer some signal mark of Her Royal favour upon the Right honourable Miss Betty Boothroyd for her eminent services during the important period in which she presided with such distinguished ability and dignity in the Chair of this House; and assuring Her Majesty that whatever expense Her Majesty shall think fit to be incurred upon that account this House will make good the same.

Address to be presented to Her Majesty by such Members of this House as are of Her Majesty's Most Honourable Privy Council or of Her Majesty's Household.

Britain is proof that democracy can work in the strangest of ways (even in utter contempt of elementary rules of grammar and language in its own records of its strange ways). It is an odd democracy, but its oddness comes from it being British, from its having emerged over the centuries as integral to the slow and quirky evolution of Britain. It was never created but has grown out of history to where it stands today and from where it continues to evolve. Observing democracy at work in Britain is to be reminded that there is in practice no such thing as democracy; there are only democracies that all do it in their own way, sometimes strangely, sometimes outrageously, sometimes even undemocratically. No prescription is available for correct procedures of democracy.

British democracy works, but it does not work particularly well. One might think it performs poorly because of its odd and old-fashioned ways, but that is hardly the case. Having an unelected upper house in Parliament, for example, is clearly undemocratic. But it is also an arrangement that probably improves the quality of decision making, or at least sometimes prevents outright bad decisions from slipping through. There are very good reasons to recommend that the British abolish the House of Lords and many of its other peculiarities, and that could even make British democracy more democratic. But it would not necessarily improve its quality of performance. What causes British democracy to work less well than it should and could is found more in defects in its architecture and less in the democraticness of its procedures.

Britain is a case study in a top-heavy democracy. What is democratic in the British regime is located predominantly in Parliament and has little support from below. The distance from ruled to rulers is immense. The chain of command linking citizenry and decision making, which in the Norwegian case in appendix B was observed to be weakening, is nearly nonexistent. On the one hand this alienates citizens from democratic rule, and on the other hand it invites nondemocracy to crowd in and fill the void. British democracy is in these ways representative of the state of advanced democracy, although the weakness of the architecture is possibly more pronounced than in some other countries.

The lesson from Britain is that democratic reform should start in the foundations rather than with procedures. There is a lively constitutional debate in Britain about proportional representation, reforms in the House of Lords, devolution to the regions, and such matters. These are important and interesting questions but, from the point of view of democratic quality, still secondary. For improvements of performance in British democracy, indeed in modern democracy generally, we should go directly to the main links between citizenry and rule. Those links need to be maintained and held strong. Citizens need to see that the rule they live under is *their* rule. Openings for nondemocracy need to be shut down.

From where we stand today in the democracies I uncomfortably call advanced, and from what I have learned from looking long and hard inside them, two recommendations for reform present themselves as fundamental. First, we must rebuild local democracy where, as is near universal, it is in decline. It is in local politics and governance that democracy is made visible and tangible for citizens where they live and in their ordinary business of life. Where local democracy is feeble or absent, what remains is what the political scientist Willy Martinussen called *the distant democracy*. It is local democracy that is the building block; it's what holds up the whole edifice.

Second, we need to give citizens reasons to be involved in politics by holding nondemocracy at bay, which is to say the transgression of economic power into politics. Start by denying political parties subsidies, be it from private donations or the public purse, and force them to compete for members, depend on members, and answer to members. I have defined democracy as a structure of power in which ultimate control sits with citizens. When money is allowed to be used as a political tool, the polity tilts towards being undemocratic by my definition, even if democratic forms are preserved. In *How Democratic Is the American Constitution*, Robert Dahl questions whether America is, in fact, ruled democratically. I agree with that question, if partly for other reasons, and not only in America. British democracy is wide open to the abuse of economic power. In Scandinavia, the political parties have given themselves a license to live lavishly off the public purse. In Europe, from one country to another, democracy is deeply tainted by corruption. For the sake of democracy it is urgent, and possible, to shut economic power out from democratic politics.

The funding of parties from private or public donations is not necessary for democracy. Party budgets can be kept within boundaries by limiting parties to revenues from membership fees. This would in one blow both shut out the influence of big money and make membership the basis of party power.

Party spending could be held down with the help of capping rules. The control over funding could be handed over to citizens. With capping, total funding would be known. That could then be allocated from the government through vouchers distributed to citizens for them to distribute to politicians and organizations of their choice. All other funding, including from candidates' or officials' own sources, should be treated as corruption. This is an example of a range of reform proposals I make aimed at giving ordinary citizens more economic power.

I offer these two recommendations as my priority ones: let local democracy in and shut the power of money out. These are simple, practical, and elementary proposals. They are not difficult to implement, and there are no prohibitive costs that stand in the way, economically or otherwise. They are alone enough to turn the tide from more distance to more nearness in democracy and to strengthen the capacity of democracies to produce trust and authority.

But there is more that can and should be done.

My third recommendation to the democracies that consider themselves advanced: Pursue supernational power with democratically grounded political power beyond the nation-state. Democracy is located on the national stage. It is challenged by the might of supernational power from above in addition to weaknesses in the foundations below. The trick here is to globalize democratic power without undermining the authority of national legislatures.

Fourth, respond to the challenge of multiculturalism. The homogeneous society is a thing of the past. Minorities are now culturally and ethnically defined. They need recognition, empowerment, and integration. I return to these two recommendations below, as well as to the matter of local democracy.

Fifth, reshape the welfare state. Where social protection is not universal, extend it and eradicate poverty. Salvage social care from, as I have described it, "chaos, mess, scandal, abuse and inefficiency." Give workers ownership of their pensions by redistributing that ownership to them from both employers and public bureaucracies.

Sixth, encourage democratic values. "The prospects for stable democracy are improved if its citizens and leaders strongly support democratic ideals, values, and practices. The most reliable support comes when these beliefs and predispositions are imbedded in the country's culture and are transmitted, in large part, from one generation to the next. In other words, the country possesses a democratic political culture. . . . Lucky is the country whose history has led to these happy results!" So wrote Robert Dahl in *On Democracy*—I cannot avoid referring yet again to the wise observations of that man! Lucky, yes, but it is not only luck. Values can be fostered. They are fostered in the institutions in which values are learned, honed, and preserved. If we take care of our institutions, as I have said in chapter 6, and invest money and support in families and schools, for example, it should be possible to extract real freedom from the promise of liberty.

To invest in schools, invest above all the concern of parents. Let all schools be for-pay schools, and let all parents pay for the schooling of their children. Allocate to all parents, rich and poor alike, their share of the school budget for them to use to pay for the schooling of their children. Move economic power from authorities to people. Give *all* parents what rich parents already have and appreciate, the freedom and power to buy schooling for their children from the school of their choice.

Family analysis tends to get muddled by moral hang-ups of various kinds. I try to avoid that as far as possible by analyzing families as organizations in which, as in any organization, efficiency rests on resources and shared beliefs and conventions. The family efficiency I am concerned with above all is in the rearing of children. I recommend that we invest economically in families, in particular, to give parents the resources they need in time and money to realize their family aspirations.

In family organizations, no less than other organizations, efficiency comes from the cooperation that is made possible by togetherness. We should therefore encourage togetherness in the rearing of children. There will be lone-parent families, and they should benefit from investment as much as other families. There is no good reason to think that lone parents are less capable parents than others, but the job of raising children is in practice a bigger one than we should expect single parents to manage comfortably on their own. Togetherness is advisable for the additional resources it brings to the job. It may also be morally advisable, but it is not necessary to go into that. It is advisable on grounds of efficiency.

To encourage togetherness is also to encourage family conventions that stimulate family projects of trust and cooperation. The rise of informal cohabitation in its modern guise as a basis for family formation has brought with it much more change in family conventions than one might think a simple formality could cause. It is eating into the partners' ability to trust their union and is contributing to making modern families more "me" projects and less "we" projects. In my analysis, it makes sense not only to encourage togetherness but also to encourage that togetherness be grounded in a formal contract, in the convention called marriage.

Finally, seventh, recognize the deficit of quality in *real existierende Demokratie*. The superiority of democracy to any other known form of rule is not in doubt. We should and must celebrate democracy and cheer it, but also protect and improve it by not succumbing to the temptation to think it is assured or that we have arrived. There is much to do: we need to encourage reform and to discourage complacency.

Local Democracy

The meaning and purpose of local democracy is in flux. Across the democratic world we see interested, engaged, and active citizens who are disenchanted with democratic governance. What they are disenchanted with in particular is local government: they do not see enough democratic purpose there to absorb their interest and involvement.

Local democracy has usually had the form of a minidemocracy in local areas: local elections for local governments. That form of local democracy is in decline. Central governments have a tendency to take control and decide what local governments must do. In Britain, for example, local democracy has been all but suspended by overrule from Whitehall. The turnout in local elections is down to 20 to 30 percent and in many places to less. To reinvigorate local democracy by admonishing people to vote where they have rightly decided there is not much point in voting is not an idea that will take us very far.

For better local democracy we need, first, to decentralize power. There cannot be local democracy unless there is local power. This means localities must be trusted to use their power according to their own priorities. If there is local democracy, localities will differ in policy—in social policy, in school policy, in transportation policy, and so on. If we are unable to accept difference, we are unable to accept local democracy. Central governments must control their urge to always standardize.

Second, we will need to decentralize not only power but also responsibility, say, the responsibility of taxation. The decline of local democracy is driven in part by structural contradictions. Most public services are delivered locally. When decision making is centralized, central government has power without responsibility and local government has responsibility without power. In most democracies, there is a tug of war between central and local government. Local governments always want more power but not always more responsibility and central governments always want to shift responsibility but not always power. We need a straighter division of labor between central and local government. That will tend to be resisted from both central and local government, if for different reasons. These are therefore constitutional matters that will need to be laid down in rules of democratic governance that are binding on the parties in the geographic power struggle.

Third, we need to think very seriously about new forms of local politics. The formality of the minidemocracy is not attractive to assertive citizens. There must be a reason for that. It would seem that a small-scale copy of national democracy in local arenas may not be the best form of democracy on that level. We are so used to thinking that democracy *is* electoral democracy that wherever we look for democracy, that is what we look for. But that may be too simple a model. Perhaps we should think of the democratic architecture less as replicas of the same thing on different levels and more as the right thing at each level.

A response to the dilemma that active citizens are politically passive may be emerging in the yet tentative thinking that goes under the name of *deliberative democracy*, as developed by Amy Gutman, Dennis Thompson, and others. This is, of course, not an alternative to representative democracy but a supplement to it. Deliberative democracy is an idea of direct and continuous popular participation in political decision making. That cannot be but a good idea in democracy, but it is also an idea it has been difficult to make practical. Proposals for making democracy more deliberative on the national scene tend to be gimmicky, as for example in Bruce Ackerman and James Fishkin's idea of a "deliberation day," a national day off now and then for everyone to spend discussing politics. The problem of implementation has caused some thinkers, such as Ian Shapiro, to dismiss the whole idea as pie-in-the-sky. It seems to me, however, that both proponents and opponents of deliberative democracy are looking to the wrong scene for it to be played out. Democratic thinking is so geared to national politics that the local level tends to be overlooked. Bring local democracy in and the knot is untangled. On the one hand, local politics is the stage on which deliberative democracy could be more than a fancy idea. On the other hand, deliberative democracy is the idea that could reverse the decline of democracy in local politics. A model of representative democracy on the national level and participatory democracy in local arenas may be more in tune with contemporary expectations than the traditional model of different levels of representative democracy.

These ideas, tentative and unrefined as they are, are for my part inspired by years of following and debating trends in local democracy in my home country, Norway. In that country, the principle of local autonomy has deep roots in the political culture. Yet local democracy is in decline. I have come to the view that this is a result of careless thinking. Local government is in large measure about the delivery of services. Issues of cost and efficiency are therefore essential. The danger is that these issues come to be seen as the only important ones. But municipalities have *two* functions. They are arenas of service delivery *and* arenas of democratic deliberation and competition. The centralization of power is often seen to be in the interest of efficiency (if often mistakenly). To counterbalance that pressure, we need a strong awareness of local government as an arena of democracy. What I have seen in this one country—and I am sure that is also the case elsewhere—is that it is now increasingly difficult to hold on to the very *awareness* that local politics is not just management but also *democracy*.

GLOBAL DEMOCRACY

One of my questions in chapter 1 is what it is that is or is not democratic. My answer there is "polities." Well, that answer is not wrong but nor is it fully correct. The site of decision making is not always a polity, at least not if we think that polities are clearly demarcated—for example, geographically (a nation or a municipality) or by membership (an association).

The most studied polity in political science is the nation-state. However, there is a great deal of decision making that matters a great deal to citizens and that is not national decision making. Not only is decision making local, there is also decision making above nation-states.

On that level, decision making takes place in global markets and in international and supranational agencies. While there is consequential decision making outside of the nation-state, democratically grounded political power is confined within it. Hence, citizens are subject to decisions over which they exercise no democratic control. That is not supposed to be the case: it is undemocratic.

The most sophisticated experience in the democratization of supranational decision making is in the European Union. Member countries have delegated decision making power upwards and sought to give that power democratic grounding in a directly elected European Parliament. Democratic innovation is evolving but, so far, unsuccessfully. It is broadly recognized that there is a democratic deficit in European integration and that no European *demos* is evolving that could underpin democracy on an all-European level. Citizens are conspicuously disinterested in the democratic experiment that is put before them. Voter turnout in European elections is in most countries much lower than in national elections and has declined while integration has increased. The recent attempt to write a European Constitution failed spectacularly, first because the framers offered no idea for Europe to ground a constitution in and then because voters turned down the bureaucratic tract they were presented in lieu of a visionary charter.

Again, the thinking seems to be the same rigid one as for local democracy, namely that democracy on whatever level must be a replication of national democracy. But why should supernational democracy necessarily be a copy of the way we do democracy in nations?

The European experience so far is that political power is delegated upwards at the expense of the role, strength, and importance of national parliaments. That is causing citizens serious concern because it remains that it is to their national parliaments they predominantly look for protection and security of freedom. This is a problem that needs to be confronted; in Europe it has been evaded. We are already in danger of losing local democracy. We need supernational democracy but not at the expense of national democracy.

If we should look for more democracy on the local level than in national politics, we should look for less on the supernational level. Supernational arenas are hardly polities that are themselves meaningfully democratic or nondemocratic in the way we would see a country as democratic or not. They are less that that, really just sites of decision making. The issue is more about that decision making being democratically accountable than about re-creating a fully fledged democracy on yet another level. It would seem simpler and safer to build on the existing institutions of democracy and more difficult and risky to create new ones at their expense and far removed from the reach of citizens. After all, we need to confront not only decision making in Europe but also in powerful global settings, such as the International Monetary Fund or the World Trade Organization.

As it happens, direct elections are not the only way to obtain accountability. There is also the time-honored procedure of *indirect* elections. The argument here for indirect elections is, of course, not that this is in itself a better form of democracy or more democratic but that it is a way of building a democratic structure of decision making at levels where direct elections do not work or are not practicable. In Europe, the method of indirect election could produce a European legislature with a popular mandate to take on full legislative power and do so while at the same time strengthening, rather than weakening, national legislatures. It is also a model that could easily be applied in the governance of global agencies.

In the case of the European Union, let the European Parliament be elected by and among the elected members of national legislatures. European elections would then be contained in national elections, and European politics would figure in those campaigns. This would give more attention to European matters than now, with poorly attended European elections fought with indifference. It would also bring new substance to and enliven national elections, something that is badly needed in its own right. It would put European issues on the agenda of debate in national settings. National legislatures, instead of being sidelined, would have a direct role in Europe. Members of the European Parliament would be accountable to their national legislatures and thereby to voters. The European Parliament would consist of elected members and be democratically credible and accountable.

A European Parliament does not need to sit continuously. It could meet, say, twice a year for, say, two months at a time. It would pass European law, appoint the executive, adopt its budget, and undertake oversight. Parliamentary subcommittees could meet at other times. Members of the European Parliament should continue to serve as members of national parliaments, which would assure their accountability and overcome the feeling of distance between citizens and the European Parliament. Members of national legislatures could be elected with substitutes who could serve in the absence of those serving in the European Parliament and its committees.

An aspect of globalization is de facto legislative power moving gradually to supranational agencies and courts, be they regional or global. This is happening in areas such as financial regulations, environmental protection, trade, and labor rights. It is something that should be encouraged further. Effective environmental husbandry, for example, must be global. A mechanism that works in Europe to fill its democratic deficit could serve as a model in other areas for national legislatures to delegate power to supranational bodies without undermining themselves as powerful, relevant, and democratic assemblies in which citizens see reasons for trust.

CULTURAL FEDERALISM

Inside the nation-state, there is local decision making. I have discussed local democracy above, but there is another dimension to it, that of minorities. Local democracy is a kind of minority democracy, it is a way of protecting geographically defined minorities against the dangers of oppressive majority rule. However, minorities are not necessarily local. Cultural minorities may be dispersed throughout the territory of the nation-state and may not be easily identified by location or membership—no one is in a formal meaning a member of an ethnic group—but they are minorities all the same. Democratic thinking has long recognized formal minority protection as a democratic virtue. Should that be extended to cultural minorities? If so, how?

These questions are in one way uncomfortable. They imply the slicing up of a population into groups by cultural belonging. This is not necessarily helpful for social cohesion or necessarily a good way of distributing respect. It could be divisive, even dangerously so. It might be seen to be offensive to classify citizens by group membership instead of just accepting each person as an equal in his or her own right. We all have multiple identities, Amartya Sen reminds us in *Identity and Violence*, and no one is only this or that kind of a person. What we should strive for is autonomy and individual respect rather than group justice on some more or less arbitrary rationale of group identity.

Still, there *are* cultural minorities, and minorities need protection. There are questions here that need reflection, and I think it is worth the time and effort to engage in this reflection although I presently do not know with confidence where such reflection should lead.

The democratic protection of local minorities is institutionalized in various forms of geographic federalism, be it formal federalism as in Germany or the United States, for example, or quasi-federalism in more or less local autonomy in nonfederal nation-states. This, I think, we can easily see as a matter of what I have called security of freedom. These are arrangements that help local minorities to feel confident that their interests are protected in the national polity. They are instruments of minority integration.

Once we recognize cultural minorities, the question presents itself of whether we need to think of some kind of cultural federalism within national polities. I think "once we recognize" is the appropriate terminology. For example, aboriginal minorities in many countries have suffered the oppression of not having been recognized as minorities, and it is only with the emergence of that recognition that the slow process of integration has been possible. In Europe today, "new" ethnic and religious minorities suffer the same oppressive lack of recognition. The denial in French schools of Muslim girls' right to dress as they like is only an extreme and visible example.

The U.S. Constitution of 1787 recognized the principle of minority rights by giving geographical minorities extensive protections. The first addition to it, added without delay, is the so-called Bill of Rights contained in the first ten amendments. This is a constitution that is strong on rights, including minority rights. But it is one that has proved incapable of providing security and integration to social minorities, as Alexander Aleinikoff finds in *Semblances of Sovereignty*. The obvious case is that of African Americans, but Aleinikoff lifts forth other categories: Native Americans, citizens of acquired territories (such as Puerto Rico), and immigrants. He tests the capacity of the Constitution for integration into "full and equal citizenship" by observing the situation of marginal minorities. And finds it wanting. For example, the Supreme Court has sanctioned practices that have denied these groups normal constitutional protections against arbitrary legislative and administrative treatment. The lesson must be that a general recognition of rights, even extensively and including minority rights, is not necessarily a sufficient basis for integration. Specific recognitions and arrangements for cultural minorities may be needed.

What might cultural federalism look like? I know not and have no ready answer. The one example I am able to point to is that of the Sami minority in Norway (and equally in Finland and Sweden). Until two generations ago, this was an oppressed, ignored, and discriminated-against aboriginal minority. Today it is a culturally proud minority that is finding its place in the larger nation on equitable terms. (The process is, however, not completed. Legal rights to land and water in the traditional Sami areas, which are inhabited by both Sami and non-Sami, remain to be settled.)

Its integration has not taken the form of absorption into the majority but, to the contrary, of specific recognitions of its cultural rights, for example, the right to use Sami languages in schools. This has required a lengthy process of national deliberation, including extensive government-sponsored studies of this specific minority's specific rights. It has required a constitutional amendment that enshrines a duty on the national government to respect and protect Sami rights. It has required a formal recognition of the Sami as an aboriginal minority according to international treaties. And it has included the establishment of a Sami Parliament outside of the national parliament, elected by the Sami themselves, with certain legislative powers in mainly cultural affairs pertaining to the Sami irrespective of where they should happen to live in the country, be it in their traditional territories in the north or, for example, in the national capital. There has also been financial support for the purpose of economic integration. That has been important but not decisive. If this minority has moved from oppression to integration, that has been thanks to a detailed institutionalization of visible cultural respect and protection.

What general lessons, if any, can be drawn from this example is an open question, except the far-reaching practical demands that need to follow from awarding cultural minorities their obvious right to recognition.

Freedom Yet Again

Freedom is what democracy is finally for. My argument for democratic reform is that it is necessary to protect democracy. My argument for protecting democracy is that we need democracy so we are able to live freely and to have our freedoms protected.

The great result of Isaiah Berlin's work on freedom, I said in chapter 6, is that he established the priority of elementary liberty in any broader concept of freedom. But there is, of course, more to his legacy. There is an insistence that ideas matter. We need to think carefully about how to understand freedom and its use. If we do not, and just take it as a matter of doing our own thing, we subject ourselves to danger. And then there is the modesty of what he asked for in the name of freedom—not for everything, but for what really matters. Berlin agreed with Aristotle in warning against false concepts of liberty.

When the most powerful politicians in the world (said a good colleague) put the word "freedom" into every second sentence of their speeches, you know there is something wrong. What is wrong cannot be that they speak for freedom, but something is definitely uncomfortable if "freedom" becomes a signal that makes others in the world tremble with fear. There are ideas about freedom that may endanger freedom; that in a nutshell is what Berlin wanted us to understand. Any powerful idea is dangerous because if used carelessly or maliciously it may legitimize bad power. The idea of freedom should be used with care and modesty. Freedom is not for whatever; it is, we should insist, always for what there are reasons to have and want. There is no freedom of choice without choice of purpose. Reason is built into freedom once we recognize that freedom is more than a good, that it is a value.

The difference in world politics, I think, is that when freedom combines with power without modesty, it *does* become an idea the powerless have reason to fear. It becomes what others insist on and they are told to obey. On the other hand, being in power is no reason not to speak for freedom, but if that is done with modesty I think those in power will speak as much to themselves about duties as to others about obedience.

The Liberal Vision Yet Again

A long project on good government has taken me from cost-benefit analyses of social policy towards a vision of modernity as liberal order. When I now consider the stuff of this project in hindsight twenty to twenty-five years after it got started, I find that what I've learned comes down to two messages.

One goes to the quest for benevolent rule. That rests on a fine balance between assertiveness and restraint in government—so fine a balance that many commentators have thought the effort is doomed to fail on one side or the other. My message has been and remains affirmative on the possibility of politics.

The second message goes to the quality of democracy. The temptation today is to take democracy to be victorious and to celebrate, but that is to neglect very severe weakness in the machinery of democracy and the frailness of democratic values; it is to lead ourselves down the road to Tocqueville's soft despotism. If democracy fails in the delivery of authority and trust, what *could* be benevolent rule might collapse into disorder or coercion. Democracy's friends should now sound loud and clear a warning about democracy's quality.

The Truth About Class Inequality

IN A PAPER published in *Citizens, Families, and Reform* (1997), I challenged what had become a strongly recommended conclusion in sociology about trends in class inequality (in a body of literature that, for convenience, I will refer to as the class-inequality literature).[1] The paper was a product of three years of collaborative work with Ottar Hellevik, and a separate paper under his name with similar criticism was published simultaneously in *Acta Sociologica*.[2] These criticisms resulted in a process of debate and reassessment.[3] It is now possible to sum up and conclude.

THE STABILITY THESIS

In *Social Mobility and Class Structure in Modern Britain* (1980), the authors followed trends in class inequality and social mobility over a period of roughly fifty years leading up towards 1980. The final conclusion was that in spite of a massive thrust of upwards social mobility, "no significant reduction in class inequalities was in fact achieved."[4] This I call *the stability thesis*.

The stability thesis was subsequently confirmed and reconfirmed in further analysis on British trends: "the terms of the competition between the classes has shown little sign of change"; "we have found that substantial absolute rates of upward and downward mobility coexist alongside relative class-mobility chances which have remained largely unchanged . . . in most of [the twentieth] century up to the present day."[5] In a new development, the thesis was found to apply not only over time within countries

This is a revised version of a paper presented to the Department of Sociology seminar at Oxford University on 31 October 2005. I am grateful in particular to Richard Breen for helpful suggestions on that occasion. As ever in this project, I am grateful to Ottar Hellevik for close and fruitful cooperation. First published in Czech Sociological Review 2006, no. 3.

[1] Ringen 1997a, ch. 5.

[2] Hellevik 1997.

[3] Marshall and Swift 1999, 2000; Hellevik 2000, 2002b; Ringen 2000, 2000b, 2005a; Swift 2000; Kivinen et al. 2001, 2002.

[4] Goldthorpe et al. 1987, p. 328.

[5] Heath and Clifford 1990, p. 15; Marshall et al. 1997, p. 59.

such as Britain but also in comparisons between countries, including between European ones with a recent historical experience of democracy and of communist authoritarianism: "in most countries there has been little change in socioeconomic inequality of educational opportunity." Across advanced societies "there are more opportunities for mobility now than in previous decades. However, the distribution of these enhanced opportunities across classes is quite another matter."[6] In *On Sociology* (2000), Goldthorpe argued that years of "technical advances in social mobility research have ... led to empirical findings on temporal constancy and cross-national communality" in the relevant kind of class inequality, and that this "might be regarded as the main achievement to date of class analysis as a research programme."[7]

Much is obviously *not* at issue: the existence of class inequality in Britain and elsewhere, the fact of upwards social mobility over time in Britain and elsewhere, the fact of social difference on many dimensions between European and other countries. Rather, the stability thesis says that in spite of everything that has changed over time and everything that is different between countries, one thing at the heart of social life has remained remarkably stable over time and constant in space, and that is class inequality.

The Challenge

Class analysis is, among other things, an analysis of social inequality through the prism of class. My background was a different one: the analysis of social inequality through the prism of income distribution and poverty.[8] My research has been, as is the class analysis in question, on trends over time and differences and similarities in space and has coincided with the class analysis in the periods covered and the kinds of countries compared. It is also similar in relying on the analysis of large data sets, often data sets carefully rearranged for comparative robustness. However, my conclusions were totally at odds with those of the class analysts. I had consistently recorded changes over time and differences in space. That record is confirmed in other work on income distribution.[9] In poverty research, a separate stability thesis was suggested, starting with Townsend's *Poverty in the United Kingdom* (1979) and in further work under

---

[6] Shavit and Blossfeld 1993, p. 19, Marshall et al. 1997, p. 3.
[7] Goldthorpe 2000, pp. 163, 257.
[8] E.g., in Ringen 1987, 1988, 1997b; Ringen and Uusitalo 1992.
[9] E.g., in Atkinson 1995a; Atkinson et al. 1995.

that inspiration.[10] That proposition has been effectively refuted, however, and the evidence is now firm that poverty rates typically show patterns of change over time within countries and of difference between countries, including rich countries.[11] The body of literature I refer to here I will, for convenience, call the income-inequality literature.

The class analysis in question is highly technical in methodology. It rests crucially for its conclusions on the reading of mobility-table data through odds ratios. A major advantage of that methodology is argued to be "that these ratios constitute the elements of log-linear models."[12] Hellevik's background for our joint project was as a methodologist and as the author of textbooks in statistical methodology.[13] He was skeptical of some uses of log-linear regression analysis in sociology, which he saw as a complicated and impenetrable way of doing what could usually be done by simpler and more transparent techniques. He was therefore, although for reasons other than mine, also distrustful of the research underpinning the stability thesis.

We resolved to join forces to reinvestigate the class-inequality research and the stability thesis. This research had long been under criticism from others.[14] However, much of that criticism, certainly from fellow sociologists in Britain, had failed to penetrate the methodological complexities of the research being targeted and had therefore had limited impact. We decided to go back to basics and explore the methodological foundations.

Empirical research on class inequality and mobility consists in the reading of mobility tables. If we are interested in trends or differences in inequality, which is the issue here, we need to observe consecutive mobility tables to see if some display less or more inequality than others. Table A.1 shows two simple mobility tables of class background and educational attainment for two imaginary populations of one thousand persons. The question here is whether different displays of data such as these show the same or a different degree of inequality.

A mobility table contains two sets of distributional data. The first set consists of two marginal distributions—say, the proportion of the population with a working-class background, a middle-class background, and so on and the proportion that finishes education at the basic level, that

---

[10] Incidentally inspired by a concept of relative poverty that has many similarities with a concept of relative class inequality that has been used in parts of the class inequality-literature, e.g., Erikson and Goldthorpe 1992.

[11] See, e.g., Ringen 1988; Atkinson 1998; UNDP [annual]; UNICEF 2005. See also www.lisproject.org.

[12] Erikson and Goldthorpe 1992, p. 56.

[13] Hellevik 1984, 2002a.

[14] E.g., Pahl 1989; Sorensen 1991; Holton and Turner 1994; Crompton 1996; Saunders 1990, 1995, 1996.

Table A.1
Two Class-Education Mobility Tables, Imaginary Populations

	Section A (O-R association = .58; Gini distribution = .26)			Section B (O-R association = .58; Gini distribution = .17)		
	Low Education	High Education	N	Low Education	High Education	N
High class	100	200	300	48	252	300
Middle class	250	150	400	156	244	400
Low class	250	50	300	197	103	300
N	600	400	1,000	401	599	1,000

Source: Hellevik 1997, Ringen 1997.
Note: O-R association = ln(odds-ratio high class/low class); Gini distribution estimated from Lorenz curve of share in higher education to each class.

goes on to secondary education, and so on. The second set consists of the conditional distributions in the space defined by the two marginals, say those originating in the working class and finishing education at the basic level, those originating in the middle class and going on to university education, and so on.

Marginal and conditional distributions are related. If something changes in the marginal distributions, something has to change also in the conditional ones. If, for example, the number of places in higher education is increased and those places are taken up, the new students have to come from somewhere, so a higher proportion of people from at least one social class, possibly several or all, will end up in higher education.

Everyone agrees that mobility tables contain data on inequality, but the story of inequality cannot be read directly out of the table; the data need to be interpreted. For example, if again the number of places in higher education is increased and new students are recruited from all classes by background (as in section B compared with section A in table A.1), is the result more inequality or less?

The interpretation of mobility tables that is behind the stability thesis is based on the following logic. The marginal distributions are seen to display social structure, class structure and the structure of education in our case. Inequality, or at least some kind of inequality, sits not in the social structure but in how people are distributed within that structure. Therefore, only the conditional distributions contain data on the relevant kind of inequality. Furthermore, some of the information contained in the conditional distributions is really structural data in disguise, for example, the effect in the conditional distributions that follows directly from changes in the marginal distributions. Therefore, the correct reading on trends in inequality is to identify changes in the conditional distributions after "subtracting" or controlling for those changes that follow directly from changes in the marginals: "the pattern of association net of the effects of the marginal distributions."[15] For example, if yet again the number of places in higher education is increased there would by this logic be no effect on the relevant kind of inequality unless one could identify changes in the conditional distributions beyond those that come directly as a result of the added number of places. The odds ratio technique is said to be *margin-insensitive*.[16] In the example in table A.1, both sections by this measure show identical degrees of inequality.

This may look impressive but is in fact a bizarre way of reading mobility-table data for the purpose of interpreting inequality. If we are interested in changes in inequality, why remove from our vision certain changes in inequality because they are changes that have a certain cause, in this case, changes in inequality which follow directly from changes in the social structure? Why not do the obvious thing and read the whole picture? The odds ratio reading appears partial. Intuition suggests that it would be safer to interpret the message contained in the table through a complete analysis that reads all the data.

That's what we proceeded to do. Instead of odds ratios we adapted the standard technique in the income-inequality literature of Gini indices estimated from Lorenz curves to the analysis of mobility-table data.[17] That reading interprets mobility-table evidence by taking note of both marginal and conditional distributions. As can be seen in table A.1, this reading shows there is less inequality in section B than in Section A.

From these examples, we moved on to real data. We took the case of class background and educational attainment, one of the associations that was found to have remained roughly stable over decades in Britain.[18] We reanalyzed the British mobility data in which our colleagues had found stability of class inequality. We kept everything the same except the statistical technique. We read the same mobility tables with the same data for the same country for the same period.

As can be seen in table A.2, the two ways of reading the same data give totally different results. In the period covered, the overall level of educational attainment in the population increased sharply. While the odds ratio reading shows stable inequality (or at least no clear trend up

---

[15] Erikson and Goldthorpe 1992, p. 56.
[16] The methodology is explained in Erikson and Goldthorpe 1992, ch. 2.
[17] The technique is explained in Hellevik 1997; Ringen 1997a.
[18] E.g., in Heath and Clifford 1990.

Table A.2

Class Association and Class Distribution of Higher Educational Attainment in Britain by Birth Cohort

	Birth Cohorts			
	1930–39	*1940–49*	*1950–59*	*1960+*
O-R association	.46	.43	.50	.44
Gini distribution	.24	.20	.15	.11

Source: Heath and Clifford 1990, Hellevik 1997, Ringen 1997.

Note: Higher education = O-level equivalent and higher. The proportion in the cohorts (all classes) attaining that level of education increased from 28 percent in the 1930–39 cohort to 68 percent in the 1960+ cohort.

or down), we saw in our reading of the same data a straight, sharp, and remarkable reduction in class inequality of educational attainment.

What then is the true story of class inequality, stability and similarity or change and difference?

WHY THE QUESTION MATTERS

The terms of the debate were set in my book *The Possibility of Politics* (1987). There, I observed, by way of conclusion, that my findings "count as rather encouraging ones for the strategy of seeking to attack social inequalities via legislative and administrative measures of a piecemeal kind."[19] That was a riposte to the first edition of *Social Mobility and Class Structure in Modern Britain*, in which the authors had observed that their findings "count as rather grave ones for . . . the strategy of seeking to attack social inequalities via legislative and administrative measures of a piecemeal kind."[20] This debate is, above all, about substantive issues in social policy. Crudely, if the stability thesis is true, the welfare state is in vain.

The class-inequality literature has produced a string of dismal conclusions to that effect following the lead of *Social Mobility and Class Structure in Modern Britain* in 1980. For example, with support in the stability of odds ratios as reproduced in table A.2: "Neither the meritocratic reforms of the 1944 Act nor comprehensive reorganisation can, in this respect at least, be said to have succeeded."[21] And further, "the advantaged social classes have been able to outmanoeuvre the social reformers. . . .

[19] Ringen 1987, p. 207.
[20] Goldthorpe et al. 1980, p. 252.
[21] Heath and Clifford 1990, p. 15.

Legislation may change the rules of the game, but the players who are most motivated to succeed may be able to adapt their strategies so that they succeed in the new game just as they did in the old." The consequence "of post-war economic growth was not that it facilitated egalitarian reform but rather that it obscured its failure. The reformers underestimated the resistance that the class structure can offer to attempts to change it: or, to speak less figuratively, the flexibility and effectiveness with which the more powerful and advantaged groupings in society can use the resources at their disposal to preserve their privileged positions." "[T]he post-war project of creating in Britain a more open society, through economic expansion, educational reform, and egalitarian social policies, has signally failed to secure its objective." "[T]he impact of educational reforms on changes in educational stratification seems to be negligible. Nowhere have they reduced inequalities of educational opportunity between socioeconomic strata." "Have mobility opportunities become more equal in these societies? The findings . . . suggest that the answer to this question is in all four cases negative."[22]

Beyond policy implications, methodological questions arise. When two methods for the analysis of the same data give different results, there is something unresolved that needs to be sorted out. In this case, two bodies of literature on social inequality tell contrasting stories. Either we find a way of reconciling those differences or we must conclude that the best available social research is inconclusive on major social trends.

Finally, there are broader theoretical implications in respect to the liberal vision. One expression of that hopeful outlook is a belief that social mobility is equalizing in that it causes class-linked inequalities of opportunity to be steadily reduced. This is the theory that is under attack from the stability-thesis school. "If the foregoing results are sound, they cast serious doubts on the arguments advanced by liberal theorists of industrialism."[23] In *On Sociology*, Goldthorpe dismisses the liberal theory on the argument, again underpinned by stability-thesis observations, that its predicted "withering-away of class . . . has yet to be observed."[24] What then remains is a dark undertone not only about the futility of the welfare state but more basically of the very idea of progress.

These claims on odds ratio evidence are in hindsight astonishingly strong. The stability thesis is treated as an established fact, so much so

[22] Heath et al. 1992, pp. 220, 241; Goldthorpe et al. 1987, p. 328; Marshall et al. 1988, p. 138; Shavit and Blossfeld 1993, p. 21; Marshall et al. 1997, p. 57; the cases and periods being West Germany 1976–91, Poland 1972–91, Czechoslovakia 1984–91, and the United States 1973–91.

[23] Marshall et al. 1997, p. 54.

[24] Goldthorpe 2000, p.163, the liberal theory being represented by e.g., Blau and Duncan 1967; Treiman 1970; and Kerr 1983.

that not only is it the "main achievement" of class analysis but an achievement of such dignity that "the focus of theoretical effort in the field should now be . . . to explain" that constancy and communality.[25] The implications for social policy are "grave," egalitarian reform has generally been a "failure," whole postwar projects have "signally failed," and educational reforms across a range of countries have "nowhere" reduced inequalities. No less than the liberal theory in all its glory stands accused and naked.

All this rests on a single and specific way of reading mobility tables and on that methodology alone: through odds ratios. Similar strong claims have been made for that methodology. Log-linear models "have emerged as the sociologist's most flexible yet powerful means for the analysis of mobility tables [and represent when] applied . . . to investigate the more detailed features of relative rates [a] technical innovation." This is a methodology that makes it "possible to specify the intrinsic association between variables after purging out nuisance variability in marginal distributions." "Under the logistic response model, differences in background effects . . . cannot result from changing marginal distributions of either independent or dependent variables because such changes do not affect the [measure]." "[L]ogit models [reveal] the 'pure' association between origin characteristics and educational attainment."[26] What is said to give this methodology its uniqueness of power is that it produces "margin-insensitive" measures of origin-destination associations.

Where this confidence in just this methodology and the importance of its findings comes from is something of a mystery. It is a very difficult and convoluted way of reading data, and there are very good reasons to mistrust the methodology both on its measurement validity and its normative significance.

One thing is presently *not* at issue: the usefulness or power of log-linear analysis in general, or of any other statistical technique for that matter. This is less a discussion about statistics than about the *usage* of statistics.[27]

NORMATIVE SIGNIFICANCE

The value reference shared by everyone in this debate is egalitarianism. The Hellevik-Ringen reading of mobility-table data is easily interpretable and not controversial. Provided the destination side of the table represents

---

[25] Goldthorpe 2000, p. 257.

[26] Erikson and Goldthorpe 1992, pp. 56–57. Grusky and Tienda 1993, p. vii; Mare 1981, p. 75; Breen and Jonsson 2005, p. 9.3.

[27] But for follow-ups on logistic vs. linear regression techniques in general, see Hellevik 2003, 2005.

attractive positions, it is a measure of class inequality in the attainment of those positions. From an egalitarian perspective, this is information of obvious normative significance. Class inequality thus measured persists in the data referred to here, but not on a stable level. In table A.2, for example, it is seen to have been reduced in line with the extension of educational opportunities.

The odds ratio reading, however, is all but easy to interpret. Just what is it that is being measured by odds ratios in class-mobility tables?

The answer has been a bit unclear and shifting. It was first thought that that particular reading on *class* inequality was sufficient for general pronouncements on *social* inequality. This was the interpretation in the first edition of *Social Mobility and Class Structure in Modern Britain*, hence the grave implications for "social inequalities." This position was abandoned, however, including in the second edition of that book. Class inequality now became more modestly a matter of precisely *class* inequality. In the next stage, following the results of Hellevik's and my reanalysis and in the exchange over those results with Marshall and Swift, that position also was abandoned in favor of a yet more modest view, according to which there are several kinds of class inequality and both ways of reading mobility tables are correct, albeit in respect to different kinds of inequality.

That's a step towards clarification but only a first step. In a subsequent paper, Adam Swift went back to methodological first base yet again and asked "precisely what it is that class analysis using odds ratios does and does not tell us." Here he underlines the "limitations" in this kind of class analysis and how it is a "narrower, or more carefully specified, research programme than some had realised." The consequence of this clarification is that odds ratio readings are interpreted so as not to tell us much or anything at all of normative significance about inequality: "[E]verybody can be getting better off, there can be more chances of upward mobility, the gaps between the positions that members of the . . . groups tend to end up in can be getting smaller, the distribution of opportunities to achieve absolute levels of goods can be getting more equal. More equal also can be both the distribution of opportunities to achieve [a specified standard of living] and the distribution of opportunities to buy goods. All this can happen without any increase in social fluidity between class positions."[28]

If that adds some further clarification to what is being measured, the next question is what it really *means.* "I have attempted to justify the normative significance of the findings of mobility analyses . . . involving odds ratios. But I've not sought to conceal the complexities involved in

[28] Swift 2000, pp. 664, 667.

such a justification. . . . To those who care about equality, but who also care about the distribution of things like opportunities to buy goods, social fluidity is an important part of the story. But it is only a part. A complete analysis of the distribution of *those* opportunities would involve reference to the size of the gaps between class positions as well as the extent of movement between them."[29] In other words, the "complete analysis" would be the kind of analysis Hellevik and I had conducted, which consists of reading all the distributional data in the mobility table. For the rest, the "important part of the story" is that odds ratio readings tell us *something* about *some* differences in *some* kinds of opportunity. Not about social inequality as such, not about class inequality as such, not even about class inequality of opportunity as such.

It now turns out, according to Swift, that this research program was never about inequality in a normative meaning after all, or at least not primarily so, but that it was always "explanatory rather than normative." What then gives odds ratio readings significance is that they "contribute to the explanation of these class-related phenomena."[30]

On this interpretation, the two series of statistics in table A.2 would seem not to be alternative readings of class inequality, or even different kinds of inequality, but to be one reading on inequality and one on an element in the explanation behind it. Together these data would then show a reduction in class inequality in spite of no weakening of the force of one contributing cause of inequality.

But that is not Swift's interpretation. He finds that the odds ratio reading uncovers a contributing explanation, but at the same time he interprets it as a measure of inequality, albeit only one kind of inequality. The same thing is both an explanation of inequality and itself a kind of inequality.

The logic would appear to be the following. Young people go through their early lives in search of education (or other attractive positions). We know that of those who started in a lower social class, a smaller proportion attained the higher level of education than those who started from higher social classes. That difference is explained, in part, by what is measured by odds ratios. What might justify calling that "class inequality" would be a credible assumption that those who move along the road from origins to destinations with a label of "lower class" are treated or affected differently in that process from others in ways that make it more difficult for them to attain the desired position of destination. Inequality is a normative concept. It refers to differences that are objectionable, in our case, from an egalitarian point of view. If young people from lower social

---

[29] Swift 2000, p. 675.
[30] Swift 2000, p. 676.

classes are blocked from attaining their aspirations, that would indeed be a case of class inequality.

However, to justify that conclusion and interpretation, it is not enough to establish that what odds ratios tell us is the force of a contributing explanation of class-related phenomena. It needs to be established that it is a special kind of explanation. Swift's conclusion is persuasive as far as it goes, but he has only established that we are on to an explanation of class-inequality, not that it is a class inequality explanation of class inequality.

In a contingency table, a measure such as the odds ratio uncovers whether there is a statistical association between the independent and the dependent variables and suggests the strength of that association. That there is a statistical association between class of origin and educational attainment in the displays in table A.1 and the real British data in table A.2 is clear and obvious. But it is *not* clear and obvious that this association is a case of class inequality.

From analyses of mobility tables, we are able to identify associations descriptively but nothing more. We may well think that an observed association hides a causal link from, in our case, class to education. That inference is supported by the fact that class comes first and education later, but it is still only an inference. All we can *know* is that there is an association. However carefully we analyze mobility-table data, we *know* nothing from that analysis about the mechanism(s) through which the inferred causality might work. In the class inequality literature it is said to be class inequality, but that is just a postulate.

If we have a firm theory of causality, we can take contingency-table associations as evidence of the causal force. For example, if the independent variable is vaccination or not and the dependent variable the incidence of the disease the vaccination is against, we can take the association between vaccination and incidence as good evidence of the effectiveness of the vaccination. That we can do in spite of having no observation of how the vaccine works in the immunity system of patients because we are on safe ground in assuming that is where it does its job.

In the analysis of class-mobility tables, we have no such firm theory to fall back on. We simply do not know through what mechanism(s) class background is supposed to cause differences in educational attainment, or at least there is no theoretical agreement about this.

A mobility table is a simple organization of data: marginal and conditional distributions clearly laid out. Those data as they appear on a sheet of paper, say in table A.1 or as usually with more finely grained decompositions of the marginal distributions, can be analyzed with great statistical precision. That is certainly being done in the class-analysis literature, with ever increasing technical sophistication.

However, the simplicity of the mobility table is deceptive. An organization of data that looks simple on paper is, in effect, a snapshot compilation of information about life-course movements over a very long period. The mobility table looks two-dimensional but in fact there is a third dimension in it, a dimension of time. If the destination is educational attainment, there may typically be fifteen to twenty or twenty-five years between positions of origin and of destination. If it is occupational attainment, the table may cover a span of forty to fifty or sixty years. Over a life course, a myriad of things happen to individuals that may contribute in various ways to their success in life, for example, their educational attainment.

In the class-inequality literature, the assumption is that everyone is equally motivated to seek higher education but that something descends on them in the process and shuts or opens doors to people, all depending on their class backgrounds. Halsey has likened it to "loaded dice" and suggested that what we are reading is those loadings.[31]

However, all we have to go by in support of that assumption is an observed association. In this case, that observation does not do much for us since it does not sit on any firm theory. The same observation is in conformity with utterly different assumptions about the mechanisms that may be at work. The important alternative theory to the one postulated in the class-inequality literature is that the statistical association between class and education is a result of self-selection rather than of dice or other treatments or influences being manipulated by someone else. If young people originating in different classes are differently motivated for higher education, or if there are differences in ability that are correlated with class, a statistical association between class and education might well reflect *equality* between the classes in the attainment of what their members themselves aim for, or fairness of treatment according to ability.

Socially differential motivation (or ability) might still be seen as a form of class inequality if we think that a lower level of aspiration (or skill) in young people from lower social classes is itself a legacy of class, but class legacy is not the only or obvious interpretation. We might, for example, take it more modestly as an inescapable evolutionary fact. Or it could be the result of informed and rational choice.[32]

The point here is that from the observed association, we cannot know which theory we should trust. You or I might want to believe one rather than another but the mobility table offers no help in substantiating such beliefs. If we have no firm theory of causality a priori, no reading of the mobility table can adjudicate afterwards between alternative possible theories.

[31] Halsey 1977.
[32] As argued by, e.g., Boudon 1974; Gambetta 1987.

This is, by and large, a restatement of prior criticism by, in particular, Peter Saunders.[33] That criticism has, however, pretty much been ignored in the class-inequality literature (although not by Adam Swift in his reassessment, which was why reassessment was unavoidable). Goldthorpe, for example, in *On Sociology*, where the stability thesis is "the main achievement to date of class analysis," deals with it by not mentioning it.

To sum up so far:

(1) Yes, it is established that there is class inequality of educational attainment (which, of course, comes as no surprise to anyone).
(2) Yes, it is established that there is an association between class and education as measured in mobility tables (which is also pretty obvious).
(3) No, it is not established that a class-destination association is a case of class inequality in a normative meaning. That has been postulated but not established.
(4) Hence, the only established evidence on class inequality from mobility-table analysis is that generated by Hellevik-Ringen–type readings.

VALIDITY

A final mystery now remains to be solved. If the odds ratio measures a cause of inequality and the Hellevik-Ringen reading measures the resulting distributions, how can the force of the cause have been stable when the result has changed? The question has perhaps become a rather academic one of little substantive importance, since we now know that the class-destination association does not contain established independent evidence on class inequality. But it still merits consideration, not least because this is where the discussion started.

We are forced back yet again to the question of what odds ratios measure. If we think they measure the mechanism in the process from origins to destinations that produces class inequality in the distribution of attainment—Halsey's loading of the dice in other words—the answer is that the cause cannot have maintained stable force when the resulting distribution has changed. That's simply mathematically impossible. If the loading of the dice is the same, the result will be the same. If the result changes, the loading of the dice must have changed. No difference in wording can get us around that obviousness. If instead of "loaded dice" we say, for example, "class bias of selection," "relative inequality," "relative opportunity," or "fluidity," the necessary conclusion is the same.

However, the combination of a stable causal force and a changing distributional outcome is not totally impossible. If we think the odds ratio

[33] Saunders 1990, 1995, 1996.

measures not *the* mechanism but the force of one among several causes that together produce the distributional result, the force of *that* cause could still be stable. That is perhaps Swift's interpretation, something that underlines again the "narrowness" of the research in question. If anything, then, what has been established is the stability of one contributing cause of class inequality which, on the one hand, is not a class-inequality explanation and, on the other hand, matters next to nothing for class inequality in the final distribution.

But in truth this solution, even if not impossible, feels outlandish and incredible. For example, going back to table A.2, it would seem entirely implausible in the face of the display there of changes in the class distribution of educational attainment to suggest that class inequality of opportunity has nevertheless been unchanging, yet that is the standard interpretation of data such as these in the class-inequality literature. The obvious starting hypothesis must be that when the class distribution of a good changes, the class-destination association will have been modified. To overturn a hypothesis of such apparent obviousness, we should want pretty solid evidence. No evidence of such persuasiveness is provided, however. First, the narrowness of evidence on offer would not seem to be persuasive even on its own terms. Second, even the narrow evidence as it stands does not serve to disprove the intuitive hypothesis. The reason is that odds ratio evidence is not proof of stability or not even in the class-destination association.

There is evidence that is not in dispute of stability in time and space of odds ratios. However, just as class-destination evidence is not sufficient to establish the facts of class inequality, odds ratio evidence is not sufficient to establish the facts of the class-destination association. It is the argument in the class-inequality literature, as we have seen, that the odds ratio method has a unique quality and power. It is supposed to tell the truth about the associations hidden in the conditional distributions in the mobility table with an authority that is superior to other ways of analyzing the data. That authority comes from the idea of *margin insensitivity.* "Odds-ratios are able to capture such net associations because they are margin-insensitive measures."[34]

In fact, however, odds ratios are *not* margin-insensitive. If margin insensitivity is at all a meaningful statistical concept, the most that could be said is that odds ratios are margin insensitive *under certain conditions.* The reference in statistical theory is that "the cross-product ratio is invariant under row and column multiplications."[35] That is some-

[34] Erikson and Goldthorpe 1992, p. 56.
[35] Bishop et al. 1975, p. 14.

thing, but it is less than margin insensitivity as a general quality of the odds ratio measure.

Statistical associations in contingency tables can be measured in different ways. While the odds ratio is a log-linear measure, the difference in proportions, for example, is a linear measure of the same thing. How various measures of association behave under changing marginal distributions is a pretty open question and certainly not something that can be pinned down as general margin insensitivity. Experiments show that both log-linear and linear measures of association sometimes respond to changes in the marginals and sometimes not, all depending on rather complicated constellations of conditions.[36] The postulated uniqueness of the odds ratio measure, supported by the argument of margin insensitivity, is simply a myth that has grown out of a simple statistical observation, the meaning and significance of which has been badly exaggerated and given credence by having been repeated by authors who refer to each other. The odds ratio is one of several available measures of association and not one that, for the present purpose, stands out from all others in authority.

If we return to table A.2 and re-estimate the class-education associations using instead of the odds ratio the difference in proportions (again, between high and low class), we get a different result from the odds ratio reading. The associations across the four birth cohorts are now .40, .40, .42, .33.[37] This is not radically different from the odds ratio results but sufficiently different to overturn the conclusion. From these data we would have been unable to conclude that the association has remained stable, and we would have had to conclude that the force of the causal factor measured is weaker at the end of the period than at the beginning. There is, from a methodological point of view, no less reason to trust these results than the odds ratio results.

CONCLUSION

In some recent class sociology in the tradition under scrutiny here, it would seem that confidence in the stability thesis is slipping.[38] That may be a result of new observations that do not fall in line with earlier ones or of a greater emphasis on exceptions in international comparisons, such as the case of Sweden, or variations within overall stability trends. This kind of reassessment is welcome but is of no consequence for the present discussion. The argument here is that there never was stability of class

[36] See Hellevik 2002b, 2003.
[37] Hellevik 2003.
[38] Breen 2004; see also a recent review in Breen and Jonsson 2005.

inequality in the data as analyzed and that odds ratio observations are inconclusive for this purpose. The same measure for the same purpose does not become more conclusive just because it comes to draw a more agreeable picture.

If we now go back to the beginning of the research program, we can see that the conclusion that "no significant reduction in class inequalities was in fact achieved" was, from what we now know, not supported by the evidence that was referred to. That evidence contains no established independent information about class inequality. The alleged margin insensitivity in odds ratios has turned out to be a red herring and odds ratio evidence to have less authority than had been ascribed to it. A more correct conclusion might have been that "no significant reduction in the power of one contributing cause of inequality was in fact achieved." That may not be insignificant, but it is not a conclusion about class inequality—all the less so since there is now other and clearer evidence of changing inequality in the same data. In recent political parlance, excessive and unsubstantiated conclusions and inferences were drawn from a dossier that had been (inadvertently, no doubt) sexed up.

The consequences of this reinterpretation are far-reaching. First, that original and powerful conclusion about class inequalities can now be considered overturned. It is, to be clear, overturned on its own terms. It is now also in question from new findings within its own framework, but those new findings would not have been necessary to overturn the original conclusion. The more correct conclusion about "one contributing cause of inequality" is no match. It is not the stuff of a stability thesis that there is reason to think anyone but methodologists, and hardly even they, would be able to get excited about. It is not a finding with grave implications for social policy or a basis for dismissing any postwar project or any other program of reform as failures (unless one thinks that egalitarian reform is not about equality at all but only about a narrow and specific contributing cause of it, which is not a class inequality cause and which the evidence shows is easily overridden by other causes). Nor is it a launchpad for much of an assault on any competing theory of, say, openness in society or historical progress.

Second, since the odds ratio reading does not provide established independent evidence on inequality, the Hellevik-Ringen reading, which indisputably does, stands unopposed. As a result, the apparent discrepancy between the class-inequality literature and the income-inequality literature is reconciled and the assault on liberal theory from one body of that literature refuted. The best available social research from both bodies speaks with one tongue on these major social trends and both speak a language that is in conformity with the liberal theory.

To sum up: the stability thesis was never the truth about class inequality; the grave conclusions for social policy were never supported by relevant evidence; and the liberal theory was never under credible challenge. When, in *On Sociology*, Goldthorpe argues that "the focus of theoretical effort in the field should be to explain the observed constancy and communality," he is suggesting to class sociology that it dedicates itself to explaining what has not happened.

How Good Is the Kindest Democracy?

A REMARKABLE STUDY of power and democracy has worked its way through a mass of research to a remarkable conclusion: the democratic chain of command in which governance is under the control of voters has burst, and the fabric of rule by popular consent is disintegrating before our eyes. The conclusion is not only that there are weak points in the chain but that a chain that was once solid is falling apart.[1]

This conclusion comes from an observation of democracy in Norway. Not surprisingly, that message has attracted controversy on the home front. There are, however, very good reasons to pay careful attention, and not only on the home front, to what is being said here about modern democracy.

AN EXCEPTIONAL CASE STUDY

The Norwegian Study of Power and Democracy (henceforth "the study") is quite unique in force and scope. Its task was to diagnose the health of the democratic system in an advanced democracy at the time of democracy's final victory in the great ideological wars of the twentieth century. For that purpose, it was given a practically unlimited budget. It was able to mobilize much of the country's formidable social-science community as well as strong forces in law, history, the humanities, and other disciplines. On issue after issue, careful effort was invested in summarizing the state of knowledge: the role of political parties, the political functions of courts, local democracy, associations and pressure groups, markets and economic power, the petroleum economy, global finance, journalism and media, changing gender relations, language and symbolic power, care and social services, economic democracy, minorities and multiculturalism, new information technology, foreign policy and development aid, social capital, European integration, supranational law. And so it

---

This is a revised version of a review essay published in the Times Literary Supplement *(13 February 2004) and subsequently in two versions in French, in* Courrier International *(7 July 2004) and* Le débat *(March–April 2005).*

[1] *The Norwegian Study of Power and Democracy: www.sv.uio.no/mutr/english/index.html.* See also Maktutredningen 2003 and Østerud et al. 2003.

went on. New research was initiated wherever pertinent questions presented themselves. The monarchy was scrutinized, as were minority rights for the Sami people and others, consumerism, the force of international treaties, the written constitution, science and the professions, business networks, culture and ethics, affluence, gender equity, and economic enterprise. Massive surveys were undertaken of attitudes and beliefs among political, business, and cultural elites and of citizenship and political behavior. The study looked back to power relations in the Middle Ages and the legacy of colonial subjugation (before 1814). There are case studies on such diverse issues as ethnic minority women via the politics of abortion, the regulation of cod fisheries, the privatization of the telecommunications, mergers and acquisitions by the country's most powerful corporation (Norsk Hydro)—even one of Henrik Ibsen as an observer of power! Long and short historical lines are laid out, as are tight and broad international comparisons.

The study was initiated by the Norwegian parliament, the Storting, and the job and budget put in the hands of a committee of five professors— three in political science, one in sociology and one in cultural studies— three men and two women. They started their work in early 1998 and submitted their final report in August 2003. In five years, the study produced fifty books, seventy-seven other reports, and a raft of articles in learned journals, most of them in Norwegian but some in English, by more than one hundred authors in all. In the process, the research was submitted to quality control in seminars, conferences, and workshops in which was sought the counsel of eminent scholars from many countries.

The other reason to pay careful attention is that the study has observed a democracy that is among the most robust of contemporary democracies. The Norwegians are a small population (less than five million) who live in a pretty large territory (about the size of Britain). They have a democratic tradition that goes back to 1814, when the then radical constitution that still prevails (with modifications) was adopted. That constitution remains the bedrock of the nation's identity and is celebrated in every town and village every year on May 17, Constitution Day. The country suffered five years of traumatic German occupation during the Second World War, and that experience fortified an ideology of egalitarianism, freedom, and constitutionalism.

Modern Norway emerged from poverty. The land is barren so that land wealth was virtually nonexistent. Not since the Viking age has there been a national aristocracy, and the 1814 constitution blocked its reintroduction. The rural elites were traditionally self-owning farmers, and the urban elites were high government officials and academics. Industrialization came only in the twentieth century, the bourgeoisie remains weak, and national leadership continues to be provided predominantly by the institutions of the state. In less than a century, the country metamorphosed from a state of utter destitution—from 1880 to 1920, a third of the population emigrated, driven out by poverty—to having become today nearly the richest people in the world. Affluence has been used to expand education (more than half of the young cohorts now take university-level education), put in place a redistributive welfare state that has done away with poverty, provides generous economic support to families and children, and strives to engineer gender equity with, for example, parental-leave provisions available on the condition that it is shared by the parents. In today's world, this is a cohesive society of strong families and schools, weak social conflicts, high quality of life (at the top of the UNDP's human development league table), and a contented and optimistic population (as expressed, for example, in the near-highest birthrates in Europe). By European standards, crime is low, the law lenient, and the prison population small. Governance is honest and benevolent, democratic institutions retain high legitimacy, and voter participation is comparatively high (but falling). Because of the petroleum economy, state finances are so solid that the government's problem is an unmanageable surplus. So we need to ask: if this is the kind of polity in which rule by popular consent is withering, what then is happening in more normal democracies where trust is more normally thin, economic power more normally strong, governance and public finance more normally in shambles, and conflicts more normally pronounced?

THE CHAIN OF COMMAND

On one level, this is a strictly constitutional study. It puts the formal procedures and institutions of representative democracy at the heart of democratic rule. That is to its benefit. Constitutional politics lends itself to being analyzed empirically in a tangible way so that we can know in a down-to-earth manner just what we are observing. Things become more elusive when, in the next round, it turns to the wider social environment in which constitutional procedures take place.

The chain of command addressed in the study is the one that makes constitutional procedures democratic. At one end is the voter; at the other end, political decisions. In a democracy, there is supposed to be a link to ensure that political decisions are the ones voters want made or approve of.

Voters are found to be a pretty constant entity as far as values and attitudes are concerned. They continue to see themselves as political animals. They are interested in political issues and are active in social life. If democracy is weakening, it is not from below; this is not an apathetic population, not even one in which apathy is creeping in.

But behavior is changing. Citizens are turning away from conventional forms of political participation. This is not because people are retiring from public and withdrawing into private life. It is more that they are shifting their involvement in public and social matters to other arenas and forms other than the traditionally political ones.

Voter participation in both central and local elections is trending downward. It is still relatively high compared to some other democratic countries but on a steady downwards slope: down from 85 percent to 75 percent from 1965 to 2001 in Storting elections and down from 81 percent to 55 percent from 1963 to 2003 in municipal elections. That overall slide, however, hides some crisscrossing movements. Women have caught up with men in political participation (except immigrant women). This is partly because of increasing participation among women, notably younger women, and partly because of decreasing participation among men, notably men with low education and income. The women who have entered politics are largely public-sector workers, the men moving out are largely those of the dwindling working class. In this traditionally social-democratic Scandinavian country, the labor movement is "no longer a force of political mobilization." Increasingly, the working class is the class of government workers.

While the basic and traditional form of political participation—voting—is trending down, other forms of participation are increasing, such as various forms of direct action, petitions, demonstrations, and political events and discussions, particularly locally. We might be tempted to see such forms of more direct politics as being also more democratic, but there is no change in the social stratification of participation. Middle-class citizens dominate direct participation, as they do voting, and working-class citizens remain in the background. The young, particularly young men, have more or less turned their backs on political-organization and political-party activity. Immigrants, in particular women, are strongly marginalized.

With less participation in old-fashioned organized politics, it is not surprising that political parties are in flux. The total number of party members is down by half since 1990. The once-strong link between social background and party allegiance has evaporated. In the 2001 parliamentary elections, blue-collar workers made up only 14 percent of the Labor Party's electorate, as compared with 22 percent of those voting for the ultrarightist Progress Party.

With falling membership ranks, political parties are reinventing themselves. They are becoming professional political machines in which members matter less and have less sway. This is made possible by tax-funded subsidies on a grand scale. (In some other countries, such as the United States and Britain, parties have, as is well-known, become dependent on private contributions, particularly from business. Some dislike that and want public subsidies instead. For democracy, it is bad news whichever way, and who can say what is worse?)

Not only parties but also other associations find themselves the victims of indifference on the part of those they see themselves to be serving. The twentieth century, up towards its end, was a grand movement of social organization: unions and labor organizations of various descriptions, benevolent and charitable organizations, local associations, women's organizations, temperance and lay religious movements, and later the organization of leisure in sports, travel, and culture. This, the study found, came to a halt and was reversed around 1990. Traditional organization is in decline, crowded out by what is called *here-and-now-organization* in often small, nonmembership-based, professional single-issue action groups. The man in the street who no longer cares for sedate and time-consuming organizational life also finds himself alone and isolated and with nowhere to go for collective action than to petitions, demonstrations and discussions. Diagnosis: "a democratic infrastructure in collapse."

It makes good sense to think of parties and associations as the building blocks of democracy that link together citizens and representatives. But such links can work both ways, they can be the people's tools of collective action but also instruments in the hands of elites for rallying support to causes under their control. In old Scandinavia (a social-democratic order the passing of which is regretted in this study), the network of associations that used to be known, honorably, as the popular movements and that are now in decline, were in many ways top-down structures of social control. The term "order" is much used in the summary report from the study for the way things were, and "disorder" for the way things are now. It may be that citizens disempower themselves when they allow the network of associations to disintegrate, but there is also something liberating in the clearing away of a paternalistic omnipresent cobweb of groups, and modern assertive citizens may well be satisfied to have a bit less of someone else's order weighing down on them. Still, a structure of links between the people and their representatives is falling apart, and what remains is the people on one side of the field, their representatives on the other side, and a void between them.

That is a new working environment for elected representatives. How do they and the institutions in which they work respond? Those institutions are municipal councils and the national legislature. (Norway also has regional institutions between the municipalities and the Storting but they matter next to nothing in real life and nothing at all to our story.)

This is a country of many and small municipalities, about 440 with an average population of less than ten thousand. The municipalities have been powerful units with vast responsibilities for local infrastructure and social services, and powers to match. They hold the power to tax—most income tax is collected locally—and discretion on the level of the local income tax (within limits set by the Storting). Democracy in this country has been rooted in a principle of local autonomy, but local autonomy has ceased to be a reality. The forms of local democracy are in place, but local politics has gradually become a matter of administering decisions made centrally and imposed locally. The taxing power of the municipalities is now no more than virtual power. All municipalities tax at the top of their nominal range of discretion, and even so, local politicians and administrators massively say that new duties are imposed on them by order from above at a pace that outstrips new funds. Nominally autonomous municipalities are reduced to standing with cap in hand at the finance minister's door. Local government is demoralized and voters disinterested.

Local government ideally plays two roles in a democratic system. It is supposed to be about decision making in local matters, and it is supposed to be a part of the infrastructure that links citizens and central government, in this respect not unlike nongovernmental associations. What links citizens to the national legislature is the vote. If that is all that ties together people and governance, it is less than a chain of command. Governance will be distant and citizens small. It is a function of local democracy to give citizens a reasoned feeling that they are included in the system of governance in the long periods between elections. The demise of local democracy—this is the one trend the study chose to describe as a crisis—is a further contribution to the collapse of the democratic infrastructure.

The decline of local democracy is driven in part by irrationalities in the organization of the welfare state. Welfare rights are granted mainly by central authorities but in large measure are delivered by local authorities. Citizens can without too much difficulty extract promises from the central government of more or better benefits because the central government can pass on the responsibility of delivery on to local authorities. The central government has power without responsibility, and local government responsibility without power. Citizens need feel no inhibition in making ever greater demands on their municipal authorities because their demands are sanctioned by the Storting. Nowhere in this spiral are dues and duties linked, and no one is in control. The costs are not so much in welfare-state budgets, although that too, as in the overburdening of the municipalities and their inability to work as arenas of democratic give and take.

There is less power in local government because the central government has usurped it. If that means more power to the national legislature, it could be good news for democracy. If there is more power to fight over, there is more reason to engage in fighting over it and democracy could see itself revitalized. Yet voters do not believe that parliamentary politics is becoming more relevant; they are less interested and involved, not more. The interpretation is not—to repeat an essential finding that deserves elaboration—that people are turning away from politics because of new values and attitudes. Rather they continue to be as interested in political and social issues as they have ever been but are turning away from constitutional politics because of the way constitutional politics are changing. Bluntly, rational and informed citizens are *right* to be less interested in democratic politics. In this polity, the citizens are found to be good enough and blame is allocated to those who work on their behalf.

The decision-making power of the national legislature is in decline. One reason is said to be that other more or less competing institutions are gaining power and that it then follows that the legislature must be losing out. The winners are the market, the media, and the courts. That analysis is, however, not entirely persuasive. Power is not divided in a zero-sum game. For example, there is no question that the media are in a way gaining in political power, but not really in power that is taken from the legislature. The power of the media is primarily to set the agenda and to orchestrate issues and awareness. That is clearly power of a sort but not power that is taken away from the legislature. Real political decisions are in the form of laws or law-like decisions, and such decisions are by definition made in the legislature and nowhere else. It may be that more of public debate and the presentation of politics take place in the media, but that is an enrichment rather than an erosion of democracy.

However, there is some more forceful action beneath the surface that is indeed undermining the decision-making capacity of the legislature. First, (large) economic actors have acquired one very specific new form of power that radically eats into the capacity of the legislature. That piece of power comes from economic globalization and consists in the credible threat of moving capital or economic enterprise out of the country. Legislatures make decisions that pertain to the national territory. Businesses can now credibly make it understood that if the legislature makes decisions they find unhelpful or objectionable, they may move capital, production, headquarters, or jobs out from that territory. There is nothing new in the use of economic threats in democratic-capitalist politics, but the credibility is new. This puts power in the hands of business, which is now so obvious to political decision makers that it is usually not even necessary for economic actors to display it for legislatures to bend to it. Business has acquired veto power in economic policy.

Second, in recent years a framework of supernational law has emerged, which is binding and limiting in national legislation. Supernational law comes from two sources. One is international covenants that national governments have formulated collectively and which national legislatures may subsequently give the status of national law. The prime example is the European Convention on Human Rights, which several countries—Norway being one—have incorporated onto national law. That convention is guarded over by the European Court of Human Rights, which has the last word in its interpretation. By incorporating the human-rights convention into national law, the national legislature chooses both to limit its own discretion of decision making and to subject itself and national courts to the higher authority of the European human-rights court. Norway has also incorporated two UN conventions on rights in addition to the European human-rights convention, and granted the Sami minority the formal status of an aboriginal people.

The other source is in supernational cooperation with the direct force of legislation, that is, requiring no decision on incorporation in the national legislature, principally the European Union. Here joint decisions are made that have the force of law in the participating nations. This obviously limits the decision-making power of the national legislatures. Well and good, that is as intended and as decided by those legislatures. But there is, as is well-known, a democratic deficit. EU laws are not adopted by a European legislature—the European Parliament is only a watchdog—but by the Commission under the oversight of national governments or by those governments jointly. That is perhaps slightly undemocratic, but the real problem is not so much in decision making per se as in the virtual impossibility of unmaking law once made, in particular treaty law. This gives the European Court nearly unlimited power to impose on and above national legislatures its view of what European law bids nations to do or not do. Judicial review is not "undemocratic"—if it were, there would hardly be any democracies—but unrivaled judicial review is. The country that has this power of judicial review is the United States, where the Supreme Court has vast real if not formal powers of legislation. In most democracies, judicial review is held under control by the power of the legislature to threaten the courts with counteraction if they should be inclined to take judicial review to extremes. When courts know that the legislature can strike back with new legislation, including new constitutional legislation, including possibly on the authority of the courts, they are unlikely to censure legislation if they think that could provoke "corrective" subsequent legislation. This balance of power allows us to have it both ways: the legislature being in good control of legislation but disciplined by a mild threat from the courts to stay carefully within the constitution and not infringe on the rights of citizens. The European Court is under no such threat. The final democratic deficit in the European Union is not in the power of the Commission but in the absence of a democratic legislature to balance the power of the Court. The Court does not make directives, but it decides what they and European treaty law mean and in this is, for all intents and purposes, sovereign and answers to no one. The democratic deficit does not rise from the delegation of legislative power upwards, but from the absence of democratic grounding in the institutions to which that power is delegated.

These losses of legislative power can be seen in most democracies. In the Norwegian case, there are some additional homegrown problems. One comes from what is known as *minority parliamentarianism*. Elections are by proportional representation and with easy access to representation for small parties. The result is a Storting of seven or eight parties, without stable or even recognizable majorities and oppositions, and shifting minority governments. The Norwegian experience is that voters dislike this form of disorder. Perpetual negotiations between the legislature and the executive over budgets and lawmaking are seen as quibbling and governance without direction. Voters decide the composition of the Storting but find that they are without direct influence in the formation of governments. On several occasions, they have had to swallow the humiliation of seeing parties that they have punished with defeat in the elections go on to win cabinet power.

In two referendums, in 1972 and in 1994, Norwegian voters decided against membership in the European Union. However, the country was and is entirely dependent on being inside the European system of free trade and economic enterprise. This has been solved by creating the European Economic Area, in which three countries—Norway, Iceland, and Lichtenstein—have put themselves in the situation that they are obliged to accept and comply with European law (with some exceptions) while excluding themselves from any participation in the decision making that generates that law. These nations have elected to accept passively as law what others decide. When a legislature disenfranchises itself, it is perhaps no wonder that voters ask what their vote is worth. (One is reminded of John Stuart Mill's single nonnegotiable limitation in self-determination: liberty does not include the liberty to abolish one's liberty.)

System and Citizens

Among the many merits of this study is that it has produced not only sharp conclusions and masses of evidence to support them but also its own criticism of its own interpretations of the evidence. Technically it had the status of a royal commission and, like all such commissions, submitted a formal end report. In that report, two members dissent from some parts of the majority view. The majority consists of professors

Øyvind Østerud (who chaired the committee), Fredrik Engelstad, and Per Selle, while the dissenters are professors Siri Meyer and Hege Skjeie (the two women in the gang of five). While the majority three speak in unity, the minority two dissent on slightly different grounds. But the nature of their dissent is formulated in very clear words by Professor Skjeie: "The conclusion of the majority is, bluntly, that 'rule by popular consent is withering'. I disagree."

The main source of disagreement is not in facts and analysis but in some elements of interpretation. The constitutional analysis at the center of the interpretations of the majority is an analysis of democracy as a *system*. The two minority voices want more to be said about the *persons* who are served by that system. "My starting point for the analysis of the anatomy of power is individuals and life forms," wrote Professor Meyer. We now know a good deal about the system; what has happened to the people who live under that system?

Is Norway a classless society? The answer is not straightforward. This has long been a society of softly drawn class divisions, and divisions by property and economic power have probably continued to soften (although income inequality has, as elsewhere, increased a bit in recent years). But the study finds that what emerges is not classlessness but new class divisions. At the bottom of the social ladder is no longer a working class (to mention) or the poor (to mention) but an excluded service underclass originating in immigration and identifiable to some degree by ethnicity and race. Norway has today nearly the highest level of immigration in Europe, and much of that immigration is, in the local terminology, *fremmedkulturell*—foreign-cultural. First-and second-generation immigrants make up 20 percent of the population in the capital.

Have women won emancipation? In education, pretty much; in political life, pretty much; and in public sector employment, including academia, pretty much. This has been helped forward by an extensive use of politically imposed quotas and various forms of affirmative action. But in economic life, more broadly speaking, no. Here Norway compares unfavorably with many other European countries and the United States. The labor market is strongly segregated by gender. Increasing female labor-force participation is explained almost totally by new jobs in the public sector, and there is a high prevalence of part-time employment among women. Women have made very little inroads into employment and, in particular, high-level employment in the corporate sector.

Have minorities won emancipation? Norwegian culture has long been seen to be homogeneous, both by the Norwegians themselves and by observers from the outside. It has been seen as homogeneous because of an absence of sharp class divisions, which is correct, and a perceived absence of minorities, which is false. The minorities have been there but for a long time did not have recognition as minorities. The largest minority is the Sami population, probably about sixty to seventy thousand people. Other "old" minorities, some very small, are Jews, Gypsies, travelers/tinkers, and Finns. For these peoples, there has been a remarkable process of recognition and of cultural restitution over the last two or three decades. The Norwegian majority is coming to recognize and accept minorities and minority rights, much aided as usual in this country by public policies, and are slowly learning to accept its culture as a multicultural one.

For the new minorities, however—that is, those originating in the country's unexpected experience of immigration—it is different. There is a pronounced and well-funded public policy of integration, but it is probably a long haul for "Norwegians" to be able to recognize "non-Norwegians" as "Norwegians."

If we measure the quality of a democracy not only in its constitutional procedures but also in the underlying social structures, the question is whether this is a population of increasing or decreasing equity in autonomy and dignity. Are ordinary people experiencing empowerment? Are previously excluded groups emancipated?

In some respects—a neutral observer would probably say to a considerable degree—the answer to these questions is in the affirmative. The situation of the old minorities is radically transformed. In the case of the Sami, this is institutionalized in group rights being written into the constitution, a Sami parliament elected by the Sami population and with some legislative authority, and their important recognition as an aboriginal people. The political situation of women is transformed, women having attained practical citizenship on a par with men. (What we are to make of women's conspicuous absence from corporate employment and power is not easily said. It could be that they are sensible enough not to want to have their lives destroyed in the corporate jungle; one hopes so.)

The trend in social relations is not universally democratic—there is the notable exception of an emerging immigrant underclass. But by and large, this is a society in which rights and powers of self-determination are being dispersed in the population and not reined in. The difficulty for the study's interpretation of its evidence is that much of this movement towards a more democratic social structure comes from uses of political power that are also taken as evidence of the retreat of political power. Improvements in the rights of minorities and of women, for example, come in part from the incorporation of supernational conventions into national law. The study runs into trouble with itself when it interprets deliberate political decisions to strengthen the rights of citizens as a democratic problem. It is true that constitutional institutions thereby bind and limit themselves and limit their own discretion in future decision making, but when that is done by shifting power downwards from collective institutions to citizens individually, we should probably take this to be better and not poorer democracy. There are costs, particularly that power is given away to supernational courts that operate outside of and above the polity, but the benefits are on the democratic side of the scales.

THE WAY TO REPAIR DEMOCRACY IS TO REPAIR DEMOCRACY

This meticulous study of a democracy—which is clearly, in Lijphart's terminology, a kind and gentle one—shows above all how unfinished and imperfect real democracies are, even when they are at their best. Citizens depend on democratic governance for their freedom. The continuation of governance that citizens can trust to protect their freedom because it is they who control it and not it them, is not something we can take for granted. Nor should we allow ourselves to be persuaded that our government does what we want of it simply because it goes through the motions of democracy.

The main conclusion offered by the study, and from which I started this essay, is actually a double conclusion that responds to two hypotheses: first, that there are breaches in the democratic chain of command and, second, that this is related to or caused by "disintegrations" in the broader environment in which the procedures and institutions of representative democracy operate, that is, by forces outside of those procedures and institutions themselves.

The evidence firmly supports the first hypothesis. If we test the quality of representative democracy by the solidity of the chain of command, the trend in the performance of this solid and well-established democracy is correctly described as decline. That is indeed a remarkable finding.

The second hypothesis is partially successful. The evidence supports it, as far as the international environment goes. Both political and economic power is increasingly exercised above and outside of the nation-state, that is, beyond the reach of national democratic institutions. While within the nation-state the chain of command from below is weakening, outside of the nation-state a new chain of command is emerging from above that limits and directs national legislation but over which citizens (and their representatives) have virtually no say or control.

It is, however, unsuccessful as far as the national environment goes (and this is what the study continues to debate into its end report). A dispassionate reading shows up a country in good order economically and socially in which representative democracy is in decline not because citizens are apathetic and social structures disintegrating but in spite of cohesion and vitality in values and social life.

The failed half-hypothesis is no less notable and important than the successful one-and-a-half. This failure adds strength to the confirmation of the first hypothesis. When representative democracy is seen as a chain of command from voters to political decisions, the quality of representative democracy is in decline whenever weaknesses arise in that chain. That is true even if citizens remain committed to democratic values, because they lose their grip on what their representatives do. It is true irrespective of whether or not the power of the legislature declines, because when representatives become less accountable there is increasing danger that they may legislate against the will of citizens. Had the conclusion been that society is disintegrating and with it democracy, it would have been devastating but trivial. The conclusion that democracy is in decline in spite of social cohesion is remarkable.

Pulling together what is confirmed and what not, the message of the study is that the decline in the quality of representative democracy is found, with some international pressures aside, in the constitutional procedures and institutions themselves: in the demise of local government, in election and party systems, in the lack of accountability in the welfare state, in the courts and judicial review. That is fortuitous for the practical business of protecting and improving democracy. It means that the best way to repair democracy is to repair democracy. We do not need to wait with democracy until we have repaired society and capitalism. We can take on democracy directly.

What Does a Good Press Look Like?

IN FEBRUARY 2003, a scandalous book was published in Paris in which *Le Monde*, by many held to be the world's best newspaper, was accused of being a part of the French establishment rather than its watchdog.[1]

In the 2002 BBC Reith Lectures, Onora O'Neill spoke of the breakdown of trust and accused the British press, by many held to be the world's best, of contributing by not being adequately accountable.[2] Is there such a thing as a good press?

THE FRENCH CASE

"Nothing is more apt to surprise a foreigner, than the extreme liberty, which we enjoy in this country, of communicating whatever we please to the public, and of openly censuring every measure, entered into by the king or his ministers. If the administration resolve upon war, it is affirmed, that . . . they mistake the interest of the nation. . . . If the passion of the ministers lie towards peace, our political writers breathe nothing but war and devastation."

You would be excused for thinking this to be a comment on current politics, but it was in fact written in 1741, by David Hume in his essay *Of the liberty of the press*. In 2002, the *Financial Times* published a series of interviews with foreign business leaders living in Britain. They lavished praise on British society and its way of life—except for the press, which one after another lashed into for its intrusiveness.

Hume went on to ask how this state of affairs had come about. His answer was that press freedom had arisen from the way politics worked in Britain, particularly the tendency to have a strong government, something that encouraged opposition to take refuge in the press. That question I will not pursue further, but it is worth being reminded that the

This is a slightly revised version of an essay published in The British Journalism Review *2003, no. 3, which in turn was based on a lecture to the* Reuters *Programme on Journalism at Oxford University earlier that year. I am grateful to Paddy Coulter for the invitation to give the lecture, to him and the Reuters Fellows for a stimulating debate, and to Bob Pinker and Bill Hagerty for assistance in making a talk into a paper.*

[1] Péan and Cohen 2003.
[2] O'Neill 2002.

eccentric British press did not fall out of the sky yesterday; it has long been here and fits snugly into a larger political jigsaw puzzle.

My question instead is whether the British press is a *good* press. I think it still stands out in its freedom, pluralism, and aggressiveness—but is it *good*?

France offers an excellent laboratory of comparison. The French press is *different*. It is smaller and less competitive. With about the same population, total newspaper circulation is only about half of that in Britain, and the number of titles, including regional and local papers, is smaller. There is nothing resembling British tabloid journalism, or Sunday newspapers worth mention. The regulatory regime is stricter, with statutory provisions for the protection of privacy. France is one of only three countries in Western Europe (with Ireland and Portugal) without an independent self-regulatory press council. The press itself is hierarchical with a single dominating newspaper holding the undisputed top position: *Le Monde*.

That is without question a newspaper of exceptional quality. Its coverage of national and international affairs is exemplary, in business, culture, and sports no less than in politics. Its reports are detailed, thoroughly researched and trustworthy. It carries lively debates and comments and treats correspondence from readers with respect. One might well complain that it is austere and not very entertaining, but it has never offered itself as entertainment. Or you may find that most of its articles are too long to be absorbed in their full richness, but then it is not a paper that does not ask something of its readers. A daily dose of *Le Monde* (as I know from having lived in France) does leave one with a feeling of being reliably informed about the world in which one lives.

But is it *good*? And by extension, if judged by the quality of its standard bearer, is the French press good?

On 9 June 2000, *Le Monde* carried one of its most dramatic ever front pages on which, across the top, Paris was branded "capital of electoral fraud." (See box.) The story took up several pages and laid out in detail a system of deep and persistent electoral fraud in the French capital, in particular in the famed Fifth District on the left bank, the power base of political leaders such as President Jacques Chirac (once the mayor of Paris) and the then mayor, Jacques Tiberi. That is a splendid front page. Here, it would seem, is a newspaper that not only informs its readers about current affairs but is independent and critical to such a degree that it threatens the established power in the heart of Paris.

However, a closer reading would reveal that the story behind the headlines was not what the paper's own reporters had dug up but one that had been exposed by political activists working outside of the press. What is remarkable in that story is not that there was fraud but that it was exposed. That Paris was politically corrupt was known by *everyone* for

---

Paris, Capital Of Electoral Fraud.

Judicial Inquiries Show That, Over A Long Time, The Universal
Suffrage Has Been Perverted In Paris.
Fictitious Voters, False Addresses, Material Benefits For
Ballots: A System Organized By The RPR.
A School case: The 5th Arrondissement, The Turf Of
The Paris Mayors.
—*Le Monde*, 9 June 2000, Top Front-Page Headlines

---

years before the newspaper chose to expose it in this way. The coverage
in *Le Monde* on that day was not news as far as the corruption was concerned but mainly in that a public secret had been openly declared. And
that had been done not by this excellent newspaper or others in the press,
but by activists on a mission to bring to the surface what everyone knew
but no one spoke of.

How could it happen that rampant political corruption was known to
thrive in the nation's capital without having been confronted decisively
in a newspaper of undisputed quality? A partial explanation might be in
France's press laws, which give persons and institutions extensive protection against press intrusion. Under that legal system, it is dangerous for
editors and journalists to engage in critical investigative journalism except
when they can back their stories up with watertight proof. Investigative
journalism does not usually start from that basis. It is more likely to start
with some suggestion of impropriety and then to roll on to reveal either
the truth of impropriety or its absence. In Britain the press can, without
too much risk, engage in more or less speculative investigation. If it is
eventually revealed to have made groundless accusations against someone, it can then be taken to task, but preventing a newspaper from starting
the process is difficult. All the paper needs is to be able to argue that it is
raising questions that are in the public interest to investigate. The burden
of proof lies with those who might want to stop it. In the French case this
is much more difficult. Suggestions of impropriety can, unless provable,
be slapped down with the law in hand. This prevents newspapers from
starting the ball rolling, all the more since the meekness of competition
does not push editors towards risk.

But although legislative framework and competition no doubt play a
role, I do not think this explanation takes us very far. The political corruption in Paris was so well-known that it would not take much investigation
to prove it—as, after all, freelance activists were able to do, no doubt with

fewer investigative resources than *Le Monde* possessed, had its editors chosen to put their star reporters on the case. Behind the legislative framework is a culture, and although "culture" is a vague and plastic term, it makes sense to say that what stood between *Le Monde*, with its perception of itself as a newspaper of superior quality and the telling of a simple truth was more culture than laws.

If the British press, as Hume suggested, is as it is because of the political system in which it works, so also the French press. French political life is hierarchical. Its center is in Paris, and in Paris it is dominated by an elite reared in *les grands ecoles* and in the ENA, l'École nationale d'administration, a peculiarly tight political-administrative-business-intellectual elite. If the way politics operates in Britain encourages an oppositional press, the way it operates in France encourages an elitist press. And that is the press France has, itself hierarchical and the newspaper that stands at the top of that pyramid aligned with the national elite.

This press culture came dramatically to light at the end of François Mitterand's presidency (1981–95). It transpired then that the French people did not know the true biography of the man who had been their president for fourteen years. He had a background as an official in the Vichy collaboratist administration during the Second World War. He suffered from cancer during his time in office, having been diagnosed with prostate cancer a few months after his first election. At his reelection in 1988, his life expectancy was about one year. (That he survived another eight years was a medical miracle.) The president's health was a sensitive issue because the end of his predecessor Pompidou's term was marred by the embarrassment that he was clearly seriously ill while his administration insisted that he only had a cold, in a rather Soviet style of deceit. This prompted Mitterand to pledge to French voters that they could trust him to be straight and open about his health, something that was subsequently revealed to have been a fourteen-year lie. A married family man, he had a mistress and with her a daughter. None of this was reported in the French press. It was common knowledge among editors and journalists but was not made public until late in his last term, and then only when Mitterand himself decided to make his life story known (for mysterious psychological reasons by which he effectively chose to destroy his own reputation).

Why did the French press not tell the French people the truth about their president? The answer, strangely enough, lies in the matter of the mistress and the daughter. Not even French press laws stood in the way of making this public. That was entirely a matter of culture—of something being regarded as private. Whether or not it is relevant for the public to know of the love life of the president (I think it is, certainly when it is institutionalized in a second family) is beside the point of our argument.

Any normal curious reader would want to know; the president wanted it kept quiet; editors knew but did not publish it. The press had trapped itself into a conspiracy of silence with the president and with others in the elite who were in the know. The press, the president, and other insiders shared an interesting secret that they were keeping from the public, whom they deemed not mature enough to know. Through such consort, and disregard for the public, the press kills itself off as the controller of power. This is elitism on display. No censorship is needed because a culture is in place in which order is maintained.

THE JOB OF THE PRESS

We are now by stealth coming back to the question of the good press. In the French case I have described *Le Monde* as a newspaper of exceptional quality, and I think no sensible reader could judge it differently. But I am not persuaded that it is a good paper or that the press of which it is a part is a good press. What, then, is a good press?

In an open and democratic society, the press has a job to do; it has a purpose. It is as good as it does its job. That may sound obvious and elementary but is far from it. I listen carefully to what is being said when people complain about the press, and what I usually hear are complaints about standards, not about performance. Baroness O'Neill's complaint, for example, is about, as she sees it, the low standard of reporting.

Standards are relevant, of course, but they are not what the press is about. They are the means by which it does its job, but they are not the job. Its excellence lies in its performance. It is therefore performance we need to scrutinize first. That done, we can and should ask if it is performance by proper standards. But looking to standards first is like praising a painter for the way he holds the brush irrespective of how he applies the paint.

The job of the press is to enlighten the public and to educate and entertain it. It is to inform the political process. It is to serve as an arena of deliberation. It is to hold to answer those who exercise power. Let us for simplicity say that the job has two elements, to inform the public and to scrutinize power.

If the job were only to inform, we could judge the press on a single standard. Does it tell us what we need to know, and does it do so truthfully? But if the job is a mixed one, we do not have that luxury. We need to consider several criteria at the same time, criteria which may well be in conflict with each other. Is the press disposed and able to take on power in such a way that those who hold it know that they are being held to answer? And does it also inform us adequately?

Were the press to accept only a duty of information, it would let us down on the essential democratic job of scrutinizing power. If it were unprepared to investigate uses and abuses of power, there would be things we need to know that we were not being told, and it would let us down on both accounts. In order to be able to display power at work, it may need to sacrifice some accuracy of information. There is something paralyzingly puritanical and bloodless in the opinion that standards are holy and paramount. That is to ask for a pretty press with no bite.

THE BRITISH CASE

The British press is not always a pretty sight, but it does its job. That is not owing to one or two quality papers, although they are there, but to its structure: the combination of quality broadsheets and aggressive tabloids, of nationals and locals. It comes from competition, from the absence of privacy legislation, from cautious self-regulation, and from a tradition and culture of critical independence. Many in Britain deplore the aggressiveness of the tabloids, but they should not fret. The threat to the quality of the British print press does not come primarily from the nastiness of the tabloids but, if anything, from a decline in the broadsheets. There, the best standards are in the obituary pages, which are outstanding, and in sports and arts reporting. Political reporting, for the most part, is poor, obsessed with Westminster and covering the broader political process badly, and dominated by an excessive deadweight of columnists and commentators, many of whom are former editors beyond their sell-by date who do not report goings-on but express opinions, usually of little use to anyone.

Without question, British tabloid journalism can be awful. Take, for example, the case of "Mary Bell." This was the pseudonym of a forty-one-year-old woman who, at age eleven, had brutally killed two boys, aged three and four. She had subsequently been under treatment and (in April 1998) lived a normal life under a new identity with a fourteen-year-old daughter. A book was published on her case, without revealing her identity, which attracted much attention.[3] The daughter did not know her mother's dark history. Within a day or two of the book's publication the tabloids had hunted down Mary Bell in her new identity and put her on their front pages, knowing that would give the daughter knowledge of her mother's background.

[3] Sereny 1998.

More stories of the same kind could be told, stories that reflect very badly, indeed, on the press. But they are, for all their nastiness, still stories of bad standards and not of bad performance.

The stories I have told regarding the French press are very different: good standards of bad performance. A press that is a pretty sight but does not do its job.

Taking the British and French stories together, I think there are three lessons here. First, in the French case, it would seem that the legal framework and culture put standards before performance. That experience suggests that standards can be too strongly regulated in law or protected in the culture of the press, which can cause its performance to suffer.

Second, in the British case, the question is whether arguments of performance are given such weight that editors are able to disregard standards. The British press would certainly not merit a clean bill of health on standards, but since the establishment of its own regime of self-regulation with the Press Complaints Commission in 1991, the trend has been towards better standards, in particular on privacy.[4] This experience suggests that careful self-regulation of standards can be effective without a cost in lower performance.

Third, the combined experiences suggest that there is a trade-off. The French press buys standards and pays with performance. The British press buys performance and pays with standards. Of course, the French press could pull itself together and perform better and the British press could clean up its act, but if perfection is not available, which it never is in human affairs, we may have to choose where we want our mistakes and costs to fall. Is it in standards or in performance we would prefer the press to fail? The occasional lapse in standards is unfortunate, sometimes very unfortunate for those who suffer; the persistent failure of performance is a democratic disaster.

The truth about the British press—and that includes the electronic media as well as the print press—is that it is simply *brilliant*. Compared with anywhere else in Europe and beyond, it is informative, lively, varied and pluralistic, entertaining and often funny, politically vibrant—and it is independent, critical, irreverent, and, thank God, intrusive. It does its job. The press culture accepts and cherishes a certain degree of healthy ruthlessness. Regulate out that spirit and much becomes lost. No one who has been outside of Britain and seen the tedious and inept press—as opposed to the occasional quality paper—most democracies are burdened with would in their right mind want that instead of what the Britons have.

---

[4] See the PCC's February 2003 Submission to the Culture, Media and Sport Select Committee of the House of Commons, ppcpapers.org.uk.

True, in doing its job it sometimes overdoes it, and the British press does have a nasty streak. It is trying to curtail this so as to avoid political regulation—successfully, says the regulator. To their credit, British legislators have held back from tying the press up in a straitjacket of privacy laws. Better to allow the occasional visible failure in standards than to engineer systematic and hidden failures in performance.

It is a popular myth that the press is held in disregard by the public and that journalism is the least trusted profession, along with used-car dealers and real estate agents. In fact, however, British journalists enjoy a remarkable degree of trust. Radio and television news reporters are at the very top of league tables of trust, along with family doctors and schoolteachers. Journalists at broadsheets and local papers are high up on the scale, alongside judges. Only journalists in "red-top" tabloids are down towards the bottom with the real estate agents.[5] All of which suggests a healthy state of affairs in the relationship between press and public.

Those of us who like to comment on public affairs usually like to ask what should be done and feel obliged to offer our earnest suggestions for action. As far as the British press is concerned, it is gratifying to be able to recommend that nothing that is not already being done needs doing. Rather, we should enjoy our blessed state and, with Hume, unashamedly rejoice that at least in this, we do it better than most others.

---

[5] See, e.g., YouGov, February/March 2003, www.YouGov.com.

The Flat-Tax Issue

DIRECT TAXES are progressive when higher incomes are taxed at a higher rate than lower incomes. A regime of strongly progressive rates is not economically and politically possible. Since only moderate tax progression is within reach, is it worth the trouble?

There is today a political movement that says that it is not and that argues the case for a flat tax regime.[1]

There is also a good deal of academic interest in the flat-tax issue.[2] This is the sister idea on the tax side to that of a basic minimum income on the benefit side (see appendix E). These ideas are carrying through to practical experimentation and implementation, particularly in democratically immature countries in East Central Europe.

If the alternatives are a moderately progressive or a flat income tax, there are good arguments against the deceptively simple idea of taxing all citizens at a flat rate. First, it is not necessary. A moderately progressive tax is politically possible and neither politically nor economically costly. Second, a moderately progressive tax *does* redistribute income in a useful direction. The scope for redistribution may be rather limited but it is real and is something that should not be given away unless there are very good reasons to do so.

However, the most important argument against the flat tax and in favor of a moderately progressive one is that the former would protect and the latter undermine the capacity of the tax regime to preserve its perception of fairness. That, again, is a necessary quality in the tax regime for its utility to the government in its power to tax.

The power to tax depends on a government's ability to persuade the middle class to let itself be taxed. The tax burden is effectively carried by the middle class, and the middle class holds the political power to resist taxation. Middle-class taxpayers always want to pay lower taxes and always look for flaws in the tax system, real or imagined, which they can use as pretexts to resist taxation. A flat-rate income tax would give the majority of taxpayers an argument of some justification for persuad-

[1] Péan and Cohen 2003.
[2] O'Neill 2002.

ing themselves that they are paying more than they should and the rich less than they should. The willingness of the middle-class majority to underwrite public spending depends on its perception that the rich pay at least a bit more than they do. Hence, the innocent-looking flat-tax idea is really a Trojan Horse in any regime of public policy that would inevitably erode the power to tax. It is not a technical or economic argument about simplicity in taxation, but an intensely political argument on the scope of public policy.

The Basic-Minimum-Income Issue

HERE IS A MAGIC FORMULA that deserves to be shot down because it is a bad and muddled idea but that, surprisingly, is managing to make itself attractive.[1]

A basic income is "an income paid by the government to each full member of society, with no conditions, irrespective of other income or property, of working or not, of family circumstances, and so on."[2] Already in this definition there is a problem, in that transfer income is not really paid by the government but by other citizens through taxation. Why should each citizen have an unconditional right to a basic income paid to him by his fellow citizens? "Everything that is morally and practically sound in the universal basic income can be achieved by other policies, and the ends that are peculiar to the UBI lack moral and practical force."[3]

The main ethical argument that is advanced in favor of a basic income is that everyone needs at least some income to be a citizen and to have freedom. Therefore, at least a minimum income should be assured to all. The premise in this argument is correct, but the conclusion is wrong. To say that everyone needs income is not to give a reason why governments should pay more income to those who already have income. It is correct that social policies should assure a national minimum, but this can only be done through some patchwork of arrangements. It is correct that social provisions should be as simple, straight, and nonbureaucratic as possible but, unfortunately, no single-formula watertight safety net is devisable. If it were, we would have it.

If a basic income were introduced *instead of* existing arrangements of income support, there would be losers, and the losers would be among those who depend on the existing arrangements of support. This would create new poverty, and citizens in need would be abandoned. Complex patchworks of income support may often have evolved into a true mess of bureaucracy and inefficiency, but that is no reason to throw everything out in despair in favor of a system that, as a matter of principle, does not direct support to where it is needed.

[1] See e.g. www.etes.ucl.ac.be/BIEN.
[2] Van Parijs 1997, p. 35.
[3] Galston 2000, p. 1.

A basic income is not necessarily argued as a safety net. In the most ambitious case for the basic income idea, put forth by Philippe van Parijs, it is not assumed that a basic income is necessarily on a level to sustain basic needs or that it necessarily replaces other forms of income support. His case for basic income is that this is the most effective way to achieve "real freedom for all." That argument, however, is self-defeating. Real freedom means not only formal freedom but real opportunity to choose the kind of life one might wish to lead. However, a basic income that does not substitute for other forms of income support and must be financed from a politically feasible tax level would be pitiful and would give no one any opportunity for choice of lifestyle when the means are wasted by being shared equally among all, including those who already have real freedom. "For all" must mean to the benefit of the least advantaged; compare my discussion of the difference principle in chapter 3. But if means are limited, the least advantaged would be worse off, be it in opportunity or standard of living, if these means were shared equally among all rather than distributed according to need.

Further arguments that are made in favor of a basic income are mainly technical and deceptively attractive: it is administratively simple, and there is no poverty-trap problem. For these arguments to be valid, however, the basic income would have to replace other provisions, such as child allowance, housing allowance, and means-tested income support. That would only be acceptable if the basic income could give those most in need a socially acceptable standard of living—or actually a higher standard of living than under any alternative arrangement of income support for the same means. But a basic income that is shared among all could not be on a level that would ensure a decent standard of living. It would be a national minimum on which no one could live and could therefore not substitute for other arrangements. Simplification in income support is certainly desirable, but although a basic income could itself be simple (as could any other form of income support on its own), it would in practice add another element of complexity since it could not eliminate the need for other forms of support. Simplicity or complexity in income support depends on how different arrangements of income support go together, not on any single arrangement on its own. Adding a new arrangement to an already complex patchwork does not create simplicity but adds complexity.

Since a basic income would be paid unconditionally, there would be no loss of transfer income involved in taking work or increasing work income. Hence, presumably, no poverty trap is created. That might be true if the basic income were the only form of income support, but that is not possible. If the basic income were adequate to live on, it would discourage work totally. That level of basic income would be morally impossible, even if it were politically possible, which anyway it is not because it could not be funded. If the basic income were inadequate to live on, it would enforce work on the poor while allowing the nonpoor to work less. Those unable to find work would be abandoned with nothing but an inadequate basic income and become destitute, or they would need some other form of additional income support, in which case they would be back in the classical poverty trap.

In Britain, where income support depends heavily on means-tested arrangements, Tony Atkinson has suggested a basic income as a way of escaping means-testing and the known disadvantages and weaknesses of such arrangements.[4] Heavy reliance on means-testing should be avoided, but that does not require an alternative in which resources are wasted by being spread out to those who already have adequate incomes. Atkinson's proposal is for a *participation income*—a basic income (which would be below a subsistence income) to all who are participating in socially useful activity, both paid and unpaid work, or have a good excuse for being nonactive, such as illness. But that would just be a little bit of income to mainly those who are not in need and nothing at all to most of those who are in need. Or in other words, again, there would still have to be means-tested or discretionary income support behind the participation income— in which case nothing is gained.

The arguments against the basic income are both ethical and technical. A basic income would involve payment of income from the government to persons and households who have no need for this income. This is not only bizarre; it is objectionable. There is no goodness involved in any action by governments unless it is for a good purpose. Giving money to those who already have enough of it is not a good purpose.

A basic income would involve an unconditional payment of income to persons who are just unwilling to work. This is defended by van Parijs on the argument that real freedom must involve the freedom to live a life that does not include working. That, however, seems to rest on a notion of citizenship as a matter of rights only, a concept of citizenship that is by definition an impossibility since there can be no rights except those that are accepted by others as duties. Free citizens do have rights, but within the constraint of concern for each other. Real freedom may well include the right to not work but not the right to require others to carry the cost of that indulgence. People who are *unable* to take on normal duties, such as to work in order to support themselves and their family, are in need, and there is a good reason that they should have help. People who are able but *unwilling* to work are free riders. For governments to encourage and support free riding is not only foolish, it is bad ethics.

[4] In Atkinson 1995a, ch. 15.

The technical argument against a basic income is cost. A basic income sufficient to live on would require a politically impossible tax level. (And anyway, there would seem to be no purpose in taxing all income earners for the purpose of giving all income earners a transfer income, as compared with taxing income earners by ability for the purpose of distributing transfers by need.) A basic income that is affordable would be useless to the poor and pointless to the nonpoor.

The Index Problem

YOU AIM TO measure or portray something statistically. You have found out that you need several bits of information to do so. You have resolved what the appropriate indicators are and have collected the relevant data, which you have laid out in front of you. The question then presents itself of how to pull those data together into an unambiguous measure or a definite portrait of the thing you are interested in. That's the index problem, how to provide *one* answer to a question when that answer depends on several bits of data.

One way to do this is to aggregate the data into a single figure on a numerical scale. Let's call that *indexing*. A well-known example is the price index for the measurement of inflation, in which price movements on a range of commodities are aggregated into a single overall price trend. A more exotic example is *the discomfort index* suggested by the American economist Arthur Okun as the sum of the rate of inflation and the rate of unemployment.

The reason indexing is a problem is that it is often difficult to find a nonarbitrary way of doing it. That again is difficult because even if it should be clear what the appropriate indicators are that would go into the index, we may not know what weight to give each indicator. In the price index, the price of a commodity, say milk, is weighted by what proportion spending on that commodity makes up in average total household spending. That is a scientifically acceptable way of doing it because it makes good sense and because the weights are not decided by what the scientist might happen to think they should be. In the discomfort index, Okun just added the two figures he thought were the relevant ones, which is to say that he gave each indicator equal weight. That could be considered less scientific because it was just a convention he chose to use without justification in any guideline of authority as to the actual contribution of inflation versus unemployment to discomfort.

If we don't have an objective criterion of weighting, an index will by definition be more or less arbitrary. (Even indices build on "objective" criteria, such as the price index, are in some respects arbitrary, of course, but I leave that aside here.) If that is the case, we might well ask if there is any point in trying to pull the data together in a composite index. The relevant information is there for all to see; why not just present it as it is without imposing on the data the straitjacket of an index? After all, if we collapse several bits of data into a single number, we lose a good deal of information in the process, which may seem careless if we know that the index we create is of dubious validity.

That is a strong argument against indexing, but it is not fully persuasive. For one thing, we *always* rely on conventions of some kind or other in any effort at measurement, and indexing is in that respect not extraordinary. As long as we use sensible conventions and explain the procedures, there is nothing unscientific in it. For example, a good scientific principle, if the weights are not objectively known, is to go by the simplest possible assumption. That would usually be to give each indicator the same weight unless there are good reasons that recommend a different convention. Okun's procedure, then, was pretty good science. That's the procedure I have used in chapter 1 in my index of democratic quality.

Furthermore, there are advantages in indexing. Some information gets lost, but something else is gained. If we just present an array of data and say that this is what the measure of the thing we are interested in is made up of and leave it at that, we and those whom we address may well feel that we have not finished the job and told our story through to its conclusion. This is a very strong instinct in any empirical research, so much so that indexing is often seen to be the obvious and unquestionable final step in the research process. For example, if we define the standard of living as made up of income and leisure, the instinct will be to pull this into a single measure so as to be able to rank everyone on a final scale. Otherwise, it will be unresolved whether A is better off than B if A has more income than B but B more leisure than A. Anything that is unresolved is, of course, intensely disturbing to the scientific mind.

By experience, the presentation of data in a cluster of indicators, as I have done in chapter 4, is often felt to be unsatisfactory and inconclusive. If you present the relevant data as a cluster of indicators rather than a single index number, although you are being more informative, you may find it difficult to make others interested in listening to you. If you pull it together into an index (and give that index a striking name), although you are being less informative, you are more likely to make people sit up and listen because what you have to say appears more authoritative and final. This is perhaps paradoxical, since the index that people are prepared to pay attention to may well be a less reliable basis for making up one's mind about the matter than a survey of the whole range of data, but such is human nature when it comes to numbers. That's why many UN agencies regularly produce reports based on "league tables" of countries in their areas of work. Everyone knows that any league table is bound to give a more or less arbitrary ranking of nations, but we also know that indices and league tables have to power to concentrate minds. There is nothing frivolous in this. For example the UNDP's Human Development

Index has probably contributed to an improved understanding in the world of the problems of poverty and underdevelopment in a way that would not have been achieved had the scientists stopped short of aggregating their development indicators into an index.

So there are arguments for both solutions, and we might ask when to index and when not? One possible answer is that indexing is only prudent if we have objective criteria for the allocation of weights. Although that might be a good cautionary rule, it is probably not one many scientists would like to subject themselves to. If there are good substantive reasons to aggregate data into an index, and that includes a desire to make one's message heard, indexing can be done safely enough with the help of transparent assumptions even if we have very little to go on for deciding on the weights. That's not where the problem lies.

If we narrow the issue down to applied policy research (and set aside considerations that are exclusively scientific in basic research), what we should be guided by, I think, is the purpose of the enterprise. We are now in the business of informing citizens and decision makers about matters relevant to the formation of opinions and policies. We can think of that job in two ways. We can imagine that the objective is to assist towards rationally informed decisions or to assist towards a rational political process.

In the first case, we should expect citizens and decision makers to be in demand of the most conclusive information possible. The scientists' job is then to tell them as precisely as they can how matters stand that are relevant to the decision problem. For example, if the central bank is considering whether or not to change the base interest rate, it needs to know how prices are developing. That includes a measure of total inflation—a price index in other words. The central bank needs much more information than this, but it is difficult to see how it could act rationally on interest rates without the help of a price index. The responsibility of the scientists must then be to be helpful and pull the price data together into an index as best they can. That is the solution demanded in the enterprise we are concerned with, and it is to that solution scientists should apply their craft. In the case of the price index, this represents no great problem since a credible basis of weights is available. But the reason the scientific job here should include indexing is not that a credible technology is available. That is fortunate but is not the reason. What calls on scientists to carry their measurement forward to an index is the nature of the demand for information that arises from the enterprise the research is seen to serve.

In the second case, the enterprise to be served is not limited to solving the decision-making problem at the end of a political process but goes to the rationality of the process itself. The job of the scientist is now not so much to guide decision makers towards good decisions as (assuming we are in a democracy) to guide citizens towards rational deliberation. That is a job of extraordinary importance in a democracy where good decisions are by definition the decisions that result from a rational process of deliberation.

Rational deliberation depends, as does rational decision making, on information, but not exactly on the same kind of information. While decision making depends on disputes being closed so that decision makers can get on with it, deliberation depends on disputes being opened up, encouraged, and guided forward. That would lead us to see the problem of indexing, and particularly of the weighting of indicators, in a new light. When weights cannot be allocated objectively, it often means that the business of weighting and thereby of indexing is in reality a normative and political problem. If the standard of living is made up of income and leisure, you and I will possibly have different opinions about the relevant importance of those two factors. If so, we should not think it is for scientists to decide for us how they ought to be weighted. Rather, that is something we have to resolve ourselves through careful deliberation, or leave it unresolved. If applied research is seen to serve the rationality of the democratic process, which is to say the process of managing normative problems, it should seek to lay out relevant issues for deliberation but not preempt the democratic nature of deliberation by seeking to impose "scientific" solutions on what are in reality normative problems.

In principle, indexing without "objective" criteria assumes that the process of deliberation over the normative problem of weighting has been completed so that we are ready to move forward to decision making on the basis of a more or less agreed-upon weighting of the arguments relevant to the decision at hand. In theory, therefore, in applied policy research in a democracy, indexing is recommended only if we can be confident that there has been adequate deliberation over the normative issues involved. If that is not the case, if the enterprise at hand is instead that very deliberation, the recommended procedure would be to put relevant information before citizens without preempting deliberation by indexing prematurely. Indexing without deliberation might be described as a form of scientific transgression into matters that pertain to the democratic process. If indexing means the processing of data into an unambiguous measure or definitive portrait of an underlying concept, say poverty, that processing is now a political task more than a scientific task.

A more simple terminology might be to distinguish, as I've done in chapter 4, between measurement and social reporting. Measurement is about resolving how factual things really stand. Social reporting is about informing a process geared to resolving political, normative, or moral questions. The problem of poverty, I have suggested, is a moral problem. Its severity is therefore not subject to being measured in the strict meaning of that term, but can only and finally be established through deliberation. Therefore, the way to use policy research to assist that enterprise is by social reporting. Therefore, again, indexing does not recommend itself, and I hence refrain from trying to express the severity of the problem in any single figure and consequently from indexing. I present what I think is the kind of information that is needed to make a judgment on the severity of the problem, but I approach that only by way of discussion and without pretending that I have a scientific measure of it.

In chapter 1, I explore democratic quality. This I take on as a straight matter of measurement. I do that, as in the exercise on poverty, with the help of assorted indicators but in that case, since I see it as a measurement problem, I do not stop with the presentation of the indicators and data but pull it all together into a final index. Since I have no objective criteria to resort to for weighting, I use the simplest-assumption procedure and give all the indicators the same weight.

Social Anchorage

FROM 1972 TO 1976, I was a member of a team that conducted a large study of living conditions in the Norwegian population.[1] A part of that study was to map out in detail the social distributions of well-being, and it turned out that those distributions were not in all respects as predicted.

BACKGROUND

I came into unexpected territory when exploring the distribution of well-being as expressed in social indicators of functional health. Those indicators were correlated with various independent variables, including importantly income and class. The correlations were teased out in the usual way, with various statistical techniques from bivariate percentage tables to multivariate regression equations. The result in this case was the expected cluster of negative correlations between social position and health, some statistically significant and others not.

Although entirely predictable in its results, that exercise left me deeply dissatisfied. I was looking for associations between sociologically crucial variables: social position and health. We had excellent data from a massive survey designed for the purpose and knew from our experience with those data that we were using tested and robust questions and indices. But no matter how aggressively I attacked the data with cross tabulations and regressions, only some modest correlations were to be found that sometimes recommended themselves by being statistically significant. The hypothesis was, of course, that social position would come through as an effective predictor of well-being. In a way that hypothesis was confirmed—the null hypothesis of no association was generally disproved—but, I felt, not in a powerful or persuasive way. Very little seemed to emerge from this particular analysis of any real importance for understanding how well-being was distributed in the population. I was not satisfied to conclude that well-being is distributed (pretty) independently of social position; that just goes against the grain of sociological evidence and would in any event not have been supported by other findings within

[1] Rødseth at. al. 1976.

the larger study. There was something wrong; something was being missed in the way the problem was approached.

Pondering this, it struck me that there might be another way of thinking about social position. The conventional idea, which I had been following, was that a person's social position is defined by what differentiates him or her from others: men are different from women, the highly educated different from those with less education, the rich different from the poor, and so on. Well and good, and for many purposes this is, we know, an analytically powerful idea. But not for this purpose, it seemed. I was at the time (and still am) working under the influence of the sociology of Emile Durkheim and even more the great Norwegian sociologist and ethnographer Eilert Sundt. They both argued, from their own empirical research, that quality of life is influenced as much by what binds people together as by what separates them. Why not think about social position in terms of bonds between people?

A reason for starting from that end was that the indicators of well-being I was exploring were what might be called action indicators. Functional health is about being able to *do* things. This is well-being not so much in the meaning of *having* as of *doing*.[2] That understanding of well-being goes to the power of and wisdom in action. What Sundt and Durkheim argued was precisely that it is for the mastering of action that individuals seek, need, and benefit from bonds to others.

The resulting study was first published in Norwegian in 1975 and again in a collection of essays in 1997, under the title *Den sosiale forankring—social anchorage*.[3] This work is not previously published in English. I reproduce its main logic and findings here for two reasons. First, it was an experimental work with results that for me confirmed an idea about individual and society, an intuition that it is through *attachments* in community that individuals are in a position to realize themselves. That intuition has stayed with me and is relevant here to the view of freedom that a free life rests on the ability to exercise restraint, and that again comes from how people are able to depend on each other rather than being at liberty from each other. Second, it gives an illustration of the power of simplicity in statistical methodology, which is a subtext in the present book.

METHODOLOGY

For an operational definition of social position along these lines, I took inspiration from an elegant study in which social position was defined in

---

[2] I here follow Allardt 1975. See also Nussbaum and Sen 1993.
[3] Ringen 1997d.

what I here call the conventional way, a study by Johan Galtung of how people's opinions on foreign policy could be seen as a function of their social position.[4] He thought that people could be located socially along a dimension from center to periphery. A society "belongs" to those who are at its center, while those who are located towards its periphery have less ownership and integration in it. That, he thought, would influence their view on social and political issues, and he developed a range of hypotheses on that in respect to issues in foreign and defense policy. To test those hypotheses, he used data from opinion surveys in the Norwegian population, collected by the Gallup Institute. These data contained a limited set of variables, which constrained him in the operational definition of his independent variable. The solution he chose was to use eight indicators of social position, to dichotomize each indicator, and to turn that into a simple additive index based on the number of indicators on which each person's position was "central" or "peripheral." That resulted in an index ranging from 0 (central position on none of the indicators) to 8 (central position on all). His dimensions of social position were gender, age, education, income, location ecologically, location geographically, occupational position and occupational sector. Being male was central and female peripheral, being thirty to fifty-nine years of age central and younger or older peripheral, having more than primary education central and only primary or less peripheral and so on.

In this study, very clear associations were found between social position and political behavior, beliefs, and attitudes, generally in conformity with reasonable hypotheses. Methodologically, the study was striking for its simplicity in its definition of the independent variable. The beauty of that, I thought, was how the hypothesized associations were uncovered with clarity with the most elementary of methodological tools. That, in my opinion, lent extra credence to the findings.

Following that example, I restarted for my own purpose from an idea that individuals in society find themselves surrounded by life arenas, the nearest arena being family, the next one friendship, the next one again work life, and finally beyond that associational and political life. The position of an individual in these arenas could be either that he or she has an attachment of integration or not. The more arenas in which a person has that attachment, the more his or her life is one of social anchorage, and the less of attachments the more his or her life would be one of social isolation. From that, I devised an elementary index of the Galtung type, based on the number of arenas in which each individual had an attachment of integration. Attachment was seen as a matter of either/or, and I assumed that the arenas were all equivalent so that attachment was at-

[4] Galtung 1964.

tachment and none of the arenas in this respect more or less important than any of the others. The resulting index, then, had five values, from the most integrated (persons with attachment in all four arenas) to the most isolated (persons with attachment in none of the arenas).

Attachment in the family arena was defined as being married or not (this was before informal cohabitation had become widespread), in the friendship arena as having or not having any good friend(s) living nearby, in the economic arena as being in gainful employment or not, and in associational life as being active or not in any political or social association. Only persons between thirty and seventy (the retirement age at the time) were included in the analysis. All data were from our own sample survey. (Technical matters of data treatment and analysis are reported more fully in the original publication. The number of respondents was 1,927.)

RESULTS

I did two sets of analysis. First, using the complete index, I established the association between social anchorage and the indicators of functional health, for which I had found very limited association with social position as defined conventionally. The results of that analysis are reported in table G.1, at the end of the appendix. The associations are now clear and strong. From this I concluded that social position defined in terms of anchorage is a powerful predictor of well-being, at least in the *doing* understanding of well-being.[5]

Second, I undertook a series of analyses based on an idea of social anchorage as a resource. There are, we may hypothesize, psychological benefits in living in integration with others as compared with living in social isolation, and there are practical benefits, such as having social networks to draw on for help and support. Such benefits to the individual, if we follow Durkheim and his notion of solidarity, would depend on a quality of mutual dependency between individual and group. The individ-

---

[5] In the original work, these and other associations were tested against various control variables, including age and gender. The indices of anchorage had some correlation with age and gender so that some associations were somewhat modified by these controls. That, however, does not materially change the results as presented here. First, the reason the indices have some correlation with age and gender is that there are real sociological differences between women and men and between age groups in social anchorage, which is to say that the real associations are precisely those that are identified in the bivariate analyses. Second, some associations were modified when subjected to statistical controls but only moderately and not so as to change the general pattern of clear and strong associations. The controls therefore served to confirm the identified associations as real and not statistically spurious.

ual needs the disciplining and guiding authority of the group but also depends on that authority being constrained, so as not to become overwhelming, by a dependency in the group on his contributions to it.

This mutuality we can think of in my model as a matter of attachments in several arenas at the same time. Take, for example, a person who is without attachments in family and economic life but who has good attachments of friendship. She is not isolated, but her relationship to surrounding groups is one-dimensional. She can draw on the support of friends, say in a confrontation with public authorities, but in her relationship to those friends she lacks the counterbalance of autonomy that would come from other attachments outside the friendship arena.

I sought to shed light on these matters by looking into one or another life arena and taking the quality of a person's situation in any arena to be a function of her anchorage outside of that arena, for example, associational activity as a function of anchorage in family, friendship, and work life. Practically, that meant using reduced indices of anchorage in three arenas rather than all four, and indices then ranging from 4 to 0 rather than from 5 to 0, as above. As dependent variables, I used what seemed to me the most relevant indicators from those available in the survey. These results are reported in table G.2, at the end of the appendix.

Here I pursue five hypotheses. First, from anchorage comes a subjective feeling of well-being. This hypothesis gains support in section A of table G.2. People who have social anchorage in family, work, and associational life are less likely than others to feel life to be slow and dreary in their free time.

Second, from anchorage comes self-assurance and good judgment. This hypothesis gains support in section B. Persons who are without anchorage in family, work, and associational life are not more likely than others to have been the victims of violence but are much more likely to entertain a fear of becoming exposed to violence. It also gains support in section C, which gives various indications of political alienation and confidence in one's control over one's own life.

Third, from anchorage comes ability and power of action. This hypothesis gains support in section D, which shows that persons without anchorage outside of associational and political life have less initiative to make themselves informed about their society (by reading newspapers regularly) and that they are less likely to participate in politics (by voting).

Fourth, from anchorage comes an opportunity to mobilize others in practical support. This hypothesis gains support in section E, which shows that persons with anchorage in family, work, and associational life are also more likely than others to have good friends.

Finally, from anchorage comes activity. This hypothesis gains support in section F, which shows that people who enjoy social anchorage are more likely than others to be active in economic, political, and associational life.

What, then, can one conclude from this experiment? There are limitations, of course. This was an elementary study that uncovered some associations between social position as understood in a certain way and certain indicators of well-being. That is in itself a fine result. Finding predicted associations of significance between independent and dependent variables is pretty much what we can hope for in empirical social research. When we find strong associations, we have a good result. When these are associations that appear in repeated analyses, we have good results that we can start to feel confident about. When the pattern of associations conforms to expectations under a credible theory, we can start to hope that we are on the trail of social mechanisms. When the relevant theory suggests where cause and effect are located in the predicted associations and the empirical results comply, we can start to suggest how those mechanisms may work.

All this was achieved, and for me, that was a source of great satisfaction. I was able to feel that something significant had been uncovered, all the more since I had first undertaken a more conventional analysis that had uncovered next to nothing of the associations that were subsequently proved to be there to be uncovered, and all the more since the associations I eventually did find were exposed with the help of elementary tools and transparent methods. Still, it *was* a study of associations and, as usual, causal mechanisms may be suggested but not proved. I suggest that social anchorage is a cause of well-being, sound judgment, power of action, and the like, but there may obviously also be causal effects that run the other way.

That qualification given, it was nevertheless my feeling at the time I did the study, and still today, that the strength and pattern of associations uncovered should be taken as powerful evidence that it is sound and fruitful to think of the position and life chances of individuals in society— from their subjective feeling of well-being to their power to shape their own lives—as strongly influenced by how their lives are linked with the lives of others. An individual may shake off or be without such constraining influences, and in that sense be at liberty to do as he wants, but then also be at risk of seeing his life float aimlessly because it is lived without anchorage.

TABLE G.1
Health Indicators as a Function of Social Anchorage (percentage in each category).

Indicators	1	2	3	4	5	6	7	8	9	10
Anchorage										
4	4	4	8	10	19	10	23	12	4	5
3	3	7	12	14	26	15	24	14	6	11
2	13	20	32	23	38	29	31	23	10	21
1	21	32	48	28	46	39	35	29	15	23
0	29	47	64	39	61	57	32	36	32	39

Indicators:
1 = Unable to walk up stairs.
2 = Unable to walk for fifteen minutes.
3 = Unable to run fifty meters.
4 = Suffering from tiredness over several weeks.
5 = Insomnia.
6 = Anxiety, disquiet.
7 = Unable to relax in free time.
8 = Having been unable over long periods to maintain normal activities due to ill health.
9 = Regular user of sleep-inducing medication.
10 = Regular user of tranquilizing medication.

TABLE G.2
Well-being, Judgment and Activity as a Function of Social Anchorage (percentage in each category).

Indicators	Section A	Section B		Section C					Section D		Section E	Section F						
	1	2	3	4	5	6	7	8	9	10	11	12	13	14	15	16	17	18
Anchorage																		
3	2	2	3	48	43	27	28	19	2	6	7	4	3	0	53	20	40	26
2	6	2	9	55	54	35	30	23	3	10	14	5	5	0	29	13	34	44
1	16	2	14	63	59	40	36	24	6	15	14	7	7	1	20	10	26	55
0	29	3	17	62	69	59	41	38	10	28	21	11	13	2	7	3	10	83

Indicators:

1 = Free time often feels slow and dreary.
2 = Exposed to violence or threat of violence during past year.
3 = Often feel fear of violence or threat of violence.
4 = People like me can vote in elections but otherwise have no influence (% agreeing).
5 = Politics is too complicated for people like me (% agreeing).
6 = Making plans for the future is not much use (% agreeing).
7 = What one achieves in life is determined by the conditions one comes from (% agreeing).
8 = Life is a result of luck and chance (% agreeing).
9 = Reads no newspaper regularly.
10 = Did not vote in the last national elections.
11 = Have no good friends living nearby.
12 = Temporarily absent from gainful employment.
13 = Work-disabled.
14 = Unemployed.
15 = Member of trade union or similar association.
16 = Member of political party or association.
17 = Member of civic association.
18 = Not a member of any association.

References

Abel-Smith, B., and P. Townsend. 1965. *The Poor and the Poorest*. London: Bell.

Ackerman, Bruce, and Anne Alstott. 1999. *The Stakeholder Society*. New Haven, CT. Yale University Press.

Ackerman, Bruce, and James S. Fishkin. 2004. *Deliberation Day*. New Haven, CT. Yale University Press.

Aleinikoff, T. Alexander. 2002. *Semblances of Sovereignty: The Constitution, the State, and American Citizenship*. Cambridge, MA: Harvard University Press.

Alkire, S. 2002. *Valuing Freedoms*. Oxford: Oxford University Press.

Allardt, Erik. 1975. *Att ha—att älska—att vara*. Lund. Argos.

Altman, Daniel, and Anibal Perez-Liñán. 2002. "Assessing the Quality of Democracy. Freedom, Competitiveness and Participation in Eighteen Latin-American Countries." *Democratization* 9, no. 2, pp. 85–100.

Anckar, D., and J. Anckar. 2000. "Democracies without Parties." *Comparative Political Studies* 33, no. 2, pp. 225–47.

Andreß, H. J., ed. 1998. *Empirical Poverty Research in a Comparative Perspective*. Aldershot. Ashgate.

Aristotle. 1995. *The Politics*. World's Classics. Oxford: Oxford University Press.

Atkinson, A. B. 1998. *Poverty in Europe*. Cambridge: Cambridge University Press.

———. 1995a. *Incomes and the Welfare State*. Cambridge: Cambridge University Press.

———. 1995b. *Public Economics in Action: The Basic Income/Flat Tax Proposal*. Cambridge: Cambridge University Press.

Atkinson, A. B., B. Cantillon, E. Marlier, and B. Nolan. 2002. *Social Indicators: The EU and Social Exclusion*. Oxford: Oxford University Press.

Atkinson, A. B., Lee Rainwater, and Timothy M. Smeeding. 1995. *Income Distribution in OECD Countries*. Paris. Organisation of Economic Co-operation and Development.

Atkinson, A. B., and J. E. Stiglitz. 1980. *Lectures in Public Economics*. London: McGraw-Hill.

Auerbach, Alan, and Martin Feldstein, eds. 2002. *Handbook of Public Economics*, vol. 1–4. Amsterdam. North Holland Elsevier.

Baldwin, Peter. 1990. *The Politics of Social Solidarity*. Cambridge: Cambridge University Press.

Barbados Ministry of Social Transformation. 2003. *National Strategy Plan*. Bridgetown, Barbados. MST.

Barber, Benjamin R. 1984. *Strong Democracy: Participatory Politics for a New Age*. Berkeley: University of California Press.

Barr, Nicholas. 1998. *The Economics of the Welfare State*. Oxford: Oxford University Press.

Bauman, Zygmunt. 2001. *Community*. Cambridge: Polity.

Becker, Gary S. 1981. *A Treatise on the Family*. Cambridge, MA: Harvard University Press.

Beckles, Hilary McD. 2004a. *Great House Rules: Landless Emancipation and Workers' Protest in Barbados 1838–1938*. Kingston, Jamaica. Ian Randle.

———. 2004b. *Chattel House Blues: Making of a Democratic Society in Barbados*. Kingston, Jamaica. Ian Randle.

———. 1990. *A History of Barbados*. Cambridge: Cambridge University Press.

Beetham, David, Sarah Bracking, Iain Kearton, and Stuart Weir. 2002. *International IDEA Handbook on Democracy Assessment*. The Hague. Kluwer International.

Berger, P.L., and R.J. Neuhaus. 1977. *To Empower People: The Role of Mediating Structures in Public Policy*. Washington, DC. AEI.

Berlin, Isaiah. 2002a. *Liberty*, ed. Henry Hardy. Oxford: Oxford University Press.

———. 2002b. *Freedom and Its Betrayal: Six Enemies of Human Liberty*, ed. Henry Hardy. London: Chatto & Windus.

Beveridge, William H. 1942. *Social Insurance and Allied Services*. London: HMSO.

Bishop, Y.M.M., S. E. Fienberg, and P. W. Holland. 1975. *Discrete Multivariate Analysis*. Cambridge, MA: MIT Press.

Blau, P. M., and O. D. Duncan. 1967. *The American Occupational Structure*. New York: Wiley.

Boix, Charles. 2003. *Democracy and Redistribution*. Cambridge: Cambridge University Press.

Bollen, Kenneth, and Robert W. Jackman. 1989. "Democracy, Stability and Dichotomies." *American Sociological Review* 54, no. 54, pp. 612–21.

Bollen, Kenneth, and Pamela Paxton. 2000. "Subjective Measures of Liberal Democracy." *Comparative Political Studies* 33, no. 1, pp. 58–86.

Bojer, Hilde. 2003. *Distributional Justice: Theory and Measurement*. London: Routledge.

Boltvinik, J. 2003. "Poverty Measurement Methods. Typology, Limitations and Problems." Working paper, Colegio de Mexico.

Booth, C. 1892. *Life and Labour of the People of London,* vol. 1. London: Macmillan.

Boudon, Raymond. 2003. *Raison, bonnes raisons*. Paris: Presses Universitaires de France.

———. 2002. *Déclin de la morale? Déclin des valeurs?* Paris: Presses Universitaires de France.

———. 1997. *L'Art de se persuader*. Paris: Fayard/Seuil.

———. 1995. *Le juste et le vrai*. Paris: Fayard.

———. 1974. *Education, Opportunity and Social Inequality*. New York: Wiley.

Bourdieu, P., and I. Wacquant. 1992. *An Invitation to Reflexive Sociology*. Chicago: Chicago University Press.

Bradbury, Bruce, Stephen P. Jenkins and John Micklewright, eds. 2001. *The Dynamics of Child Poverty in Industrialised Countries*. Cambridge: Cambridge University Press.

Brady, D. 2003. "Rethinking the Sociological Measurement of Poverty." *Social Forces* 81, pp. 715–52.

Breen, R., ed. 2004. *Social Mobility in Europe*. Oxford: Oxford University Press.

Breen, R., and J. O. Jonsson. 2005. "Inequality of Opportunity in Comparative Perspective. Recent Research on Educational Attainment and Social Mobility." *Annual Review of Sociology* 31, pp. 9.1–9.21.

Brennan, Geoffrey, and James M. Buchanan. 1985. *The Reason of Rules*. Cambridge: Cambridge University Press.

———. 1980. *The Power to Tax*. Cambridge: Cambridge University Press.

Briggs, Asa. 1961. "The welfare state in historical perspective." *Archives européennes de Sociologie* 2, no. 2, pp. 221–59.

Bryan, Frank M. 1995. "Direct Democracy and Civil Competence." *Good Society* 5, no. 1, pp. 36–44.

Buruma, Ian. 1999. "The Man Who Would Be King." *New York Review of Books*, 10 June.

Callan, T., B. Nolan, and C. T. Whelan. 1993. "Resources, Deprivation and the Measurement of Poverty." *Journal of Social Policy* 22, no. 2, pp. 141–72.

Capaldi, Nicholas. 2004. *John Stuart Mill*. Cambridge: Cambridge University Press.

Casper, Gretchen, and Claudio Tufis. 2002. "Correlation versus Interchangeability. The Limited Robustness of Empirical Findings on Democracy using Highly Correlated Datasets." *Political Analysis* 11, no. 2, pp. 1–11.

Castles, Francis G. 2004. *The Future of the Welfare State*. Oxford: Oxford University Press.

Cohen, G. A. 2001. "Freedom and Money." *Revista Argentina de Teoria Juridica* 2, no. 2, www.utdt.edu/departamentos/derecho/publicaciones/rtj1/primeraspaginas/index.htm.

Coleman, David. 2005. "Facing the 21st Century. New Developments, Continuing Problems." In Macura et al. 2005.

Coleman, James S. 1990. *Foundations of Social Theory*. Cambridge, MA: Harvard University Press.

———. 1971. *Resources for Social Change*. New York: Wiley.

Commaille, Jacques. 1997. *Les nouveaux enjeux de la question sociale*. Paris: Hachette.

Cammaille, Jacques, and François de Singly, eds. 1997. *The European Family: The Family Question in the European Community*. Dordrecht, Netherlands: Kluwer Academic.

Commission on Private Public Partnership. 2002. *Building Better Partnerships*. London: Institute for Public Policy Research.

Crompton, R. 1996. "The Fragmentation of Class Analysis," *British Journal of Sociology* 47, no. 1, pp. 56–67.

Crouch, C., and A. Heath, eds. 1992. *Social Research and Social Reform*. Oxford: Clarendon.

Dahl, Robert A. 2001. *How Democratic Is the American Constitution?* New Haven, CT: Yale University Press.

———. 1998. *On Democracy*. New Haven, CT: Yale University Press.

———. 1989. *Democracy and Its Critics*. New Haven, CT: Yale University Press.

———. 1985. *A Preface to Economic Democracy.* Berkeley: University of California Press.

———. 1971. *Poliarchy: Participation and Opposition.* New Haven, CT: Yale University Press.

Dasgupta, P. 1993. *An Inquiry into Well-being and Destitution.* Oxford: Oxford University Press.

Diamond, Larry. 2002. "Elections without Democracy. Thinking about Hybrid Regimes." *Journal of Democracy* 13, no. 2, pp. 5–21.

Diamond, Larry, and Leonardo Morlino, eds. 2005. *Assessing the Quality of Democracy.* Baltimore, MD: Johns Hopkins University Press.

Donnison, David. 1982. *The Politics of Poverty.* Oxford: Blackwell.

Doyal, L., and I. Gough. 1991. *A Theory of Human Needs.* London: Macmillan.

Dunn, John. 2000. *The Cunning of Unreason.* London: HarperCollins.

Durkheim, Emile. 1897. *Le suicide, étude sociologique.* Paris: Alcan.

Eklund, Robert B., ed. 1998. *The Foundations of Regulatory Economics*, vols. 1–3. Cheltenham, UK: Edward Elgar.

Eliasson, Nils. 2001. *Protection of accrued pension rights.* Lund, Sweden: Faculty of Law.

Elklit, Jørgen, and Palle Svensson. 1997. "What Makes Elections Free and Fair?" *Journal of Democracy* 8, no. 3, pp. 32–47.

Elster, Jon. 2000. *Ulysses Unbound.* Cambridge: Cambridge University Press.

———. 1999. *Strong Feelings.* Cambridge, MA: MIT Press.

———. ed. 1998. *Deliberative Democracy.* Cambridge: Cambridge University Press.

———. 1989. *Nuts and Bolts for the Social Sciences.* Cambridge: Cambridge University Press.

Erikson, Robert, and John Goldthorpe. 1992. *The Constant Flux: A Study of Class Mobility in Industrial Societies.* Oxford: Oxford University Press.

Erikson, Robert, Erik Jørgen Hansen, Stein Ringen, and Hannu Uusitalo, eds. 1987. *The Scandinavian Model: Welfare States and Welfare Research.* New York: M.E. Sharpe.

Ermish, J. F., and M. Francesconi. 2001a. "Family Structure and Children's Achievements." *Journal of Population Economics* 14, no. 2, pp. 249–70.

———. 2001b. "Family Matters: Impacts of Family Background on Educational Attainments." *Economica* 68, no. 270, pp. 137–56.

Esping-Andersen, Gøsta, with Duncan Gallie, Anton Hemerijck, and John Myles. 2002. *Why We Need a New Welfare State.* Oxford: Oxford University Press.

Evans, Geoffrey. 1958. "Ancient Mesopotamian Assemblies." *Journal of the American Oriental Society* 78, no. 1, pp. 1–11.

Farber, Daniel A., and Suzanna Sherry. 2002. *Desperately Seeking Certainty: The Misguided Quest for Constitutional Foundations.* Chicago: University of Chicago Press.

Ferrera, Maurizio, ed. 2005. *Welfare State Reform in Southern Europe.* London: Routledge.

Fincher, R., and J. Niewenhuysen, eds. 1998. *Australian Poverty: Then and Now.* Melbourne: Melbourne University Press.

Finer, S.E. 1997. *The History of Government*, vols. 1–3. Oxford: Oxford University Press.

Fitzgerald, Garret. 2003. *Reflections on the Irish State*. Dublin: Irish Academic Press.

Fleming, Daniel E. 2004. *Democracy's Ancient Ancestors*. Cambridge: Cambridge University Press.

Flora, Peter, and Jens Alber. 1981. "Modernization, Democratization, and the Development of Welfare States in Western Europe." In Flora and Heidenheimer 1981.

Flora, Peter, and A. J. Heidenheimer, eds. 1981. *The Development of Welfare States in Europe and America*. New Brunswick, NJ: Transaction.

Friedman, Benjamin M. 2005. *The Moral Consequences of Economic Growth*. New York: Knopf.

Friedman, Milton, and Rose Friedman. 1979. *Free to Choose*. New York: Harcourt Brace Jovanovich.

Friedman, Thomas L. 2005. *The World Is Flat: A Brief History of the Twenty-first Century*. New York: Farrar, Straus and Giroux.

Galston, William A. 2000. "What About Reciprocity?" *Boston Review*, October/November.

Galtung, Johan. 1964. "Foreign policy opinion as a function of social position." *Journal of Peace Research* 1, 206–31.

Gambetta, Diego. 1988. *Trust: Making and Breaking Cooperative Relations*. Oxford: Blackwell.

———. 1987. *Were They Pushed or Did They Jump?* Cambridge: Cambridge University Press.

Gates, William H., and Chuck Collins. 2003. *Wealth and Our Commonwealth: Why America Should Tax Accumulated Fortunes*. Boston: Beacon.

Gershenkron, Alexander. 1962. *Economic Backwardness in Historical Perspective*. Cambridge, MA: Harvard University Press.

Gershuny, Jonathan. 2000. *Changing Times: Work and Leisure in Postindustrial Society*. Oxford: Oxford University Press.

Gilbert, Neil. 2002. *Transformation of the Welfare State: The Silent Surrender of Public Responsibility*. New York: Oxford University Press.

———. 1983. *Capitalism and the Welfare State*. New Haven, CT: Yale University Press.

Gilljam, Mikael. 1988. *Svenska folket och löntagarfonderna: En studie i politisk åsiktsbildning*. Lund, Sweden: Studentliteratur.

Glennerster, Howard, John Hills, David Piachaud, and Jo Webb. 2004. *One Hundred Years of Poverty and Policy*. York, UK: Joseph Rowntree Foundation.

Goldthorpe, John. 2000. *On Sociology*. Oxford: Oxford University Press.

Goldthorpe, John, with C. Llewellyn and C. Payne. *Social Mobility and Class Structure in Modern Britain*, 2nd ed. Oxford: Oxford University Press.

———. 1980. *Social Mobility and Class Structure in Modern Britain*, 1st ed. Oxford: Oxford University Press.

Goodin, Robert E., Bruce Headye, Ruud Muffels, and Henk-Jan Dirven. 1999. *The Real Worlds of Welfare Capitalism*. Cambridge: Cambridge University Press.

Gordon, D., and P. Townsend, eds. 2000. *Breadline Europe: The Measurement of Poverty*. Bristol, UK: Policy.

Gordon, Margaret S. 1988. *Social Security Policies in Industrial Countries*. Cambridge: Cambridge University Press.

Gough, Ian. 2000. *Global Capital, Human Needs and Social Policies*. London: Palgrave.

———. 1979. *The Political Economy of the Welfare State*. London: Macmillan.

Griffin, James. 1996. *Value Judgement*. Oxford: Oxford University Press.

Grusky, D. B., and Tienda, M. 1993. "Foreword." *In* Shavit and Blossfeld 1993.

Gustafsson, B., ed. 1999. *Poverty and Low Income in the Nordic Countries*. Aldershot, UK: Ashgate.

Gutmann, Amy, and Dennis Thompson. 2004. *Why Deliberative Democracy?* Princeton, NJ: Princeton University Press.

———. 1996. *Democracy and Disagreement*. Cambridge, MA: Harvard University Press.

Habermas, Jürgen. 1990. *Moral Consciousness and Communicative Action*. Cambridge: Polity.

———. 1984/87. *The Theory of Communicative Action*, vols. 1–2. Cambridge: Polity.

Hagenaars, A. 1986. *The Perception of Poverty*. Amsterdam: North-Holland.

Hall, Robert E., and Alvin Rabushka. 1995. *The Flat Tax*, 2nd ed. Stanford, CA: Hoover Institution Press.

Halleröd, B. 1999. "Economic Standard of Living: A Longitudinal Analysis of the Economic Standard among Swedes 1979–1995." *European Societies* 1, no. 3, pp. 391–418.

———. 1995. "The truly poor: direct and indirect consensual measurement of poverty in Sweden." *Journal of European Social Policy* 5, no. 2, pp. 111–29.

———. 1998. "Poor Swedes, Poor Britons: A Comparative Analysis of Relative Deprivation." In Andreß 1998.

Halleröd, B., and M. Heikkilä. 1990. "Poverty and Social Exclusion in the Nordic Countries." In Heikkilä et al. 1999.

Halsey, A. H. 1977. "Towards Meritocracy? The Case of Britain." In Karabel and Halsey 1977.

Hansen, Erik Jørgen, Stein Ringen, Hannu Uusitalo, and Robert Erikson, eds. 1993. *Welfare Trends in the Scandinavian Countries*. New York: M. E. Sharpe.

Harrington, M. 1962. *The Other America*. New York: Macmillan.

Hart, H.L.A. 1979. "Between Utility and Rights." In Ryan 1979.

Heath, A. F., and P. Clifford. 1990. "Class Inequalities in Education in the Twentieth Century." *Journal of the Royal Statistical Society*, series A, 153, no. 1, pp. 1–16.

Heath, A. F., R. M. Jewell, and J. K. Curtis. 1987. "Trendless Fluctuation: a reply to Crewe." *Political Studies* 35, no. 2, pp. 256–77.

Heath, A. F., C. Mills, and J. Roberts. 1992. "Towards Meritocracy? Recent Evidence on an Old Problem." In Crouch and Heath 1992.

Hedström, P., and S. Ringen. 1987. "Age and Income in Contemporary Society." *Journal of Social Policy* 16, no. 2, pp. 227–39.

Heiberg, Marianne, Geir Øvensen, and others 1994. *Palestinian Society in Gaza, West Bank and Arab Jerusalem: A Survey of Living Conditions*. Report 151. Oslo: Fafo.

Heikkilä, M., B. Hvinden, M. Kautto, S. Marklund, and N. Ploug, eds. 1999. *Nordic Social Policy*. London: Routledge.

Heller, Patrick. 2000. "Degrees of Democracy. Some Comparative Lessons from India." *World Politics* 52, no. 4, pp. 484–519.

Hellevik, Ottar. 2005. "Linear versus logistic regression when the dependent variable is a dichotomy." Working paper, Department of Political Science, University of Oslo.

———. 2003. "Kvantitativ analyse: statistisk raffinement versus mening." *Sosiologisk tidsskrift* 10, no. 3, pp. 54–74.

———. 2002a. *Forskningsmetode i sosiologi og statsvitenskap*, 7th ed. Oslo: Universitetsforlaget.

———. 2002b. "Inequality versus association in educational attainment research: Comment on Kivinen, Ahola and Hedman." *Acta Sociologica* 45, no. 2, pp. 151–58.

———. 2000. "A less biased allocation mechanism." *Acta Sociologica* 43, no. 1, pp. 80–83.

———. 1997. "Class Inequality and Egalitarian Reform." *Acta Sociologica* 40, no. 4, pp. 377–97.

———. 1984. *Introduction to Causal Analysis*. London: George Allen & Unwin.

Hill, Kim Quaile. 1994. *Democracy in the Fifty States*. Lincoln: University of Nebraska Press.

Hills, John, and Kitty Stewart, eds. 2005. *A more equal society? New Labour, poverty, inequality and exclusion*. Bristol, UK: Policy.

Hirshman, Albert O. 1970. *Exit, Voice, and Loyalty*. Cambridge, MA: Harvard University Press.

Holmes, Stephen. 1995. *Passions and Constraint*. Chicago: Chicago University Press.

Holmes, Stephen, and C. Sundstein 1999. *The Costs of Rights: Why Liberty Depends on Taxes*. New York: Norton.

Holton, R., and B. S. Turner. 1994. "Debate and Pseudo-Debate in Class Analysis: Some Unpromising Aspects of Goldthorpe and Marshall's Defence." *Sociology* 28, no. 3, pp. 799–804.

Hood, Christopher C. 1983. *The Tools of Government*. London: Macmillan.

Horowitz, Irving L. 1999. *Behemoth: Main Currents in the History and Theory of Political Sociology*. New Brunswick, NJ: Transaction.

Howell, William G., and Paul E. Peterson. 2002. *The Education Gap: Vouchers and Urban Schools*. Washington, DC: Brookings Institution Press.

Huber, Evelyn, Dietrich Rueschemeyer, and John D. Stephens. 1997. "The Paradox of Contemporary Democracy. Formal, Participatory and Social Dimensions." *Comparative Politics* 29, no. 3, pp. 323–42

Huntington, Samuel P. 1996. *The Clash of Civilizations and the Remaking of the World Order*. New York: Simon & Schuster.

———. 1991. *The Third Wave: Democratization in the Late Twentieth Century*. Norman: University of Oklahoma Press.

Iazzetta, O., G. O'Donnell, and J. Vargas Cullel. 2004; *The Quality of Democracy in Latin America: Theory and Applications*. Notre Dame, IN: University of Notre Dame Press.

Immergut, Ellen, Karen M. Anderson, and Isabelle Schulze, eds. 2006. The Handbook of West European Pension Politics. Oxford: Oxford University Press.

Inglehart, Ronald, Miguel Basañez, Jaime Díez-Medrano, Loek Halman, and Ruud Luijkx, eds. 2004. *Human Beliefs and Values: A Cross-Cultural Sourcebook Based on the 1999–2002 Values Surveys*. Madrid: Siglo XXI.

Inglehart, Ronald, Miguel Basañez, and Alejandro Moreno. 1998. *Human Values and Beliefs: A Cross-Cultural Sourcebook*. Ann Arbor: University of Michigan Press.

Inkeles, Alex, ed. 1991. *On Measuring Democracy: Its Consequences and Concomitants*. New Brunswick, NJ: Transaction.

Iversen, Torben. 2005. *Capitalism, Democracy, and Welfare*. Cambridge: Cambridge University Press.

Jacobsen, Thorkild. 1970. *Toward the Image of Tammuz and Other Essays on Mesopotamian History and Culture*. Cambridge, MA: Harvard University Press, 1970.

Jahanbegloo, Ramin. 1992. *Conversations with Isaiah Berlin*. London: Peter Halban.

Janowitz, Morris. 1976. *Social Control of the Welfare State*. New York: Elsevier.

Jones, Catherine, ed. 1993. *New Perspective on the Welfare State in Europe*. London: Routledge.

Joshi, H., and H. Davies. 1993. "Mothers' Human Capital and Childcare in Britain." *National Institute Economic Review* 182, pp. 50–63.

Kahn, Alfred E. 1988. *The Economics of Regulations: Principles and Institutions*. Cambridge, MA: MIT Press.

Kangas, Olli, and Joakim Palme, eds. 2005. *Social Policy and Economic Development in the Nordic Countries*. London: Palgrave Macmillan.

Kangas, O., and V. M. Ritakallio. 1998. "Different Methods—Different Results? Approaches to Multidimensional Poverty." In Andreß 1998.

Karabel, J., and A. H. Halsey, eds. 1977. *Power and Ideology in Education*. New York: Oxford University Press.

Katzmann, Robert A. 1989. "The American Legislative Process as a Signal." *Journal of Public Policy* 9, no. 3, pp. 287–305.

Kerr, C. 1983. *The Future of Industrial Societies*. Cambridge: Harvard University Press.

Kiernan, K. 1992. "The Impact of Family Disruption in Childhood on Transitions Made in Young Adult Life." *Population Studies* 46, pp. 213–34.

Kivinen, O., S. Ahola, and J. Hedman. 2001. "Expanding Education and Improving Odds. Participation in Higher Education in Finland in the 1980s and 1990s." *Acta Sociologica* 44, no. 4, pp. 171–81.

Kivinen, O., J. Hedman, and S. Ahola. 2002. "Changes to Differences in Expanding Higher Education. Reply to Hellevik," *Acta Sociologica* 45, no. 2, pp. 159–62.

Klein, R. 2001. *The New Politics of the National Health Service*. Harlow, UK: Prentice Hall.

Klingeman, Hans-Dieter, and Dieter Fuchs, eds. 1995. *Citizens and the State*. Oxford: Oxford University Press.

Kolberg, J. E., ed. 1992. *The Study of Welfare State Regimes*. New York: M.E. Sharpe.

Korpi, Walter. 1983. *The Democratic Class Struggle*. London: Routledge & Kegan Paul.

Korpi, Walter, and Joakim Palme. 1998. "The Paradox of Redistribution and Strategies of Equality," *American Sociological Review* 63, pp. 661–87.

Kwon, Huck-ju, ed. 2005. *Transforming the Developmental Welfare State in East Asia*. London: Palgrave Macmillan.

———. 1998. The *Welfare State in Korea: The Politics of Legitimation*. London: Macmillan.

Lagos, M. 2003. "A Road with No Return?" *Journal of Democracy* 14, no. 2, pp. 163–72.

Laslett, Peter. 1971. *The World We Have Lost*. London: Methuen.

Laumann, E. O., ed. 1970. *Social Stratification: Research and Theory for the 1970s*. Indianapolis: Bobbs-Merrill.

Layard, Richard. 2005. *Happiness: Lessons from a New Science*. London: Allen Lane.

Lestaeghe, R. 1995. "The Second Demographic Transition in Western Countries: An Interpretation." In Mason and Jensen 1995.

Lewis, Bernard. 2004. *From Babel to Dragomans: Interpreting the Middle East*. New York: Oxford University Press.

Lijphart, Arend. 1999. *Patterns of Democracy*. New Haven, CT: Yale University Press.

Linz, Juan J., and Alfred Stepan. 1996. *Problems of Democratic Transition and Consolidation*. Baltimore, MD: Johns Hopkins University Press.

Lipset, Seymour Martin. 1960. *Political Man*. London: Heinemann.

Lipset, Seymour Martin, and William Schneider. 1983. The Confidence Gap. New York: Free Press.

Mack, J., and S. Lansley. 1985. *Poor Britain*. London: Allen & Unwin.

Macura, M., A. L. MacDonald, and W. Haug, eds. 2005. *The New Demographic Regime: Population Challenges and Policy Responses*. New York: United Nations.

Maktutredningen. 2003. *Makt og demokrati: sluttrapport fra Makt- og demokratiutredningen*. Oslo: NOU 2003.19.

Manin, Bernard. 1997. *The Principles of Representative Government*. Cambridge: Cambridge University Press.

Mansbridge, Jane J. 1980. *Beyond Adversary Democracy*. New York: Basic.

Mare, R. D. 1981. "Change and Stability in Educational Stratification." *American Sociological Review* 46, no. 1, pp. 72–87.

Marshall, A. 1920. *Principles of Economics*, 8th ed. London: Macmillan.

Marshall, Gordon, and Adam Swift. 2000. "Reply to Ringen and Hellevik." *Acta Sociologica* 43, no. 1, p. 85.

———. 1999. "On the Meaning and Measurement of Inequality." *Acta Sociologica* 43, no. 1, p. 84.

Marshall, Gordon, Adam Swift, and Stephen Roberts. 1997. *Against the Odds: Social Class and Social Justice in Industrial Societies*. Oxford: Oxford University Press.

Marshall, G., H. Newby, D. Rose, and C. Vogler. 1988. *Social Class in Modern Britain*. London: Hutchinson.

Marshall, T. H. 1963. *Class, Citizenship, and Social Development*. Chicago: University of Chicago Press.

Mason, K. O., and A.-M. Jensen, eds. 1995. *Gender and Family Change in Industrial Countries*. Oxford: Clarendon.

Mason, Mary Ann, Arlene Skolnick, and Stephen D. Sugarman, eds. 2003. *All Our Families*, 2nd ed. New York: Oxford University Press.

Mayer, S. E., and C. Jencks. 1988. "Poverty and the Distribution of Material Hardship." *Journal of Human Resources* 24, no. 1, pp. 88–113.

McRae, Susan, ed. 1999. *Changing Britain: Families and Households in the 1990s*. Oxford: Oxford University Press.

Mesure, S., ed. 1996. *La rationalité des valeurs*. Paris: Presses Universitaires de France.

Mieroop, Marc van de. 1999. *The Ancient Mesopotamian City*. Oxford: Oxford University Press.

Mill, John Stuart. 1859/1991. *On Liberty and Other Essays*. World's Classics. Oxford: Oxford University Press.

Mishra, Pankaj. 2004. *An End to Suffering: The Buddha in the World*. New York: Farrar, Straus and Giroux.

Mkandawire, Thandika, ed. 2004. *Social Policy in a Development Context*. London: Palgrave Macmillan.

Mommsen, W. S., ed. 1981. *The Emergence of the Welfare State in Britain and Germany*. London: Croom Helm.

Moran, Mary K. 2005. *Liberia: The Violence of Democracy*. Philadelphia: University of Pennsylvania Press.

Moynihan, D. P., T. M. Smeeding, and L. Rainwater, eds. 2004. *The Future of the Family*. New York: Russell Sage Foundation.

Munch, G. L., and J. Verkuilen. 2002. "Conceptualising and Measuring Democracy. Evaluating Alternative Indices." *Comparative Political Studies* 35 (February), pp. 5–34.

Myrdal, Alva, and Gunnar Myrdal. 1934. *Kris i befolkningsfrågan*. Stockholm: Tiden.

Nash, Andrew. 1999. "Mandela's Democracy." *Monthly Review* 50, no. 11, pp.

Nolan, B., and C. T. Whelan. 1996. *Resources, Deprivation and Poverty*. Oxford: Oxford University Press.

Norris, Pippa, ed. 1999. *Critical Citizens: Global Support for Democratic Governance*. Oxford: Oxford University Press.

Nozick, Robert. 1974. *Anarchy, State, and Utopia*. New York: Basic.

Nussbaum, Martha C. 1999. *Sex and Social Justice*. New York: Oxford University Press.

Nussbaum, Martha C., and Amartya Sen, eds. 1993. *The Quality of Life*. Oxford: Oxford University Press.

O'Connor, James. 1973. *The Fiscal Crisis of the State*. New York: St. Martin's.

O'Neill, Onora. 2002. *A Question of Trust*. Cambridge: Cambridge University Press.

OECD. 1986. *Living Conditions in OECD Countries*. Paris: Organisation for Economic Co-operation and Development.

———. 1982. *The OECD List of Social Indicators*. Paris: Organisation for Economic Co-operation and Development.

———. 1981. *The Welfare State in Crisis*. Paris: Organisation for Economic Co-operation and Development.

Offe, Claus, ed. 2003. *Demokratisierung der Demokratie: Diagnosen und Reformvorschläge*. Frankfurt: Campus.

———. 1984. *Contradictions of the Welfare State*. London: Hutchinson.

Offer, Avner. 2006. *The Challenge of Affluence*. Oxford: Oxford University Press.

———, ed. 1996. *In Pursuit of the Quality of Life*. Oxford: Oxford University Press.

Okun, Arthur. 1975. *Equality and Efficiency: The Big Tradeoff*. Washington, DC: Brookings Institution Press.

Orshansky, M. 1969. "How Poverty Is Measured." *Monthly Labour Review* February, p. 2.

———. 1965. "Counting the Poor. Another Look at the Poverty Profile." *Social Security Bulletin* 28, p. 1.

Østerud, Øyvind, Fredrik Engelstad, and Per Selle. 2003. *Makten og demokratiet*. Oslo: Gyldendal Akademisk.

Pahl, Ray. 1989. "Is the Emperor Naked? Some Questions on the Adequacy of Sociological Theory in Urban and Regional Research." *International Journal of Urban and Regional Research* 13, no. 4, pp. 709–20.

Parr, Susan J., Robert D. Putnam, and Russel J. Dalton. 2000. "A Quarter Century of Declining Confidence." *Journal of Democracy* 11, no. 2, pp. 5–25.

Péan, Pierre, Philippe Cohen. 2003. *La Face Caché du Monde*. Paris: Mille et une Nuits.

Pen, Jan. 1971. *Income Distribution*. Penguin.

Piachaud, D. 1981. "Peter Townsend and the Holy Grail." *New Society* 57, pp. 419–21.

Piachaud, D., H. Sutherland, and T. Sefton. 2003. *Poverty in Britain: The Impact of Government Policy since 1997*. York: Joseph Rowntree Foundation.

Pierson, Paul 1994. *Dismantling the Welfare State?* Cambridge: Cambridge University Press.

Pigou, A. C. 1920. *The Economics of Welfare*. London: Macmillan.

Pontusson, Jonas. 1992. *The Limits of Social Democracy Investments Politics in Sweden*. Ithaca, NY: Cornell University Press.

Popper, Karl. 1945. *The Open Society and Its Enemies*, vol. 1–2. London: Routledge & Kegan Paul.

Preston, S. H. 1984. "Children and the Elderly: Divergent Paths for America's Dependents." *Demography* 21, pp. 435–57.

Proyecto Estado de la Nación. 2001. *Auditoría Ciudadana sobre la Calidad de la Democracía 1–2*. San José, Costa Rica: Editorama.

Putnam, Robert D. 2000. *Bowling Alone: The Collapse and Revival of American Community*. New York: Simon and Schuster.

Putnam, Robert D., and K. Goss, eds. 2002. *Democracies in Flux: The Evolution of Social Capital in Contemporary Society*. New York: Oxford University Press.

Rainwater, L. 1974. *What Money Buys*. New York: Basic.

Ravallion, M. 1996. "Issues in Measuring and Modelling Poverty." *Economic Journal* 106, pp. 1328–43.

Rawls, John. 1985. "Justice as Fairness, Political Not Metaphysical." *Philosophy and Public Affairs* 14, no. 3, pp. 223–51.

———. 1971. *A Theory of Justice*. Cambridge, MA: Harvard University Press.

Raz, Joseph. 1986. *The Morality of Freedom*. Oxford: Oxford University Press.

Reich, Gary. 2002. "Categorising Political Regimes. New Data for Old Problems." *Democratization* 9, no. 4, pp. 1–24.

Rieger, E., and S. Leibfried. 2003. *Limits to Globalization: Welfare States and the World Economy*. Oxford: Blackwell.

Ringen, Stein. 2006. *The Possibility of Politics*, 3rd ed. New Brunswick, NJ: Transaction.

———. 2005a. *Citizens, Families, and Reform*, 2nd ed. New Brunswick, NJ: Transaction.

———. 2005b. "Liberty, Freedom and Real Freedom." Pts. 1 and 2. *Society* 42, March/April, pp. 36–39; May/June, pp. 42–48.

———. 2005c. "Problém chudoby—několik doporučení k definici a měření." *Sociologický časopis/ Czech Sociological Review* 41, no. 3, pp. 125–39.

———. 2004a. "Demokrati, velstand og ansvar: Frihetens problem i en verden av mistro." *P2 Akademiet* 29. Oslo: Transit/NRK.

———. 2004b. "A Distributional Theory of Economic Democracy." *Democratization* 11, no. 2, pp. 18–40.

———, ed. 2004c. *Norges nye befolkning*. Oslo: MandagMorgen.

———. 2004d. "The Powerlessness of Powerful Government." Paper presented to the Second Edmond Mokrzycki Symposium of the Polish Academy of Sciences, Warsaw, 19–20 November 2004.

———. 2004e. "Wealth and Decay." *Times Literary Supplement*, 13 February 2004.

———. 2003a. "Fewer People: A Stark European Future." *Times Literary Supplement*, 28 February 2003.

———. 2003b. "Why the British Press Is Brilliant." *British Journalism Review* 14, no. 3. pp. 31–59.

———. 2002. "Helvetius and Friends." *Times Literary Supplement*, 15 November 2002.

———, ed. 2000a. *Hva skjer med demokratiet?* Oslo: Fafo. www.fafo/pub/rapp/928/index.htm.

———. 2000b. "Inequality and Its Measurement." *Acta Sociologica* 43, no. 1, p. 84.

———. 2000c. *Utfordringer til demokratiet*. Oslo: Verdikommisjonen. Also in Ringen 2000a.

———. 2000d. *Veien til det gode liv*. Oslo: Erling Kagge.

———. 1999a. "Demokratiet lider av dårlig demokratiforståelse." *P2 Akademiet* 24. Oslo: NRK.

———. 1999b. "Familie og produksjon." In K. Christensen and L.J. Syltvik, *Omsorgens forvitring?* Bergen, Norway: Fagbokforlaget.

———. 1999c. "Reason, Democracy and Reform." In M. Potucek, *Ceska Spolecnost na konci tisicileti.* Prague: Karolinum.

———. 1998a. *The Family in Question.* London: Demos.

———. 1998b. "The Great British Myth." *Times Literary Supplement,* 23 January 1998.

———. 1998c. "Social Security, Social Reform, and Social Assistance." In D. Peters, *Social Protection of the Next Generation in Europe.* The Hague: Kluwer.

———. 1998d. "Verdi og frihet." *Nytt Norsk Tidsskrift* no. 4. pp. 365–69.

———. 1997a. *Citizens, Families, and Reform.* Oxford: Oxford University Press.

———. 1997b. "The Experience of Income Redistribution." In N. Keilman, J. Lyngstad, H. Bojer, and I. Thomsen, *Poverty and Economic Inequality in Industrialized Western* Societies. Oslo: Scandinavian University Press.

———. 1997c. "The Open Society and the Closed Mind." *Times Literary Supplement,* 24 January 1997.

———. 1997d. *Reformdemokratiet: Forankring, frihet og velferd.* Oslo: Universitetsforlaget.

———. 1996. "Households, Goods, and Well-Being." *Review of Income and Wealth* Series 42, no. 4, pp. 421–31.

———. 1995. "Well-Being, Measurement, and Preferences." *Acta Sociologica* 38, no. 1, pp. 3–15.

———. 1993. *Democracy, Science, and the Civic Spirit.* Oxford: Oxford University Press.

———. 1991a. "Do Welfare States Come in Types?" In P. Saunders and D. Encel, *Social Policy in Australia: Options for the 1990s.* Sydney: UNSW Social Policy Research Centre.

———. 1991b. "Households, Standard of Living, and Inequality." *Review of Income and Wealth* Series 37, no. 1, pp. 1–13.

———. 1988. "Direct and Indirect Measures of Poverty." *Journal of Social Policy* 17, no. 3, pp. 351–65.

———. 1987. *The Possibility of Politics: A Study in the Political Economy of the Welfare State.* Oxford: Oxford University Press.

———. 1986. *Svensk inkomstfördelning i internationell jämförelse.* Stockholm: Ministry of Finance.

———. 1985. "Toward a Third Stage in the Measurement of Poverty." *Acta Sociologica* 28, no. 2, pp. 18–30.

———. 1984. *Er velferdsstaten realistisk?* Oslo: Tiden.

———. 1981. *Hvor går velferdsstaten?* Oslo: Gyldendal.

Ringen, Stein, and Brendan Halpin. 1997. "Children, Standard of Living, and Distributions in the Family." *Journal of Social Policy* 26, no. 1, pp. 21–42.

Ringen, Stein, and Peter Hedström. 1990. "Age and Income in Contemporary Society." In T. M. Smeeding, M. O'Higgins and L. Rainwater, *Poverty, Inequality and Income Distribution in Comparative Perspective.* London: Harvester Wheatsheaf; Washington, DC: Urban Institute Press.

Ringen, Stein, and Hannu Uusitalo. 1992. "Income Distribution and Redistribution in the Nordic Welfare State." In J. E. Kolberg, *The Study of Welfare State Regimes*. New York: M.E. Sharpe.

Ringen, Stein, and Kari Wærness, eds. 1982. *Sosialpolitikk i 1980-åra*. Oslo: Gyldendal.

Robbins, Lionell. 1932. *An Essay on the Nature and Significance of Economic Science*. London: Macmillan.

Rødseth, Tor, Gudmund Hernes, Asbjørn Aase, and Stein Ringen. 1976. *Levekårsundersøkelsen: Sluttrapport*. Oslo: NOU 1976.28.

Rogoff, Natalie, and Stein Ringen. 2005. "Eilert Sundt." *Dictionnaire de la pensée sociologique*. Paris: Presses Universitaires de France.

Rosanvallon, Pierre. 1995. *La nouvelle question sociale*. Paris: Seuil.

———. 1981. *La crise de l'État-providence*. Paris: Seuil.

Rose, Richard. 1994. "Postcommunism and the Problem of Trust." *Journal of Democracy* 5, no. 3, pp. 18–30.

———. 1984. *Do Parties Make a Difference?* 2nd ed. London: Macmillan.

———. 1976. "On the Priorities of Government: A Developmental Analysis of Public Policy." *European Journal of Political Research* 4, no. 3, pp. 247–89.

Rose, Richard, and Guy Peters. 1978. *Can Governments Go Bankrupt?* New York: Basic.

Rothschild, Emma. 2001. *Economic Sentiments: Adam Smith, Condorcet, and the Enlightenment*. Cambridge: Harvard University Press.

Rowntree, B. S. 1901. *Poverty: A Study of Town Life*. London: Macmillan.

———. 1941. *Poverty and Progress*. London: Longmans Green.

Rowntree, B. S., and G. R. Lavers. 1951. *Poverty and the Welfare State*. London: Longmans Green.

Ruggeri Laderchi, C., R. Saith, and F. Stewart. 2003. "Does It Matter that We Do Not Agree on the Definition of Poverty? A Comparison of Four Approaches." *Oxford Development Studies* 31, no. 3, pp. 243–74.

Ruggles, P. 1990. *Drawing the Line: Alternative Poverty Measures and Their Implications for Public Policy*. Washington DC: Urban Institute Press.

Rui, Sandrine. 2004. *La démocratie en débat*. Paris: Armand Colin.

Runciman, W. G. 1966. *Relative Deprivation and Social Justice*. London: Routledge & Kegan Paul.

Ryan, Alan, ed. 1979. *The Idea of Freedom*. Oxford: Oxford University Press.

Sachs, Jeffrey D. 2005. *The End of Poverty: Economic Possibilities for Our Time*. Penguin.

Saunders, Peter, ed. 2005. *Welfare to Work in Practice*. Aldershot: Ashgate.

Saunders, P. 1996. *Unequal but Fair? A Study of Class Barriers in Britain*. London: Institute of Economic Affairs.

———. 1995. "Might Britain Be a Meritocracy?" *Sociology* 29, no. 1, pp. 23–41.

———. 1990. *Social Class and Stratification*. London: Routledge.

Scanlon, T. M. 1998. *What We Owe to Each Other*. Cambridge: Harvard University Press.

Schokkaert, Erik, ed. 2001. *Ethics and Social Security Reform*. Aldershot, UK: Ashgate.

Schumpeter, Joseph. 1952. *Capitalism, Socialism, and Democracy*. London: George Allen & Unwin.

Seeleib-Kaiser, Martin. 2002. "Globalisation, Political Discourse and Welfare Systems in a Comparative Perspective: Germany, Japan and the US." *Czech Sociological Review* 38, no. 6, pp. 749–69.

Seip, Anne-Lise. 1994. *Veiene til velferdsstaten*. Oslo: Gyldendal.

Sen, Amartya [A. K.]. 2006. *Identity and Violence: The Illusion of Destiny*. New York: Norton.

———. 2005. *The Argumentative Indian: Writings on Indian History, Culture and Identity*. London: Allen Lane.

———. 2002. *Rationality and Freedom*. Cambridge: Harvard University Press.

———. 1999a. "Democracy as a Universal Value." *Journal of Democracy* 10, no. 3, pp. 3–17.

———. 1999b. *Development as Freedom*. Oxford: Oxford University Press.

———. 1983. "Poor, Relatively Speaking." *Oxford Economic Papers* 35, no. 2, pp. 153–69.

———. 1981. *Poverty and Famines*. Oxford: Oxford University Press.

Sen, Amartya, and J. Foster. 1997. "Inequality after a Quarter Century." In A. K. Sen, *On Inequality*, 2nd ed. Oxford: Clarendon.

Sereny, Gitta. 1998. *Cries Unheard*. London: Macmillan.

Shapiro, Ian. 2003. *The State of Democratic Theory*. Princeton: Princeton University Press.

Shavit, Y., and H.-P. Blossfeld, eds. 1993. *Persistent Inequality: Changing Educational Attainment in Thirteen Countries*. Boulder: Westview.

Siaroff, Alan, and John W.A. Merer. 2000. "Parliamentary Election Turnout in Europe since 1990." *World Politics* 50, no. 5, pp. 916–27.

Simon, Herbert A. 1983. *Reason in Human Affairs*. Stanford, CA: Stanford University Press.

Skocpol, Theda. 1992. *Protecting Soldiers and Mothers*. Cambridge, MA: Harvard University Press.

Smith, Adam. 1776. *An Inquiry into the Nature and Causes of the Wealth of Nations*.

———. 1759. *The Theory of Moral Sentiments*.

Sorensen, A. 1991. "On the Usefulness of Class Analysis in Research on Social Mobility and Socioeconomic Inequality." *Acta Sociologica* 34, no. 1, pp. 71–87.

Stedman Jones, G. 2004. *An End to Poverty?* London: Profile.

Stiglitz, Joseph. 2000. *Globalisation and Its Discontents*. London: Allen Lane/Penguin.

Stouffer, S. A., E. A. Suchman, L. C. DeVinney, S. A. Star, and R. M. Williams. 1949. *The American Soldier: Adjustment during Army Life*. Princeton: Princeton University Press.

Swaan, Abram de. 1988. *In Care of the State*. Cambridge: Polity.

Sundt, Eilert. 1993. *Sexual Cuatoms in Rural Norway*. Ames: Iowa State University Press.

———. 1980. *On Marriage in Norway*. Cambridge: Cambridge University Press.

Swift, Adam. 2000. "Class Analysis from a Normative Perspective." *British Journal of Sociology* 51, no. 4, pp. 663–80.

Taylor, Charles. 1991. *The Ethics of Authenticity*. Cambridge, MA: Harvard University Press.

———. 1979. "What's Wrong With Negative Liberty?" In Ryan 1979.

Terum, Lars Inge. 1996. *Grenser for sosialpolitisk modernisering*. Oslo: Universitetsforlaget.

Titmuss, Richard M. 1968. *Commitment to Welfare*. London: Allen & Unwin.

———. 1958. *Essays on "The Welfare State."* London: Allen & Unwin.

Tocqueville, Alexis de. 1935, 1840. *De la démocratie en Amérique*. Paris.

Townsend, P. 1985. "A Sociological Approach to the Measurement of Poverty— A Rejoinder to Professor Amartya Sen." *Oxford Economic Papers* 37, no. 4, pp. 659–68.

———. 1979. *Poverty in the United Kingdom*. London: Penguin.

Travers, P., and S. Richardson. 1993. *Living Decently: Material Well-being in Australia*. Melbourne: Oxford University Press.

Treiman, D. J. 1970. "Industrialization and Social Stratification." In Laumann 1970.

UNDP. [Annual.] *Human Development Report*. New York: Oxford University Press for the United Nations Development Programme.

UNICEF. 2005. *Child Poverty in Rich Countries 2005*. Report Card no. 6. Florence: UNICEF Innocenti Research Centre.

———. 2000. *League Tables of Child Poverty*. Report Card no. 1. Florence: UNICEF International Child Development Centre.

UNPF. 2002. *The State of the World Population 2002*. New York: United Nations Population Fund.

van den Bosch, K. 2001. *Identifying the Poor*. Aldershot, UK: Ashgate.

van Parijs, Philippe. 1997. *Real Freedom for All*. Oxford: Oxford University Press.

van Praag, B., and P. Frijters. 1999. "The Measurement of Welfare and Well-being: The Leyden Method." In D. Kahneman, E. Diener, and N. Schwarz, *In Well-Being: The Foundations of Hedonic Psychology*. New York: Russell Sage.

Vedung, Evert. 1995. *Informative styrmedel*. Uppsala, Sweden: University of Uppsala, Department of Political Science.

Veit-Wilson, John H. 1986. "Paradigms of Poverty. A Rehabilitation of B. S. Rowntree." *Journal of Social Policy* 15, no. 2, pp. 69–99.

Venturi, Franco. 1979. "Venise et, par occasion, de la liberté." In Ryan 1979.

Verdikommisjonen. 2001. *Sluttrapport 1–3*. Oslo: Office of the Prime Minister.

Wærness, Kari. 1981. *Kvinneperspektiv på sosialpolitikken*. Oslo: Universitetsforlaget.

———. 1978. "The Invisible Welfare State: Women's Work at Home." *Acta Sociologica* 21, Supplement.

Webster, Charles. 1998. *The NHS: A Political History*. Oxford: Oxford University Press.

Wellings, Kaye, and Jane Wadsworth. 1999. "Family Influences on Teenage Fertility." In McRae 1999.

Whiteford, P. 1997. "Measuring Poverty and Income Inequality in Australia." *Agenda* 30, no. 3, pp. 325–49.

Whitehead, Laurence. 2004. "The Dark Side of Democratization: 'Dysfunctional' Democracies in South America." Working paper, Nuffield College, Oxford.

Wilensky, Harold L. 1975. *The Welfare State and Equality.* Berkeley: University of California Press.

Wills, Gary. 2001. *Venice: Lion City.* New York: Simon & Schuster.

Wolfe, Barbara. 2001. "Public Programmes Create Private Incentives and Disincentives toward Work." In Schokkaert 2001.

Wolff, Edward N. 1996. *Top Heavy: The Increasing Inequality of Wealth in America and What Can Be Done about It.* New York: New Press.

Index